Yair Davidiy

TH

TRIBES

Sub-Title:

The Israelite Origins of Western Peoples

First Published:
Hebron, Israel 1993
2nd edition:
Jerusalem, 1999

Third Edition
5765-2004
Jerusalem,
Israel

Cover design by
Oriel P. Davidi

R-D

RUSSELL-DAVIS

ISBN   965-90255-3-X

Address for Correspondence (2004):

Yair Davidy
Brit-Am Israel
P.O.B. 595
Jerusalem 91004
ISRAEL

britam@netvision.net.il

0546-423196
http://www.britam.org/

THE TRIBES

The Israelite Origins of Western Peoples

(Third Edition)

**The Location of the Lost Tribes of Israel in
Western Europe, the British Isles, North
America, Australia, New Zealand,
and South Africa:
Giving the Identity of Each
Individual Tribe Today**

Written by Yair Davidiy
and Published
in the Zionist State of Israel
in that section of the Land
of Israel that has been
partially liberated by
the Jewish People
on your behalf

The Tribes: Table of Contents Page

CHAPTER ONE

THE TRIBES: INDEX OF MAPS

Letter of Commendation from
Rabbi Abraham Feld
Maccabee Institute
for Emergency Rescue,
Educational, and Social Aid
P.O.B. 1438

Jerusalem 91004

Israel

Upon reading Mr. Yair Davidiy's book on the dispersion of the lost ten tribes, and contemplating on how most people will receive this as startling new information I was reminded of a law that U.S. President Bush recently endorsed.

On March 20, 1992 the President signed a historic Joint resolution of both Houses of Congress recognizing the Seven Noachide Laws as the "bedrock of society from the dawn of civilization" and urged America to "return to the moral and ethical values contained in the Seven Noachide Laws" (H.J. Res 104, Public Law 102-14).

This House Joint Resolution Public Law 102-14 is at once recognition of Torah's relevancy and a basis for a common denominator among all the nations of the world.

In much the same way, Mr. Yair Davidiy's scholarly work stands as testimony to a common heritage and bloodline that so many people share unbeknownst to themselves.

Mr. Davidiy is a first class historian and has produced an astonishing book. He is writing in the spirit of the Gaon Elyahu of Vilna, who sent emissaries looking for the lost tribes.

Indeed the Jerusalem Talmud declares in the days to come the ten tribes will be righteous converts (Sanhedrin, 10).

Thus Mr. Davidiy's masterly documented and profoundly thoughtful work is helping bring the world forward in the dynamic process of Redemption.

i

We of Mossad Maccabee have only the highest praise and respect for this valuable contribution to understanding our roots and heritage.

July 4, 1993

Fondest regards and blessings,
Avraham Feld
Director of Volunteers
Supervisor of Crisis Intervention Team.

Foreword to the Second Edition of *The Tribes*
Rabbi Abraham Feld
Maccabee Institute
for Emergency Rescue,
Educational, and Social Aid

A fellow in a large, fancy car pulls up to a youngster on a bicycle:

"Hey kid, where is Center Street?" –asks the driver.

"Don't know, Sir," says the kid.

"Well, where is Hennicks Road?"

"Don't know, Sir,"

"OK. Where is Hill Side Avenue?"

"Sorry. Don't know that either."

"Well kid, don't you know anything?"

"At least sir, I know I ain't lost!"

We are blessed with another edition of *The Tribes* by Yair Davidy. where directions are given helping people find their way back home.

The Chariot ("Mercavah") vision of the prophet Ezekiel hinted at the awesome renewal of God's presence from a ruined and desecrated Jerusalem. The Talmud (Baba Batra 14b) points out how towards the end of the Book of Ezekiel the Prophet closes with words of profound comfort. His message teaches the exiles, who felt they were dry bones with no part in the future of Israel, that indeed they would share in the glorious future. The message of comfort includes the reconciliation of the Lost Ten Tribes with Judah, a future messiah descended from David, and the rebuilding of the Temple. Something very unique about the Book of Ezekiel is that whereas other prophets spoke in sweeping generalities, Ezekiel spoke in very exact terms of height and length in measurements of the Third Temple. This makes for a heightened sense of reality to identify with. It gives us the blueprint or more graphic framework in which to place our hopes for a redeemed world.

When God showed Ezekiel the vision of the future Temple, Ezekiel declared, Master of the Universe, we are now in exile in the Land of our enemies and you instruct me to tell Israel the exact form of your house! There is nothing we can do! Why should we not leave the matter until we come home and then you may tell them? God replied: "Ezekiel, is it right that just because my children are in exile the building should be neglected?" The very study of the building plans of the Temple is considered an especial merit conducive to its eventual construction. Go tell them to sincerely learn the Temple's construction and I will give them abundant reward as if their study was actually the construction of the Temple (Tanchuma, Tzav.14). This Midrash is much in the spirit of Hosea 14:(2)3: "However, you have declared we may substitute the prayer of our lips for the sacrifice of bullocks✶." When Israel recites the Scriptural verses of the various offerings (be they animal, bird, or agricultural) God says, I will consider their recital as if they had brought the sacrifice and forgive them their offences (Tannis 276, Megilla 31a). The Torah in Leviticus 6:18 writes that, This is the Torah (i.e. teaching) of the sin-offering to clearly show that whoever is studying the teaching concerning the offering is considered as if he/she had actually brought the offering (Menachos 110;a).

The ancient message describing how important and precious it is to study the Temple may perhaps apply in some measure to the study of the future redemption and whereabouts of the Lost Ten Tribes. Certainly we are comforted by this study. It creates new insights and understandings of numerous Biblical texts, of history, archaeology, and of philosophy. This study definitely deserves our support and encouragement.

When the world will be finally redeemed and the Third Temple built – What will it all have been for? We see very clearly from the words of Ezekiel 11:20, –"That *they may walk in my statutes and keep my ordinances and do them* and they shall be my people and I will be their God". Ezekiel 37:24: "And David my servant shall be king over them; and they all shall have one

---

✶ [Hosea 14:2] take with you words, and turn to the LORD: say unto him, take away all iniquity, and receive us graciously: so will we render the calves of our lips.

iv

shepherd. They shall also walk in my judgments, and observe my statues, and do them".

The living commandments of the Torah are the eternal vehicles and cords of love to bind us to God (Deuteronomy 4:5-8, Deut. 10:12-13, Deut. 29:28-29 Psalm 111:7-8, Psalm 119:44, 72, 97, 155, 163, 165 Psalm 19:8-9 Zechariah 14:16 Malachi 3:22 1-Kings 8:46-50 Genesis 4:6-7 Isaiah 45:15, 17 1-Kings 15:11 2-Kings 22:2 Genesis 26:5 Deut. 30, Num.12:6-8, Deut.34:10, Isaiah 2:2

In the works of Yair Davidy we can see a reflection of Ezekiel. Yair Davidy with his exact measured analysis of Tribal Identity is reminiscent of the Prophet Ezekiel with his exact detailed vision. In both instances we are inspired and given hope. The vision of Ezekiel is on an inspired Divinely approved level while the other is on a simple analytical plane. The study of Yair Davidy may lack an absolute Divine stamp of approval but it is logical and is in accordance with the texts. The Maccabee Insitiute has witnessed Yair Davidy uniting people and bridging gaps, as Ezekiel did. Yair Davidy through his writings and lectures has inspired many people to renew themselves. This too is reminiscent of the vision of Ezekiel and the revival of the dry bones. This message of Ezekiel ch.37 precedes the re-union of "the rod of Judah, and the children of Israel his companions" with the rod "For Joseph, the rod of Ephraim, and all the house of Israel his companions" (Ezekiel 37: 16).

One of the purposes of the dispersion of the Ten tribes of Israel was to bring about a social and ethical improvement and enrichment of the nations. They were to repair the social fabric of the societies they found themselves in. The organization *Brit-Am* of Yair Davidy through its link with the *Maccabee Institute* is involved with social and moral concerns as well. The aim is that charity (Tsedakah) be practiced according to the highest ideals of historic Orthodox Judaism. The Hebrew word "Tsedakah" denotes more than philanthropy. It is more than mankind's humanity to mankind -as noble as that is. "Tsedakah" means justice. Giving is not merely an act of pity and charity but the correct right thing to do. It is simple justice.

This is Judaism in action. Judaism is inherently a way of life with an exclamation mark on just action and righteous living.

The Maccabee Institute is an expression of *Brit-Am* and Yair Davidy. Together they are involved in a host of wholesome projects that are dedicated to making the world a better place for you and me. There is, for example, a big brother/big sister program, aid to the physical and mentally challenged, youth programs –i.e. preventing teenagers from committing suicide, and getting kids off the streets and into school. The JOB (Just One Break) program sets young people up with satisfying worthwhile jobs. In addition we have clothing distribution to needy families and new immigrants.

One aspect of the Maccabee Institute's social welfare and educational outreach is a category by itself. Here we are speaking of activities in redeeming people from emergency captive-like situations, for example complex cases of drug and alcohol addictions, situations of extreme abuse and very dangerous cults.

Some Biblical verses that can be loosely applied to the Maccabee Institute's activities are: "You shall not harden your heart or close your hand" (Deuteronomy 15: 7). "You should not stand idly by the blood of your neighbor" (Leviticus 19:16). "He shall not rule harshly over him in your sight" (Leviticus 25:53). When one evades the above obligations one trespasses Biblical prohibitions. Inactivity in obligatory cases causes nullification of the following injunctions and positive commandments:

"If you forbear to deliver those that are drawn to death and those that are ready to be slain" (Proverbs 24:11).

"You shall love your neighbor as yourself," (Leviticus 19:18).

"Your brother shall live with you. You shall open your hand to him," (Leviticus 25:35-36).

The great rewards for those who give Tsedakah are clearly written in the Bible and Talmud. Rav Abahu, for example, said, If you see a person distributing his money for Tsedakah know that his wealth will increase- as it is written in the Book of Proverbs 4:24 "There are people who scatter and increase."

The Tractate Gittin 72 explains the verse in the Prophet Nahum, 1:12, "Thus says the LORD, if they are in full strength and even many, they will be sheared and he will pass, and even though I have afflicted you I will afflict you no more." If a person sees that his livelihood is being constricted he should give charity from it, and all the more so if it is plentiful. So what is the meaning of the above phrase, "they will be sheared and he will pass"? In the Yeshiva of Rabbi Yishmael it was taught, One who shears off some of his wealth and uses it for charity will soon be delivered from the punishment of Gehinom. It is comparable to two sheep that have to pass through a rushing stream. As soon as one gets shorn of its fleece it is able to cross the stream whereas the unshorn sheep cannot. The verse in Nahum continues, "And even though I have afflicted you." Mar Zuta explains, Even a poor person who himself survives on charity should give something to charity out of what he has. The verse continues, "I will afflict you no more." Rav Yosef taught, "He will no longer be afflicted with poverty."

Charity annuls harsh decrees and can rescue a person from death (1-Kings ch.17, Proverbs 10:2 11:4, Shulchan Aruch, Yoreh Deah 247, Rama).

It is understood in the Torah that through tithing one might become very wealthy:

"Honor the LORD with your capital, and with the first fruits of all your increase. So shall your barns be filled with plenty, and your presses shall burst out with new wine" (Proverbs 3:9-10).

"Bring you all the tithes into the storehouse, that there may be food in my house, and prove me now herewith, says the LORD of Hosts, if I will not open to you the windows of heaven, and pour you out a blessing, that there shall not be room enough to receive it" (Malachi 3:10).

"And the work of righteousness shall be peace" (Isaiah 32:17). The word translated from the Hebrew as "righteousness" is "Tsedakah", otherwise used to denote "charity." The deed of charity leads to peace. Thus no bad

vii

consequences result from giving charity. We continuously ask the Almighty to listen to us, so should we listen to the pleading for charitable requests. We should also remember that this world undergoes a cyclic pattern and sooner or later the descendants of those who are now rich or well off may well be impoverished. If you have been merciful to others mercy is in turn shown to you and to yours in a way that you would want it to be.

In addition there exists the need for giving tithes to and/or investment in *Brit-Am Israel*. More research must be done, the results published and brought to the attention of as many people as possible. We need state-of-the-art audiovisual presentations, lectures, graphical representations, books, pamphlets, and extensive guided tours of the center of Jerusalem as well as of the countryside of Israel. The *Brit-Am Israel* endeavor as it encompasses Talmud Torah (–the study of the Torah) is one of the commandments for which there is no prescribed limit. A monumental project would be to establish a fellowship for advanced research and scholarship on the Tribes and related topics. A think tank of scholars could come up with original insights and publish their findings.

All of these worthy projects need your encouragement, prayers, gifts, and support.

In the words of Dr. Rabbi Abraham Heschel though we are differentiated concerning the law we are united in our being accountable to God. We are objects of God's own concern, precious in his eyes. Our concepts of what ails us may be different but the anxiety is very similar. In time of need we have the same feeling of shame, of sorrow, of sighing, and the same necessity to obey and do what we must.

All of mankind can find meaning and proximity to God through the Bible: "I call heaven and earth to bear witness that any person, Jew or Gentile, man or woman, freeman or slave, if his deeds are worthy, then Divine Inspiration will descend upon him" (Tana DeBei Eliahu 9). To quote the Sage and Prophet Joel, "I will pour out My spirit on all flesh" (Joel 3:1).

In my approbation to Yair Davidy's work *Lost Israelite Identity* I quoted the Midrash emphasizing that he who hopes and trusts in God will be saved. "Turn ye to the stronghold ye prisoners of hope" (Zechariah 9:12). "For they shall not be ashamed that wait for me" (Isaiah 49:23), where the word translated as "wait" is the Hebrew word (*kivah, tikvah*) actually meaning "hope." When burnt offerings and peace offerings cannot be offered it is required that we hope Rabbi Heschel the survival of holiness in the history of the Jews is a verification of the Bible. The Bible is a unifying factor for many of us. Its revelation to Israel continues as a revelation through Israel. The Protestant Pastor, Christian Furchtegott Gellert was asked by Frederik the Great, "Herr Professor, give me proof of the Bible, but briefly for I have little time." Gellert answered, "Your majesty, the Jews."

The existence of the Jews is indeed testimony to the God of Abraham. Loyalty to the laws and teachings of Moses is a light illuminating those who practice them and those who are aware of them. So too is the revelation of the Identity of the Lost Ten Tribes a witness to the presence of God in the world. Many of us enjoy a shared commitment to the Hebrew Bible, to commandments, justice, mercy, contrition, sensitivity to the sanctity of life, recognition of the involvement of God in history, prayer, and whatever else we can gain through Torah knowledge.

There are times when we all stand together and see our faces in the mirror, the anguish of humanity and its helplessness, the perplexity of the individual and the need for Divine Guidance. We are called to praise God and to do what is required of us. We all have a task in this life and fulfilling this task is a commandment. Knowing our Tribal Identity can help us realize our individual and national tasks. "I am a companion of all who fear you, who keep your precepts" (Psalms 119:63). We rejoice wherever His name is praised, His presence sensed, His commandment done.

We are happy to welcome this second edition of The Tribes by Yair Davidy. The scholarship, insights, and keen analysis of history and destiny should lead to further study and investigation. This work has opened before us the doors of knowledge and it is up to us to walk through those portals.

May we soon see the realization of the following esoteric and beautiful passage from our Oral Tradition:

YALKUT SHIMEONI, SONG OF SOLOMON 905.

"BEHOLD THOU ART FAIR, MY LOVE, YEA PLEASANT, ALSO OUR BED IS GREEN"

SONG OF SOLOMON 1;16.

"ISRAEL SAYS: BEHOLD THOU ART FAIR, MY LOVE – WHEN YOU WILL TAKE RETRIBUTION FROM THE WORSHIPPERS OF IDOLS. YEA PLEASANT – WHEN YOU PAY THE REWARD OF THOSE WHO FEAR YOU. ALSO OUR BED... : THESE ARE THE "TEN TRIBES." *[IN HEBREW BED IS "ERES" WHILE TEN IS "ESER" AND USES THE SAME LETTERS, AND "OUR BED" (ERSEYNU) SOUNDS LIKE "OUR TEN" (ESEREYNU).]* THEY ARE THOSE WHO WERE EXILED BEYOND THE SAMBATION RIVER. THE EXILES OF JUDAH AND BENYAMIN [I.E. THE PRESENT-DAY "JEWS"] ARE DESTINED TO GO UNTO THEM AND BRING THEM BACK IN ORDER TO MERIT WITH THEM THE MESSIANIC ERA AND LIFE IN THE WORLD-TO-COME. THIS IS AS IT SAYS, "IN THOSE DAYS THE HOUSE OF JUDAH SHALL GO UNTO THE HOUSE OF ISRAEL AND THEY SHALL COME TOGETHER OUT OF THE LAND OF THE NORTH UNTO THE LAND THAT I HAVE GIVEN FOR AN INHERITANCE UNTO YOUR FATHERS"

(JEREMIAH 3;18).

Avraham Feld,
POB 1438,
Maccabee Institute,
Jerusalem,
Israel.

PROLOGUE

THE LEGACY

Beginning

This book shows how most of the ancient Israelites were exiled and lost their identity and that today their descendants are to be found mainly amongst the "Gentile" peoples of North America, Northwest Europe, Australia, New Zealand, and South Africa. The present day Jews in the Diaspora and Israel are mainly descended from only two of the original twelve tribes whereas the offspring of the remaining majority are in the above areas.

Not only are the ancient Israelites proven in general to have migrated to the west where their children formed eventually the nations of Great Britain, Eire, France, Holland, Belgium, Switzerland, Denmark, Norway, Sweden, Finland, the USA, Canada, Australia, New Zealand, and South Africa. But *also* individual Israelite Tribes are specifically identifiable as historical groups (such as the Angles, Jutes, Franks, etc.) who settled in definite areas. Different segments of each tribe tended to congregate together in the same places so that their descendants are now concentrated each in its own country which thus belongs to whatever specific tribe gained predominance within its boundaries.

It will be demonstrated how from the Tribes of Joseph (Ephraim and Menasseh) the present day English-speaking nations were formed. The Tribe of Reuben became dominant amongst the French, Benjamin became the Belgae, Zebulon

1

forefathered the Dutch, Dan the Danes, Naphtali the Norwegians, and Gad the Swedes. The Fins of Finland came from Issachar, Simeon, and Gad; Asher gave rise to the Scots, Issachar to the Swiss, and so on. Some elements from each Tribe also mixed in with those of other tribes. Clan appellations amongst the Israelite Tribes are seen to have often been preserved by the Israelites in their places of exile and throughout the course of their wanderings. Their descendants are therefore often identifiable today according to the same names.

These claims are not far-fetched. They are supported by Biblical, Historical, and other evidence. Much of our proofs are, in effect, even recognized by the academic world, which simply has not sufficiently co-related the information in its possession and not drawn the necessary conclusions from evidence it already acknowledges. It is not being said that ALL the peoples in the discussed nations are of Israelite descent. It is, HOWEVER, being stated that the overwhelming majority of the Lost Ten Tribes are in those very areas, that they significantly influence national characteristics, and that their numbers must be substantial possibly in some cases forming a majority of the population.

Similar claims regarding the Israelite origin of the British and others have been made in the past though the evidence presented herein is more far reaching, better substantiated, and more conclusive and convincing than anything advanced heretofore.

Some attempt has been made to present the case objectively though it should be realized that both the personal disposition of the present author as well as the nature of the account do not permit the extensive consideration of every contradictory opinion. This work is largely a collection of facts, each of which has been checked, cross-referenced, and evaluated in its own right. Be that as it may, the account given within relies on the sum of related data every piece of which needs to be considered as part of the whole body of evidence. Every proof adduced reinforces the overall picture and is in turn itself further confirmed by the total context.

Many of the conclusions reached, though sometimes seemingly obvious, are in effect potentially revolutionary in their implications.

It is hoped, therefore, that the present exposition will receive the appreciation it deserves without individual qualms or prejudices being allowed to blur the import of the book or its real significance.

The goal of this work is primarily a study that it is hoped will lead to a deeper and more widely spread understanding of Israelite Tribal Identities in the light of Biblical and Historical truth. This book helps clarify the truth of the Bible. Reading the Bible and studying its content is what we all need to do today, more than ever before. Not only is this obligation vital to us now, it is also not difficult. With a little effort and perseverance Bible study becomes enjoyable and gives life to its adherents. **The Tribes** provides information concerning the identity of that people which the Bible primarily speaks about and who on the whole are still unaware of their Israelite and Tribal Identity.

The peoples identified within the following pages as descendants of Israelite Tribes need too gain a deeper appreciation of themselves as they now are and once were. The account contained within bears a far-reaching message concerning the modern-day power struggle, Biblical prophecy and outlook, and the personal appreciation many people should have for themselves. The Jewish people and many "Gentiles" in the West are Tribal-brothers. They are by ancestry all "Israelites". On the other hand, this work is as important to the Jewish people in equal measure as it is to those identified as descended from the Lost Ten Tribes of Israel.

The Hebrew Exiles in Europe and Britain

The Blessings of Abraham

According to the Bible, Abraham was chosen to be the forefather of a nation through whom all the families of the earth would be blessed (Genesis 12:2), who would keep the way of the LORD to do justice and judgment (Genesis 18:19), and who would themselves become numerous, great, mighty, and blessed (Genesis 22:16-19). The blessings, in effect, were given unconditionally ("By myself have I sworn, says the LORD", Genesis 22:16) and were more a means to achieve, rather than an effect, of the ordained national role. Abraham begat Isaac, and Isaac begat Jacob who was renamed "Israel" (Genesis 32:28) who had twelve sons and these became the twelve tribes of Israel.

The Peoples of Israel Split into Two Separate Kingdoms

Under kings Saul, David, and Solomon the twelve tribes were united in one kingdom which, at various stages, controlled a significant portion of the Middle East. King David, from the Tribe of Judah, established the capital at Jerusalem within which his son Solomon built the Temple. In the reign of King Rehoboam, son of Solomon, ten of the northern most tribes seceded and formed their own kingdom (1-Kings 12:20-23), which was referred to as "Israel", (e.g. Hosea 5:5). The remaining tribes who remained faithful to the House of David were called "Judah". From inhabitants of the Kingdom of "Judah" are descended the modern Jews, though many individuals from the northern seceding tribes also made their way south (e.g. 2-Chronicles 15:9). In the course of time, these too became part of the Jewish nation.

All Inhabitants of the Northern Kingdom Are Exiled

In approximately 740-720 BCE the Northern Kingdom of Israel was conquered by the Assyrians and all of its people were exiled (2-Kings 17:18). Sennacherib, the king of Assyria[1], also exiled more than 200,000 people from the kingdom of Judah which number, at that stage, must have accounted for a good portion of the total Judean population. It follows that those Israelites exiled by the Assyrians included many from Judah. Those in Judah however, who were not exiled, numbered many from the northern tribes who had made their way south previously. Even so, it is conventionally accepted to name those exiles taken away by the Assyrians **"The Lost Ten Tribes"** after the original body who broke away from Judah. The Lost Ten Tribes were destined to lose their identity. The exile appears to have been complete. There are **no** definite archaeological remains pertaining to Israelites in the northern

"Israel" area[2] and dating from after the Assyrian exile. Some later traditions indicate that a small percentage did remain and these either joined their brothers in "Judah" or else amalgamated with the "Samaritans" who were foreigners settled by the Assyrians in place of the evacuees (2-Kings 17:24)[3]. Nevertheless, the overwhelming majority of Israelites had been taken away to places named in the Bible, in Talmudic literature, and other sources, to locations wherein Israelite presence is confirmed by archaeological evidence and popular legend. The exiled Israelites are often identifiable in their places of exile by the very same Tribal and Clan names they had before their exile. They were destined to play an important role in human history.

What Happened To the Exiles?

The Israelites had been exiled because they worshipped other gods and followed pagan customs (2-Kings 17:7-23). In their places of exile the Israelites were to continue on the whole their idolatrous practices and adoption of foreign ways. Despite their imitation, throughout the ages, of the peoples surrounding them, the Hebrew nature of the exiles was to reassert itself from time to time. These arousals of the Israelite national and tribal character enabled the realization of their inherited mission to tame and humanize the pagan world. The present book, here and there, analyses this mission and discusses prophecies concerning its fulfillment, though the major emphasis will be on **historical proofs** identifying the historical and modern-day offspring of the Lost Ten Tribes. This will be done by generally connecting peoples with the exiles. Not only are specific peoples identified with the exiles in general but also they are directly identified as members of Israelite Tribal-clans within the Israelite Nation! The Israelites were transported en-masse partially by ship to Spain and the west and from there they moved to Gaul and the British Isles but mainly they were sent to areas in northern Mesopotamia and to Hara. From those regions they later moved northward into "Scythia" (roughly the area encompassed in the past by the USSR) whence they migrated in several waves to the extreme north and west of Europe from which their descendants settled North America, Australia, New Zealand, and South Africa. The peoples in these said nations today are thus in the Biblical and historical sense

5

brothers of the Jews who came from the remaining southern kingdom of Judah and comprised the second half of the Hebrew nation with the Lost Ten Tribes comprising the remainder. The Jews and the Lost Ten Tribes together form the Israelite or HEBREW nation.

Who are the Hebrews?

The word "HEBREW" is a transliteration of the Hebrew word "Ibri", or "Ivri" and has been understood as meaning "descendant of Eber" or "someone from over the river Euphrates" though in Scripture the name is allocated only to Israelites (Iben Ezra on Exodus 21:2). The name "IBRI" may be literally understood also as meaning simply "outsider" and is derived from the root "aver" or "over" (עבר) which, in both English and Hebrew connotes "above and beyond"[3] . The first Hebrew in the Scriptural sense was Abraham the Hebrew. A Midrash (Genesis Rabah 42) says that: All the world stood on one side while Abraham the Patriarch stood **over** on the other. Abraham was the forefather of the Twelve Tribes of Israel. Ten of these Twelve Tribes disappeared and were lost. Part of the Lost Ten Tribes gave rise to peoples who moved from the Middle east to Spain and from there to France, Holland, Ireland, and Britain. They called themselves "Hiberi" or Hebrews and received Celtic culture. They were joined by other Israelites who advanced overland and had either also received aspects of "Celtic" civilization or that of the Northern "Germanic" peoples. Out of the original twelve tribes only two remained in the Land of Israel to be historically identified. The remaining two tribes absorbed some refugees and migrants from the other Tribes and together they became the Jews of history. The Jews were named after "Judah" who was the dominant tribes amongst them. The Jews were exiled from their land and suffered persecution and unjustified hostility for more than two thousand years but at least they retained knowledge of their identity..

What Happened To the Land of Israel?

The Land of Israel ("Palestine") passed from Roman hands into that of the Byzantines, thence the Persians took control, followed by the Arabs, the European Crusaders, again the Arabs and finally the Turks.

Zionism (Restorationism) was also a British Movement!

English, French, and Jewish thinkers beginning from the 1600's began (sometimes independently of each other) to advocate the establishment anew of a Jewish State in the Land of Israel. In Britain this line of thought was known as Restorationism and it was paralleled amongst the Jews by Zionism. In the late 1800's the Jewish Zionist movement was formed to work for the formal reconstitution of a Jewish National Presence in Israel. At the same time Jewish settlement in the Land increased significantly. The Turkish rulers of Palestine and the local Arabs were essentially hostile to this movement but the British used their influence and became the semi-official protectors of the Jewish presence. The British also made periodical attempts to alleviate the conditions of the Jews in Continental Eastern Europe where they were severely persecuted.

The long apparent British ambition to found a Jewish State within the area of ancient Israel has been described by Franz Kobler:

"Nowhere more than in Britain has the idea of the Restoration of the Jews been developed into a doctrine and become the object of a movement extending over more than three centuries. Only in Britain the leading spokesmen of many generations have been inspired by the vision of a revived Israel. Only there the creation of a Jewish National Home has been a serious and almost continuous political issue which was finally translated into reality..."

" The idea of Israel's Restoration is rooted in the fundamentals of the Commonwealth, Inseparable... from the character and history of the British nation in spite of a temporary abandonment..."

"The movement [i.e. Restoration of the Jewish Independent Kingdom] [is].. an integral part of British religious, social and political history forming a parallel, not an annex, of the histories of Jewish Messianism and Zionism .... The recognition of Israel's Restoration as an organic part of British political ideas.... [is] .. a genuine religious, humanitarian and political trend within British history."
Franz Kobler, "THE VISION WAS THERE", UK 1956 pp.7-9.

In 1914 the Turks joined the Germans and Austrians and fought against Britain and her allies in the First World War. With the impending defeat of Germany and Turkey the question arose as to the fate, after the war, of the non-Turkish states in the Turkish Empire, including that of the "Palestine" area.

British Ambivalence

The Government of Great Britain issued the Balfour Declaration (1917) which declared the purpose of establishing a Jewish State in the areas of modern day Jordan and Israel. Henceforth the British and Jewish Zionists began to lay the foundations for Jewish Restoration. Despite several attempts by the British establishment to renege on their undertaking, it was the British who supplied the infrastructure and much of the economic base for the coming state of Israel, This continued almost to the very last minute of British presence in the area. On the other hand it was British arms, training and citizens who helped the Arabs in their attempt to destroy this very entity. From the beginning, the British administration had suffered from an ambivalent attitude and in the 1930's the anti-Jewish tendency appeared to have gained an upper hand. The British under Arab pressure restricted Jewish immigration to "Palestine".

Traitors within France

In 1933 Hitler came to power in Germany and many Jews made desperate attempts to escape from Europe. Most of these attempts were successful even though Jewish refugees were not welcomed in many countries. With the outbreak of War the Germans conquered regions that contained Jewish citizens and refugees and these were murdered by the Nazis. France had accepted more Jewish refugees from Germany than any other country. France was defeated but before capitulating the French Army gallantly protected the British forces who were miraculously enabled to escape at Dunkirk. France however was riddled with right-wing pro-German anti-Jewish elements. It was the enemies of the Jews of France herself who betrayed France from within. Hitler had reactionary elements in France working on his behalf. These formed the basis of the Vichy Government in southern France that co-operated with the Germans. To some degree ethnic divisions may be distinguished between those Frenchmen who willingly submitted to Hitler and those who did not.

The Attitude of the Peoples to the Holocaust

Britain (more than any other nation apart from France) had accepted a good number of Jewish refugees but then decided to drastically reduce admission. Economic reasons, as well as anti-Semitism or the fear of arousing it, were among the reasons for these restrictions. Open or concealed hatred of the Jews was often a motivating factor all over the world in denying the Jews refuge. Every country on earth closed its doors against Jewish refugees. This policy continued during the Second World War to a degree. Some of the officials responsible knew that the results of this policy meant death for those of Jewish descent who fell into German hands but others were not so aware. Despite all this it is doubtful if anything really could have been done on a large scale other than defeat the Germans which is what was done. Claims to the contrary appear to be illusionary departures from the reality as it then was.

Claims against the Allies include the following: 1. They did not accept Jewish refugees before the War. 2. They did not bomb Auschwitz and the other camps. 3. They did not warn the Germans that atrocities would be punished. 4. They did not "barter" Jewish lives for goods when the Germans offered to do so towards the end of the War. 5. They closed the doors to Palestine. Some of these claims have something in them and some do not.

Concerning (1) they were not aware that the Germans were about to conquer Europe and kill all the Jews they could find. Perhaps they should have been but they were not and neither was anybody else, including most of the Jews in Europe itself. Before the War Jewish refugees from Germany usually managed to find refuge in other countries. Those who went to places that the Germans later conquered were killed but no-one foresaw this eventuality at the time.

2. Bombing Auschwitz and the camps (if indeed it was possible) underestimates the determination of the Germans to kill Jews at all costs and however they could.

9

3. Warnings not to harm the Jews were in fact issued in some cases but it was also feared that their results could be counter-productive. The conditions were those of total warfare and antisemitism was actually popular especially in Eastern Europe. In Hungary Roosevelt threatened to bomb Budapest if the persecution of the Jews did not cease and this threat influenced the Hungarian Government to lessen the persecution. Wallenstein of Sweden and Lotz of Switzerland in Hungary saved numerous Jews and they were acting on behalf of the USA in coordination with their own governments.

4. There was no real possibility of "bartering" Jewish lives for goods. Hitler would never have allowed it. Suggestions to the contrary by the Nazis appear to have been part of a German trick to sow discord between the Allies and Russia who already suspected the Allies of wanting to see Russia broken. The Germans were killing Jews even at great expense to their own war efforts.

5. The British restricted Jewish entry to Palestine because they feared Arab reactions. Jews who illegally attempted to reach Palestine were either allowed to stay in the Land of Israel or interned on Cyprus. A different policy could have saved more Jewish lives but how many is uncertain and those responsible were not necessarily aware of this possibility at the time. The measure of hostility towards the Jews from other peoples at that time is not appreciated. At the beginning of the War Turkey had instituted anti-Jewish measures but the USA pressured her to desist from them. Spain was neutral and allowed the entrance of refugees though at one stage she considered handing them over to Germany. A thinly veiled threat from Churchill caused the Spanish to think again. Things were done on behalf of the Jews. It may not have been enough but it was something and it was done by those who themselves were fighting for their own existence. Things were done and they were done mainly by the Western Allies whom we believe to constitute the Lost Ten Tribes of Israel. In the cases of not-totally Axis-dominated nations such as Hungary, Turkey, and Spain the Allies did exert effective pressure on behalf of the Jewish people.

The Germans and Austrians had began the SECOND WORLD WAR and conquered most of continental Europe. They proceeded to exterminate the Jewish people, men, women, and children. They were helped to murder Jews by Ukrainians, Latvians, Lithuanians, Romanians, Croatians, and others. More than six million Jews were killed. In Poland some people rescued Jews, though the anti-German Polish resistance movements themselves frequently also murdered Jews fleeing from the Germans. This was done as a matter of policy and in some cases had priority over the struggle against Germany. After the War Poles who had helped rescue Jews often had to keep it secret lest their fellow citizens murder them or their kin[4]. This was not the case in Germany. The consistency of the German attitude was not always a conscious one. Nevertheless most Germans to some degree accepted the Nazi aims. In the Bulgarian parts of Bulgaria-proper the Jews were protected though the Jews of Bulgarian-Macedonia were handed over to German forces for extermination. In Western Europe the Danes, Belgians, Dutch, and French, at great risk to themselves, often helped Jews escape or gave them shelter, though in some of these countries the Germans had helpers in murdering the Jewish people. The Italians often quite heroically helped save Jews yet had allied themselves to Hitler and worked for a Nazi victory.

The British Saved Mankind and Delivered the Jews from Destruction!

The British remained unconquered and the only determined unbeaten opponent of the Germans, from the beginning of the War until its end, was Great Britain and Her Dominions. At one stage Britain (and her "daughter" Dominions) stood alone against the victorious conquering Germans. The British could have made a separate peace on favorable terms with Germany but even if the British Government had wanted to (and it did not) the British people would not accept anything less than continued struggle for complete victory. The anti-Jewish policies of the Nazis even from before the beginning of the War was the major single factor in turning British public opinion against Germany[5]. The USA actively supported Britain on the material level turning

11

itself into one vast hinterland-producing area for the British effort. The USA and Russia after being attacked joined Britain against Germany. Ultimately Great Britain, Australia, New Zealand, South Africa, and Canada, together with the USA and USSR, defeated Germany and the German allies, Italy, Croatia, Hungary, Rumania, and the Baltic States. Despite everything, those Jews who did survive owe their lives, in a sense, to the Allies' victory.

The Betrayal of the Jews

Both before the War and during it, it may have been possible to save the lives of a more Jewish refugees than actually were saved if there had been somewhere to settle them in. France, Britain and the USA received many and most other places very little. Even Britain and the USA did not receive as many as they could have. Australia and South Africa closed their doors. After the WAR these same places (Australia, New Zealand, Canada, the USA, Britain, etc.) were often enthusiastic (and at other times at least willing) in re-settling millions of non-Jewish refugees and immigrants from Russia, the Ukraine, Latvia, Lithuania, Hungary, Germany, Italy, Pakistan, Africa, Asia, and so on. From reading accounts and official reports concerning the fate of the Jews during the Holocaust years when the Jews needed to be helped an unmistakable impression is received. Some of the authorities in potential host countries would rather have left the Jews to their fate than help them, especially if help meant accepting them into their own countries[6]. **Jews were not welcome (to say the least) in several cases.** This throws a serious question on the degree of Israelite ancestry claimable by the said nations. It does not nullify such claims but it means that they must be qualified and **the presence of non-Israelite elements existing alongside the Israelite ones seriously taken into consideration!** On the other hand some effective policies were undertaken. The positive actions on behalf of the Jews were nearly always due to people identified in this work as coming from "Lost Ten Tribes" Israelite stock. In France people of Protestant Huguenot descent were especially active in doing all that they could to rescue Jews and whole villages participated at great risk to themselves. The fact that the WAR against the Nazi evil was fought, maintained, and eventually won was also due mainly to people identified by us as descended from Israelites. Despite everything, one aspect of the whole War effort had the goal to ensure Jewish survival.

The German Plan to Exterminate Britain.
Traitors To Britain Were Anti-Jewish!

The Germans had found the Dutch too pro-Jewish and not sufficiently "Aryan" in outlook. They intended to deport all of them to Poland which would be depopulated of its Polish inhabitants. In the Second World War they had attempted to conquer Britain. They had plans, if successful, to deport all of the male population as slave labor to the Continent: Females (if they survived) would be fertilized by SS men. Professor Dr. Franz Six was to be in charge of Britain. He later indoctrinated the Killing Squads (Einsatzgruppen SS) in Russia.

<<Hitler agreed with every word; his great respect for the Anglo-Saxon race had made it all the harder for him to enter this life-or-death struggle which must end with the destruction of one of them." Peter Townsend, "Duel of Eagles", 1971, p.45.

Compare Robert Payne, "The Life & Death of Adolf Hitler" U.S.A. 1973, p.400: <<Among the many plans submitted to Hitler and approved by him was a comprehensive plan for transporting the greater part of the male population to work in factories in Germany. Orders concerning the Organization and Function of the Military Government of England, a thick compendium of rules and regulations to be followed by the German administrators of the conquered territory, called for all able-bodied men between the ages of seventeen and forty-five to be sent to Germany as slave-laborers. The women of England, with the help of the SS, would produce a new race of Anglo-Germans. The entire intelligentsia and all the Jews would be liquidated. SS Colonel Professor Dr. Franz Six, a former dean of the faculty of political science at the University of Berlin, was placed in charge of the liquidation and deportation of Englishmen. SS offices would be established in London, Bristol, Birmingham, Liverpool., Manchester, and Edinburgh. Colonies of Englishmen would be established in the Baltic States".

The above documented plan only represents part of the actual eventuality. The plan was that set out for the best of circumstances from the German point of view. It reflects German susceptibilities prior to action. Hitler considered England "the enemy above all enemies" (Payne p.343). The fate of the English in practice was liable to have been even worse than the plan indicates.

<<I am sure that Hitler would not have hesitated for a moment to employ atom bombs against England. I remember his reaction to the final scene of a newsreel on the bombing of Warsaw in the autumn of 1939...Hitler was fascinated. The film ended with a montage showing a plane diving toward the outlines of the British Isles. A burst of flames followed and the island flew into the air in tatters. Hitler's enthusiasm was unbounded. "This is what will happen to them!" he cried out, carried away. "That is how we will annihilate them!">> Albert Speer, "Inside The Third Reich", New York, 1971, p.303.

The Germans were developing means of mass-sterilization. They meant to eliminate the British people as we know it. They Even so, there existed fringe elements within certain sections of British society who had appeasing tendencies towards the Nazis both during the War and after it. It was these same "conciliatory" elements in many cases who later strengthened the anti-Jewish sentiments expressed in official policy regarding Palestine.

To sum up: The whole world east of the Rhine actively participated in killing the Jews. The British and Americans were against it and did what they could to prevent it but there were elements amongst them that strongly did not want "too many" Jews in their own country or in "Palestine," or elsewhere. There were also elements who were anti-Semitic outright. These were a minority but had influence at crucial moments. Elements who were anti-Jewish were often in effect proven to be traitorous to the Allied cause.

After the War the Jews in Palestine, reinforced by survivors from Nazi Europe were faced with a coalition of hostile Arab forces partly backed, armed and trained by the British and including the presence of British military personnel.

14

Fiction between the Jews and British had been growing due to the British restricting Jewish immigration to Palestine (including that of those who had no-were else to go)♥, and not allowing the Jews to defend themselves against Arab terrorism. In addition anti-Semitic elements in the local British Palestinian administration and in the British Government had increased in influence.

Why Did Britain Renege?

The British attitude in Palestine resulted from a mixture of anti-Semitism in certain circles together with a misplaced colonial tradition of protecting the "natives". The results of this characteristic had already been seen elsewhere: British concern for the Red Indians in North America at the expense of the British descended white settlers was one of the causes of the American War of Independence against the British. In South Africa, British protection of the "blacks" discriminated against Dutch Boer and British settlers. In New Zealand, British policy had favored Maori natives over immigrants from Britain[8]. In Palestine the British often attempted to be impartial but suffered from a conflict of interests. Prior to the Second World War, a British officer (**Orde Wingate**) under directions from the British Army helped found the Jewish Fighting Forces and formulate military concepts that ultimately led to Jewish victory. Orde Wingate, incidentally, believed in the Bible, realized that the British descend from the Lost Ten Tribes[9] and dreamt of leading an independent Jewish Army. He was transferred against his will from "Palestine" and in the Second World War liberated Ethiopia from the Italians. Later in Burma

---

♥ The most traumatic event in this regard was probably the "Struma" affair. The Struma was an unseaworthy boat into which 769 Jewish refugees had been crammed. They were fleeing from Romania where the local populace had turned almost "cannibalistic" in its treatment of the Jews. The boat docked near Istanbul and the passengers requested entry visas to Palestine but were refused. The Turks then cast the boat adrift and refused help even though the British had relented and agreed to take in the children. The boat was then sunk by a Soviet submarine in February, 1942. Only two of the passengers reached shore one of whom was shot by the Turks and the other survived. At the time it was not known that the Soviets were responsible for sinking the ship nor was the attitude of the Turks publicized. In the eyes of many Jews in Palestine the British were responsible as in some way they may well have been. For details see, "Death on the Black Sea. The Untold Story of the STRUMA and World War II's Holocaust at Sea", Douglas Frantz and Catherine Collins, USA, 2003.

he caused the Japanese to divert their forces and thus probably ensured the Allied victory against the Japanese. In "Palestine", in addition to Orde Wingate, many of the British personnel were pro-Jewish in practice.♦ At one stage the British had actually executed hundreds of Arab rebels and otherwise disposed of many more. The British position was never really clear, even to themselves, and both Arabs and Jews felt discriminated against. There were also many British soldiers and administrators were anti-Semitic and openly sided with the Arabs. In British Governmental circles men such as **Lloyd George** and **Winston Churchill** were strongly pro-Jewish and Zionistic but they were restrained and hampered by their colleagues and by people in lower echelons. Despite everything, on the whole, the Jews benefited from the British presence. Even though some Britons worked against it **most of the British public (in Britain) continually favored the establishment of a Jewish state**! It was a succession of British Governments who let their own people down by being less pro-Jewish than they should have been. The British had ruled in Palestine where Jews and Arabs were fighting each other. Both resisted the British until the British decided to leave. Newly-released documentation suggests that the British Labour Government envisaged an Arab victory over the Jews which would result in the British being called back to serve as "Protectors" of a truncated Jewish entity centered on Haifa[10]. Pro-Jewish (or just fair-minded) elements however amongst the British forces evacuating Palestine helped the Jews save themselves from the defeat they were intended to suffer .

After the establishment of the State of Israel Winston Churchill in the House of Commons stated that the anti-Jewish policies of some British Governments had been mistaken and called for Reconciliation[11]. For the sake of perspective it should

---

♦ Wingate had been preceded by Colonel John Henry Patterson (1867-1947). Patterson was born in Dublin of Protestant origin. Like Wingate he intensely believed in the Bible. Also like Wingate he believed that the British were descended from the Lost Ten Tribes of Israel. Patterson had been the Allied commander of the Zionist Mule Corps that saw service against the Turks in Gallilopoli. He later commanded the Jewish Legion that fought east of the Jordan in the First World War on behalf of the British. Like Wingate Patterson was a zealous Zionist. He was a friend of the Zionist leader, Zeev Jabotinsky.

be recalled that the British feared Communist expansion and that the Jewish international consensus regarding Communism was at first unclear. Jews on the Continent had been horribly oppressed and persecuted. In Russia many Jews had been forced by the authorities to abandon their religion. Some had found refuge in Revolutionary movements. These were a small percentage of the Jewish people but for the Revolutionaries they were qualitatively important. Quite a few of the early Communist leaders were Jewish even though the Communists as a whole were mortal enemies of the Jewish people. Communism was then a serious threat. In addition at that time many other Jews had Socialist and extreme liberal sympathies. These were identified as potentially "Communist" and the "Communist menace" was regarded with a partially-justified hysteria in certain circles. The British also had important oil interests, hopes of retaining their Empire, numerous Moslem subjects in India and Malaya and other areas, and there were other considerations. A parallel case in some respects is that of South Africa, and how many liberal Anglo-Saxon Gentiles and Jewish intellectuals supported the South African whites in the past even though the whites may have been objectively relatively more justified than any other group in prevailing circumstances? The South African whites were forced to place their very existence in danger mainly due to pressure from their liberal Anglo-Saxon and Jewish brothers. It should also be remembered that Anti-religious Jews in and outside of Israel and including members of some of the Israeli Governments have on occasion been almost as anti-Jewish as some of the British sometimes were. [*The Oslo Agreements of 1993 and everything that sprang from them are an example. These Agreements gave weapons and a power base within the Land of Israel to Arab murderers whose declared intention was to kill as many Jews as possible. These Agreements were sanctioned without any justification by numerous leaders in the Jewish community.*] It is also worth highlighting some of the positive pro-Jewish aspects the British Administration in Palestine did have when an overall view is taken:

<<The British kept their promises to the Zionists. They opened up the country to mass Jewish immigration; by 1948, the Jewish population had increased by more than tenfold. The Jews were permitted to purchase land, develop agriculture, and establish

17

industries and banks. The British allowed them to set up hundreds of new settlements, including several towns. They created a school system and an army; they had a political leadership and elected institutions; and with the help of all these they in the end defeated the Arabs, all under British sponsorship, all in the wake of that promise of 1917. Contrary to the widely held belief of Britain's pro-Arabism, British actions considerably favored the Zionist enterprise.>> Tom Segev, "One Palestine Complete", USA, 2001, p.5

<<The British had found an underdeveloped country when they arrived, and they left behind much progress, especially among the Jews. But they also left behind much backwardness, especially among the Arabs.>> Segev, p.9.

<<Pollock [a British military administrator in Palestine] and others like him wanted the state administration to continue to function properly, and so they did in fact make a great effort to transfer it to the Jews. Some functions were handed over to the municipalities, others to the Jewish Agency. In addition, the evacuation plan, from south to north, left responsibility for Jewish population centers in British hands, almost to the very last minute, thus impeding Arab war plans>> Segev, p.513.

The State of Israel and Non-Jewish "Israelite" Support

At all events, despite the attacks of hostile Arab states, the Jews won their War of Independence and the State of Israel came into existence in 1948. President Truman insisted that Israel be allowed to retain the Negev area thus doubling the size of the new country. For a limited time after its inception the State of Israel enjoyed the aid of individual Frenchmen and the general support of France. Britain remained ambivalent, though in 1956 Britain, France, and Israel were allied in military action against Egypt. At that stage the USA was antagonistic. In 1967 Israel fought a war against the Arab States surrounding her and was victorious. After 1967 the USA became Israel's main (and almost only) backer and also materially supported her. President John Kennedy told Golda Meir that the relationship between the USA and Israel was comparable to that between the USA and Britain. President Nixon was a genuine friend of Israel and so were most other American leaders such as President Reagan and President George Bush . Millions of Jews had been imprisoned in eastern Europe, Ethiopia, and the USSR and it was largely due to US influence and often active intervention that many of these were enabled to emigrate to Israel and elsewhere. The USA did, however, have its own anti-Jewish and anti-Zionist elements and these, on occasion, did damage to the Israeli cause, or at least tried to. The USA at times openly used its overwhelming influence to attempt the manipulation of Israeli society and government. The establishment of left-wing governments in the State of Israel and forced agreements that enabled the Palestinian Arabs to arm themselves and seriously endangered Israel was due to American and European interference in Israeli affairs.

On the other hand Israel received much support from Fundamental "Evangelicals" in the USA and elsewhere. Throughout the Western World and especially the English-speaking areas Christians have recently began to search for their "Hebrew" roots. The more Biblically orientated they are the more this phenomenon occurs and it is usually accompanied by increasing sympathy for and support of the Jewish State of Israel. By "Hebrew" roots the Christians intend the sources of their religious faith but we would say that an inner arousal of their ancestral Hebraic sources is also a factor.

A very large proportion of those who have supported and helped the Jews and the State of Israel were descended from Israelites as proven in this work. Often those few friends whom the Jews had were both of Israelite origin and also believed strongly in the Bible. In the USA this phenomenon was and is especially noticeable. There were also occasions when the USA seemed to regard Israel almost as an expression of part of itself and act accordingly though at other times Israel was treated with barely-subdued hostility.

On the whole it may be said that since the eighteenth century (and to an extent well before) most countries of the world were anti-Jewish while the USA, Britain, and France, and related nations in Western Europe and overseas were ambivalent with a favorable attitude prevailing more often than not. This book brings proof that part of the reason for this "Ambivalence" was HEREDITY. There is a familial relationship between western peoples and the Jews which at times is instinctively felt and expressed. The Lost Ten Tribes having

19

migrated westward is the best factual explanation of this feeling.

Inheritance

A significant and influential portion of the peoples in northwest Europe, Britain, and North America have the same ancestry as the Jews. This fact has influenced the historical behavior of the said peoples.

It is generally accepted that these peoples have always been attached to the Bible, especially to the "Old" (Hebrew) Testament. On the whole their overall national tendency has been a striving for the general good and justice for all. It is obvious that these goals have not been achieved but attempts have been made and for that matter no claim is being made that all of these peoples are Hebrew or that Hebrew ancestry is always good. A specific influence is being considered as attributable mainly to the contribution of definite groups who, to some degree, probably merged with others of possibly opposing inclinations.

The Promise to Abraham – A Prerequisite for Greatness

Abraham was the first ancestor of the Hebrew nation and of him it was stated:

"ABRAHAM SHALL BECOME A GREAT AND MIGHTY NATION, AND ALL THE NATIONS OF THE EARTH SHALL BE BLESSED IN HIM... HE WILL COMMAND HIS CHILDREN AND HIS HOUSEHOLD AFTER HIM, AND THEY SHALL KEEP THE WAY OF THE LORD, TO DO JUSTICE AND JUDGMENT; THAT THE LORD MAY BRING UPON ABRAHAM THAT WHICH HE HATH SPOKEN OF HIM" (GENESIS 18:17-19).

This blessing infers that becoming "a great and mighty nation" was not only an effect but also a PREREQUISITE of having all the nations of the earth being blessed in him and of doing justice and judgment. Similar verses in the Bible expound on this theme and add detail to it. We will return to this subject. The doing of justice was to be especially associated with the Tribe of Joseph.

Colonialism Was Beneficial

The nations identified in this book as being of the Israelite seed of Abraham were those who mainly conducted European colonialist policies from the eighteenth to twentieth centuries. The overall effects of colonialism, in most cases, were very beneficial -despite claims to the contrary. French, British, and Dutch colonialism put a stop to internecine warfare, ended human sacrifice and slavery, founded and/or improved irrigation-systems, reformed agricultural practices and public hygiene, built bridges, roads, public works, and so on. Wherever they ruled the local population greatly increased in numbers, in health, and in respect for basic human dignity. The colonial powers also often (but not always) made large profits for their own citizens and helped themselves by exploiting opportunities for investment, which the subject countries offered. This investment usually benefited all parties. This was part of the blessing of Abraham, the power was given and it was used for good, even though in some cases the initial conscious motivation in colonization was a lust for power and material gain. In the case of the British, colonies often accrued to the Empire due to dynamics beyond the conscious control of the British themselves! The overall effect of colonization was beneficial, and altruistic motives were also present and implemented. Even today these peoples remain the only real morally motivated advancers of international justice in this world. Even if this morality is often misapplied or self-serving or strangely selective there does exist a genuine will to do the right thing overall and on the whole the effects are positive.

We Are Not Racists!

Another point is that the above statements and the historical material revealed in this book are not coming to support any racialist or other theories. All of mankind is descended from one ancestor. The characteristics of everyone else are potentially present somewhere in each of us! The peculiar behavior of any group may, in part, be attributed to the effects of climate, environment, geographical location, historical factors, and cultural influences, all of which are largely beyond the control of whoever is affected by them. NEVERTHELESS, for whatever reason, a promise was made to

Abraham which was unconditional and which had therefore, at some time, to occur; and to some extent so it has -in the above mentioned nations. Whatever caused this occurrence in the immediate sense is relatively inconsequential.

The historical proofs in this book, thus, have potential significance beyond that of academic study. The said evidence may be of importance in helping many peoples understand both their own past and their present obligation and potential. An important message of this book involves the ancestry of many people in the western world today for whom the historical study indicates Israelite ancestral identities and these entail both hereditary characteristics and obligations.

The exiles from the Northern Kingdom were taken in part overseas to Spain and its region and from there they moved to Ireland, Britain, and Gaul. Others were moved to the fringes of the Assyrian Empire, Northern Mesopotamia, the Caucasus and Zagros Mountain areas and Eastern Iran. From these regions they were to move into Europe and Eurasia and eventually converge on the west in the process adopting aspects of "Celtic" and "Germanic" civilization. They had been transferred at the first en-masse from the LAND OF ISRAEL. In Israel they had been part of a Twelve Tribed Nation, each tribe being divided into smaller familial groupings and sub-clans. The Assyrian directed relocation of these "Israelites" was accompanied by the partial breaking up and scattering of the Tribal units. Nevertheless, enough of the original organizational patterns were to be maintained in the places of exile to enable the identification of historical groups with Israelite entities and to trace their subsequent movements.

The identifiable Israelite descended peoples were destined to reach and settle in West Europe, where too, the same Tribal and Tribal clan equations are possible. What exact percentage of Israelite parentage exists in the relevant nations wherein these groups settled is uncertain but it appears to be substantial. At all events, wherever else parts of the Lost Ten Tribes of Israel may or may not be, their overwhelming majority migrated to the above mentioned areas, as the following pages show.

The identifiable Israelite descended peoples were destined to reach and settle in West Europe, where too, the same Tribal and Tribal clan equations are possible. What exact percentage of Israelite parentage exists in the relevant nations wherein these groups settled is uncertain but it appears to be substantial. At all events, wherever else parts of the Lost Ten Tribes of Israel may or may not be, their overwhelming majority migrated to the above mentioned areas, as the following pages show.

AND YE ANSWERED ME, AND SAID, THE THING WHICH THOU HAST SPOKEN IS GOOD FOR US TO DO [DEUTERONOMY 1:14]

SO I TOOK THE CHIEF OF YOUR TRIBES, WISE MEN, AND KNOWN, AND MADE THEM HEADS OVER YOU, CAPTAINS OVER THOUSANDS, AND CAPTAINS OVER HUNDREDS, AND CAPTAINS OVER FIFTIES, AND CAPTAINS OVER TENS, AND OFFICERS AMONG YOUR TRIBES [DEUTERONOMY 1:15]

AND I CHARGED YOUR JUDGES AT THAT TIME, SAYING, HEAR THE CAUSES BETWEEN YOUR BRETHREN, AND JUDGE RIGHTEOUSLY BETWEEN EVERY MAN AND HIS BROTHER, AND THE STRANGER THAT IS WITH HIM [DEUTERONOMY 1:16]

YE SHALL NOT RESPECT PERSONS IN JUDGMENT; BUT YE SHALL HEAR THE SMALL AS WELL AS THE GREAT; YE SHALL NOT BE AFRAID OF THE FACE OF MAN; FOR THE JUDGMENT IS GOD'S: AND THE CAUSE THAT IS TOO HARD FOR YOU, BRING IT UNTO ME, AND I WILL HEAR IT [DEUTERONOMY 1:17]

AND I COMMANDED YOU AT THAT TIME ALL THE THINGS WHICH YE SHOULD DO [DEUTERONOMY 1:18]

CONVENTIONAL MAP OF THE TRIBAL ALLOCATIONS WITHIN THE LAND OF ISRAEL PRIOR TO THE EXILE

THE EXPANSION OF ISRAELITE TRIBES IN BIBLICAL TIMES

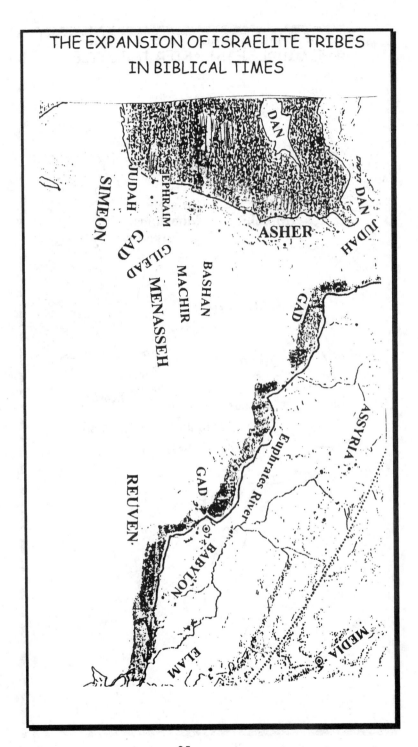

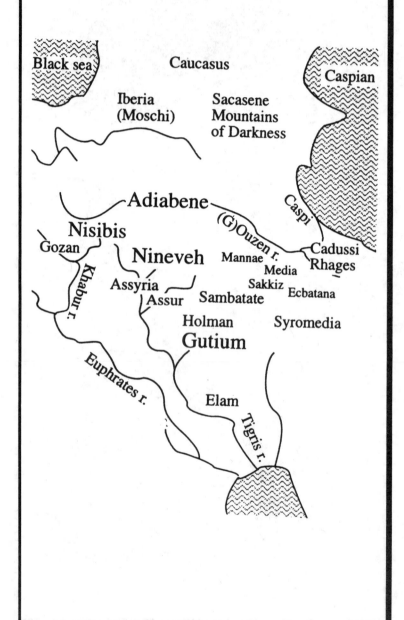

AREAS OF EARLY ISRAELITE SETTLEMENT IN
THE MIDDLE EAST AFTER THE EXILE

1

THE HISTORICAL
BACKGROUND

According to conventional history, the British Isles, Gaul (France and Belgium), and the West European coastline, in ancient times, were settled by peoples of Celtic culture. Prominent elements amongst the Celts included the Galatians (also known as the Galli) in Gaul, the Cymbri in Denmark, and the Cimry and Caledonians in Britain. These groups were ascribed Cimmerian origin by Classical writers[1], which is substantiated by archaeological evidence and other sources. The Cimmerians had first appeared on the fringes of the Assyrian Empire in the Middle East shortly after the majority of northern Israelites had been exiled, and all areas of their early appearance were those to which Israelites had been transported. The Cimmerians moved to the west where they merged with and transformed Celtic civilization which they came to dominate.

In the period 50 BCE to 450 CE the Cimmerian-Galatian sphere in the west was overrun by a host of newcomers, such as, the Danes, Vandals, Goths, Suebians, Angles, Jutes, and Franks. All of these peoples were akin to each other and also had ancestral links with the Galatian peoples they were conquering. These nations had advanced via Germany and Scandinavia from further east, from the area of "Scythia" that encompassed Russia, Siberia, and even what is now northern China.

Prior to their being in "Scythia" these same peoples had been found on the fringes of the Assyrian Empire, in northern Mesopotamia, the Caucasus and Zagros mountain areas and in eastern Iran. They had previously been transferred en-masse from the LAND OF ISRAEL. In Israel they had been part of a Twelve Tribed Nation, each tribe being divided into smaller familial groupings and sub-clans. The Assyrian directed relocation of these "Israelites" was accompanied by the partial breaking up and scattering of the Tribal units. Nevertheless, enough of the original organizational patterns were to be maintained in the places of exile to enable the identification of historical groups with Israelite entities and to trace their subsequent movements.

The identifiable Israelite-descended peoples were destined to reach and settle in Western Europe, where too, the same Tribal and Tribal clan equations are possible. What exact percentage of Israelite parentage exists in the relevant nations wherein these groups settled is uncertain but it appears to be substantial. Wherever else parts of the Lost Ten Tribes of Israel may or may not be, the overwhelming majority migrated to the above mentioned areas, as the following facts show.

SEE, I HAVE SET BEFORE THEE THIS DAY LIFE AND GOOD, AND DEATH AND EVIL;

IN THAT I COMMAND THEE THIS DAY TO LOVE THE LORD THY GOD, TO WALK IN HIS WAYS, AND TO KEEP HIS COMMANDMENTS AND HIS STATUTES AND HIS JUDGMENTS, THAT THOU MAYEST LIVE AND MULTIPLY: AND THE LORD THY GOD SHALL BLESS THEE IN THE LAND WHITHER THOU GOEST TO POSSESS IT.

BUT IF THINE HEART TURN AWAY, SO THAT THOU WILT NOT HEAR, BUT SHALT BE DRAWN AWAY, AND WORSHIP OTHER GODS, AND SERVE THEM;

I DENOUNCE UNTO YOU THIS DAY, THAT YE SHALL SURELY PERISH, AND THAT YE SHALL NOT PROLONG YOUR DAYS UPON THE

LAND, WHITHER THOU PASSEST OVER JORDAN TO GO TO POSSESS IT.

I CALL HEAVEN AND EARTH TO RECORD THIS DAY AGAINST YOU THAT I HAVE SET BEFORE YOU LIFE AND DEATH, BLESSING AND CURSING: THEREFORE CHOOSE LIFE THAT BOTH THOU AND THY SEED MAY LIVE:

THAT THOU MAYEST LOVE THE LORD THY GOD, AND THAT THOU MAYEST OBEY HIS VOICE, AND THAT THOU MAYEST CLEAVE UNTO HIM: FOR HE IS THY LIFE, AND THE LENGTH OF THY DAYS: THAT THOU MAYEST DWELL IN THE LAND WHICH THE LORD SWARE UNTO THY FATHERS, TO ABRAHAM, TO ISAAC, AND TO JACOB, TO GIVE THEM.

[DEUTERONOMY 30:15-20]

The Exile

The original Twelve Tribes of Israel had split into two kingdoms. Two tribes comprising "Judah" were in the south, and the ten tribes of "Israel" were in the north. The Ten Northern Tribes were entirely taken away by the Assyrians to places in northern Mesopotamia, to the Caucasus area and to Eastern Iran.

The Bible says that: "The King of Assyria took Samaria, and carried Israel away **into Assyria**, and placed them in **Hala**, and in **Habor**, and in the **cities of the Medes**" (2-Kings 17:6).

The Bible also mentions "**Hara**" (1-Chronicles 5:26) in Eastern Iran as a place of exile. The Talmud and archaeological findings enable the identification of these places of re-settlement. Shortly after the exile and re-settlement every one of the said places became a center for a group of peoples who then appeared for the first time. They are known to history as the Cimmerians, Scythians, and Guti or Goths. It will be shown that these entities were (at least in part) the Lost Ten Tribes of Israel!

The bulk of the Israelites had been exiled in the period 730-710, or earlier. In about 707 BCE, a people named "Gimirae" were reported from the region of Mannae[2]. These are the Cimmerians. They were referred to as "Outcasts" by the

Assyrians[3]. They had been subjects of Assyria but had rebelled and broke away. The Prophet Amos (Amos 4:3 as translated into Aramaic by Targum Yehonathan) had previously foretold that the northern tribes would be "cast-out" to the Mountains of Mannae. Apart from their being in Mannae, the Cimmerians were also reported as at first centered in the region of Iberia[4]. The Cimmerians killed the king of neighboring Urartu ('Ararat) and overran his land. They also defeated and killed Sargon, king of Assyria, in 705. Sargon was replaced by Sennacherib (705-681) who beat off the Cimmerians. After this a portion of the Cimmerians invaded the Land of Phrygia in Northern Turkey .

The Cimmerian king was called by the Assyrians *"King of the Umman Manda* [i.e. Cimmerians], *king of the Sakae* [Scyths] *and Guti* [Goths]"[5]. In the dialects of the area *Umman Manda* could mean "People [Umman] of Manasseh."♥ The Cimmerians and Scythians were essentially different branches of the one people: They were called *Umman Manda* by the Assyrians at that time. Later the Babylonians would apply the term to the Medes who took the place of the Scythians. In one Assyrian document the Cimmerians are referred to as "Amuru" and the Cimmerian king is termed "King of the Amuru". "Amuru" means Amorite but in Assyrian usage the expression meant "Dweller of the Land of Israel" or "Previous Dweller of the Land of Israel and/or Syria"[6]. In the Assyrian inscription "Syrians" (Achlamu) are explicitly spoken of separately as adversaries of the "Amuru": Since the term in general had come to be applied to either Israelites or Syrians and in this case the Syrians are spoken of separately it therefore follows that by "Amuru" Israelites are intended! That portion of the Cimmerians that invaded Phrygia were soon driven out of Anatolia and crossed the Bosporus into Europe. Jerome (on Zecharia 10:11), the

---

♥ In Aramaic, Persian, and other northern dialects at that time the Hebrew "d"-sound was often changed for "s", thus "Manasseh" becomes "Manda". An analysis of the term "Umman Manda" shows that it was first applied to "Semitic" nomads from the geographical area of the Israelite Tribe of Manasseh in the eastern region of Ancient Israel adjoining the Euphrates River, see Michael C. Astour, "Ezekiel's Prophecy of Gog and the Cuthean Legend of Nathan-Sin." Journal of Biblical Literature (JBL), vol. 95/4 (1976), 567-99. The Assyrians called the Cimmerians and Scythians "Manda". After the Cimmerians had left the area the Later Babylonians applied the term to the Medes

translator of the Bible into Latin, had heard from Jewish sages the tradition that Israelites, exiled by the Assyrians, reached the Bosporus where Turkey joins Europe and from there headed north, i.e. into Europe. These Cimmerians, traveling via the Balkans and Danube valley, eventually reached Gaul, the British Isles, and Scandinavia They became the major factor in "Celtic" Civilization.

Meanwhile, the rest of the Cimmerians who had not been driven into Phrygia but had remained on the fringes of the Assyrian Empire managed to recuperate. By the end of Sennacherib's reign they had gained control of Mannae. They posed a serious challenge to Sennacherib's successor, Essarhaddon (681-669 BCE).

At first Essarhaddon beat the Cimmerians, some of whom joined his forces[7]. In about 676 a new element, known as "Ishkuza"[8] emerged from the Cimmerian ranks. These are identified with the Scythians whom the Persians and Babylonians referred to as the "Saka": The terms "Ishkuza" and "Saka" are both forms for the name "Isaac". Abraham the patriarch had been promised: *"In Isaac will your seed be called"* (Genesis 21:12). After their first appearance, the Scythians and Cimmerians are recognizable as distinct entities though, in effect, both bodies were combinations of Scythians proper, of Goths, and of Cimmerians in varying proportions.

In 673 King Esarhaddon of Assyria slew the Scythian king who was then replaced by Bartatua. Bartatua became the Scythian ruler and entered into alliance with the Assyrians. He married the daughter of Esarhaddon. The Assyrian Empire at that stage was troubled by rebellious Medes, Mannaens, Cimmerians, and others. From being allies of the Assyrians the Scythians progressed to hold the Assyrians in some type of subservience for 28 years[9]. For a period they took control over much of the Assyrian Empire. According to Herodotos they ruled it. They established a center at Beth Shean in the former land of northern "Israel"✦. Archaeological finds testify to Scythian presence throughout the Israelite region[10]. The Scythians attacked Egypt and raided the Philistine city of Ashkelon. At this stage the Jews of Judah in the south who had not been exiled but had remained on part of their own land centered around Jerusalem were ruled by king Josiah ben Amon (628-609 BCE). During his reign, the Scythians were taking over control from the Assyrians, attacking the Philistines and setting themselves up in Beth-Shean and over portions of the former land of Israel. King Josiah of Judah was also extending his influence into that very same area! King Josiah had made himself independent of Assyria, smashed idols (2-Chronicles 34:4-7) that represented Assyria's authority[11], and established colonies in northern Israel, at Megiddo, in the north near Beth-Shean, and in Philistia on the coast[12]. King Josiah also had a presence in Beth-Shean (which was considered the Scythian headquarters) itself! A stone monument with an inscription of King Josiah testifies to his suzerainty over the Beth Shean area[13].

The Scythians, as well as king Josiah, attacked Philistia. The Scythians later also maintained a presence in Philistia[14] alongside the Judaean colonies that were there. In other words, the Scythians and Judeans of King Josiah were in the same areas, undertaking the same activities, and must have been working hand in hand[15].

At this same time, in eastern Iran (in the region of Hara and Bactria), there arose a religious reformer named Zarathustra. The original doctrine of Zarathustra (ZOROASTER) was monotheistic and even **Biblical** in character[16]. After Zoroaster's death, his religion was taken over and altered by the Median tribe of Magi. The original message had been Hebraic but the Magi made it pagan. Zoroaster, according to Iranian tradition had been taught by the prophet Jeremiah or by one of

---

✦ Pliny N.H.5;16, Avi-Yonah quotes Eusebius and G. Syncellus to the effect that the Scythian presence in the Land of Israel was co-eval with the reign of Josiah ben Amon, king of Judah. According to Georgius Syncellus (Chron. 1:405) the origin of the name Scythopolis for BETH-SHEAN (also known to Josephus, Ant. xii. 85 sect 34..., Eusehius OS 237:5, and others) was the presence in that city of a body of Scythians from the time of Psammetichus I (664-610 BCE) see M. AVI -YONAH, "The Beth Shean Valley" (Hebrew) 1962 in "The 17th Archaeological Convention. Israel Exploration Society".

Jeremiah's pupils[17]. Zoroaster himself had Scythian familial connections[18]. Some reports identify Zoroaster as an Israelite[19]. Zoroaster was linked to both the Scythians and to the Hebrews. Zoroaster is an additional indication that the historical Scythians were to a significant degree of Israelite origin.

Eventually, after enduring Scythian subjection and witnessing the partial disintegration of their Empire, the Assyrians attempted to re-assert themselves. At this stage, ca. 616 BCE, the Medes and Babylonians were in open revolt. About two years later, in 614 the Medes began to besiege Nineveh, the Assyrian capital. The Assyrians were supported by part of the Mannaeans and by Egypt. The Scythians of the time were divided. Some Scythians already sided with the enemies of Assyria. The most powerful section of the Scythians however at first seemed more inclined to support Assyria versus her besiegers than to be against her. The Medes, Babylonians, Guti, Gimiri (Cimmerians), and others were combined against Assyria. Scythians from Bactria-Hara and from the city of Ecbatana were called to Assyria's help. [Ecbatana in Media was THEN a Scythian center but later became the capital of Media][20]. When the Scythians arrived at NINEVEH they were somehow persuaded to change sides and to join the besiegers[21]. According to a Babylonian inscription, Nineveh was taken and sacked by the allies with the Umman-Manda (meaning in this case, the Scythians) taking the leading role. Shortly afterwards all of the other Assyrian cities received similar treatment. The Assyrian Empire was destroyed.

Meanwhile, an Egyptian army under Pharoah Neco had been marching to the aid of Assyria. King Josiah of Judah attempted to stop the Egyptian progress. The King of Egypt tried to dissuade him: "HE SENT AMBASSADORS TO HIM, SAYING, WHAT HAVE I TO DO WITH THEE, THOU KING OF JUDAH? I COME NOT AGAINST THEE THIS DAY, BUT AGAINST THE HOUSE WHEREWITH I HAVE WAR" [2-Chronicles 35:21]. The expression the Egyptian used to denote the Scythian side to the conflict is "house", i.e. not your house but the other (Scythian) house. This is an unusual choice of expression. There were two Houses of Israelites: the House of Judah and the House of Israel (2-Samuel 2:7 Jeremiah 11:10). Pharoah Neco was distinguishing between the two. King Josiah would not heed and was killed fighting Pharoah Neco at

Megiddo. The Egyptians continued northward, only to be defeated at Carchemish (2-Chronicles 35:20-25).

King Josiah of Judah had died fighting on the Scythian behalf. After having defeated the Assyrians and the Egyptians, the Scythian leaders were invited by the Medes to a feast. The Medes got the Scythians drunk and then massacred them (Herodotus 1;106). After this the Medes and Babylonians divided the former Assyrian Empire between themselves. The Babylonians conquered Judah and exiled its inhabitants to Babylon. Later, the Medes lost supremacy to their allies, the Persians. Cyrus the Persian king conquered Babylon and allowed the Judeans to return to their land. As for the Ten Tribes, Medes, Babylonians and Persians were to progressively drive the Israelite-Scythians out of the Middle East area and into the north. From the north the Scythians were eventually to continue westward into Europe.

PARALLELS BETWEEN SCYTHIANS AND ISRAELITES

Were the Israelites Scythians??

Talmudic sources and connected Commentaries state that King Josiah ben Amon of Judah sent Jeremiah the prophet to bring back the Lost Ten Tribes. They say that some few of them did in fact return temporarily (Arakin 33a, Megilla 14b, Rashi on Sanhedrin 94a)! They later again left the land of Israel according to the sources and returned to their places of exile✱. This all happened in the time of Jeremiah the Prophet. The religious reformer bearing a Biblical-type message and known as Zoroaster appeared in Scythian areas in the time of Jeremiah.

During the reign of King Josiah of Judah and in the time of Jeremiah the Scythians had settled for a time in the Land of

---

✱ Rabbi S. GOREN, "Torat HaShabbat. VeHamoed" quotes Nachmanides (Ramban) on Ketuboth 25a. See also similar remarks by NACHMANIDES in "The Book of Redemption", concerning the Census of Ezra and the fact that no members of the Lost Ten Tribes are recalled therein. See,
"The Return of the Lost Tribes. What Does the Bible Say?" which is a translated excerpt from Nachmanides in the magazine "Brit-Am" issue 1:1 [The article has been posted on the Brit-Am Web site]. Nachmanides on Gittin 33;a
See also the Artscrolls "Schottenstein" Edition of the Talmud, Arakin, p.12b note 15 for additional sources.

Israel and had made it a center of theirs. King Josiah of Judah died fighting on the side of the Scythians. After Josiah's death the Scythians departed from the Land of Israel.

The Scythians bore Tribal names similar to Israelite ones, they identified their ancestor with JOSEPH of Israel✿. Scythian artwork was of Israelite-Phoenician origin[22].

The events of the Scythian-Assyrian epoch were also echoed in Biblical Prophecy. The prophets largely predicted events that in their fullness will occur in the Messianic era. Nevertheless, they often presented their account of the future in the description of events happening in their own time or not so long afterwards and thus history may be considered to repeat itself[23]. There are a few Biblical passages concerning the fall of Nineveh, the Assyrian capital that may be best understood in light of the Scythian-Judean symbiosis in the reign of King Josiah. The fifth chapter of Micah, for instance, speaks of a ruler coming out of Beth Lehem. King Josiah was a descendant of David, who came from Beth Lehem. *"The remnant of his brethren"* returning unto the Children of Israelis is spoken of (Micah 5:3) and refers to the partial (and temporary -then) re-settlement of Israelite Scythians in the former Land of northern Israel. The important verses, for our consideration, are Micah 5:5-8:

AND THIS MAN SHALL BE THE PEACE, WHEN THE ASSYRIAN SHALL COME INTO OUR LAND: AND HE [i.e. Assyria] SHALL TREAD IN OUR PALACES, THEN SHALL WE RAISE AGAINST HIM [i.e. against Assyria] SEVEN SHEPHERDS, AND EIGHT PRINCIPAL MEN.

✿ Irma HAYNMAN, "The Syncretic Creed of Hellenized Jews From Tanais (Northern Black Sea Region), Jerusalem 1994. Haynman shows that the Scythian inhabitants of Tanais on the Dan River estuary, the Royal Scythians and the Parthians revered a figure named Aspourgos. The name Aspourgos, Haynman says, derives from the same root as the name Joseph and later Aspourgos was identified with Joseph. Our position has been that from the beginning Joseph and Aspourgos were one and the same. Haynman bases her case mainly on findings from the city of Tanais on the Don River. This city was identified by the historian of Iceland, Snorre Sturlasson, as " Asgard" meaning the ancestral home of the Scandinavian forefathers.

AND THEY SHALL WASTE THE LAND OF ASSYRIA WITH THE SWORD, AND THE LAND OF NIMRUD IN THE ENTRANCES THEREOF....
AND THE REMNANT OF JACOB SHALL BE IN THE MIDST OF MANY PEOPLE AS A DEW FROM THE LORD.
AND THE REMNANT OF JACOB SHALL BE AMONG THE GENTILES IN THE MIDST OF MANY PEOPLE AS A LION AMONG THE FLOCKS OF SHEEP..."

Again, the main point of these passages may be applicable only to the Messianic era yet it is also descriptive of our explanation of the Israelite-Scythian equation. The Assyrians, at first, came into the land of Israel and trod it down, including the Royal palaces, as archaeological excavations of Samaria have proven. They then exiled all of the surviving inhabitants. From their places of exile, the Israelite-Scythians made peace with Assyria, then became *"Shepherds"* i.e. allies and protectors of Assyria. After that the Scythians graduated to become the effective rulers of the Assyrian Empire, i.e. they became the *"eight principal men"* or rulers spoken of by the Prophet Micah. Finally the Israelite-Scythians destroyed the Assyrian cities and wasted *"the land of Assyria with the sword"*, just as Micah describes.

Similarly, the Talmud says (Shabbat 147) that the Lost Ten Tribes came to a calamity because of the *"Wine of Phrygia"*[24] and perhaps the reference is to the same drunken feast that caused the Scythian leaders to be killed and to lose control of the Assyrian empire. Other parallels can be drawn between descriptions of the exiled Israelites and the Scythians but for the moment the point has been made. Secular sources repeat about the Scythians what Biblical and Talmudic reports say concerning the Ten Tribes. The Scythians were therefore Israelites or at least Israelites were one of the components of the Scythian Union. The Scythians had been part of the Cimmerians and regarding the Cimmerians we have additional evidence indicating an Israelite origin. The facility with which the Israelite-Scythians evidently took control of the Assyrian Empire is comprehensible once we realize that after their Exile

Israelites had quickly become prominent in Assyrian administration and Military Forces.

The Assyrians had employed the exiled Israelites in complete cavalry and chariot units, as archers, specialized individuals, and as general auxiliary manpower[25]. The first cavalry unites in the Assyrian Army were Israelite or Syrian in origin. Later, a general in Sargon's forces was named "Hilkiyahu" which is a Hebrew name[26]. Lists have been discovered in Nineveh (one of the Assyrian capitals) of cavalry units from Israelite Samaria and other records of charioteers bearing Israelite names[27].

A list has been found containing *"the names of many, perhaps most, of the top officials and the equestrian officers in Sargon's army"*[28]. This list mentions 13 equestrian officers from Israelite Samaria. The commander of the known Israelite Samarian unit has the same rank as the twin brother of King Sargon and was considered about the seventh most important man in the kingdom[29]. The personal bodyguard of Sennacherib was a unit from Lachish[30] in Judah of Exiles who were taken away together with the Ten Tribes and were to be counted as part of them. Improvements in fortifications undertaken by the Assyrians may also be attributed to Israelite influence. The same applies to irrigation projects and engineering works undertaken throughout the new territories conquered by Assyria. Israelite influence was everywhere. Israelites had also been settled throughout the Assyrian Empire especially in areas that came to be considered Cimmerian and Scythian centers. The Israelites then disappear and their place is taken by the Scythians who take over the Empire, ally themselves with Judah, and fulfill the role attributed to the Ten Tribes.

The Lost Ten Tribes of Israel were therefore to be found amongst the Cimmerians, Scythians, and Goths. Specific groups from these peoples may be identified with Israelite clans. These will be shown to have settled in Western Europe where many of their descendants are still to be found today.

MOVEMENT OF ROYAL SCYTHS (SCYTHAE BASILOI) TO THE BALKANS THEN TO SOUTHERN POLAND (SOURCE OF VISTULA RIVER) THEN TO SCANDINAVIA VIA JUTLAND

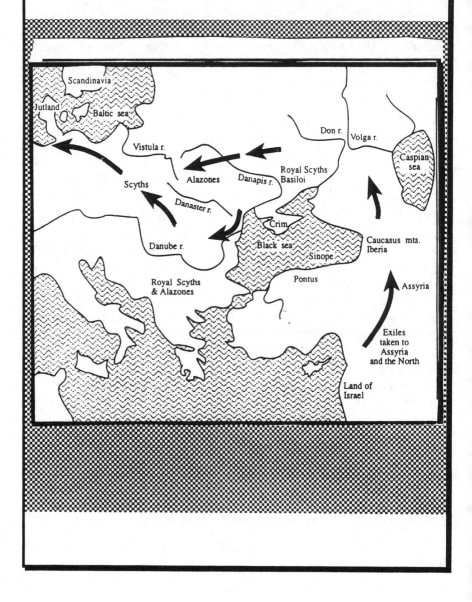

2

THE SCYTHS, ISRAEL, AND PHYSICAL TYPES

Scyths and Goths

We have seen how the Israelites in their places of exile had formed the Cimmerian, Scythian, and Guti nations. It may be that non-Israelite nations were also part of these groups or later came to be identified with them. The Cimmerians were forced out of Anatolia via the Bosporus. They entered the Balkans whence they continued into north and Western Europe. Part of the Cimmerian host had consisted of segments from the Guti and Saki. Segments from these last two bodies split off from the Cimmerians and remained in the Balkans for a time. They became known to history as the **Getae** and **Daci**[1]. The Getae and Dacae were renowned for their monotheism and for their sense of justice. They too were to be pushed northward. Ptolemy reported them as being in Scandinavia under the names "Gutae" and "Daucae". English tradition[2] said that Getae and Dacae were amongst the Anglo-Saxon led forces that conquered England. The Getae were regarded as part of the Gothic[3] nation.

39

The main portion of the Gothic peoples had been attached to the Scythians. Unlike the Cimmerians, the bulk of the Scythian host at first remained in the Middle East area. The Scythians overpowered the Assyrian Empire but afterwards lost control to the Medes, Babylonians, and Persians. Consequently, the Scythians were also pushed northward into the steppes of Southeast Europe, Southern Russia and Central Asia. In the 500's and 400's BCE bands of Scythians made their way to Western Europe. In the West they merged with the Cimmerians who had gone before them to form Celtic and Galatian civilization. Most Scyths, however, did not head westward at first but settled in the region of "SCYTHIA". The name "Scythia" is usually applied to the region of Southern Russia. The term however could encompass all the Northern Eurasian area from the borders of China to the confines of Germany and even beyond. Much later it appears, that the Romans used the term "Scythia" for Britain and Scandinavia. We employ the term to cover all those regions initially controlled by the Scythians meaning mainly Southern Russia and Southeast Europe.

The Scythians of Scythia may be culturally differentiated: The Scythians were divided into western and eastern sections with the Sarmatians between them. The Scythians in the east are often referred to in historical works as "Sacae" though strictly speaking "Sacae" is another name for Scythians in general.

The Scythians in the west were the Scythians of Classical history. Amongst these the Royal Scyths (Basiloi), Alans, and Alazonians were predominant. The Western Scyths were pushed further westward by the Sarmatians who attacked them from the east. In the 500's and 400's BCE they entered the Balkans (southeast Europe) but further Sarmatian and other pressures pushed them northward. In the 300's and 100's BCE the Royal Scyths, via Poland, entered Scandinavia which originally was named "Scathanavia"[4] or "Scatenauge"[5] in their honor [*"Scat" means Scyth*]. Scandinavian mythology, art styles, and religion all recall their Scythian origin[6].

Associated with the Scyths were the Goths. The Goths (called also "Gudo" and "Guti") had, in effect, remained largely attached to the Scythian hosts with whom they were often identified. The Goths were a widely scattered nation. Branches of the Goths, apart from those who became known as Getae in the Balkans, were to be found as Gothones on the Baltic coast, as "Guti" east of the Urals, and as Goths along the Black Sea northern shore. In the east, the Guti are also often referred to in historical literature as "Yueh-chi"[7] or as "Massagetae". The Gothic-Guti and the Sacae and related groups dominated the area of Central Asia up to, and for a time into, present-day China. The Chinese[8] described them as green-eyed and red-haired, which description is confirmed by wall-paintings[9] and mummified[10] bodies. The said findings reveal, on the whole, a blue-eyed people with blondish hair, though many darker types were also present.

From the east all of the Scythian peoples eventually moved westward. They moved in waves of migration. The Goths also moved westward and settled partly in southern France and in scattered areas throughout Europe. A major portion of the Goths settled at an early stage in Sweden where they are still distinguishable today. The historical Goths were dominated by Israelite Tribes that had once dwelt East of the Jordan. The name of the Israelite Tribe of **Gad** in Biblical Hebrew could be pronounced as "Goth"!

Many of the early Scythians were described as fair and of an apparent "Nordic" type appearance. This leads to a consideration of the question whether or not this phenomenon had existed previously amongst the ancient Hebrews.

The Physical Anthropology of
the Ancient Hebrew Peoples

The Israelites of old were regarded by the Egyptians as people from the land of Amuru, meaning the land of the Amorites which the Israelites conquered. Another term applied to the general Syrian area was "Retenu". The name "Upper Retenu"[11] corresponded to the geographical space encompassed by the Land of Israel, according to the Bible. People from the area known as "Amuru" or "Retenu" after ca.1400 BCE were presumably Israelites. They are depicted[12] on Egyptian monuments as red, blonde, or black-haired with frequent blue eyes and red beards. Illustrations of individuals with this appearance are automatically assumed to pertain to the Israelite or "Syrian" area. Another blonde blue-eyed people depicted on Egyptian monuments were the so-called "Libyans" and it has now been proven that these were not dwellers of "Libya" but rather of the Nile Delta and of Hebrew origin[13].

On the Egyptian pictures skins of individuals from the Israelite or "Syrian" area are often light colored and pinkish[14]. **In addition darker individuals from these same areas are also depicted and sometimes they are the majority.** The identification of the "Amuru" people depicted with Israelites may be confirmed from illustrations of an Egyptian monarch and his campaign against the Tribes of Israel: In about 924 BCE the king of Egypt, Shishak, invaded Judah and the (then) separate state of North Israel. Pictures of the campaign of Shishak reveal him receiving homage from the King of Judah and from the heads of cities and dignitaries in Judah and throughout northern ISRAEL. The personages depicted are of "Amuru" type and these pictures are sometimes even used as typifying the Egyptian depiction of "Amuru" characteristics. In the said context "Amuru" in effect often meant Israelite. It seems that the ancient Hebrews were a people of mixed kinds. This concept is apparently confirmed by Talmudic sources. One Midrash (Genesis Rabah 98;5) says that amongst the Tribes of

Simeon and Levi were very light-colored types ("bohakanim"). On the other hand, a Talmudic source (Mishna Negaim 2;1) says that Israelites (meaning in this case, the Jews of Judah) are mainly of an intermediate type coloring being neither black like a "Cushi" (Negro) nor light like a "Germani". "Germani" in Talmudic terminology (Aruch HaShalem) meant someone from the far north at that time or who looked like people from that area and the term could be applied (Maimonides) to a very light colored person like part of the people of Scandinavia. Joseph, the son of Israel, was described in a Midrash (Genesis Rabah 86;3) , as looking like a "GERMANI" (i.e. like someone from the North, "very white", fair, according to Maimonides) and in another passage (Talmud Sota 36) as having a face that was "pink like a rose" . It follows that Joseph was considered as having been of Nordic appearance which was a known familial trait since Joseph is also said to have looked exactly like his father. [*On the other hand it may be that Joseph was exceptional in this regard*]. Joseph (Ephraim and Manasseh) was the leading tribal group in the Northern Kingdom. The above sources indicate that the original twelve tribes of Israel were of mixed physical types and that in some tribes or geographical regions one kind was more dominant than others. It has also been stated that the Tribes tended to marry only within themselves and thus physical differences between different tribes were emphasized[15]. The claim may also be made that peoples of the same areas of otherwise entirely different physical characteristics often have the same coloring*. A mixed genetic stock of similar but different variations will produce over a

---

* R.B. DIXON , "The Racial History of Man", N.Y. & London 1923, p.32 ff. Dixon claims that examination and measurement of skeletal remains shows the Nordic peoples to be of mixed "Caspian" and "Mediterranean" origin with an addition of NEGROID or rather "proto-Negroid" features. He claims that all peoples who have congregated in the Scandinavian and Baltic areas including proto-Negroid, proto-Australoid, Alpine, Mediterranean, and Caspian types have been "bleached" by an unexplainable but demonstrable process. Even animals from this area have been so affected.

long period more often the type that is most adaptable to the surrounding environment. This is not evolution. It is adaptation of an already existing physical entity (i.e. a group of people) to empirical circumstance in accordance with its already existing genetic potential.

The suggestion that physical environment influences inherited appearance and that the Israelite Tribes were of differing types, should not surprise anybody -both ideas are indicated in the Bible and in Oral Tradition.

Genetics in the Bible?

Regarding external influences, it is related in the Book of Genesis how Jacob was set to mind flocks of sheep and goats belonging to his father-in-law, Laban (Genesis 30:31-43). The sheep were either all white or of mixed-coloring whereas the goats were all black or mixed-colored. Laban separated all the mixed-colored out leaving only the pure colored in Jacob's care.

Jacob had only entirely black goats and entirely white sheep. There were no mixed coloreds left with him. Nevertheless, according to the Law of Genetics (as explained by Professor Y. FELIKS , "The Animal World of the Bible," Tel Aviv 1962) part of the pure-colored animals left with Jacob were probably the offspring of mixed-colored and pure-colored mating who appeared pure-colored yet retained the Genetic potential for mixed-coloreds within them. Jacob placed rods peeled in certain patterns in the watering-troughs of the "STRONGER" (Genesis 30:41) beasts before their mating and so produced mixed-colored lambs. The Hebrew word translated as "stronger" (*Mekusherot*) actually more correctly means the "first-to-breed" (Rashi, Onkelos) . "But when the cattle were feeble he put them [*i.e. the rods*] not in" (Genesis 30:42). The Hebrew word ("atufim") translated here as "feeble" is interpreted in the Aramaic translation to mean "late coming" ("lakashiut") meaning late to breed. Jacob placed the rods in the watering troughs when the animals that were sexually precocious came to drink. He took the rods out of the water when the late sexual developers approached. In animals and plants, crossbreeds often breed earlier. In other words the account may be understood as saying that Jacob placed the peeled-rods before those animals that were of mixed parentage with a mixed genetic constitution even though externally they appeared to be pure-breeds. Those that were "the first-to-breed" would have been the ones with parents of each type. Jacob was inspired to utilize external influences in order to activate inherent genetic potential since he placed rods only before those beasts that were of mixed parentage and acted accordingly by maturing earlier. The rods may also have acted as some type of catalyst. This does not mean that no miracle was involved since Jacob apparently succeeded far beyond what he could have been expected to by the Laws of Nature alone. Nevertheless Jacob did act rationally.

In addition to the above we have the proven influence of the environment on physical type.

Environmental Influence?

It used to be believed that head shapes are inherited and that different craniological indexes (the relative proportions of width to length, etc) reflect differing origins. There is something in this assumption. In some cases it holds but in other cases it does not. Children of Sicilian immigrants to the USA had rounder heads than their parents whereas the offspring of East European Jews had longer ones than their own forebears. The head shapes of children whose parents had moved from one area of Germany to another were often found to be more similar to those of their neighbors than those of their progenitors. In the State of Israel: <<*It is possible to see a difference in the head shape of the immigrant populations, children of the migratory waves of the 1920s, that came to Israel from Europe (Ashkenazic Jews): The head shape of the second generation, born in the land, was different on the average from that of their parents and had changed to become narrower and longer, similar to that of the*

45

local populations (of Jews from eastern countries and beduin)>> Dr. Yose NAGER, "Mi Anachnu?" Israel, 2003. On the other hand other populations in the Land of Israel such as the Christian Arabs and Druze tended to have rounder head shapes. A lot of contradictions exist on this subject: Kurds and Armenians have lived besides each other for centuries but have entirely different head shapes. The inhabitants of Central Europe were longheaded until the Middle Ages when they changed to predominantly round heads. The same applies concerning the Amerindians who at that time inhabited the central regions of North America. In both cases no recorded incursion of newcomers is known to have taken place but rather an unexplained change occurred in the existing populations.

Patriarchal Mixed Marriages?

As for different types having been present in the ancestry of Israelite Tribes from the very beginning, Jacob (i.e. Israel) the Fore-Father was twin-brother to Esau who was "Admoni" (red-haired)◘ and hairy (Genesis 25:25) whereas Jacob was smooth-skinned (Genesis 27:11) David, King of Israel, was also an "Admoni" (1-Samuel 16:2) meaning red or golden haired. Laban, the father-in-law of Jacob has a name meaning "Whitish" and which is cognate with the English word "blond"[16]. On the other hand the Shepherdess in the Song of Solomon (1:6) announces, "I am black but comely..." The Tribal Patriarchs all took women from different nations and in the course of time the separate genetic potentials combined with differing environments would have produced distinctly different types. The area of ancient Israelite settlement contained climates varying from the semi-tropical to the Alpine.

◘ Genesis 25:25 "Admoni" sometimes translated as "ruddy" but more correctly meaning "red-haired" or "golden-haired".

According to the Bible and later Jewish legends (as recorded in "Seder HaDorot", and "Sefer HaYashar") the tribal Heads married women from various nations[17]. Joseph married an Egyptian woman (Genesis 41:45)[※]. Machir, son of Menasseh had an Aramaean concubine (1-Chronicles 7:14). Reuben married a Hivite. Levi and Asher married descendants of Eber. Judah had one Canaanite and one Semite wife. Zebulon married a Midianitess and Issachar a descendant of Sem. Benjamin married a daughter of Zimran, son of Abraham and Keturah. Dan took a daughter of Lot, nephew of Abraham. Naphtali took a daughter of Nahor, as did Gad, and so on. The Apocryphal Book of Jubilees (ca. 200 BCE?) also says that the Tribal Patriarchal heads married women from different nations and mentions Canaanite, Egyptian, Semitic, and Mesopotamian women. Whether all of the above traditions are correct or not, they do reflect the apparent reality of some mixing with other nations whilst retaining an Israelite Tribal identity that is Biblically and historically acceptable. Intermarriage of the Tribes with different nations combined with other factors must have produced different types, and this with the later influence of varying physical environments is enough to explain the superficial differences amongst the descendants of different Israelite Tribes today.

[※] The Ancient Egyptians were mainly of Mediterranean Hamitic type similar to the Berbers of North Africa. The British and Americans are descended largely from Joseph whose wife was Egyptian. It is interesting to note that the Older methods (including Craniology) classifies the present-day British as being fifty-percent Mediterranean (like the Ancient Egyptians) and fifty percent Nordic.

THE MIGRATIONS

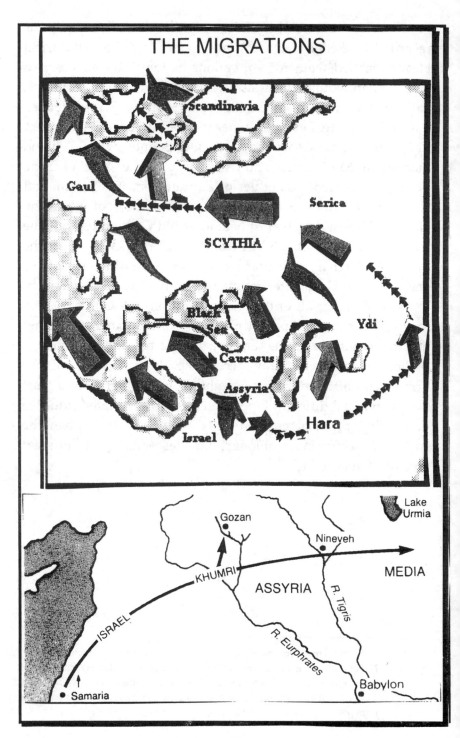

Regions of Cimmerian & Scythian Activitiy

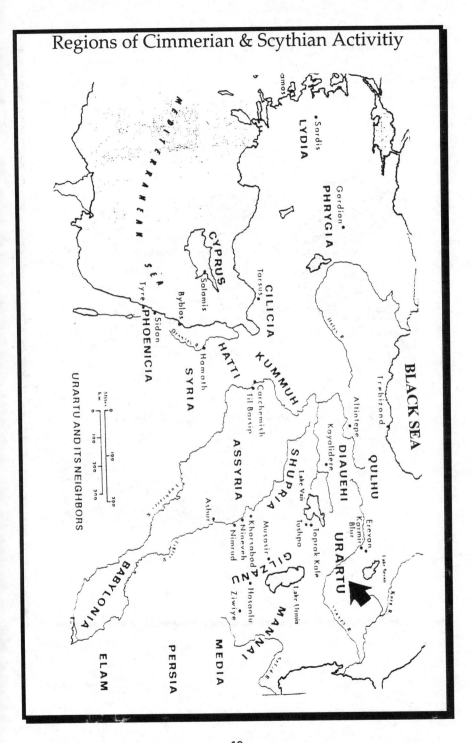

URARTU AND ITS NEIGHBORS

49

HARA AND IT IS SURROUNDINGS

3

THE ISRAELITE NATIONS COME TO EUROPE

Major Migratory Movements

A brief summary of ethnic migrations pertinent to our study may help simplify the overall picture[*]:

1. ✦Movement by Sea

Most of the Israelites were exiled to the north. A portion however were transported overseas in Phoenician and Philistine ships working for the Assyrians (Amos 1:6-10). The transported Hebrews were taken to Spain, Gaul, and Britain. Those taken to Spain later moved northward into Gaul or crossed over to Britain and Ireland. Proof for the transportation of Israelites to the West by Sea is obtainable from the Hebrew Bible, Biblical commentaries, traditions, legends, archaeology, and historical writings[1]. The transportees merged with other Israelites who had moved overland and been influenced by Celtic civilization.

---

[*] Dates used are only rough approximations and in accordance with conventionally accepted reckoning that may yet have to be revised.

2. ✣ Movement by Land Northward

Ca.740-720 BCE: The Assyrians moved masses of Northern Israelites (and other Syrians and Phoenicians) to Northern Mesopotamia and to Hara in eastern Iran. They became identified with the Cimmerians, Scyths, and Goths.

3. ✣ Cimmerians to Europe and Galatian-Gaul

♦ Ca. 640 BCE: The first waves of Cimmerians via Turkey and the Anatolian Bosporos were driven into Europe whence they made their way west to Gaul and Britain becoming known as Celts and Galatians. The Galatians were identifiable in Europe with both part of the Celts and Belgae and with early groups in Germany. Even though the Cimmerian-descended Galatians had migrated to Western Europe at an early date, Galatian expeditions were undertaken back from the west towards the east. These resulted in Galatians being present also in several eastern regions including parts of Scythia and the Galatian region of Turkey. At the same time the Galatian center remained in Western Europe. The Galatians were descended from Israelite Tribes (Reuben, half-Menasseh, and Gad) that had once been located in the Land of Israel east of the Jordan River. This area had been known as "Gilead" and "Bashan". The name of the Galatians was sometimes rendered as "Galadi" and is derived from the Hebrew form of Gilead. Gilead is also the name of a son of Machir from the Israelite Tribe of Manasseh whose descendants formed part of the Galatians and related peoples.

♦ The Galatians had a tendency to merge with, or join in alliance to, the Goths. The Goths came from Gad which Tribe had adjoined and confederated with Machir from Manasseh in the Land of Israel. We will see recurring patterns of specific Israelite Tribes linking up with each other.

4. ✱ First Scythian Movements to Europe

Ca. 550 BCE: The movement of Scythians from the Middle East to north of the Caucasus began in earnest with the penetration of Scythia. Offshoots from this movement reached into Western Europe and Gaul. A significant presence was established within the area of Poland whence Scandinavia and the West were later to be reached. The Scythians west of the Caspian Sea were dominated by the Royal Scythians. Those east of the Caspian Sea became culturally differentiated from those to the west and so for convenience sake are referred to as "Sacae" even though technically the term "Sacae" could originally have referred to all Scythians.

5. ✱ Royal Scythians Move Westward

Climate changes in Scythia caused "Sarmatian" groups to push the Royal Scyths westward in the period 300-100 BCE. The Royal Scyths re-settled at first in the area of Bulgaria, then after renewed pressure continued north, ultimately to reach Scandinavia which was named "Scatanavia" (Land of the Scyths) and "Basilia" (Pliny N.H. 27;35). The Royal Scythians had been named "Basiloi". This name came to mean "monarchs" or "royals" in Greek but it was not originally a Greek word. The area of Israel east of the Jordan known as "Bashan" had also been called "Basil".

6. ✱ Royal Scythians to Scandinavia

The Huns emerging from Mongolia or further east from 200-160 BCE attacked the Aseir (Wusun), Goths, and Sacae and caused these peoples to war amongst themselves. These events were followed by a climate change which, after 120 BCE, caused the desolation of Chorasmia (east of the Caspian Sea) which previously had been heavily populated. Goths and Sacae began to move westward and Scandinavia was re-populated in the period 100 BCE-100 CE These movements caused a chain reaction and immigrations into Scandinavia included Royal

Scythians moving northward from the Balkan area. The Baltic coast was also heavily settled in this time, and from there more tribes were to move westward.

7. ✦The **Belgae**

After 200 BCE the Belgae from the East began occupying nNorthern Gaul. They were associated with, or accompanied by, a group ultimately hailing from the Middle East and Syria and known linguistically as "The Northwest Block"[1]. They arrived in Europe via Anatolia and the Crimean region of Southwest Scythia. Culturally these peoples were Galatian and Celtic. Groups of Belgae also occupied parts of Britain and Ireland.

8. ✦ **Eastern Scythians Move West**

Later, from eastern Scythia, in the decades 70-50 BCE, the Western Sienbi and the Northern Hun group of Hugie, Dingling, and Gienkun moved westward. The Northern Hun group in Scythia had encompassed several smaller tribes at least some of whom were of Israelite origin. They began to re-appear from 50 BCE in the Rhine area of Western Europe and within a hundred years had taken over the region. Archaeological evidence shows that in the time of Caesar the area of "Germany" east of the Rhine had had a type of culture (termed the "La-Tene" culture) similar to the Celtic type in Northern Gaul of the Belgae and Treveri[2]. By 50 CE[3] this culture had been completely destroyed and the region resettled by peoples bearing previously unknown names such as the Chatti, Chasuarri, Angrivarri, Ampsivarri, etc. The following examples of peoples who migrated from Scythia to Europe have the name by which they were known in the west followed in brackets by that which they had previously been called in Scythia: The Chauki (in Scythia "Cachage Scythae"), the Tubantes (Tabiene), Bructeri (Bactria), Chatti (Chatae Scythae), and the associated groups of Varni (Varini), Tigorini (Taguri),

Angiloi (Augali-Aegeli,), Jutes (Iatii), Sasons (Sasones) and Scoti, Esci (Ascotacae), as well as Alans (Alans), Tectosaces (Tectosace Scythae), As (Asi), and quite a few others listed in the following pages. The area of Germany, like Scandinavia, received Tribes coming from Scythia and about to continue westward into Gaul and Britain. ["Gaul" is a term generally inclusive of modern France, Belgium, Switzerland, and Holland.].

9. ✦ Suebi and Saxons Move Westward

From 150-350 CE continuous warfare instigated by the Huns in East Scythia caused many more peoples to move westward amongst whom were the eastern branch of Sienbi in ca. 170 CE [*The western branch of Sienbi had previously gone to Europe in about 60 BCE*]. In Europe the Sienbi were generally referred to as Suebi. This movement out of Scythia to the West caused the existing peoples in Germany in the period 200-300 CE[4] (and in some cases somewhat before that time) to be replaced by bigger groups who absorbed them. The larger groups included the Saxons, Franks, Alemani, and so on and the Suebi. The Suebi appear to be the only major body remaining as an independent entity. They had acted as precursors to the newer arrivals. They were to be closely associated with the Saxons and Alamans who settled Alsace and Switzerland.

Many of the peoples arriving in the west came via Scandinavia or had had components in the Scandinavian region. This explains why traditions attribute a Scandinavian origin to some of these groups. The Scandinavians themselves believed that they came from (or via) Scythia.

The movements were of peoples coming from Scythia via Scandinavia and the Baltic Coast, and in the south via the Balkans. These migrations could be gradual. For instance, wooden chamber graves are noticeable in southern Poland from before 200 BCE. These graves it has been suggested (by

W.E. Filmer)[5] were modifications of former "Royal-Scythian" type and they are connected with the movement of the Scythians to the north and west. After 100 BCE the same type of grave is evident on the north Baltic coast and a hundred years later re-appears in Jutland (Denmark) where it continued for several centuries. From Jutland emerged many of the invaders of England.

The movement westward could also be quite sudden. Events on the borders of China or even deep within China sometimes had direct connection to movements in the west. Peoples of nomadic disposition would traverse the distance. Chain reactions of one group pushing forward another would also occur. It should also be noted that by about 200 BCE several Scythian nations were already dispersed with parts deep in Asia and other sections penetrating Europe. Suebi, Goths, and Saxon groups were widely spread, as were others. Pockets of Alans[6], for instance, are discernible from the borders of China to the European Carpathians and were eventually to be found in Brittany[7] of Gaul on the Atlantic Coast.

10. ✤ The Huns Push Saxons, Franks, and Others Westward

In the years 350-450 CE the Huns moved en-masse out of "Scythia" (Eurasia) into Europe forcing most of the peoples in Scythia to accompany them or else to flee for their lives. As a result of the Hun invasions the Saxons, Franks, and Alamans received a large augmentation of manpower with the addition of new clans which (in the case of the Saxons) included those identified as Huns proper[8]. In response to Hun pressure these greatly increased bodies overran the Western Roman Empire and settled Gaul and Britain. Goths, Vandals, Visigoths, and others also conquered formerly Roman countries. In most cases however, the conquerors were numerically insignificant when compared to the native populations. The whole process of movement, on the whole, was to continue till about 500 CE with an invasion by the "Vikings" some time later. In this period the white peoples of the East, described by the Chinese, were to disappear almost entirely and re-appear in Europe. Examination of events in the east enhances understanding of the "Great Migrations" period. It also adds an additional confirmatory dimension to the body of evidence connecting the migrating peoples and their modern "European" descendants with The Lost Tribes of Israel.

11. ✤ The Danites and Nephtalites Move to Scandinavia

A good portion of the Naphtalite horde had remained to the east of Scythia. In the 450-500 CE period the Naphtalites began to move west eventually entering Scandinavia in the 500's and 600's CE. The Naphtalite horde included the Danes who re-settled Denmark possibly via Sweden. The Naphtalites themselves settled mainly in Norway. Sweden was populated by Goths and by Suiones[9] descendants of Shuni (pronounceable as "Su-oni") son of Gad (Genesis 46:16).

12. ✤ The Viking Invasions

The continued migrations to Scandinavia resulted in over-population, the pushing outwards of coastal populations, and subsequent overseas colonization. The Scandinavians overseas were known as the Vikings.

13. ✤ The Normans

The Vikings settled in England, Ireland, Normandy (France), and elsewhere. In Normandy the Vikings accepted French Culture and were called Normans. From Normandy they invaded England in 1066.

14. ✤ The Getae and Daci

A portion of the Cimmerian-host in its trip westward had remained in the Balkans and became known as the **Getae** and **Dacii**. The Getae were a Gothic people who had been culturally influenced by the neighboring Thracians. The Getae and Dacae had an aversion to images, certain similarities to the Celtic druids[10], and were Monotheists as well as believing in an after-life. Most of the Getae and Daci in the period 100 BCE-100 CE moved to the north toward the Baltic and Scandinavia and eventually participated in the Anglo-Saxon invasions of Britain. The Roman Imperialists exterminated those who remained behind in "Dacia" of the Balkans. The Getae had been linked with the Agathyrsi from whom emerged the Khazars and Picts.

15. ✦ The Picts and Khazars

Some groups of Sacae-related Israelites including bands of Goths and Naphtali remained in the Caucasus region and adjoining areas of Scythia. These were eventually to amalgamate with the Agathyrsi and form the **KHAZAR** nation which converted to Judaism. Some of their descendants are to be found today amongst the modern Jews. The real core of the Khazar nation federation was centered on the Akatziri or "Agathyrsy" as the Greeks called them. The Agathyrsi had had at one stage a section on the Baltic coast and another in Pontus by the Caucasus. At some time between 50 BCE-300 CE (more likely closer to the latter date) the Agathyrsi sent a contingent across the sea to Scotland where it became identified with the **PICTS** (*Servius on Aenid 4.v.146*). The Picts were to act more as accomplices than as opponents to the Anglo-Saxon invasion. The Picts were formidable warriors and seriously perturbed all who stood against them. The Agathyrsi-Picts intermixed with peoples in Scotland who had been there before them and are therefore mistakenly identified with them. The Agathyrsi (Akatziri) in Europe were described by Jordanes (the Gothic historian) as being an extremely brave people.

The Khazars, who came from the Agathyrsi, were to convert to Judaism and had their own belief in having once been part of the Israelite nation. The Khazars were centered in Southern Russia but a small colony also existed in Sweden[11]. The Khazars in Sweden had connections to the Anglo-Saxon colony of Hedeby in North Germany before the Angles and Saxons moved to Britain[12]. The Khazars and the Goths in early Medieval times were identified by Medieval Chroniclers with the **Lost Ten Tribes of Israel**. Similarly, the Historian Gildas in Britain (500s CE) appears to have identified the Celtic inhabitants of Britain as Israelites. The Anglo-Saxon Bede identified the English physically with the people of Israel. The Franks and Visigoths in the 7th century had similar notions[13]. Historically many of the peoples who came westward were considered Gothic though the Goths-proper settled in Sweden. There exist traditions placing Israelite Tribes in areas of Sacae and Gothic habitation and their Tribal names correspond with those of Israelite entities. The parallelism between the Scyths and Israel has also been shown. The Scyths, Goths, Cimmerians and related groups of Scythia were all one people, from one original stock, which was Israelite. From these nations emerged those of Western Europe.

The "Barbarian" nations who invaded Northwest Europe derived from forces of the Scyths and Goths, who in turn had once been together with the Cimmerians. The Cimmerians had previously gone west and become part of the "Celtic" peoples whom the "Barbarians" were now conquering.

The above list traces all the invaders of West Europe back to the Cimmerians, Goths, and Scythian Sacae. The Scythian origin of the "Barbarian" invaders of northwest Europe strengthens the case for the nations in question having significantly large Hebraic elements in their ancestral stock.

SCANDINAVIA

Scandinavia was destined to serve as a place of settlement for many of the Scythian peoples and as an area of transit for others on their way west. A clarification of Scandinavia's history facilitates the explanation of Scandinavia's role. Several distinct periods are observable:

♦ 1. The Bronze Age, which ended about 500 BCE and culminated with the almost-complete depopulation of Scandinavia. The founders of this civilization had come from the Middle East, from Israel, and in part moved to Ireland and Britain. They are recorded in Irish tradition as the People of Dana.

♦ 2. The era between 100 BCE and 100 CE in which Scandinavia was re-populated, especially by Royal Scyths and Goths.

♦ 3. A century of disturbance (300's- 400's CE) in which Scandinavia was apparently conquered and in which many Tribes left and headed further west.

♦ 4. The arrival of new peoples from east Scythia in the 500's and 600's CE culminated in the 700's experiencing overpopulation and unsettlement which led to the Viking oversea expeditions. Later arrivals in Scandinavia provide plentiful evidence of having arrived from the "Sacae" areas in east Scythia. This evidence consists of legends, art, customs, archaeological findings, and demographic factors.

Evidence of Scythian Origins

It may be shown that the "Barbarian" newcomers emerged from Scythia from several viewpoints: **Demographically**, Germany at that time could not have supported the millions of people in the Barbarian forces. The archaeological and historical evidence indicates that most of Germany was relatively unpopulated, uncultivated, and not amenable to large groups of settled (non-nomadic) peoples. The same applied for the rest of northern Europe. In east Scythia there had existed settlements of numerous civilized peoples of so-called **"Nordic" appearance** who **disappeared** shortly before the Barbarians were first recorded in Western Europe. The "Barbarians" who suddenly appeared in Western Europe had **traditions** that they came from Scythia[14] and their **artistic styles** are actually identical to those known from the Scythian areas[15].

They had similar "Shamanistic" Scythian religious beliefs and customs[16], they wore the same armour[17], and fought with the same tactics. The Scythian peoples were destined to disappear from Scythia in the period between 300 BCE to ca. 600 CE. Just as the Scythians were leaving Scythia, they began to appear in the west as "Barbarians" largely after passing through Scandinavia, Pannonia (Hungary), and Germany.

The similarities between the Scythians and the "Barbarians" who invaded the West are acknowledged and discussed by modern scholars. They however tend to assume that the "Barbarians" came from Scandinavia and Germany and simply absorbed "Scythian" influences through a process of cultural osmosis and also that some Scythian or Sarmatian bodies had been confederated into the essentially "European" Barbarian hosts[18].

In 700 BCE **Germany** had been practically uninhabited[19]. Later, a few isolated peoples did settle in Germany but these are archaeologically and linguistically indistinguishable from their Celtic, Thracian, or Illyrian neighbours[20]. Scandinavia at one stage had supported a rich and advanced Bronze Age civilization which, due to invasions and climatic change, virtually disappeared leaving the region almost deserted until about 100 BCE[21] when it was repopulated as described by peoples emerging from Scythia. Neither Scandinavia nor Germany of that time could have supported the masses of peoples who came to the west after ca.200 BCE; nor are there any intermediate stages of significance, which show any cultural osmosis from Scythia taking place. The Barbarian nations (such as the Franks, Anglo-Saxons, Danes, Vandals, Goths, Alemans, Alans, Vikings, etc.) already possessed their "Scythian" characteristics when they first appeared.

The Romans who encountered the "Barbarians" on their borders, fought against them whilst at the same time enlisting them in their armies, and wrote about them, had essentially correct information concerning their origins. They considered the Goths to be Scyths and the Scyths of Scythia to have become, under different names, the Barbarian nations[22] of the west who were pushing against the Roman frontiers which they often reached via Germany.

In the period of the Great Migrations described above, especially after 400 CE, groups of settlers and military elites from the Scythian area were to be found in Scandinavia and throughout those areas of Germany from which emerged the hosts participating in the Anglo-Saxon invasions of Britain. This is confirmed by recent Scandinavian and German archaeological findings[23].

It is now generally agreed that the Barbarians did not originally speak an Indo-European language though at some stage they came to learn one "badly" in a linguistic sense. In Germany, they conquered and/or adjoined Indo-European "natives" with whom they forbade intermarriage[24] though they interacted linguistically and culturally. After the Scythian Barbarians left "Germany", going to France, Holland, Britain, Switzerland, and elsewhere, the native "Germans" re-asserted themselves. Meanwhile hordes of Slavonic and other peoples swept into Germany in the 500's CE to fill the vacuum left by the evacuating Scythian Israelites. These peoples were later "Germanized" through colonies of German natives settling amongst them, pressures by German Rulers, and the policies of the Catholic Church. The process of Germanizing the Slavonic peoples of Germany, including those in Bavaria, continued into the twentieth century.

The invaders of Britain after 400 CE were headed by the Angles, Jutes, and Saxons. Parallelisms exist between Anglo-Saxon culture and that of Scythia. They had emerged mainly from Scythia and passed through Scandinavia and/or Germany without sojourning for an appreciable time.

The Israelite Origins of the "Barbarian" Peoples

Proof that the "Barbarian" invaders of Western Europe were largely Israelite consists of the following facts:

✷The places they emerged from in Scythia had been those identified with specific Israelite clans whose names often correspond with those of the relevant groups in Scythia.

✷The names of these peoples in Western Europe frequently correlate to those of Israelite entities as does their relative positioning to each other - as explained elsewhere.

✷They descended from Scythian or Scythian- connected peoples and independent proofs showed a Scythian-Hebrew linkage;

✷Their language is consistent with that of Northern Israelites having spoken a Phoenician influenced Hebrew dialect and having been exposed to strong Median, Persian, and other "Indo-European" influences.

✷Their mythical ancestors and some of their customs also prove their Hebrew origins.

✷ Their national character on the whole is often that which would be expected of Hebrews who had lost all knowledge of their real origins.

✷ They gave rise to certain nations in Western Europe. The Bible and to Rabbinical Sources declare that the Lost Ten Tribes of Israel will be in "islands", "on the coast", by the Atlantic Ocean and in the north and possessing other characteristics. All of these taken as a comprehensive whole are applicable only to the West European peoples of today and their descendants.

Language

The Scythian-Gothic nations had emerged from Scythia. In east Scythia, -at least in the area east of the Caspian Sea whence the Sacae (Anglo-Saxons) were once centered, Aramaic was spoken[25]. Aramaic is closely related to Hebrew. Some of the Israelite Tribes had spoken Aramaic while others used a type of Hebrew influenced by Aramaic, or Aramaic influenced by Hebrew. Aramaic was one of the official languages of the

Assyrian Empire. The Old Anglo-Saxon English language is a composite dialect and contains many Hebrew words. Linguistically, the west Barbarians may originally have spoken Hebrew or a related Semitic dialect. There is nothing to obviate such a possibility since new languages were sometimes learnt and old ones forgotten in historical experience. The Normans, for instance, came from Scandinavia and settled en-masse in Normandy, France, but within two generations they had forgotten their parent language and knew only French!

Terry Marvin **BLODGETT** in 1981 published a Ph.D. Thesis ("Phonological Similarities in Germanic and Hebrew", The University of Utah, 1981) in which he proved that the original tongue of the northern "Barbarians" was Hebrew. Blodgett, now Professor of Languages, Southern Utah University, Cedar City, Utah, USA, showed how it is agreed that approximately one-third of all Germanic vocabulary is of an unknown (non-Indo-European) origin. "Also the Germanic sound shifts and gemination* are not to be explained on the basis of Indo-European linguistics".

These foreign non-Indo-European elements can be attributed (says Blodgett) to Hebrew incursions recognizable in the areas of phonology [speech sounds], morphology [word formation], and lexicology [word elements]. "English, Frisian, Dutch, Flemish, High and Low German, Danish, Swedish, Norwegian, and Icelandic, as well as the extinct languages of Gothic, Old Norse, Old Saxon, and others comprise one of the Indo-European groups of language commonly called Germanic. On a broader scale, the Germanic branch of languages shares many features in common with the Italic, Greek, Celtic, Slavonic, Indo-Iranian and other Indo-European groups". Even so, the Germanic branch of these languages has a non-"Indo-European" component comprising approximately one-third of the total: It is this element that Blodgett identified as

---

* Gemination: Doubling of consonants, e.g. "bid" becomes "biddan" in Old English; the "d" is pronounced twice.

HEBREW!!! Blodgett proved his case using terminology and a great many examples of a technical nature. A crude but reliable enough explanation of the overall tendency of Blodgett's work is as follows:

At some early stage, there occurred a series of sound shifts in the Germanic language or languages, the Indo-European "bhrator" became "brother", "peter" became "father", etc., e.g. "p" became pronounced as "f", "t" became "th", "k" became "ch", b, d, and g also changed.

Opinions concerning the date of this Germanic Sound Shift give dates varying from 2000 BCE to 9 CE. On the one side, John T. Waterman ("A History of the German Language", 1966) says "the general consensus of scholars is that the Germanic Sound Shift began probably not much before the fifth century B.C., and that it was essentially completed by the last pre-Christian century", i.e. from ca. 400 BCE to 100 BCE. Waterman bases his case on the fact that words in Germanic borrowed from Greek in the 400s BCE also underwent the shift whereas words taken from Latin in the first century BCE did not.

<<On the other hand, Heinz F. Wendt ("Sprachen", 1977) believed that the shift had been essentially completed by 500 B.C.>> Overall it seems to be accepted that the shift occurred around 500 BCE give or take a century or two. All Germanic dialects took part in the shift so it is assumed that the change took place whilst the parent groups were still in the north, - in Scandinavia and Northern Germany. The period of 500 BCE (for the said "Sound Change") is the one most authoritative opinion seems to converge on. Whether it occurred before 500 BCE or in the following era the most important point for us is recognition of the fact that it did occur.

A lot of reasons have been proposed to explain this shift but the bottom line is that the Cause is generally ascribed to ethnic factors implying racial mixture. "S. Feist thinks that the northern peoples were originally non-Indo-European, who learnt their Indo-European from the broad-headed Alpine race." Waterman and others basically held similar opinions. It is the northern areas of Scandinavia and Germany at that time that were linguistically less Indo-European.

We have shown above that in the period under consideration newcomers from Scythia were in the area and that in East Scythia Aramaic was used as a major language.

The Scythians in East Scythia must have used Hebrew as well as Aramaic. New works by Scandinavian scholars such as Dr. Kjell Aartun[26] and Orjan Svensson (of Blekinge in Sweden) have proven that the first Runic inscriptions in Scandinavia were written in dialects derived from Hebrew and Aramaic [27]!! Early Nordic dialects as well as early English ones still retained a large number of Hebrew and Aramaic words and Hebrew characteristics. Remnants of these are still to be found in the English language.

The Germanic Sound Shift can best be explained by the mass presence of former Hebrew-speakers. The same changes that occurred in Germanic occur in Hebrew according to fixed Grammatical and phonetic rules. Blodgett points out that people who from birth made the said changes would naturally have tended to speak as if the changes also held in a foreign language that they may have been forced to use at short notice. Even sophisticated technical details concerning rules of the Sound Shift in Hebrew were continued into Germanic.

Additional linguistic evidence confirms the presence of Hebrew speakers amongst the early Northern Peoples. *"The Origin of Modern Culture Languages and their Derivation from the Hebraica,"* by Professor Karl Rodosi, 1891, also adequately proves that the so-called Germanic tongues must have been formed by peoples who originally spoke Hebrew. The implications of these studies are applicable to West Europeans but do not encompass most of the modern Germans. The case is similar to that of the present inhabitants of Jamaica who now

66

speak English though only a portion of their ancestors came from Britain. An idea of the affinity between English and Hebrew may be also obtained from Isaac Mozeson, "The Word," NY, 1989. Mozeson says (p.1), <<Hebrew vocabulary has as much affinity with English as it has with Arabic. More English words can be clearly linked to Biblical Hebrew than to Latin, Greek, or French>>.

Thus, the Israelites became the Cimmerians, Scyths, and Goths, and these became the Barbarian invaders of Western Europe Other proofs exist confirming these conclusions. This evidence includes the retention of Israelite Tribal and Clan names by the migrating bodies. It also involves the continued, or renewed, employment of traditional Israelite Tribal symbols by modern nations amongst whom there exists a definite presence of that very same tribe to whom the traditional symbol belongs. In nearly every case the National symbols correspond with the Israelite Tribal emblem of whatever Tribe became dominant within the nation concerned! Nations in whom a specific Israelite Tribe settled developed national characteristics that derived from the tribe.

"Tracing the Dispersion"
by Terry M. Blodget

Extracts

<<Indo-European had six verb tenses. Hebrew, on the other hand, contained only two tenses (or aspects), dealing with actions either completed or not completed. Germanic, likewise, reduced its number of tenses to two-past and present. The other tenses in modern Germanic languages have developed out of combinations of these two original tenses.

<<Verb forms in the two language groups also contain similarities. The Hebrew verb kom, kam, kum, yikom ("to arise, come forth"), for example, compares favorably with modern English come and came, Old English cuman, and German

kommen, kam, gekommen ("to come forth, arrive, arise"). According to this formula, words brought into Germanic after 700 B.C. had a tendency to modify their spelling in three ways:

<<First, in most Germanic dialects, the words changed in spelling according to the sound shift. Hebrew, on the other hand, changed only in pronunciation; spelling remained the same.

<<Second, the vowels in the initial syllables were frequently dropped in written Germanic forms because Hebrew words usually carried the accent on the last syllable. Compare Hebrew daraq and English drag. Occasionally, if the initial consonant was weak, the entire syllable dropped out, as in Hebrew yalad ("male offspring, son") and English lad, and in Hebrew nafal ("to fall") and English fall.

<<Third, Hebrew used a tonal accent (a vocal emphasis featuring a tone or sound in part of a word) rather than a stress accent (a vocal emphasis featuring increased volume in speaking part of a word), but this changed to a stress accent in the Germanic dialects. However, the effects of the Hebrew tonal accent are evident in Germanic. The Hebrew tone, which usually appeared in the final syllable, was often represented in written Germanic by one of four tonal letters-l, m, n, or r. Compare Hebrew satat ("to place, found, base, begin") with English start (r represents the Hebrew tone), and Hebrew parak ("to be free, to liberate") with English frank ("free; free-speech"-in which p was shifted to f, the unaccented a was deleted, and n was added for the Hebrew tone).

<<Similarities in Hebrew and English words point to their common roots.

Some Hebrew-English Cognates

Hebrew	English
KAHAL, KAHALAH "to call"	CALL
OBER, OVER "to cross over"	OVER
DOR, DUR "to rotate, turn aside, enter a dwelling"	DOOR Entrance to dwelling
GADAR "to surround, enclose, to collect"	GATHER
HARAP, HARAPAH "to pluck [a harp], to harp at, to scold"	HARP
DARAG, DARAGAH "to go by steps, to walk or ascend with difficulty"	DRAG
BALAK, BILEK, BLIYK "to make empty, void" ("void of light") ("void of vegetation, pale") ("void of color") ("void of marks")	BLACK BLEAK BLEACH BLANK
SHAPAH "to form, carve, shape, create"	SHAPE

<<Biblical Hebrew contained relatively few root words-originally only a few hundred-but from these roots, words were formed in great variety. Most of these formations were made by exchanging vowels, adding prefixes or suffixes, and doubling consonants according to certain rules. Literally thousands of words similar to these roots, and to the multiple forms that developed out of these roots, appeared in Germanic dialects between 700 and 400 B.C. One example is the Hebrew word

dun or don. The root is "dwn" [don] and is related to the root 'adan ("to rule, to judge, to descend, to be low, area ruled or judged, area of domain"). The proper name Dan ("judge") is related to this root. Out of this root also developed the Hebrew word 'adon ("Lord, Master"). These words remind us of the Anglo-Saxon word adun, out of which the English word down (the noun form means "hill, upland") developed and the area ruled was don, or its modern counterpart town. It is also interesting to note that the Hebrew word 'adon ("Lord") and its root 'adan ("to rule, judge") compare well with Odin and Wodan, two names from different dialects for the highest Germanic god.

<<Changes in language provide only one kind of linguistic evidence we can use to identify the dispersion of Israel. Other linguistic evidence can be found in place names and in the names of various ancient peoples who lived north of the Middle East following the captivity of Israel. Many of these people migrated farther north and west into Russia, Scandinavia, Europe, and Britain.

<<The Dariel Pass, also called the Caucasian Pass...begins near the headwaters of the Euphrates River and leads north through the Caucasus Mountains. At the turn of the century, Russian archaeologist Daniel Chwolson noted that a stone mountain ridge running alongside this narrow passage bears the inscription Wrate Israila, which he interpreted to mean "the gates of Israel."[28]

<<A number of other geographical locations in the area of the Black Sea have names that suggest Hebraic origins. For example, the names of the four major rivers that empty into the Black Sea seem to have linguistic ties to the tribal name of Dan. They are the Don (and its tributary the Don-jets), the Dan-jester (now Dnestr), the Danube (or Donau), and the Dan-jeper (now Dnieper). North of the Caspian Sea is a city called Samara (Samaria). There is also a city of Ismail (Ishmael) on the Danube, and a little farther upstream is a city called Isak (Isaac).

SCYTHIAN PATHS OF MIGRATION
EXILED FROM ISRAEL, THE LOST TEN TRIBES WENT NORTH AND THEN WEST!!

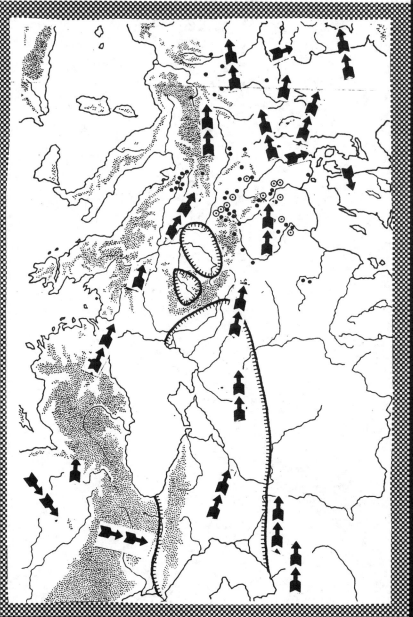

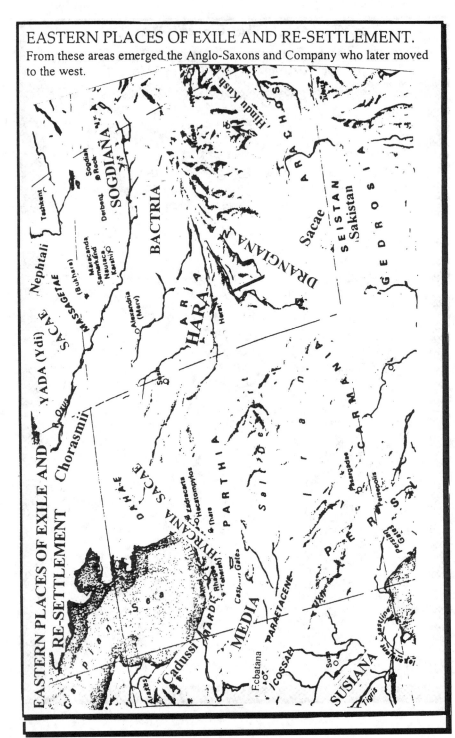

EASTERN PLACES OF EXILE AND RE-SETTLEMENT.
From these areas emerged the Anglo-Saxons and Company who later moved to the west.

HARA AND NEIGHBORHOOD

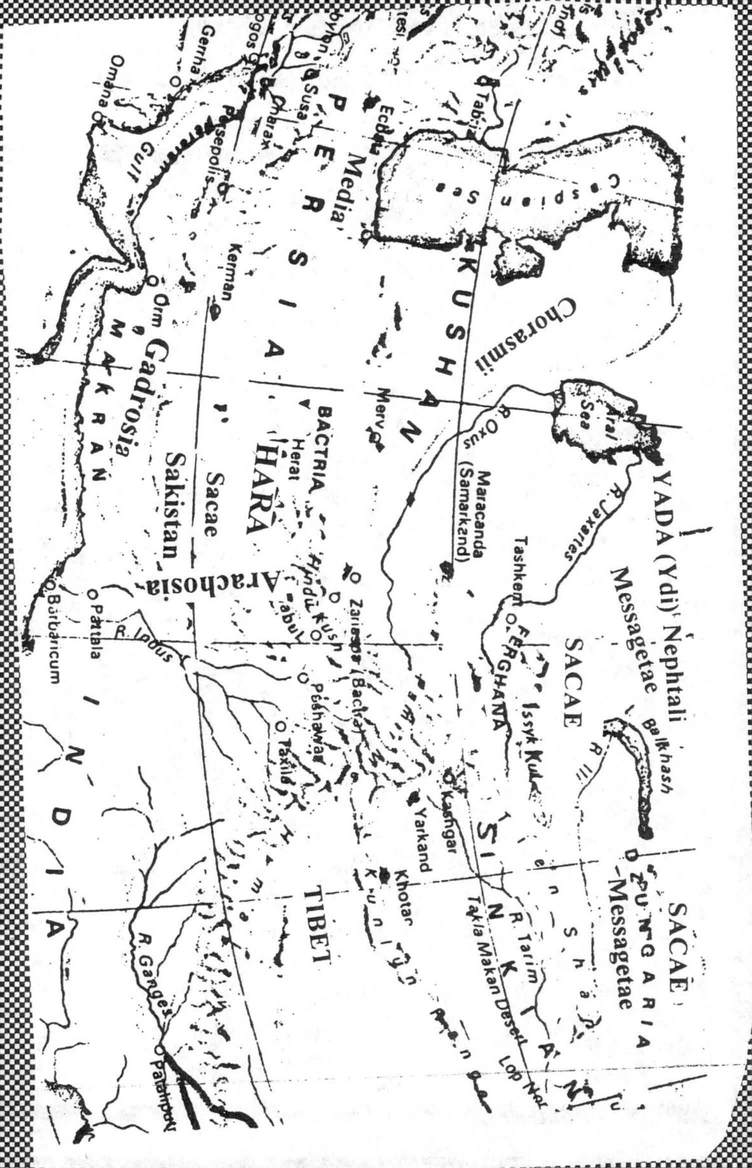

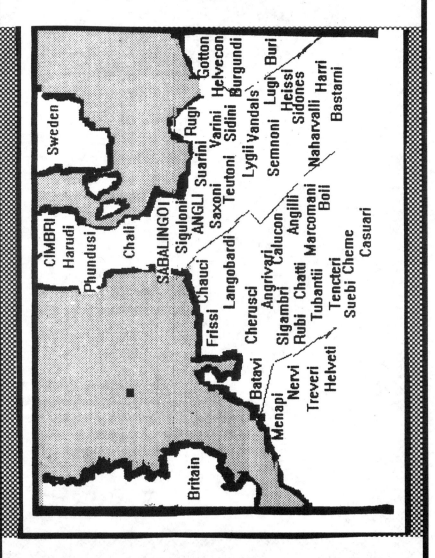

Central Europe Prior To The Anglo-Saxon Invasions Of Britain And The Frank Incursion Of Gaul

Based On Ptolemy And Tacitus

4

THE EXILES' FIRST
LOCATIONS

Prior to the Exile of the Northern Ten Tribes there had originally been Twelve Israelite Tribes, each tribe being divided into familial clans listed in the Books of Genesis (ch. 46) and Numbers (ch.26) with additional information being found in the Book of Chronicles and elsewhere in the Bible. All together there were seventy Israelite family units the overwhelming majority of whom were exiled and even those who were not are proven to have had substantial portions of themselves amongst the exiles. These Tribal Clans often became at some time or other national groups in their own right. Each individual Tribe will be discussed in the following chapters. We will also further clarify what has been said above regarding the routes of migration to the west. It will be shown how in the Land of Israel before the exile, in Scythia after exile, and later in Western Europe after the evacuation of Scythia, the same relative tribal formations were maintained and similar characteristics exhibited.

The Northern Ten Tribes of Israel had been conquered and exiled by the Assyrians. They were taken at first to several areas which are designated, by Biblical and Talmudical sources, as Halah, Habor, the River Gozan, Cities of the Medes[1], Hara[2], the Snowy Mountains[3], Caspii[4], Mountains of Darkness[5], Har-Mannae[6], Sambation[7], Afrikey[8], and so on. The said names often prove to be alternative appellations for the same or adjacent locations.

The exile of the northern Israelites by the Assyrians is described in the Book of Kings that speaks of the capture of Samaria and exile of Israel. "Samaria" was the name of the northern Israelite capital and is sometimes used as an eponym for the Northern Kingdom.

"THE KING OF ASSYRIA TOOK SAMARIA, AND CARRIED ISRAEL AWAY INTO ASSYRIA, AND PLACED THEM IN HALA, AND IN HABOR, BY THE RIVER OF GOZAN, AND IN THE CITIES OF THE MEDES" (2-KINGS 17:6).

The exile took place in several stages and before the exile of "Samaria" (Manasseh, Ephraim, and Zebulon), the Tribes to the north (Dan, Asher, Issachar, and Naphtali) had been taken away by the Assyrian monarch who *"carried them captive to Assyria"* (2-Kings 15:29). Likewise, the tribes east of the Jordan (Reuben, Gad, and half Manasseh) had been carried *"unto Halah, and Habor, and Hara, and to the river Gozan"* (1-Chronicles 5:26).

The place of exile nominated as **"Assyria"** refers to the province by that name which encompassed most of Mesopotamia[9] and extended into the Zagros Mountains in the east, while in the west it reached unto the shores of the Black Sea. **Halah, Habor**, the **River Gozan**, and many of **the cities of the Medes** were within the confines of **"Assyria"** or close to its fringes. **"Hara"** was much further to the east in the region straddling the borders of present day Iran and Afghanistan. "Hara" encompassed places named Aria, Ariana, and Arachosia, by the Greeks[10]. "Hara" was called "Haraiva" and "Hare" by the Persians[11], and known under its correct name "Hara" to the Medes[12], just as it is still called "Hara" by the locals today[13]. It is crossed by the Hari Rud or "River of Hara" and contains the city of Harat.

The Assyrians ruled the Hara area and all of the surrounding region and settled a portion of the Israelite tribes there in, specifically part of those tribes from east of the Jordan: Rueben, Gad, and half Manasseh, since only concerning their exile is the name "Hara" mentioned:

"THE GOD OF ISRAEL STIRRED UP THE SPIRIT OF PUL KING OF ASSYRIA, AND THE SPIRIT OF TIGLATH-PILNESER OF ASSYRIA, AND HE CARRIED THEM AWAY, EVEN THE REUBENI, AND THE GADI, AND THE HALF TRIBE OF MANASSEH, AND BROUGHT THEM UNTO HALA, AND HABOR, AND HARA, AND TO THE RIVER OF GOZAN UNTO THIS DAY" (1-CHRONICLES 5:26).

Assyrian control of the Hara area is proven by inscribed claims of Assyrian monarchs to have received tribute from Magan and Meluhha which nations (in neo-Assyrian nomenclature) were either by the Indus delta or to the east of it[14]. Hara adjoined Bactria and Roman and other accounts related that the Assyrian Semiramis (wife or widow of "Pul"*): had conquered Bactria to the north of Hara as well as parts of India to its east[15]. The Assyrians sent frequent expeditions to Mount "Bikni" meaning the "Mount of Lapis Lazuli" and most (if not all) the lapis lazuli of Assyria came from Badakhshan to the northeast of "Hara"[16]. According to Greek and Iranian sources the Assyrians had planted colonies in the region of Kabul and Gandhara to the east of Hara[17]. Indian scripts also recall the "Asurya" with their god "Asura" (meaning the Assyrians with their deity "Ashur") who had colonies in Hara and Sakastan[18]. Assyrian cultural influences in this area and cultural influences from this area on Assyria confirm the Assyrian presence in this region[19].

According to local tradition the eastern part of Hara ("Ghor"), where the Hari River rises, was once settled by a people referred to as "Assakan" and "Bnei Yisral" or Children of Israel[20]. "Assakan" was shortened to "Sak" or "Sok" and local Muslim lore equated the term with the name "Isaac", father of Israel[21]. A dialectical variation of "Assakan" is Afghan[22] and the

---

* re Pul and Semiramis see "Lost Israelite Identity" by Yair Davidy

names "Bnei Yisral" and "Afghan" were applied later to a group from Armenia who settled in the area **after the original "Bnei Yisral" and "Assakan" had moved out**[23]. The newcomers eventually moved further east into modern Afghanistan. They did not apply the names "Afghan" and "Bnei Yisral" unto themselves until fairly recently and then only within a few literary circles[24]. Some Israelite and/or Jewish elements may have been absorbed amongst one or two of the various "Afghan" groups and these in turn influenced the whole. The Royal family, for instance, had a tradition that they descended from the Tribe of Benjamin[25]. Even so, most Afghans never seem to have identified themselves as Israelites and are antipathetic to the very idea[※]. They are the first to admit that the names "Afghan" and "Bnei Yisral" were first applied to them by foreigners[26]. By their own admission they received these names from other peoples. They themselves say that they received the names due to the original holders of these names having moved out of the area that they came to occupy. The existence of these names is evidence that a section of the Israelite nation had once been in that area. The original dwellers are apparently to be identified with the historical "Sok" or "Sakae" (meaning Scythians) who were in the Hara region at least from around 600 BCE [27] or earlier. They had been settled there by the Assyrians, and had a tradition that King Solomon of Israel had once ruled over them[28]. From the Saka descend the Anglo-Saxon invaders of Britain.

[※] The Afghans also had traditions that they were descended from Esau the brother of Jacob. In their eyes this made them kindred of the Romans and Byzantines. Another tradition said that they were descended from the Koresh tribe in Arabia and thus related to Mohammed. They had additional traditions of like nature. Other peoples in Afghanistan (unrelated to the Afghans or Pathans) also claim descent from Israel. There had once been a sect in the region that adopted Jewish customs. Later members of this sect and/or genuine Jews of the region had been forced to become Muslims. They retained some of their customs and traditions that were in turn adopted by some of their neighbors. These phenomena of adopting the names of other tribes and the customs and traditions of neighboring peoples are frequent patterns in the history of Central Asia and of Eurasia in general.

According to Indian records a people known as "Yavanas"[29] had occupied the area of Hara. The "Yavanas" were not a Greek people, even though "Yavan" means Greece. The term "Yavana" may be traced to Alexander the Great of Macedon (after 330 BCE) who established Greek ruled kingdoms east of the Caspian Sea, in Bactria and Sogdiana. The term "Yavana" thus became applied, in Indian Literature, to the residents of these areas, including the neighboring province of "Hara". The "Yavanas", in the original Indian sense of the term, were a people associated with (or sometimes identified as) the Sakae, Goths, and Parthians who all dwelt in the Hara region[30], and who were all of Hebrew descent. The Yavanas were a monotheistic people centred on "Hara" and considered to be connected with the Assyrians[31], which is consistent with their having been exiled to Hara by the Assyrian establishment.

As noted above, the Israelite Tribes of Reuben, Gad, and half-Manasseh, which had previously dwelt in that part of the Land of Israel to the east of the Jordan River, were the tribes who according to the Bible had been resettled in **HARA**. The names of peoples in the neighborhood of Hara correspond to those of the Tribes who had been sent there and to those of clan-names within those tribes. Reuben, for instance, was represented by the Reubenite clan of CARMI (Numbers 26) in the region of CARMANIA which adjoined Gadrosia (of Gad) south of Hara and encompassed Makran, named after Machir, who had dominated the half tribe of Manasseh, east of the Jordan (Joshua 17:1).

Hara largely received only part of three of the exiled tribes even though other tribes were later to be found close by. Apart from Hara, most of the exiles were resettled in northern Mesopotamia and its neighborhood: in Hala, Habor, the River Gozan, and in cities of the Medes (2-Kings 17:6).

"Halah" is identified in the Talmud as Holwan[32] (also referred to as "Holman"[33]) which was in the Zagros Mountains east of the Tigris River. This was the area ascribed in later

Assyrian writings to the "Yasubi"[34] and "Yasubgalli"[35] which names, in Semitic dialect, mean "Joseph" and "The Exiles of Joseph." Here too, were the SAMBATAE and the city of "Gomara"[36] and the adjoining "Sabatus"[37] River. The name "Sambat" (in Hebraic Greek) implies Sabbath so the appellations "Sambatae" and "Sabbatus" (referring to the Lower Zab River) gave rise to the legend of the River Sambation which stopped flowing every Shabbat and besides which the Lost Ten Tribes were said to be located, in part[38]. Historically, this region was one of the Scythian centers. The city "Gomara" stood on the site of Sakkiz, the Scythian capital. Later the Scythians were to move northwards and re-locate themselves in southern Russia. The names "Sambation" and "River Sabbath" appear to have moved with the Scythians to the Don and Danaper Rivers[39], and were given to those rivers. The name "Sambation" is also recorded as a personal name in the Scythian city of Tanais[40]. The city "Tanais" at the River Don estuary was probably know as "Dan" and social arrangements were determined by a cult based on traditions derived from the Biblical figure of Joseph[41]. Early Jewish tradition equated the Sambation River with the River Don[42].

To the east of Holman and the Sambatae were the Sagartii, Syromedia, and the city of Ecbatana. The Sagartii were called "Asakarti" by the Medes and Persians and were in the area to which part of the Tribe of Issachar had been taken, according to Jewish legend. "Syromedia", reported Ptolemy, was that part of Media to which "Syrians" had been removed and, in Classical terminology, "Syria" encompassed the former Land of Israel. "Ecbatana", in the Talmud, is referred to as "Hamadan" (its more popular name) and is considered one of the "Cities of the Medes" to which Israelites were exiled[43]. Historically, Hamadan, though at first a Median city, later served as a Scythian centre[44], and then after the Scythians had been expelled from the Middle East it reverted to the Medes. Other identified "Cities of the Medes" were Characene (Charach) in Elam, Saki (Hiski) in Sacasene[45] (north Armenia) and Hassaka (north of Nisibis) and the region of Moschi[46] that included Iberia[47] (Georgia) in the Caucasus. All of these areas became Scythian centers. The Scythians had first appeared in the area of Mannae, which in Assyrian terms meant the region of SAMBATAE, Holman, and Gomora (Sakkis) city.

The prophet Amos had foreseen the northern Israelites being cast out to "Harmonah" (Amos 4:3) which the King James Translation understands as meaning "into the palace" though the Aramaic Translation of this passage has a different interpretation. The Aramaic version ("Targum Yehonatan") received Talmudic approbation and frequently paraphrases the text, becoming more like a commentary. This version understood the verse in Amos as saying that the northern Israelites were destined to be cast out unto "Har-Mannae" or the Mountain of Mannae which shortly after the exile became a Cimmerian and Scythian centre, the Cimmerians and Scythians being in effect one people.

The important point in the identifications of places of exile given above and continued below is to notice the constant association of the given areas with Cimmerians, Scyths, and Goths. The Cimmerians had first appeared in Iberia (whose very name means, "Land of the Hebrews") and in Mannae and the Scythians emerged from the Cimmerian ranks[48]. The Goths were known also as Guti. They were recalled as being together with the Sakae (Scyths), and Cimmerians[49]. They had two major centers. One was in the region of Sambatae-Sagartii recalled above, and the other was in the east, to the north of Hara, though at an earlier stage they seem to have also been to Hara's south.

The place of exile called "The River Gozan" appears to be the region by the Ouzan River, which in local dialects was pronounced something like "Gouzan"[50]. Ptolemy calls this river the "Cyrus" and places the city of "Gauzania" on its banks, which is called "Ginzak" by the Talmud and identified with

Gozan[51]. In this region were the Cadussi, who were a Scythian people related to the Sakae, and, according to Pliny (N.H. 6; 18), they called themselves "Gaeli". The Celts in Britain also called themselves "GAELI" and perhaps the name is derived from the Galilee in Israel. Alternately the name could be derived from the Hebrew "Goleh", meaning exile or wander. The Scots of Scotland also understand the name "Scot" to mean "wanderer." Later in Scythia (east of the Ural Mountains) were to appear a nation named "Naphtali" and descended from the Israelite Tribe of that name. In Persian records the Naphtali were referred to as "Kadassaye"[52] i.e. Cadussi. Naphtali had been one of the tribes of the Israelite Galilee. Kadesh had been the major center of Naphtali (Judges 4:6) and from there the Naphtalites were also known as Cadussi or Kadussi. The Tribe of Naphtali, which later appeared in Scythia east of the Ural Mountains, was identical with the Gaeli-Cadussi who previously had been in the "Gouzan" area south-west of the Caspian Sea which area was one to which the Assyrians had transported Israelite exiles.

The Ouzan (or "Gouzan") River was one of two rivers named "Gozan" reported by Eberhard Schrader in his "The Cuneiform Inscriptions and the Old Testament", (London 1888, p.267). Schrader reported further that there was a place named "Halahhu" in the area of Holman (near "Gouzan") which confirms the Talmudic equation (Kiddushin 72a, Yebamot 17) of Holman with Halah, one of the places of exile.

Apart from the "Gouzan" river (in Adherbaijan), another identification of the "River Gozan" is the area Gozan (called "Gauzanitus" by Ptolemy) at the head reaches of the Khabur River from which area Assyrian inscriptions have testified to the presence of Israelite exiles[53]. In this region was the city of Nisibis[54], considered one entity with Adiabene (Hadayb), which Talmudic sources identified as the place of exile named "Habor" (pronounceable as "Khabor") which is consistent with the Khabur River receiving its name from a cognate source. In other words, both in the "Gozan-Gauzanitis" area at the head reaches the Khabur River as well as in the Ginzak-Gouzan region, further to the east by the banks of the Ouzan River, were to be found Israelite exiles. Both areas, according to the Talmud, may be considered to equate the Biblically named places of exile, even though the authorities disagree on which place is which. For the present account it is sufficient to know that Israelites were in both areas and also that both regions became centers of Cimmerian, Scythian, and Gothic activity. The Cimmerians together with the "Subartu" (after rebelling) launched attacks upon Assyria[55] from the Gauzanitis region[56]. "Subartu" was an Assyrian term for "Syrian"[57]. The word for "Syrian" in Hebrew and Semitic languages, however, was usually "ARAMI" and this nomination was applied to Israelites[58] and to the people of Judah[59] as well as to others from the "Syrian" area. Pliny (N.H. 6; 19) said that the Persians had called the Scythians "Sakae" after the nearest tribe to them but their original name, he said, had been "ARAMI" and this is consistent with their Israelite origins.

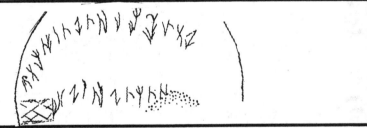

Inscription on silver bowl belonging to Sakae-Scythians, found in Kazakstan 1969, dates from ca. 400 BCE. This inscription was understood by Dr. Jeannine Davis-Kimball to be a prototype of Runic-Wrting who recognized "all the characters immediately as having identical forms with Germanic runes" and to contain the name, "*Uuilaz* or *Wilaz*, possibly an Indo-Iranian version of *Wilagaz*, or in modern English, Wily". Picture reproduced from *"The World of the Scythians"* by Renate Rolle 1980. The runes are actually a version of the Ancient Hebrew-Phoenician alphabet. Orjan Svensson ("De Blekingska Runornas Hemligheter", 2001) has proven that the oldest known runes in Sweden were written in Hebrew and Aramaic dialects.

83

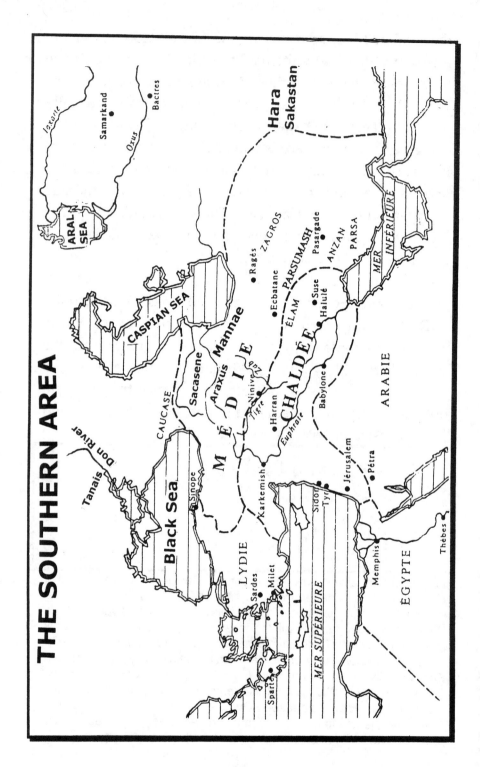

THE SOUTHERN AREA

5

THE SCYTHS OF ISAAC IN THE EAST

THE ISRAELITES IN IRAN AND EAST SCYTHIA
The Hebrews Become Cimmerians, Scythians, and Goths

An emphasized differentiation of Israelite Tribes and Tribal-clans took place after the exile by the Assyrians and subsequent migrations to Eurasian Scythia and from there moving on to Western Europe. This process occurred after the Ten Northern Tribes of Israel had separated from the Tribe of Judah. They had rejected the House of David and formed their own kingdom. The Assyrians conquered their land and exiled them. The Northern Kingdom had left nothing of substance behind it within the Land of Israel. Everything was destroyed and nearly all of the people were taken away. The exiled Hebrews were absorbed within the framework of the Neo-Assyrian Empire, taken into the army, and resettled in border regions. The Assyrian Empire under attack from without had begun to disintegrate and the Israelites were enabled to assume independence of action. A major factor undermining the Assyrian Empire was attacks by the Cimmerians. The Cimmerians first appeared in places whereto the Israelites had been exiled in the period immediately following upon their re-settlement by the Asyrians.

The Cimmerian "outcasts" brought forth a "Scythian" people named "Saca" after "ISAAC" and this people appear to have been Israelite as the Cimmeri themselves (at least in part) were. The Israelite identification of the Scythian-Sakae with the "House of Isaac" is exemplified by:

* Their being called "Arami" meaning Syrian.
* Their association with the Cadussi who belonged to the Israelite Tribe of Naphtali.
* Their connection to the Guti-Goths who were named after the Israelite Tribe of "Gad".
* Their having been in every area to which Israelites were known to have been deported to previously.
* Their partnership with King Josiah of Judah which paralleled that attributed in the Bible and Talmud to the Lost Ten Tribes.
* Their role as protectors, dominators, and destroyers of Assyria which also paralleled the role attributed by the Hebrew Prophets to the Lost Ten Tribes.
* The appearance of Zoroaster amongst them with a Hebraic message and influence of Jeremiah the Prophet who had been sent to the Lost Ten Tribes.
* In Hara one section of them had been explicitly referred to as "Sok" (Isaac) and as "Children of Israel".
* Israelite characteristics such as an aversion to images, a taboo on pork, and a cult derived from the Biblical figure of Joseph.
* Scythian artwork is typologically consistent with an Israelite origin.

Additional evidence identifying the Scythian peoples with the Hebrews is presented further on: The Scythians were to be forced northward into Scythia (Eurasia) and an examination of Scythian Tribal names in Scythia reveals

86

similarities to the names of Israelite Tribes and Tribal clans. Traditions and mythology substantiate these likenesses. The processes which caused these Scythian (Israelite) peoples to later migrate to Western Europe have been described and further signs of Israelite progeny revealed. Biblical prophecies are seen to locate the Lost Ten Tribes of Israel in northwest Europe, in Britain, and in the daughters of Britain and Northwest Europe, in North America, Australia, New Zealand, and South Africa. Our understandings of these Prophecies are confirmed by historical studies.

The Identification of Israelite Tribes

The correlation of Israelite Tribes with groups otherwise identified as Scythian is demonstrated throughout much of this work. For the present purposes the term "Scythian" may generally be considered to encompass the Scyths-proper, the Cimmerians, and the Goths. These peoples had been associated in the Assyrian ruled Middle East area. The Scyths-proper had been called "Arami", Ishkuzi, Sacae, and other appellations. The Cimmerians had been known as Gimirrae or Gamera; and the Goths were recalled as "Guti".

Classical accounts used in recounting the fate of these peoples are often not contemporary with the events described. Ptolemy, for instance, wrote his Geography about 120 CE but used sources[1] dating from many centuries beforehand, as well as those of his own time. It follows that in some cases Ptolemy recorded the same people under the same or similar names in two different regions whereas, in fact, they had migrated from one place to the other. Such cases of double reporting when combined with other evidence may actually be used as proof of the migrating paths. Analysis of Ptolemy's Maps is given in several of the following chapters.

After being expelled from the Middle East the Scyths, Cimmerians, and Goths split into several bodies of which two main groups may be roughly identified. One group went west at an early date and became associated with the Cimbrians,

Galatians, Celts, Getae, and Dacae in Europe. The other group at first went north and east into "SCYTHIA" becoming the Scythians and Goths of Classical Accounts. From this last group were to come the Jutes, Saxons, Angles, Franks, Scandinavians, Goths, and so on known to history. It is these latter peoples who emerged from "Scythia" that the historical aspects of the present book are primarily concerned with.

In Scythia the Goths split into several sections, the eastern part becoming known in the west as "Massagetae" and to the Chinese as "Gu-ti"[2] which name is sometimes (incorrectly) transliterated as "Yuehchi" or the like. Part of the Gothic confederates in the east were the Naphtalites or White Huns who included an entity named DAN. Also associated with both the Goths and Naphtalites were the ancestors of the Parthians who were destined to conquer the Persian Empire and rule over a good portion of the Middle East for about five hundred years. An account of these peoples is extremely interesting and is also important for an understanding of the present study. Nevertheless, since many different groups are involved and the sources used come from various places there exists a multiplicity of names, many of them unfamiliar to the average reader. This proliferation of appellations may cause an initial confusion. The suggested solution is to keep reading since most important points are elaborated upon several times from different aspects and with the addition of new information which maintains interest. Pliny (Natural History ca.70 CE) is a source frequently employed in studying the Historical Geography of Scythia, therefore his remark concerning this area is worth quoting: *"And in regard to no other region is there more discrepancy among the authorities, this being due as I believe to the countless numbers and the nomadic habits of the tribes"* (N.H. 6;19).

The results of this study identify peoples and places in West Europe and Britain with specific Israelite Tribes and clans. The Hebrew Tribes are traced firstly to areas of "Scythia" and with the Scythian-connected migrations to Europe they are identified once more in their new places of settlement, and the

Israelite-Scyth-European connection is re-affirmed. Each stage of the narrative is seen to provide further evidence in its own right for the Israelite derivation of these peoples.

Israelite Tribes In The Iranian And East Scythian Sphere

The Assyrians had exiled the Ten Tribes of Israel to northern Mesopotamia and to Hara (1-Chronicles 5:26) which was SOUTHEAST of the Caspian Sea. Hara became a Scythian centre and was the general region of Zoroaster (Zarathustra) who founded an originally Monotheistic Hebrew-type religion. Zoroaster was himself associated in popular tradition with both Scythians and Hebrews[3]. Both **BACTRIANA and SAKASTAN were considered part of Hara**. SAKASTAN was also called Drangiana, Seistan, and even "Scythia"[4]. SAKASTAN was peopled by Sakae (Scyths) whose presence in that region is now dated to before 600 BCE.[4] * This date is consistent with the date of Assyrian Exile and the period following it. The people of Sakastan had a tradition[5] that King Solomon of Israel had once ruled over them. Bactriana also became a major Scythian region at one stage, and the Jews of Bactria[6] believed that the Lost Ten Tribes had been in their area.

After the Medes and Persians gained control of the neo-Assyrian Empire they had began to push both the east and west Scythians northwards. The King of Persia, Darius (521-406 BCE.), claimed to rule over the Sacae who were beyond Sogdiana, meaning those in the heart of eastern Scythia. As a result of their being pushed northwards Scythian groups for a time were to be found in both the Iranian and Scythian regions [*by "Scythia" is meant the former USSR domain*]. Similarly,

---

* Sakastan is not to be confused with Sacasene which was also a Scythian center. "Sakastan" was east of the Caspian Sea by Aria (Hara) whereas "Sacasene" was part of Caucasian Armenia west of the Caspian. Strabo (11.8.14) reported, <<*The Sacae occupied Bactriana, and got possession of the most fertile tract in Armenia which was called after their own name 'Sacasene'*>>. "Sacasene" was in Armenia whereto exiled Israelites from the Ten Tribes had also been taken. The Khazars first appeared from Sacasene.

traditions concerning the Israelites have existed in both areas as exemplified in the accounts of Eldad and others.

Zebulon, Issachar, Gad, Naphtali

Eldad HaDani (ca. 800 CE) collated legends extant in his time concerning the Ten Tribes of Israel. He mentioned the Tribe of Zebulon having been east of Mesopotamia in the Paran Mountains, meaning the "Paroutas" branch of the Zagros Mountains[7]. **Zebulon** seems to have been also once located (in part) further east where there existed a kingdom called ZABULISTAN that was named after a people[8] who evacuated the region sometime prior to the Moslem period. Zabulistan[9] encompassed the area south of Kabul (in Afghanistan) and also Sakastan. The Scythian hero called "ZOHAK" had colonized it.[10]. The name "ZOHAK" is actually a variant of ISAAC. Zohak in Iranian Literature represented the Scythians.[11]. Zohak was considered an agent of the Assyrians[12] and as responsible for having settled the inhabitants of Zabulistan in their places[*]. Several Israelite groups were in the Zabulistan region. Zebulon, in Biblical and Talmudic lore, is closely connected with his brother Issachar. In the Parouta area (ascribed to Zebulon) Ptolemy recalled a people he calls Sagartii and whom the Persians termed Asakarta. The Asarkta belonged to **Issachar**. Thus, Zebulon and Issachar were together in the Parouta region. Eldad[13] said too that part of Issachar was in Carmania to the south of the Caspian Sea and another part was situated to the east of it[14]. East of the Caspian, Ptolemy recorded the Sagaruce who (like the Sagartii above) belonged to Issachar. Similarly, in Carmania were the Isatichae (says Ptolemy) who represent the other branch of Issachar mentioned by Eldad. The identifications of the Sagaruce and Isatichae with portions of Issachar correspond with the locations given to Issachar in Eldad's account. Also in Carmania, were the Pasargadae whose

---

[*] Zohak was also in effect identified with Israel, Josef **HOROVITZ**, "Hebrew Iranian Synchronism," Bombay, 1931, p.3

name means "Son-of-Gad"[15]. The Tribe of Gad was recalled throughout the Iranian neighbourhood: In **GAD**rosia, in the **GAD**anopydres of Carmania, in the **GOD**man province south of the Caspian, in the Thata**GYDES** of **SOGDIANA** and the Indus banks and in the **Gut**i-Goths of Sogdiana and beyond it. The neighboring province of Gandhara (west of the Indus River) in Old Persian was known as **Gad**ara. Also in GADrosia were the Yautiya (Utii) which name is probably the equivalent of Yatya[16] who were later recorded as an independent entity amongst the Naphtalite Huns. The Naphtalite Huns came from the Israelite Tribe of Naphtali and were later to be reported of in Russian Central Asia before migrating to Scandinavia. In Russian Scythia they reportedly had been based in part east of the Ural Mountains.

Naphtali, Judah, And Dan In Scythia

The "Naphtali" in the 400s CE had begun to be reported of in Eastern Scythia. The Naphtali were also known as Naphtalite-Huns, Eptali, and Hefthalites. They were at one stage east of the Ural Mountains and in Byzantine writings were then called "Kadassay"[17] (i.e. Cadussians) after Kadesh-Naphtali (Judges 4:6) in the Land of Israel. Previously, in ancient times the Cadussians had been located southwest of the Caspian by the area of Mannae north of Mesopotamia. Mannae was the region whereto the prophet Amos[18] foresaw the northern Israelites being exiled. Mannae had also been a Cimmerian and Scythian centre. The Cadussi had been considered a Scythian people related to the Sacae[19]. Pliny (N.H. 6;18) says that the Cadussi called themselves "Gaeli" which name the Celts in Britain were also to apply to themselves. The Apocryphal book of Tobit (Tobias) described exiles from Israel from the Tribe of Nephtali as being in the Cadussi region (Tobit 1:1-2 1:10 2:10 2:7 5:6). Along with the Scythian movement northward the Cadussi had apparently re-located themselves, which explains their identification afterwards as the Naphtalites east of the Urals. Chinese records speak of a group named "Yautya" together with the Naphtali. According to the Chinese, the "Yatya" were a section of Naphtali also referred to as "Hu" and as "Yeda"[20]. The Assyrians had termed Judeans of Judah and of Sma'al in Cilicia, "Yaeti" and "Yadi"[21] which names are similar to the appellations "Yatya" and "Yeda" for the group amongst the Naphtalites. Similarly, in Caucasian dialects "Yat"[22] or "Yet" means Jew. The Naphtalite Yaeti correspond to the Yautiya who formerly had been situated in Gadrosia and had there adjoined the Dangalai (Pliny N.H. 6;92). The Dangalai have a name implying "Dan of the Galilee". They also moved northward and were recorded by the Chinese as being near the Naphtalites in the north. The Chinese called them, "Dingling" or "Dinlin" and described them as blondish and of fair appearance[23].

The Geographer Ortellius[24] (1570) charted a map of northern Scythia in which he utilized legendary traditions. He included the Naphtalite Huns and "Danites" as part of one body from the Israelite Tribes of Naphtali and Dan. To the east of the Naphtali Ortellius located the rest of the Lost Tribes whom he said were called "Gauths". The position which Ortellius allocated to the "Gauths" corresponds to that of the Guti (Yuehchi) who neighbored the Sacae-Scyths. The Guti (Yuehchi) in the west were referred to as "Gauths," "Goths" and as Massagetae. Evidence exists indicating that the Naphtalites ultimately migrated to Scandinavia, on the whole, apart from small splinter groups, one of which amalgamated with the Khazars. In Europe the Goths, Jutes, Danes and Nephtalite "Vikings" of Norway were destined to be closely associated with each other. This association had been preceded in Scythia by the union of their immediate ancestors: The Naphtali became the Norwegians, Dan the Danes, Yadi the Jutes of Denmark, and the Guti became the Goths of Scandinavia.

The position wherein Ortellius placed the Naphtalites in Tartaria (Scythia) roughly corresponds to the area ascribed by Herodotus (4; 22) to the Thyssagatae and Iyrcae -after allowance is made for the area's remoteness and a tendency for movement. Different divisions of the Iyrcae were to be named "White Ugrians", and "Turcae"[24]. The "White Ugrians" were those Iyrcae who later joined the Khazars while the "Turcae" in Roman authors[25] represent the other section of the Iycrae who, according to tradition[26], migrated to Scandinavia. The Iyrcae had neighbored the Thyssagatae whose name is assumed to mean "Little Goths"[27]. Similarly, in Chinese literature[28], a group known as "Little Goths" (i.e. Little Gu-ti, "Sian Yuehchi") were reported from nearby Badakhshan which was northeast of Bactria and these are identified with the Naphtalites. Jewish legends[29] recalled the presence of the Israelite Tribes of Dan, Naphtali, Zebulon, and Asher in Badakhshan where the people known as "Little Goths" and as "Nephtali" are known to have been. It follows from the above that the names Thyssagatae, Little Goths, Goths, Naphtali, Iyrcae, Cadussi, and so on all applied to the same or to closely related peoples who in east Scythia had adjoined each other and who all were Hebrew.

Issachar, Reuben, Gad, And Machir In Iran And Scythia

The legends collated by Eldad[30] included the report that Reuben was (or had been) together with Issachar at the eastern end of the Caspian Sea. Eldad also placed Issachar in Carmania. Ptolemy had located the Astaveni on the eastern shore of the Caspian and these may have been the "Hetsroni" (Numbers 26:6) who were a clan of Reuben. Close by the Astaveni were, according to Ptolemy, the Sagaruce who like the Sagartii belonged to Issachar as did the Isatichae to the south in Carmania. Thus, the Astaveni of Ptolemy correspond to the Hetsroni of Reuben, while the Sagartii, Sagaruce, and Issatichae were portions of Issachar. This area east of the Caspian was that from which the Parthians were destined to emerge and to create what was probably the second (after the Romans) most powerful kingdom in the world. The Parthians, according to Chinese sources[31], came from the same stock as the Guti who are otherwise known as "Goths". The name "Goth" in

Biblical Hebrew is another form for "GAD"[*] and "GAD" is a typical root in Gothic toponomy. The Tribe of Gad had been exiled together with the tribe of Reuben and the half-tribe of Manasseh (1-Chronicles 5:25-26) to Hala, Habor, the River Gozan, and to Hara which adjoined the future region of Parthia. It appears that Reuben, as well as Gad, contributed to the Gothic entity, and it may be concluded from this and the following indications that the Parthians, at least in part, were also of Israelite descent. Both the Goths and the Arsacid rulers of Parthia were ascribed Hebraic origins in their own time (or close to it) by contemporary observers.

The half-tribe of Manasseh, which had been exiled together with Reuben and Gad, included the important clans of Machir and Gilead (1-Chronicles 2:23). The association of Machir with Gad is noticed in the south of east Iran where Gadrosia (Gad) adjoined Makran. Further north the Guti were to be associates of the Amyrgioi Scyths who, under the names of Skati Maruka and Mercians, were to participate in the invasions of Europe. In Anglo-Saxon England the kingdom of MERCIA was to become the largest and, for a time, the most important single polity.

The Amyrgioi Scyths east of the Caspian who were destined to give rise to the Mercian Saxons were descendants of Machir (or "Ha-Machiri") from Manasseh.

Early tradition spoke of the Lost Ten Tribes being in the Scythian area. This has been discussed by Andrew Colin GOW, "The Red Jews. Anti-Semitism in an Apocalyptic Age 1200-1600" NY 1995). Already in the 300s CE the Latin Tiburtine Sibyl spoke of the anti-Christ being from the Tribe of Dan and of Alexander, the Indian King who shut up Gog and Magog in the far north. The whole area of Scythia even Georgia in the Caucasus in Medieval writings could be referred to as India or

---

[*] HACOHEN ("Imri Emet", Jerusalem 1989) affirms that an unaccented "d" (ד) was pronouncable as an "English 'th'" and that a PATACH vowel tended to an "o" sound. *It follows that the Hebrew name "GAD" (גד) may alternatively be transliterated as "GOTH".*

"Cush". Josephus (Jewish Wars vii;7;4) says that Alexander the Great used iron gates to close up mountain passes so that the Scythians would not break into the civilized world. Elsewhere (Antiquities 1;b;i) Josephus identifies the Scyths with Magog. From the 1100s CE Gog and Magog were identified as the Lost Ten Tribes. Peter Comestor (ca. 1165) identified the Lost Ten Tribes with Gog and Magog whom Alexander had locked up behind iron gates in the mountains. The area of the Ten Tribes was referred to as Caspia apparently due to its proximity to the Caspian Sea. The Lost Ten Tribes were called "Red Jews" and were described as all having Red Hair. Red Hair in the Middle Ages especially in Germany was considered a negative characteristic and associated with the Jews and with Judas. The Anti-Christ and Judas were depicted as both having red hair and as both coming from the Tribe of Dan. Gow quotes David Kaufman (1892): The legend of the Ten Tribes as future deliverers of Israel was "a faith that was slumbering in the popular Jewish consciousness all through the Middle Ages" (Jewish Quarterly Review, iv, 503-508).

Passau Anonymous (1330): <<THE JEWS AND MANY JUDAIZING CHRISTIANS IMAGINE THAT THIS PEOPLE [i.e. The Ten Tribes] IS HOLY; THEY WOULD BE GLAD IF THEY WERE TO COME, AND WOULD JOIN THEIR RANKS IMMEDIATELY>>.

In Germany the Jews were believed to be in league with the devil and to be plotting with the "Red Jews" meaning the Ten Tribes to overthrow Christendom meaning in their eyes mainly Rome and Germany. Luther identified Gog and Magog with the Turks and said they were descended from "Tatars or Red Jews." The Jews also believed the Lost Ten Tribes to be in Scythia, in the region by the Caspian Sea. This belief was widespread and lasted up to the 1600s CE. Christian Gerson of Reckinghausen (a Jewish convert to Christianity, 1607) said:

"MANY JEWS BELIEVE THAT THE TEN TRIBES WHOM THE KING SALMANESSAR LED AWAY ARE STILL TOGETHER AND LIVE BEHIND THE DARK MOUNTAINS CALLED THE CASPIAN MOUNTAINS...MANY CHRISTIANS ALSO TALK ABOUT THE RED JEWS, WHOM THEY HAVE NEVER

SEEN, WHENCE COMES THE WRONGHEADED NOTION, THAT THE MESSIAH MIGHT STILL BE BORN FROM THE TRIBE OF JUDAH, FROM THE RED JEWS."

It should be noted that the Lost Ten Tribes and Gog and Magog were also identified with the Goths most of whom had long ago settled in Sweden though popular fantasy still located them in the east. An English work (one of several) published in 1607 speaks of an army of the Lost Ten Tribes arriving from the east with the aim of defeating the Turks (who then where the dominant Muslim power) and saving Christendom. At least in this latter case the Lost Ten Tribes were depicted as destined to play a positive role

At all events early Jewish sources place part of the Tribe of Manasseh in the same region wherein history records the Amyrgioi Scythians (who became the Mercian Saxons) to have been. Local names for cities and regions in the area, such as Maruka and Maracanda are derived from the name "Machir". One of these said sources is the Cochin Scroll[32], which in a preamble speaks of the Lost Ten Tribes.

[Micah 4:7] AND I WILL MAKE HER THAT HALTED A REMNANT, AND HER THAT WAS CAST FAR OFF A STRONG NATION: AND THE LORD SHALL REIGN OVER THEM IN MOUNT ZION FROM HENCEFORTH, EVEN FOR EVER.   Malbim: Judah shall be a remnant and the Ten Tribes that were cast off a strong nation.

[Micah 4:8] AND THOU, O TOWER OF THE FLOCK, THE STRONG HOLD OF THE DAUGHTER OF ZION, UNTO THEE SHALL IT COME, EVEN THE FIRST DOMINION; THE KINGDOM SHALL COME TO THE DAUGHTER OF JERUSALEM.
The future redemption will begin when Judah begins to bring in its exiles, then sets up a kingdom of its own . The Ten Tribes will follow afterwards.

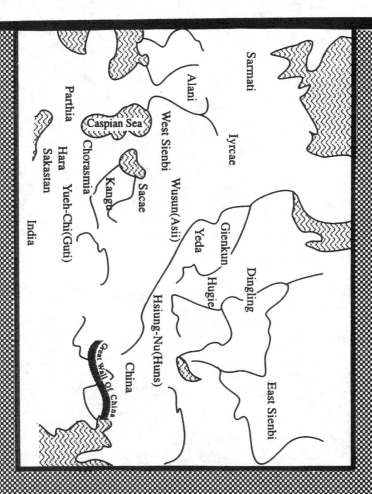

APPROXIMATE POSITIONS OF EAST SCYTHIAN PEOPLES ACCORDING TO CHINESE (AND WESTERN) SOURCES

EXCERPTS FROM THE MAP OF
TARTARIA (SCYTHIA) BY ORTELLLIUS

98

DAN, NAPHTALI AND THE GOTHS MAP OF TARTARIA: ORTELLIUS

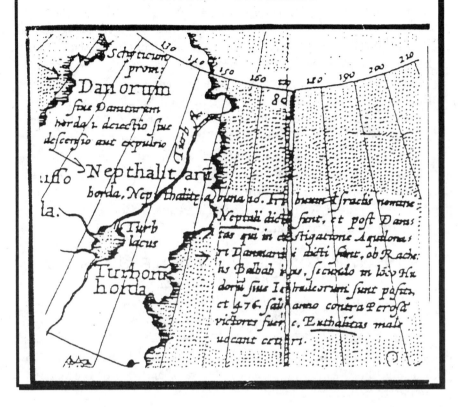

"Nephthalitarus horda, Nephtalite, a buna 10. Tribuum Israelis nomine Neptuli dictisunt, et post Danitas qui in castigatione Aquilonari Danmarcki dicti sunt, ob Rachelis Balhah ins, secundo in lici Hudora siue Iehudeorum sunt positi, et 476, Salianno contra Perosa victores suere, Euthalitas maleuvocant cetiri. Danorum: sui Daniturum horda i. deiectio siue descensio aut expulsio. Arsareth Hic 10 Tribus Secesere, et Totaroru silie Turtarorum loco Scythice substituerunt. Unde Gauths seu Gauthay a summa Dei gloria aserenda ibi dicti sunt, et hinc Cathay clarist Regnum. Argon. Christianorum olim regnu noie. Presbiteri Iois in aseirat, a D Thomas ibi ibstituum, ut Romane corresponderant ecclesie, per Presbiterum Iaem Africanuum Rome obediens et antequa a Gothan vinceretur Criue Romone nunciqiiabatur".

TRANSLATION OF THE QUOTATION FROM THE MAP OF TARTARY BY ORTELLIUS

"The Nephtalite horde, Nephthalites were from the 10 Tribes of Israel. They were called Neptuli. They were placed under the standard (eagle) of Danmarck [Dan] who had been reproved. They came from Bilhah, Rachel's maidservant. Their position was second in honor after the Judaeans. In 476 Salianno [their leader, Salt?] was victorious against Peros [the Persian monarch]. Some incorrectly call them Euthalites.

"The Danes: These are the horde of Dan who became separated and either left or were expelled.

"Arsareth: Here, the 10 Tribes were secluded. The Totarou or Turtaru in the place of the Scyths they replaced whence Gauths or Gauthay they were called (in that place) in order, they said, to give glory to God [Gauth,= Goth, =God, =Got] and here their kingdom is the famous Cathay.

"Argon. Once a king of Christians (was here) called Presbiteri Iois ((John?)), appointed by St. Thomas and in ecclesiastical correspondence with Rome (Similarly (?) the Presber Iaem [John?] of Africa is (also) obedient to Rome) [This was] before the Goths (Gothans) defeated them and killed (?) Rome's representative

6

HISTORICAL IDENTIFICATIONS

The Maps of Ptolemy

An important source of information for this study consists of the Maps of Ptolemy which depict the regions between far eastern Scythia (i.e. Serica) and Britain in the west. The relevant maps reflect the historical period from the Israelites having been resettled after their exile, moving to Scythia, and from there moving westward. By describing the Maps, the historical migrations of the Hebrew clans are illustrated and the evidence identifying these clans as Israelite is demonstrated. The historical reality of the Maps and the Tribal Identities rely on the same details and a certain parallelism between the Maps discussed and the order of Tribal identities discussed in Section One will be noticed. Some necessary repetition of imparted information occurs though in different context and in a manner complementing the overall presentation. The Maps are described moving from primary places of the First Exile south of the Caspian Sea to the Northeast and from the east, westward. They also roughly progress in a chronological order since, roughly speaking, a good portion of the Israelites did move in the same geographical direction in the same order of sequence. The first Tribes described are those of Gad, Reuben, and the half-tribe of Manasseh and these may have been the first tribes to be exiled. Most of the Tribal clans are traced to historically known

Scythian European-Celtic peoples. These were related to, or otherwise connected with, other such groups that too are proven to have belonged to the same Israelite tribe as themselves. Alternatively the other groups they were associated with prove to have been descended from part of another Israelite tribe that in Scripture was somehow especially linked to its own. Tribal origins at the group level instinctively influenced ethnic movements and bonding. The imparted information may well help interested individuals and even certain whole nations realize who they really are, or at least, who they may well be. The Maps of Ptolemy serve both to prove and to illustrate the migratory paths connecting peoples in Europe to Tribes of Ancient Israel.

The present work traces Israelite Tribes after the Assyrian Exile to Mesopotamia and Iran and their surroundings and from there to Eurasian "Scythia" and thence to West Europe via Scandinavia and Germany. The said migrations are demonstrated graphically through the use of maps based on Ptolemy's Geography. Not every point alluded herein is to be labored over, much of the information has already been given in the previous pages but the use of Ptolemy's Maps serves to confirm and enhance the overall presentation as well as being substantial proof in its own right.

Claudius Ptolemaus lived about 100-175 CE. His "Guide to Geography" is believed to have been based on an earlier work. The sources used by Ptolemy (or by whomever he based himself upon) seem to be spread over a period dating back to Herodotus (ca.450 BCE) and even beyond. A Phoenician source (Marinus of Tyre) dating from around 350 BCE has also been suggested as a source used by Ptolemy. From the time of his earliest sources to the time Ptolemy actually wrote there occurred several waves of upheaval and migrations in which many peoples were uprooted and came to traverse vast distances in relatively short periods of time. These occurrences are not generally taken account of in Ptolemy's work so that

THE SAME NATIONS CAME TO BE RECORDED IN TWO OR MORE DIFFERENT PLACES. This aspect of Ptolemy when corresponded with additional evidence is usable as further proof of the migratory process.

The Maps used are those taken from old editions of Ptolemy and may be based on those of Ptolemy himself. Alternatively, they are early compilations based on the descriptions in Ptolemy's writings.

The relative positioning in these maps is fairly accurate even by modern standards. Here and there serious errors are noticeable, and in some cases the actual placements were somewhat different. Nevertheless, the Geography of Ptolemy serves as an excellent basis for the present exposition.

THE FIRST OF THE MAPS DESCRIBED (THOSE OF HABOR, MEDIA, PARTHIA, AND HARA) REPRESENT LARGELY THE SITUATION OF THE EXILED ISRAELITES AFTER THEIR BEING RESETTLED BY THE ASSYRIANS AND SUBSEQUENT DEVELOPMENTS BEFORE THEIR BEING DRIVEN FURTHER NORTH WHENCE THEY WERE DESTINED TO INVADE AND SETTLE NORTHWEST EUROPE. IF THE SUBJECT OF ISRAELITE TRIBAL IDENTITY REALLY INTERESTS YOU: MAKE AN ATTEMPT TO FOLLOW THIS EXPOSITION ON PTOLEMY. YOU WILL FIND THE INFORMATION BOTH HIGHLY INTERESTING AND OF GREAT VALUE.

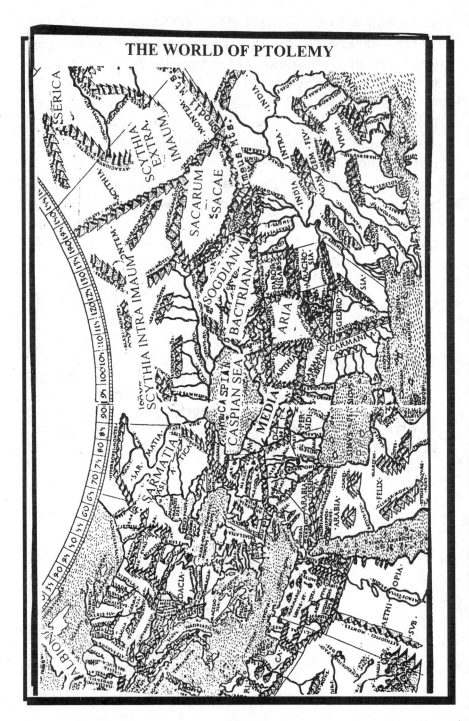

THE WORLD OF PTOLEMY

PTOLEMY'S MAP OF HABOR AND CO.

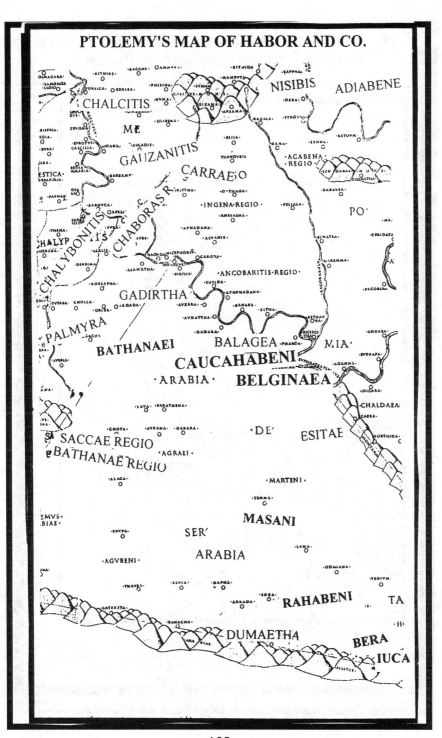

VERY APPROXIMATE POSITIONS OF SCYTHIAN PEOPLES
ACCORDING TO THE GEOGRAPHY OF PTOLEMY

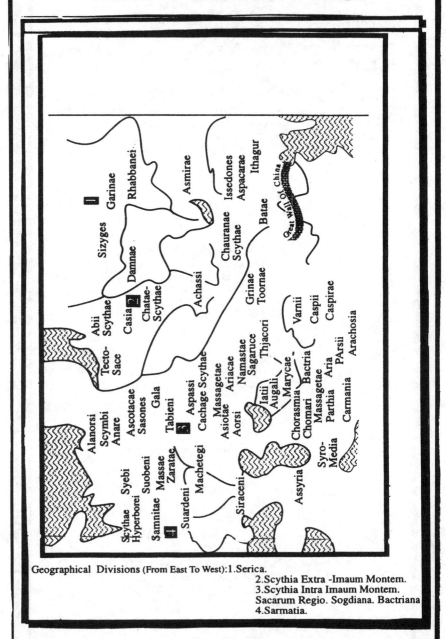

Geographical Divisions (From East To West):1.Serica.
2.Scythia Extra -Imaum Montem.
3.Scythia Intra Imaum Montem.
Sacarum Regio. Sogdiana. Bactriana
4.Sarmatia.

Explanation of the Map:

HABOR AND THE REST
The Land of Israel before the Exile:

The Map showing the location of Habor also depicts a large section of the Middle East. It shows areas settled by Israelite Tribes long before the Exile as well as regions in which Israelites were re-settled by the Assyrians after the Exile.

According to the Bible (1-Chronicles chapter 6) the Tribes of Gad and Reuben fought against Arabian tribes and settled in their lands *"until the time of exile"* (1-Chronicles 6:22). The former presence of Israelite Tribes in northern Arabia and Syria prior to the exile is recalled in some of the place-names mentioned by Ptolemy in the Land termed **"ARABIA"** on his Map.

As well as the Tribes of Gad and Reuben the area east of the Jordan River was also settled by the half-tribe of Manasseh along with a portion from Simeon and contingents from Judah, Benjamin, and other Tribes.

The clan of Yacin (Icen) from Simeon is recalled in **IUCA in the south-east near the Persian Gulf.** This clan later in Scythia became known as the Sacae-Eucae and Eucatae and in northern Europe as the Saxon-Euci and in Celtic Britain as the ICENI neighbors to the SIMENI. Boudicca, the Celtic Queen in Ancient Britain who led a revolt against Roman Tyranny belonged to the Iceni tribe. This area includes the oil-rich fields of present-day Kuwait and the Iraqi oil fields and it is interesting to note that the region once belonged to Israel.

West of Iuca is **Bera** and Beria is a clan name amongst the Tribes of Benjamin, Ephraim, and Asher. Another acceptable way of pronouncing the Hebrew spelling of "Beria" gives "Beria-g-h" or "Ver-iag" which national name re-appeared amongst Scandinavian and Khazar groups.

The name **RAHABENI** ON PTOLEMY'S MAP IS A FORM FOR REUBEN and was to be repeated in Serica (east of

Scythia) as the RHABBANAEI who gave rise to the RIBUARI FRANKS in Europe.

The name **MASANI** derives from Manasseh and the inversion of syllables ("Mas-ani" for "Man-aseh") is a common phenomenon. The Masani were later recalled in Northern Holland and from there they crossed over to England.

Further north, the **BALAGAEA** and **BELGINAEA** co-relate to the name BELAH (pronounceable as "Bela-g-h") which was a clan name from the Tribe of Benjamin and was to re-appear in the BELGAE who gave their name to BELGIUM.

CAUCHABENI means "Sons (Beni) of Chaggi" or Haggi (Num.26) whose name in Hebrew began with the letter HETH (ח) which may be transliterated either as "h" or as "ch. Haggi (Chaggi) was one of the Clans of Gad which in Scythia became known as the Cachage Scythae and as the Huga. Later in northwest Europe they were recorded as the Cauki (Chauci) or Hugo Franks. **GADIRTHA** recalls the place name Gadir. This place-name occurs several times within the Land of Israel and may also be associated with GAD. Gadira was also the name of an important port in southern Spain linked with the Phoenicians, Tarshish, and the Celts of early Ireland and Britain. Much of the region east of the Jordan settled by the Tribes of Reuben, Gad, and half-Manasseh in the Bible (Deuteronomy ch.4) is termed BASHAN WHICH IN ARAMAIC BECAME BATHAN and is recalled in **BATHANAEI** and **BATHANAE REGIO** (i.e. Kingdom of Bashan) adjacent to **SACCAE REGIO**.

The Mesopotamian Sumerians called the area of Bashan "BASIL" and later the Royal Scythians were named Scythae Basilae and these gave their name to **SCANDINAVIA** which was originally called "SCATANAVIA" or Land of the Scyths. Scandinavia according to the Roman Geographer, Pliny, was also known as "BASILIA". The Prophet Micah spoke of the Lost Tribes ultimately returning to these regions: <<LET THEM FEED IN BASHAN AND GILEAD, AS IN THE DAYS OF

OLD>> [Micah 7:14]. The Kingdom of the SACCAE (Saccae Regio) besides Bathanaea has a clear Scythian connection since "SACCAE" was the contemporary Middle Eastern term for Scyth and the name is believed to be a derivative of "Isaac". The appellation "Saxe" or "Saxon" is a further development of the same name.

The First Maps relates to the places reached by the Israelites shortly after their exile. The map shows **GAUZANITIS** and the **CHABORIS RIVER** and **CHALYBONITIS**.

In this area the presence of Israelite exiles from Samaria has been testified to by the finds of inscriptions. **Gauzanitis** has been equated with the River Gozan in the verse concerning the Assyrian deportation: *"THE KING OF ASSYRIA took Samaria and carried Israel away into Assyria, and placed them in Halah, and in Habor, the* **River Gozan***, and in the cities of the Medes"* (2-Kings 17:6). The actual places of exile are discussed more fully elsewhere. The Talmud seems to identify the River of Gozan with the Ouzan to the southwest of the Caspian Sea [*"Ouzan" is pronounced locally as "GOUZAN"*]. The Ouzan River is further to the northeast and is called the "Cyrus" by Ptolemy. The region of "HABOR" (pronounceable as "Chabor"), to which Israelites were also taken, encompassed the **CHABORAS** River area as well as **Nisibis** and the adjoining expanse of **Adiabene** according to the Talmud (Kiddushin 72, Adiabene is another name for Hadayb).

The **CHALYBONITIS** was named after the Chalybes who were descendants of the CHELUBAI (1-Chronicles 2:19) from Hetzron of Judah. They were descended from the sons of Chaleb ben Jefunai and associated with the Keni and Kenizai who were metal workers. After their exile the Chalybes were associated by the Greeks with the Cimmerians and ascribed the invention of iron processing. They were then located (after exile) in the Caucasian area of Iberia (Georgia) wherefrom the Cimmerians were first to emerge. Justin reported a group of

Chalybes under the same name in the area of Galatia in Northwest Spain where too they were noted as metallurgical experts. From Spain they apparently passed over into Ireland and Celtic Britain as did the rest of the Israelite settlers in that area.

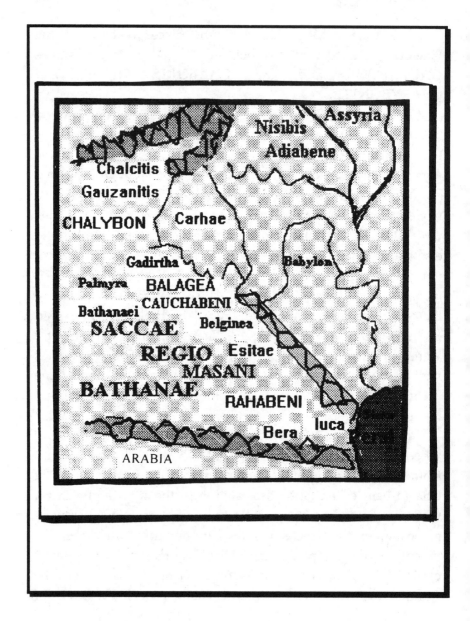

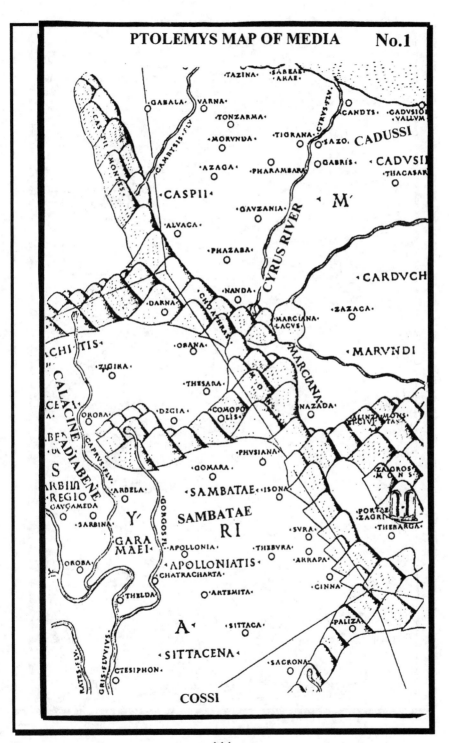

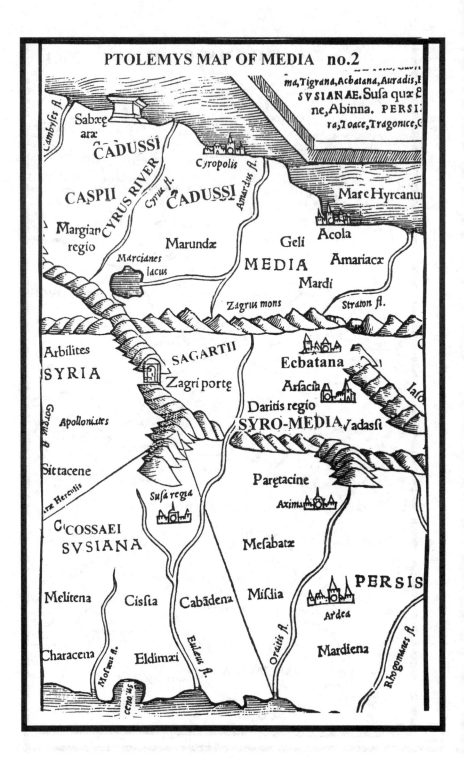

ma,Tigrana,Acbatana,Auradis,E
SVSIANAE. Sufa quæ &
ne,Abinna. PERSI:
ra,Ioace,Tragonice,C

Cambyfes fl.

Sabæe
aræ

CADUSSI

Cyropolis

CASPII

CYRUS RIVER

Cyrus fl.

CADUSSI

Amardus fl.

Mare Hyrcanu

Margian
regio

Marundæ

Geli

Acola

Marcianes
lacus

MEDIA

Amariacæ

Mardi

Zagrus mons

Straton fl.

Arbilites

SYRIA

SAGARTII

Zagri portę

Ecbatana

Arsacia

Gorgus fl.

Apolloniutrs

Daritis regio
SYRO-MEDIA Vadassi

Iafo

Sittacene

aræ Herculis

Susa regia

Parętacine

Aximu

C COSSAEI
SVSIANA

Melitena

Cissta

Cabādena

Mefabatæ

Misdia

PERSIS

Ardea

Characena

Mofæus fl.

Eldimæi

Euleus fl.

Oraitis fl.

Mardiena

Rhogomanes fl.

Explanation of the Map:

MEDIA

The Maps of Habor, Media, Parthia, and Hara all mainly depict the locations of Israelites shortly after their exile. In the Northwest of Media is "**CALACINE**". This is probably "HALAH" ("CHALACH") which along with the River Gozan and Habor was mentioned as a place of exile. **ADIABENE** (Hadayb) is identified in the Talmud with HABOR. Adiabene later became a SACAE-SCYTHIAN autonomous area within the Parthian Empire. Monbaz, the local monarch of Adiabene was descended from Sacae tribesmen who had been settled in the area by the Parthians. He may have been related to the rulers of Parthia. Monbaz converted to Judaism (Josephus, "Antiquities, Book 20, ch.2). Monbaz once helped save Jerusalem from famine, saying, "My father amassed treasures in this world, I will do so in the next". Members of his family assisted the Jews of Jerusalem against the Romans. His mother, Queen Heleni also converted and contributed artifacts of gold to the Temple. There is a street named in honor of Queen Heleni in the center of the New City of Jerusalem adjacent to the Old. To the northeast of Adiabene were the **Caspii** and Cadussi (Naphtalites from Kadesh-Naphtali in the Galilee) besides the **CYRUS** River known locally as the Ouzan or "Gouzan" as discussed above. This river was considered by the Talmud to be the River of Gozan mentioned in the Bible. The Caspii were also reported from the region of Kashmir which became a SACAE center at one stage and where too the Lost Ten Tribes were reported as having been.

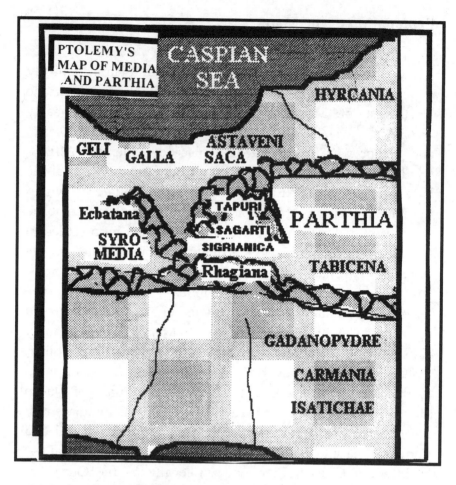

CASPIAN
SEA

HYRCANIA

GELI

GALLA

ASTAVENI
SACA

Ecbatana

TAPURI

SAGARTI

SIGRIANICA

PARTHIA

SYRO-
MEDIA

Rhagiana

TABICENA

GADANOPVDRE

CARMANIA

ISATICHAE

Explanation of the Map:

MEDIA & PARTHIA

The **CADUSSI** were a Sacae people also known as "GAELI" and as NAPHTALI and later reported east of the Ural Mountains in Scythia and in Badakhshan. East of the Cadussi was Media proper and south of Media was **Ecbatana** and Syromedia. Ptolemy stated that **SYROMEDIA** was that part of Media to which "Syrians" had been exiled. The term "Syrian" in foreign usage could encompass Israelites. In Semitic-tongues the word for "SYRIAN" is "ARAMI" and Pliny stated that the SACAE had originally been known as "ARAMI".

114

ECBATANA (Hamadan), became a Scythian capital and then later passed to Median ownership after the Scythians had been defeated and the process of expelling them from the Middle East had began. The Scythian period of Ecbatana must have begun shortly after the Assyrian exile of the Israelites. The Talmud (Kiddushin 72) states that Ecbatana (Hamadan) was one of the **"CITIES OF THE MEDES"** to which Israelites had been exiled. The Biblical expression "Cities of the Medes" probably refers to the time the Scriptural passage was written and not necessarily to the time of exile at which stage the predominant population may have been that of the transported Israelites.

According to Amos Chacham ("Safer Yishayahu") Ecbatana was more properly called "Ach-mat-ana" and rendered as "HAMATH" in Hebrew[1], being that same "HAMATH" in the list of places to which Israelites had been taken: *"From Assyria, from Egypt, and from Pathros, and from Cush, and from Elam, and from Shinar, and from HAMATH, and from the Isles of the Sea"* (Isaiah 11:11). In this list "Shinar" was not Mesopotamia (as generally supposed) but rather Pontus[2] on the southeast shores of the Black Sea which was also known as Shinar, "Cush" appears to refer to Sakastan as referred to by the Talmud though the term could also be applied to Central Asia and India in general. *"The Isles of the Sea"* listed by Isaiah in this case may have referred here both to the Aegean (Greek) Isles and to the Isles of Britain. An early sea-migration of Israelites may have reached Britain after passing through the Aegean Islands and even having sojourned therein for a period. Such an eventuality is suggested by Celtic-Irish legends. Nevertheless, overall Biblical usage appears to apply the expression "Isles of the Sea" specifically to the British ones.

The **SAMBATAE** (Map of Media no.1) gave rise to the name Sambation. The name Sambation was later transferred to the Don River in Southern Russia. Jewish tradition said that the Lost Ten Tribes were beside the Sambation River and beyond it.

When the Lost Ten (Scythian) Tribes of Israel moved, the name Sambation moved with them. From the Don (Sambation) River area came the early settlers of Scandinavia. The region of Sambatae in Media was a place of Israelite exile. The city called Gomara in the map of Ptolemy was on the site of Sakkis which was a Scythian center.

South of Syromedia (Map of Media no.2) was Persia proper and east of Persia was **CARMANIA** named after Carmi son of Reuben. Carmania is called "Germania" by Herodotus[3]. The name "GERMANI" in Talmudic usage could be applied in several ways; it was used for the sons of Gomer[4], the sons of Edom[5], and for JOSEPH of Israel[6]. The name applied to a certain physical type[7] (the so called "Nordic" one) as well as to the later inhabitants of Germany[8] in Europe. The appellation has importance in connection to the Lost Israelites as well as to several other peoples and it is these latter ones who became ancestors to some of the present day Germans.

The **ISATICHAE** in Carmania belonged to the Tribe of Issachar as did the **SAGARTII** to the west of Syromedia.

PARTHIA was destined to become a great empire (247 BCE- 224 CE) The Parthians were a combination of **APARNI** nomads and local inhabitants. Their ruling house, the Arsacids, was ascribed Israelite origins[9] and was related to the SACAE and Goths[10]. The Aparni were originally Scythians who invaded the Province of Parthia in Southeast Persia and settled there. Eventually they gained control of the Persian Empire and ruled over it by making alliances with local aristocracies and governing in a feudal fashion. In many ways their rule was quite liberal and enlightened. They fought numerous wars against the Romans and were often successful. The Parthians relied on the continuous support and manpower of the Scythians to their north. B. Philip **LOZINSKI**, ("The Original Homeland of the Parthians," 1953 Netherlands) points out that when this was no longer available (due to the Scythian peoples having moved westward) the Parthian Empire collapsed.

Many Parthians had converted to Judaism while others became Christians. Le Comte de GOBINEAU ("Histoire Des Perses", Paris 1869) considered the Pathans of Afghanistan to be offshoots of the Parthians. Steven Collins wrote extensively about the Parthians and their Israelite origins. Collins traces the Parthian Arsacid dynasty to the House of David and the Parthians in general to the Tribe of Ephraim.

Collins writes:

"EPHRAIM DOMINATED THE PARTHIAN EMPIRE, WHICH BORE THE NAMES OF THE CLANS OF EPHRAIM AMONG ITS FOUNDING GROUPS. ITS BROTHER EMPIRE, SCYTHIA, WAS DOMINATED BY THE MASSAGETAE (MANASSEH). THE EAGLE (AND THE WAR SIGN OF A CLUMP OF ARROWS) WAS ONE OF THE PRIMARY HERALDIC SYMBOLS OF THE SCYTHIANS/ MASSAGETAE."

"THE BACTRIANS, THE ERANIANS, AND DAHANITES WERE MOST LIKELY THE EPHRAIMITE CLANS OF THE BACHRITES, THE ERANITES, AND THE TAHANITES"[11]

The **ASTAVENI**, to the north of Parthia (in Hyrcania), came from Hetzron (Genesis 46:9) son of Reuben. The Tribes of Gad and Reuben appear to have been significant in Parthia which was west of **ARIA** (Hara) meaning the same Hara to which these tribes had been exiled.

"And he [i.e. the king of Assyria] carried them away, even the Reubenites, and the Gadites, and the half tribe of Manasseh, and brought them unto Halah, and Habor, and **HARA**, and to the River Gozan..." (1-Chronicles 5:26).

Hezron was also the name of one of the clans of Judah (Numbers 26:21), and a large number of Jews from Judah were later settled by the Persians in the region of **HYRCANIA**[12].

PTOLEMY'S MAP OF ARIA –
HARA of ISRAELITE EXILE (1-Chronicles 5;26).

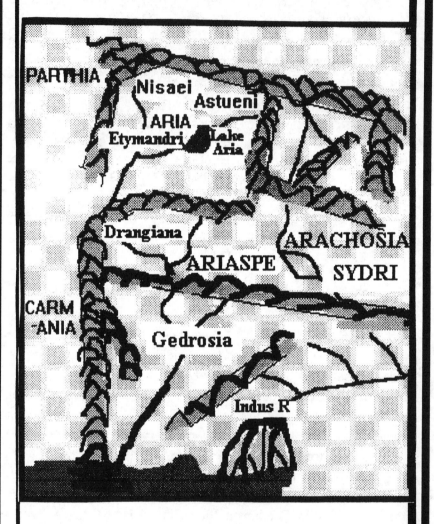

Explanation of the Map:
HARA =Aria

East of Parthia was **ARIA** known locally and to the MEDES as HARA. It is the place of exile mentioned in the Bible. Here were the **Nisaei** and the **Astueni** in the north who may also have belonged to Hezron of Reuben.

The name Nisaei is cognative with the root "NES" associated with the Scythians. The centre of the Scythians while they controlled the Assyrian Empire was Beth Shean in the Land of Israel, and Beth Shean, said PLINY, had been called "Nissa". Similarly, the Parthian-Sacae center east of the Caspian was known as Nissea and the name recurs in Sacae Israelite history.

South of ARIA was **DRANGIANA** also known as SAKASTAN and a SACAE centre whose kings claimed to have belonged to the House of David[132]. From the Sacae descend the Anglo-Saxons of England. Another name for Sakastan was Nimroz or Nimrod the legendary ruler of Assyria. The inhabitants of Sakastan according to their neighbors had been transported there by the Assyrians. They were Scythians and identified with the figure of Zohak (Isaak) and of Israel. Zohak was also in effect identified with Israel[14]. The Scythians were colonists and allies of the Assyrians and to a degree identified with the Assyrians in the eyes of their neighbors: That was why the region was nicknamed after "Nimrod", a legendary Assyrian ruler who came to represent Assyria in general in popular folklore. This has been explained by the researches of H.W. **BELLEW** ("An Inquiry into the Ethnography of Afghanistan" London, 1891). Bellew makes it quite clear that in this region and the surrounding area of Afghanistan there had existed a tradition of Israelites from the Lost Ten Tribes reaching the area. The same sources, reports Bellew and others, emphasize that the Israelites had since moved away long ago. The Sacae in effect were identified as Israelites.

GADROSIA is associated with the Tribe of Gad and to the west of Gedrosia in Carmania were the Pasargadae (according to Pliny) whose very name means "Sons of Gad". In the south of Gadrosia was **MAKRAN** possibly named after MACHIR son of Manasseh. Machir was the father of Gilead who settled on the eastern banks of the Jordan. It was the people of MACHIR who formed the half tribe of Manasseh exiled together with Reuben and Gad. One of the sons of Machir was named PERESH (Chronicles 7; 16) who may be represented by the **Parsii** to the east of Aria-Hara.

It will already have been noticed that groups identified as belonging to Reuben, Gad, and Manasseh were somehow or other centered on Aria. The same phenomenon is repeated nearly everywhere these groups were located. They had settled besides each other in the Land of Israel and they were exiled together.

Aria, Gedrosia, and Arachosia were all one geo-political entity. This is the area usually referred to as "CUSH" in the Bible as being a place of Israelite exile. "CUSH" is sometimes translated as "Ethiopia" and in Classical Literature this area was called "Ethiopia of Asia" and considered geographically a part of India. The Lost Tribes and Cush are referred to in Zephania, *"From beyond the rivers of CUSH [Ethiopia] my suppliants, the daughters of my dispersed shall bring mine offerings"*, (Zephania 3:10). The Aramaic Translation to the above verse is "Hodu" (i.e. India) for Cush indicating that the Cush of Hara-Sakastan and the neighboring area is referred to. The Talmud (Yoma 10a) has been understood as equating Sakastan with Cush. Frisian legend referred to the region of Central Asia as "India" and said that their ancestors together with the forefathers of the Saxons had dwelt there after leaving "Jerusalem" (i.e. the Land of Israel) and before moving westward.

In **ARACHOSIA** to the east of Drangiana-Sakastan were the **SYDRI** also known as the Syrakusae or "Syrians-of-Cush", and as Sygambri. The Sygambri were recalled by Justin in Bactria to the north of Aria and later settled in France as part of the Franks. Arachosia and part of Gedrosia in the Iranian areas were known as Zebulistan after the Tribe of Zebulon.

In Aria, Indian reports mentioned the presence of a monotheistic nation somehow associated with Assyria. Neighboring Aria was Drangiana-Sakastan, also called Nimroz after Nimrod the legendary Assyrian monarch, and it was believed that the inhabitants had been settled in their place by the Assyrians. The SACAE of HARA at one stage were referred to by their neighbors as "Beni-Isral" or Children of Israel and their national name of Assak, Sak, or Sok was understood to be a form of Isaac. The name "Sacae" was sometimes rendered as "Sexe" and even as "Saxon". The Saxons and the Angles were descended from these people and together with other groups that came out of Scythia, such as the Vandals and Jutes they were to become the major invaders and settlers of England in Britain.

The Sacae in Scythia were closely associated with the Guti who became known as the GOTHS in the west, and descended from the Israelite tribe of Gad.

[Jeremiah 31:8] BEHOLD, I WILL BRING THEM FROM THE NORTH COUNTRY, AND GATHER THEM FROM THE COASTS OF THE EARTH, AND WITH THEM THE BLIND AND THE LAME, THE WOMAN WITH CHILD AND HER THAT TRAVAILETH WITH CHILD TOGETHER: A GREAT COMPANY SHALL RETURN THITHER.

[Jeremiah 31:9] THEY SHALL COME WITH WEEPING, AND WITH SUPPLICATIONS WILL I LEAD THEM: I WILL CAUSE THEM TO WALK BY THE RIVERS OF WATERS IN A STRAIGHT WAY, WHEREIN THEY SHALL NOT STUMBLE: FOR I AM A FATHER TO ISRAEL, AND EPHRAIM IS MY FIRSTBORN.

Uncle Sam and John Bull

7

THE COCHIN SCROLL AND THE GOTHS

Simeon, Manasseh, And The Khazars

The Cochin Scroll is primarily a history of the Jews in Cochin, Southwest India, and only incidentally mentions the Lost Ten Tribes. The Scroll was first reported of in 1774 but is considered to have been copied from very old records. It was found written on parchment said to have been duplicated from brass plates. These plates were taken by the Dutch to Amsterdam and disappeared. According to the Cochin Scroll, some of Simeon and Manasseh settled in the Khazar kingdom to the west and east of the Caspian Sea. Others of the Ten Tribes migrated eastward: Members of the Tribes of Simeon, Ephraim, and Manasseh settled the area of Margiana (i.e. Merv, north of Hara) east of the Caspian. The Tribe of Issachar went on to the Northeast. Other Tribes, including part of Manasseh, overpassed Issachar continuing still further eastward into Tartary on the borders of China. Regarding the statement that Manasseh and Simeon settled in the Khazar region, Eldad also reported that the Khazars were descended from Simeon and other tribes according to different versions. Letters[1] ascribed to

123

King Joseph of Khazaria (ca. 960 CE) and to a subject of the Khazar Kingdom related a tradition that Simeon was the Khazars' forefather. The Khazar kingdom is usually considered as having been centered north of the Caucasus but an important component of its population derived from the region east of the Caspian, in Chorasmia. The various reports therefore agree in tracing the Tribes of Simeon and Manasseh to this area.

It should be noticed that the Israelites had been exiled in stages after being split up, but not scattered, meaning that parts of one tribe could appear together with parts of another in several areas. Likewise the nomadic lifestyle imposed upon them by geographical and political necessity meant that they were highly mobile and therefore are difficult to localize historically.

Peoples of Israelite descent, according to traditions, were to be found throughout the Scythian and Iranian areas and this corresponds with other evidence. The general tendency was for movement from the Iranian region into Scythia and then westward BUT in some cases it happened that for a period for the movement was in the opposite direction.

In those days all of Eastern Russia and parts of Northern China were populated by nomadic peoples whose dominating element, according to Chinese descriptions, were often fair skinned, fair-haired, and fair eyed though other types were also present. These peoples were identified as Scythians, and Israelite groups were part of them. The importance of the said physical description lies in the fact that it was unlike that of the Mongoloid tribes who followed after them but that it was similar to that of the European "Barbarians" whose own traditions were to claim that they came from Scythia.

Strabo (vi.7.2.) said that, <<*Most Scythians from the Caspian Sea are called Dahai, those more to the east Massagetae and Sacae, the rest have the common appellation of Scythians but each tribe has its peculiar name*>>. The Sacae referred to by Strabo mean (in this case) the Amyrgian Scyths who had been centered around Maracanda and nearby Maruka in Sogdiana. The Massagetae according to Roman reports equal the Guti or Goths[⑥]. The term "Goth" is an alternative Hebrew pronunciation of the name Gad. Manasseh and Gad had been neighbors east of the Jordan in Israel (1-Chronicles 5:26). Half-Manasseh and Gad, along with Reuben, were exiled together.

The Cochin Roll reported that parts of Ephraim, Simeon, and Manasseh, settled in MARGIANA (Merv) east of the Caspian. The name MARGIANA is cognate with that of "Maracanda" of Southern Bactria just north of Hara. In Sogdiana, to the northeast of Bactria, Ptolemy placed the Marycae and the city of Maruca, which was also derived from the same root as Maracanda. MARACANDA was to be renamed "Samarkand". Samarkand was so-called in honor of Samaria, the former Israelite capital in the territory of Manasseh. The names Maracanda, Marycae, Maruca, and Margiana were connected to that of the Sacae-Amyrgio who intermittently dominated this region. These appellations (Amyrgio, Maruca) are similar to permutations (Aimerico, Maghario, Aymeri) known in Europe for the name Machir which in Hebrew was rendered as "HaMacheri"[♥]. Similar inverted changes were used elsewhere in this same region, for instance the Sakarukae (Sagaruce) are also referred to as Saraukae. Machir (HaMachiri) in the Land of Israel had

---

[⑥]
The Romans identified the Massagetae with the Goths. "Massagetae" in the Gothic tongue of the Balkans means "Great Goths" and the Chinese applied a term (often incorrectly transliterated as "Ta Yuechi") with the same meaning to the Massagetae. This does not nullify the possibility that the name Massagetae had other origins and only later received its accepted meaning.

[♥] A Jewish Prince in south France called "Machir" and descended from King David had his name rendered (after ca. 768 CE) as Maghario, Magharius, and Aymeri, Arthur J. ZUCKERMAN, "A Jewish Princedom in Feudal France, 768-900", New York,1972, p.180, p.121. ZUCKERMAN (ibid) Aimericus = Makhir p.433. The name AMERIGO is also a derivative of MACHIR. The Continent of America was named in honour of Amerigo Vespucci, an Italian explorer. Nevertheless, the name **AMERICA** may be understood as signifying "Land of MACHIR", from the Tribe of Manasseh and historically this signification is not inappropriate.

dominated the half tribe of Manasseh on the east bank of the Jordan and his territory had included a contingent from Judah (1-Chronicles 2:21-24) descended from Yair, and neighboring the Tribes of Reuben and Gad. The Mercian Saxons and Myrings in Europe were also to be referred to as "SKATI-MARUKA"[2], meaning Scyths from Maruka (Amyrgian Scyths). They had come from around Bukhara, north of Bactria, both places being named after the BACHRI who were a clan of Ephraim (Numbers 26:35). From the Bachri came the Boruchteri who participated (along with the Frisians, Rugini, Huns, Danes, Old Saxons, according to Bede[3]) in the Anglo-Saxon invasions of Britain. Bukhara (which was also named after the Bachri) was to the north of Bactria.

In the east of Bactria were the Varni who were later termed "Varini" and were to be associated with the Angles in the North German region of Thuringia[4]. To the north on the Jaxartes River banks were the Iatii, Thacori, and Augali. After coming to Europe the name of the Thacori would be changed to Tigorini. The Iatii were referred to in the Indian Rigveda as "Yadii"[5] and probably equate the Yatya or Yeda recorded by the Chinese as part of the Naphtalites. These names ("Yatya", "Yadii", and "Yeda") are synonymous, in effect, with local appellations for Judah, meaning Jew. The Iatii in Europe were to become known as Jutes which also can be spelt similarly to North European terms for Jew. The Jutes were to settle in Denmark before participating in the invasion of England and a tradition from the Danish area related that the Jutes came from the Israelite Tribe of Judah and the Danes from Dan[6]. The Jutes, together with the Saxons and Angles, were the paramount conquerors of England. The Angles descend from the Augali who in Sogdiana neighbored the Thacori and Iatii. Herodotus (3; 92) called the Augali, "Aegli", and placed them on the outskirts of Northern Bactria. The word "AEGEL" in Hebrew means "Bull-calf". An "Aeglah" on the other hand was a heifer or female calf and the Prophet Hosea referred to the northern

126

kingdom of Israel as an "Aeglah" (Hosea 10:11). King Jeroboam had instituted the worship of bull calves at the centers of Dan and Beth-el in the Kingdom of Israel (1-Kings 12:27-30). A bull was the symbol of the Tribe of Ephraim (Numbers Rabah 2;5). Of Joseph, the father of Ephraim it had been said, *"His glory is the firstling of his bull"* (Deuteronomy 33:17). The prophet Jeremiah called the Tribe of Ephraim, "An untrained bull calf" (Jeremiah 31:18) i.e. in the original Biblical Hebrew an untrained **"AEGEL"**. The name AEGEL may have been an accepted synonym for the Tribe of Ephraim, as claimed by the foremost Jewish Biblical Commentator, Rashi[7]. In Ashkenazic Hebrew the term "aegel" could be pronounced as "angel" and in North European dialects, the name "AEGEL" was interchangeable as a diminutive form (i.e. endearing nickname) for the ethnic group "ANGLI"[8]! "Angle" and "Aegel" were alternative pronunciations or renditions of the same word in both Hebrew and European dialects! The Angles together with Jutes and Sacae descended Saxons were destined to invade and dominate England that is named after them, "Angle-land", i.e. "The Land of the Bull-Calf". They belonged to the Tribe of Ephraim who had a Bull as his symbol. From about 1712 CE the English have nicknamed themselves, "John Bull"[9] and somehow this nomination has corresponded in national consciousness with an inner self -identification.

In Scythia Ptolemy placed the ASPASSI Scythae to the north of the Iatii and Augali and the Chorasmii to their southeast. Modern scholars seem to assume that the Chorasmi and Aspassi were parts of the one people. Strabo called the Aspassi, "Atassi". He said, <<*Belonging to the tribe of the Massagetae and Sacae are also the Atassi* [i.e. Aspassi] *and Chorasmi*>> (Strabo xi.8.8.). The Massagetae (according to Ptolemy) had two sections, one in Margiana and another further east in the Sacae domain beyond the Jaxartes River. As for the Aspassi, they historically were to be connected with the Parthians who were also known as "Ashakens" and similar

127

denominations. A similarly named people were to the east of Hara, in the region of the Kophen (Kabul) where "Assakenoi" or "Assaka" were to be found. These were a part of the Sacae and were named after Isaac.

The Assakenoi were either identical with, or close neighbors of the "Aspioi" or "Aspaganoi" whose name was also to be rendered as "Isap" and "Ysuf-zi" meaning **"Tribe of Joseph"**. In other words in both Kabul (Afghanistan) and in North Scythia were neighboring peoples who bore names with the roots Ask and Asep. Scythian peoples bearing names with the root Asc, Asek , Sak, etc. are fairly common and appear to be so called since they had once belonged to the **"House of Isaac"**. Likewise, the Yasubi, Yasubgalli, Aspaganoi, Aspassi, Aspacarae, Suefs, Suobeni, all appear to have belonged to Scythian peoples, and all have names somehow connected to the same word root and probably received their appellations since they belonged to the tribe of JOSEPH.

Some scholars have claimed that some of these names derive from the Iranian "aspa" meaning horse but Irma **HAYNMAN**, *["The Syncretic Creed of Hellenized Jews From Tanais (Northern Black Sea Region)], Jerusalem 1994, proved that the use of this root-name in ethnic connotations preceded the Iranian era and was of Semitic origin and at least cognate with the Hebrew name* **JOSEPH**. *Haynman's study indicates that in the Scythian-and Parthian regions eponymous names derived from Asap were consciously equated with the Biblical Joseph!*

Traces of Israel?

By the Kophen River (Kabul) in the vicinity of the Asapaganoi (Aspioi) and Assakenoi (called "Assacanus" by Strabo 15; 27) lived the Nisaoi who it was opined had arrived with Dionysus or were descended from him[10]. Dionysus (Bacchus) was a Greek god and the Greeks were in the habit of identifying local gods or heroes with their own. The local "Indians" considered their own "Bacchus" to have come from

Assyria[11] which is consistent with his followers having been Hebrew exiles whom the Assyrians re-settled. The Greeks (in their own way) may also have identified the Greek god "Bacchus" with some famous Israelite leader of migrating Hebrews. According to Greek tradition "Bacchus" was born in the Land of Israel[12] and his nurse, says Pliny (N.H. 5;16), was buried at Nysa (Beth Shean). The only nurse buried in Biblical Writ was the nurse of Rebeccah, "Deborah", who was buried at Beth-el under an oak, called in Hebrew "Allon Bachuth", meaning "Oak of Weeping". "Bachuth" (weeping) could be pronounced "Bachus". One version of Greek Mythology ascribed the characteristics and deeds of Moses (the Israelite leader) to Bacchus. The connection with Nysa (Beth Shean) may have some significance since when the Israelite-Scythians gained temporary control over the Assyrian Empire they used Beth Shean as one of their administrative centers and attempted to re-settle there.

Sicambri And Teutons In Scythia

"Nisaoi" and similar names are often noticed in Scythian areas[14]. The capital of the Parthians in Scythia east of the Caspian was called "Nisaya"[15]. "Nes" in Hebrew means "miracle", "sign", or "emblem", and is also found in association with the name of an altar (Exodus 17:15) or its location, and with other place names. Beth-Shean in the land of Israel had once been a center for the Scythians when, in conjunction with the Kingdom of Judah, they ruled the former Assyrian Empire. Beth-Shean had been given the name "Nissa" (Pliny N.H. 5;16). Beth-Shean was in the territory of Manasseh, one of whose clans was named Shechem (Numbers 26:30) or "SECEM". The Nisaoi people in the region of Gandhara were also known as Syrakusai[16] (i.e. "Syrians of Kush") and as "SUGAMBRI"[17]. The Sugambri also were to appear in the region of Bactria as "Sigambri" where together with the Ambri[18] they met Alexander the Great of Macedon. These Sigambri probably belong to the same group as the "Secem"- Manasseh associated "Scymbi" mentioned by Ptolemy in North Scythia besides the Alanorsi. Later, in Europe, the Sigambri were known variously as "Sigambri", "Sugambri" and "Sicambri". The Sigambri (Sicambrians) were to be associated with both the Franks and Saxons. Their name is often rendered as "Sicambri" and they belonged to the clan of SECEM as did the Scymnitae **north of the Caspian Sea** (and west of the Samnitae) in Asiatic Sarmatia that was part of Scythia. "Scymnitae" means "People of Secem", i.e. of Shechem of Manasseh (Numbers 26:31). In Scythia the ASPASSI were reported by Ptolemy somewhere between the Scymbi and the Augalli (Angles) and Iatii (Jutes) and these Aspassi parallel the Aspioi to the east who neighbored the Sigambri in Gandhara. The root **"ASP"** is derived from the Hebrew "aseph" and connected to the name of Joseph who was the father of Manasseh. The Scymbi in Scythia were neighbors to the TECTOSACES who were also reported of in Gaul. Their name, "Tecto-Sace" is a combination of the Hebrew "Tahat" (pronounceable as "Tachat", i.e. "Tect") or "Tahan" (Teuton) and "Sacae". Tahan was a clan of Ephraim (Numbers 26:35) of which "Tahat" was either part (1-Chronicles 7:20) or an alternate rendition of the same appellation.

In addition, in both the Aspassi-and-Augalli region and by Gandhara were the THATAGYDES (Sattaguda) believed to be a combination of Thata and Goths[19]. Thats and Goths were also reported together on the Black Sea Shore[20]. The Thata have been identified[21] as Teutons who later received fame in Europe and were centered in northern Danish Jutland in the province of Thuith[22] (of Thy) though Ptolemy located some of them between the Saxons and Angles which groups presumably swept them up in the invasion of England. In England they were called TUIHANTI[23] and were part of the Frisians and participators in the Anglo-Saxon forces. Strabo records "SUGAMBRI" and Teutons together on the European North Sea coast. The Teutons in Europe received renown for (together with Cimbri and Ambrones) attacking Rome. Teutons and Ambrones were neighbors and allies from the North. The Ambrones derived from the Ambri who, together with the Sicambri had been reported previously in Bactria. The Sicambri were to settle in Holland, Belgium and France and belonged to the Secem clan of Manasseh. The Teutons came from Tahat (1-Chronicles 7:20) or from Tahan (Numbers 26:35) who were probably one and the same. At all events they both belonged to Ephraim who was brother to Manasseh.

Zabulistan Of Zebulon

Parts of the peoples described had been located in Gandhara (east of Hara) which, with the region surrounding it to the west and south, was known as **Zabulistan** after Zebulon, son of Israel. This region (Zabulistan) is sometimes referred to as "Indo-Scythia" by Classical writers. In addition, some Classical authors called the area south of Gandhara, "Ethiopia of Asia". The Assyrians used the term "Meluhhe"[24] for this province, which name was also applied on other occasions to Ethiopia in Africa. Josephus (Antiquities I) describes India as beginning from the Indus and its tributaries or their general region. Thus "Kush of India" or Cush India suits Zabulistan. This definition conforms to other Classical geographers.

Likewise in the Bible the expression "Cush" (translated as "Ethiopia") could be applied to both Ethiopia in Africa and to "Indo-Scythia", meaning Zabulistan. Even today the name Hindu Kush (i.e. "Cush of India") is applied to the nearby mountainous area in North Afghanistan. Twice in the Bible, "CUSH" is recalled as one of the places where members of the Ten Lost Tribes were taken to, or were to be located: One is in Isaiah 11:11 where Cush is found together with a list of other places of exile. The other is in Zephaniah (3:10) where it says, "The daughters of my dispersed shall bring mine offering, **FROM BEYOND THE RIVERS OF CUSH**". In both these two cases the Aramaic translation of Yehonatan renders CUSH as "HODU". "HODU" in Hebrew means India and this therefore

131

shows that the Aramaic Paraphraser (recommended by the Talmud) believed that "CUSH" referred to the Ethiopia of Asia[24] otherwise once known as Zabulistan. This area ("Zabulistan") was considered by Classical geographers to be part of India. At all events, the name "CUSH" had several applications one of which was to the region of Hara and neighboring areas.

Legends Concerning Hebrew Tribes
Confirmed By Tribal And Clan Names

"CUSH" as a term was applicable to the region of Cossai in Elam and also to the whole region east of Carmania including Hara. The area traversed by the Indus River with its tributaries and confluents seems to have had strongest claim to the appellation as confirmed by the expression, "Rivers of Cush" and by Yehonatan's translation of CUSH as "Hodu". Even so, it should be reiterated that, "Beyond the Rivers of CUSH", could also refer to Hara and Sakastan and all the region east of Carmania[25] including the Hindu Kush area which is beyond the Indus just east of Hara and the Hari Rud ("River of Hara")[26] south of Bactria. The Talmud has been understood to explicitly identify "Cush" with Sakastan which adjoined (or was part of) Hara southeast of the Caspian Sea. At all events, one tradition[27] from this area said that Naphtali and Zebulon lived in the Hindu Kush. Another tradition[28] placed Naphtali and Zebulon together with Dan and Asher in nearby Badakhshan. To the direct north of Badakhshan the Jews[29] of the Aral Mountains claimed descent from Naphtali but in this case, like similar ones in the region, they probably appropriated to themselves an already existing tradition of Naphtali having been in this area. Likewise, one part of Manasseh was reported in the Cochin Scroll as being on the borders of China and Tartary. Most of these traditions and others like them correspond to the tribal situation from the Scythian period. "Cush" is considered to be synonymous to "Hodu" or "India" and Frisian legends related that their ancestors along with those of the Saxons and Angles had come from "Jerusalem" and had sojourned in "India" which from the context meant somewhere in Scythia well to the east of the Caspian Sea. From "India" they migrated westward. These legends accord with archaeological findings.

The general area connected with the Tribes of Dan, Asher, and Naphtali is that of the Aral Mountains and Badakhshan which was called the "Crystal Mountain" or "Mountain of Lapis Lazuli" (Mount Bikni) whereto the Assyrians sent expeditions of conquest and subjugation. It was to be associated with the Naphtalites[30] (also called "Little Goths", and "Thyssagetae") who came from the Tribe of Naphtali but included contingents from Dan and Judah. This area was also ascribed to the Asii[31] (plural: Aseir) whose name is similar to "As" which is how the Phoenicians[32] wrote and probably pronounced Asher. The North Israel dialect of Samaria is said to have been closer to Phoenician than to Judaic-Hebrew[33]. The As (Aseir)[34] became the Scandinavian ruling class who, prior to moving northward, were to migrate west, to the Don River banks, and to beside the Caucasus yet retaining possessions and relations in the east[35]. The Asii historically are connected with the Alans northeast of the Caspian Sea. Alans, Aorsi, Aseir, and "Wu-Sun" (in Chinese records) are all considered to be the same or closely related peoples. The Alans had scattered groups from China to the European Carpathians[36]. The Alans came from Elon son of Zebulon. They were to settle in Western Europe.

The Massagetae bordered this region and they, in part, came from Manasseh. Further to the east were the ASPACARAE whose name bears the root "ASP" associated elsewhere with JOSEPH. Further considerations link the ASPACARAE with Manasseh, son of Joseph. The place of the ASPACARAE was in SERICA, i.e. Tartary, which later would have been considered as bordering China, thus confirming the Cochin Scroll which placed part of Manasseh in this region.

133

According to the Chinese, the eastern half of the Sienbi dominated the whole area of Serica. The Sienbi of Chinese chronicles became the Suebi of West European history. They also come from Joseph. They were later to be found as "Swaefs" amongst the Anglo-Saxon forces. These peoples in Scythia who are identified with Israelite Tribes were to reappear in Europe as identifiable entities under the same or similar names.

The Iyrcae And A Clarification Of The Cochin Scroll

Israelite Tribes in the Scythian region were seen to include the Naphtali who contained contingents of Dan and Judah and were linked with the Goths and Iyrcae. The "Iyrcae" in Scandinavian tradition were to be amongst the settlers of Scandinavia. The Goths belonged to the Tribe of Gad and were destined to populate Sweden.

The record of the Cochin Jews in India said that the Lost Ten Tribes had reached the region east of the Caspian. The region around Margiana had been settled by the Tribes of Simeon, Manasseh, and Ephraim, with some of Simeon and Manasseh settling in the Khazar kingdom besides the Caspian.

Historically, the Tribe of Ephraim near Margiana was represented in the Bactri (of Bactria), in the Chorasmi, Augali (Aegli), and Aspassi. Simeon north of the Caspian (a future Khazar area) was to be found in the Samnitae (reported by Ptolemy) and neighboring Zaratae, who belonged to the Zarhites of Simeon (Numbers 26:13). South of the Samnitae (north of the Caspian) were the Machetegi who came from "Maacha" (2-Kings 15:29) an important center in the Land of Manasseh in Israel and the name of the wife of Machir from Manasseh (1-Chronicles 7:16). Manasseh was also to be found in the nearby Suobeni and Scymbi. The Scymbi came from Shechem, a clan name amongst Manasseh (Numbers 26:31) [*The "sh" was freely replaced by "s", and a "b" was often inserted after "m" for euphonic reasons*]. Manasseh was also found in Margiana together with the Tribe of Gad in the Massagetae. Part of Manasseh and Issachar had continued on into Tartary that was called SERICA by Ptolemy. Since Issachar elsewhere is identified as the Sagaruce east of the Caspian and the Sagaruce were also called Saraukae, it may be that the very name of Serica (Tartary) derives from Issachar due to an inversion of syllable order which is not an uncommon phenomenon in the Scythian sphere. A major clan of Issachar was the Shimroni (Numbers 26:24) and in Serica Ptolemy mentions the Asmiraea Kingdom. "Asmirae" and "Shimroni" in Semitic dialects are synonymous. Close to the Asmiraea Kingdom were the Aspacarae whose name contains the root "Asp" which was associable with Joseph and these equal that portion of Manasseh (son of Joseph) said to have accompanied Issachar to Serica-Tartary. South of the Aspacarae in Serica, according to Ptolemy, were the "ITHAGURI" and this name may also be considered a form of ISSACHAR. Most of these peoples were to participate in the invasions of Western Europe and they are identifiable as known tribes amongst the "Barbarian" nations. The Iatii became the Jutes, the Augali the (Aegloi) Angles, the Sigambri -the Sicambri, the That -the Teutons, the Ambri became Ambrones, the Saxe (Sacae) became the Sexe or Saxons, and the Asii in Scandinavia were known as As or Aseir.

The Israelite origin of the above nations of Scythia together with evidence of their migration to Western Europe is confirmed by similarity of names and legends as well as by the Hebrew connection of related groups, such as the Parthians and Khazars, by archaeological findings, historical records, and Scriptural passages.

The Movement West

So far, Israelite tribes in Scythia and especially East Scythia have been equated with the Massagetae (Ta Yuehchi) Goths, Assi, Sakae, and their adjoining kin. Climatic changes and Hun attacks were to force all these peoples westward.

The Huns (Hsiung-nu) in about 160 BCE began their attacks against the Wu-Sun (Asii), and Yeuh-chi (Goths), which attacks had caused the displacement of the Sacae and other groups. During this period there occurred extreme climatic change. Consequently, the fertile, heavily populated, irrigated areas of Chorasmia and the region east of it had been abandoned along with numerous other centers in the Siberia (Eastern Scythia) area, from about 120 BCE.

At this very same time Scandinavia received an influx of population. The newcomers to Scandinavia had the same art styles as those previously extant in Chorasmia and its neighborhood. The repopulating of Scandinavia was to continue in full force for at least two hundred years. The movement parallels continued dislocation of nations due to warfare in East Scythia.

Scandinavian tradition traces their ancestors (according to the older accounts) to the Don River region but says that their leaders, Odin and Thor, had possessions and kinfolk further east and frequently were away on journeys in that area. In addition, they said that their ancestors, the Aseir, had been in Ydi (Ida, Yadi), east of the Caspian, before coming to the Don. Yadi was the name of both a region and a people who dwelt east of the Caspian and who were part of the Naphtalites. The Naphtalites were eventually to settle in Norway. Other traditions identify the ancestors of the Scandinavians with the "Turcae" which is the name Roman historians gave to the Iyrcae of Herodotus (who neighbored the Thessagetae), and in Chinese records (as Gaogu and Uigur) were associated with the Hugie and Dingling. These peoples (Iyrcae, Thessagetae, Gaogu, Dingling, and Hugie) were all located north of the Caspian and to the east of it. In addition, the Scandinavians attributed the main branch of their ancestral gods to the race of As, or Aseir. The As were an actual people recorded in historical documents and related to the Aorsi who were situated by the Don but had other branches further east. Strabo positioned one of these eastern branches, the Asii, in the same area allocated by Chinese sources to the WuSun thus equating the two. Also the task played by the Tokharians, Asianoi (Asii) and Sakaraucae in Roman accounts is the same as that played by the Yeuh-Chi (Gu-ti) and WuSun in Chinese ones. The area of the Asii (Wusun) in the east was also that of the land of Yadi. This was the homeland of the Aseir before their first movement westward to the Don River and thence to Scandinavia.

>><<In Asia to the east of the TANAIS (Don River) there was a land called Asaland or Asaheim (land of the Æsir); its chief city was called Asgard (Home of the Æsir). The city was ruled by a chieftain called Odin...>>

<<Asgard, in Norse mythology, is the homeland of the _Aesir,_ the race of warrior gods. It is surrounded by a high wall of closely fitted stone blocks. In the middle of Asgard lies the plain of Idavoll (or Ida) where the Aesir meet to decide important issues.>>

"Ida" is Yda or Yeda an area associated with the Naphtalites and with the ancestors of the Danes.

Scattered Positioning of the Tribes in Scythia

Another factor that deserves consideration is the scattered positioning of peoples in this area with different sections of the same nations being found in widely separated locations. The dislocation of the Gu-ti (Goths), Sacae, and Asii and Hugie (Franks) and all the others including the Sienbi was accompanied in the west by the sudden appearance of peoples like the Goths, Saxons (Sakae), Hugo-Franks, and Suebi (Sienbi, Suobeni, Syebi) in the west. The evacuation of Scythia was in stages. It was not always entirely completely in the one direction though the overwhelming tendency was westward.

The Gothic Invasions: The Goths had had a group on the Baltic shores from early times and possibly had had some long continued association with Scandinavia. With the intensified settlement of Scandinavia, came Yuehchi-Goths (also known as Massagetae) from the east. Sweden especially received a dominant Goth and Goth-related (Suion) ethnic character. The incursions into Scandinavia were too great to enable stabilized settlement and there was an almost immediate continuation westward. One section of the Goths, instead of heading west, from about 50 BCE started south and linked up with related peoples in Scythia west of the Ural Mountains and north of the Black Sea. Some of the peoples they joined with were also Gothic and together they formed an Empire stretching to Denmark and perhaps beyond. They had formed two divisions, Visigoths to the west and Ostrogoths in the east. The Ostrogoths were the dominant body. The Ostrogoths were to be attacked by the Huns and (in 374 CE) to be partially subdued by them, while the Visigoths fled towards the Roman Province of Dacia which at this stage was virtually uninhabited. The Romans granted the Visigoths refuge but abused and mistreated their wives and children. The Visigoths rebelled and thus began a series of events that led to the downfall of the Roman Empire.

Consequences of Hun Aggressions: The Great Migrations of peoples from the east to Western Europe had been caused by climatic changes and by the Huns. The Huns would attack peoples in east Scythia some of whom went west at an early stage towards Europe, others stayed within Scythia only to continue westward later fleeing from Hun aggression or serving as enforced partners in the Hunnish enterprise. Some of the movements were the result of chain reactions; people who had been displaced by the Huns would in turn displace others. As a result of the Hun initiatives the following changes were to take place: The Hugo Franks, who had mainly been part of the Hugie group in Scythia, were to conquer Gaul and settle in Holland, Belgium, and France. The Suebi (as Allemani and others) descendants of the Sienbi (called Suobeni and Syebi by Ptolemy) were to settle in Alsace, Switzerland, and Suabia, and to some extent also in Holland. [The term Suebi however later came to be applied to several different and probably unrelated groups.] The Vandals who accompanied the Goths and were associated with them were to make temporary conquests in

Gaul, Spain, and North Africa though the majority of them seem to have accompanied the Anglian forces in the domination of North England and Southern Scotland. The Sigambri from the environs of Bactria were to join the Franks in Europe. The Angles (Aegloi) from Bactria together with the Saxe-Saxons (Sakae) and Jutes (Iatii) from Scythia were to be the dominant elements in the conquest of England. The Goths warred against Rome and established kingdoms in Italy, France, and Spain. In Southern France, especially, their presence was significant, though ultimately only in Sweden did they remain as an historically recognizable entity. The Alans, from north of the Caspian Sea and Caucasus, were to form settlements in Brittany (France) and Switzerland. Other groups (such as the Lombards) who also probably emerged from Scythia and seem to have been Hebraic were (via Scandinavia) to make incursions of their own. The Lombards, for instance, settled in North Italy. In short, the Israelites became Scythian and the Scythians were to become European. The descendants of the Northern Hebrews today must be sought for in Europe more than anywhere else.

[Isaiah 49:6] AND HE SAID, IT IS A LIGHT THING THAT THOU SHOULDEST BE MY SERVANT TO RAISE UP THE TRIBES OF JACOB, AND TO RESTORE THE PRESERVED OF ISRAEL: I WILL ALSO GIVE THEE FOR A LIGHT TO THE GENTILES, THAT THOU MAYEST BE MY SALVATION UNTO THE END OF THE EARTH.

[Isaiah 49:8] THUS SAITH THE LORD, IN AN ACCEPTABLE TIME HAVE I HEARD THEE, AND IN A DAY OF SALVATION HAVE I HELPED THEE: AND I WILL PRESERVE THEE, AND GIVE THEE FOR A COVENANT OF THE PEOPLE [Hebrew: "Brit-Am"], TO ESTABLISH THE EARTH, TO CAUSE TO INHERIT THE DESOLATE HERITAGES;

FAMILY TREE OF REUBEN

REUBEN

Hanoch Phallu Hezroni Carmi
(Pallui)

Eliab

Nemuel Datan Abiram

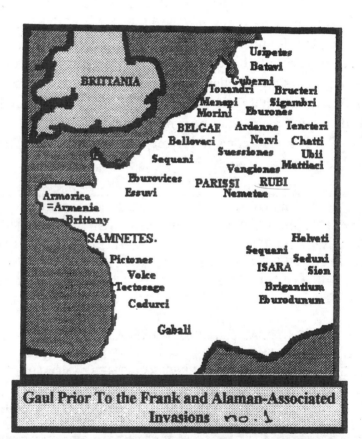

Gaul Prior To the Frank and Alaman-Associated Invasions no. 1

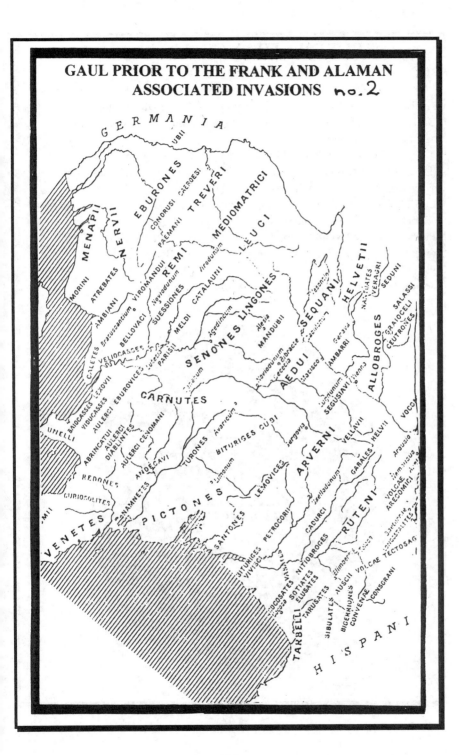

GAUL PRIOR TO THE FRANK AND ALAMAN ASSOCIATED INVASIONS no. 2

GERMANIA

UBII

EBURONES

TREVERI

CONDRUSI CAEROESI

PAEMANI

MEDIOMATRICI

LEUCI

MENAPII

NERVII

REMI

MORINI

ATREBATES

Virodunum

HELVETII

SEQUANI

NANTUATES

VERAGRI

SEDUNI

SALASSI

GRAIOCELI

CEUTRONES

AMBIANI

VIROMANDUI

SUESSIONES

Novyodunum

LINGONES

Alesia

MANDUBII

ALLOBROGES

BELLOVACI

SENONES

VELIOCASSES

Bracusantium

CALETES

MELDI

CATALAUNI

PARISII

Igedincum

Noviodunum

Cabracte

Gergovia

AMBARRI

VOCCI

AULERCI EBUROVICES

LEXOVII

Lutecia

Cenabum

AEDUI

Matisco

BAIOCASSES

VIDUCASSES

CARNUTES

SEGUSIAVI

VELLAVII

UNELLI

ABRINCATUI

AULERCI

DIABLINTES

AULERCI CENOMANI

TURONES

Avaricum

BITURIGES CUBI

ARVERNI

GABALES

HELVII

Arausia

Nemausus

VOLCAE

ARECOMICI

ANDECAVI

REDONES

NAMNETES

LEMOVICES

Uxellodunum

CURIOSOLITES

PICTONES

BITURIGES

PETROCORII

CACURCI

RUTENI

VOLCAE TECTOSAG

VENETES

SANTONES

VIVISCI

NITIOBROGES

SOTIATES

AUSCII

CONVENAE

CONSORANI

TARBELLI

TARUSATES

ELUSATES

SIBULATES

BIGERRIONES

HISPANI

REUBEN = FRANCE

The official emblem of France is its tri-color flag. Previously the symbol used was the fleur-de-lis, which had been a royal emblem since the Dark Ages. The above emblem was adopted in the Third Republic as a "quasi-official" one.

The motto means, "Liberty, Equality, Fraternity", and these qualities (for both good and bad) were exemplified in the figure of Reuben whose Tribe dominates the Israelite element in France.

LIBERTY: Reuben acted with lack of propriety towards his fathers concubine (Gen.37:22) which was taking "liberty" too far, at the expense of others. Reuben intended to set Joseph free and in effect saved his life (Gen.37:22) which is an application of the principles of both LIBERTY and FRATERNITY. At the same time Reuben was the first-born and should have acted with more authority; i. e. EQUALITY was misapplied.

8

REUBEN AND
THE "RIBUARI"- FRANKS

"AND THESE ARE THE NAMES OF THE CHILDREN OF
ISRAEL WHICH CAME INTO EGYPT, JACOB AND HIS
SONS: REUBEN, JACOB'S FIRSTBORN.

"AND THE SONS OF REUBEN: HANOCH, AND PHALU, AND
HEZRON, AND CARMI"

(GENESIS 46:-9).

The Origin of the Barbarian Franks

The exiled Israelites became Scythians or at least part of
the Scythians were Israelites. The Scythians invaded Western
Europe and were called "Barbarians". The origin of the name
"Babarian" is uncertain. It may be derived from the Semitic
"Babiru" which in Ancient Times was interchangeable with
"Habiru" meaning Hebrew[1]. The Barbarians of history emerged
from Germany and Scythia. They included Israelite, Edomites,
and others. One of the major Barbarian confederacies was that
of the Franks. The Franks were a federation of several smaller

combinations of tribes classified as Frankish and sharing some type of commonality. They seem to have been first reported about 256 CE when a group of them invaded Gaul, then passed into Spain and from there went to North Africa. Other Frankish-groups soon emerged from the northern Rhine region and began to expand in influence until they succeeded in subjugating the whole of Gaul that was then later called "France" (i.e. Land of the Franks) in their honor. A song[2] in Gaul dated from about 350 CE equated the Franks with the Persians and Sarmatians. Persians and Sarmatians had indeed neighbored the Scythians in Scythia. Other traditions (such as that of Nicholas Vignier ca. 1630)[3] said that the Franks were originally Scyths or Sarmatians. The Franks appear to have gone at first to the mouth of the Rhine and from there southwards. Old accounts[4] say that the Franks had come from the former Saxon area of Maurunganie in North Germany below the place of the Normans. The *Geography of Ravenna* (700's CE) states that the Franks had been in southern Denmark. Another source describes the Franks as, *"A people whose name of old was the Deni* [i.e. Danes]. *The Frankish people is sprung from them, so the legend relates"* (Ermoldus Nigellus 826 CE)[5]. This suggests that a part of the early Frankish leadership may once have been in Scandinavia.

Other very strong and consistent traditions[6] connected the Franks (who were also called Frakkar and "Frygges") with Phrygia, with Troy (near Phrygia in Anatolia, Turkey), and with Pannonia. Pannonia, in Roman times, referred to the area of Hungary but later usage[7] applied the term to an extended area including the north and west. Whatever areas of temporary sojourn the Frankish peoples may have been in **their primary source of origin is to be sought in Scythia east of the Caspian**. The Franks are traceable to the **Hugie**, the Tectosaces and related peoples of the Scythian steppes. The Franks were destined to move westward and conquer Celtic peoples including Galatians and settle in France. The Celts were then concentrated in Gaul (France) and Britain but had once been spread throughout much of Europe. Even before conquering Gaul the Franks had a proven ability to absorb other peoples, especially those of Celtic connection. It is possible that in the course of their movements the Franks gathered in pockets of Cimmerians and Galatians that formerly had been scattered in the Southeast European area. The Franks eventually conquered Gaul the northern part of which was populated by the Galatians. Some French writers said that the Franks were themselves mainly of Galatian origin. The Galatians or Galati were also known as Galadi and in French this is a form of the Hebrew name "**Gilead**". The Tribe of Reuben had originally settled east of the Jordan in the land of Gilead (Joshua 22:9).

The Franks in northern Europe had first been known as "**Huga**"[8] and this name is one of the indications linking them with the Hugie of Scythia. Amongst the Hugie of Scythia Tribal names (such as "Gali") associated with the Galatians existed. A Galatian connection could explain the Troy and Phrygian legendary associations of the Franks. A small but famous group of Galatians had returned from Western Europe to the east, attacked Greece, crossed over from Europe into Asia Minor and then settled in Phrygia (near Troy) in Anatolia. Some Galatians had also (at another stage) gone further eastward into Scythia and these too may have linked up with the Hugie. The Galatians were descended from the ancient Cimmerians[9] a portion of whom had previously (before moving into Europe) also sojourned for about 160 years in Phrygia. The Franks were to eventually settle in Holland, Belgium, and North France. They are mainly descended from the Tribe of Reuben though included contingents of other Israelites.

Reuben in the Middle East before the Exile and in Scythia After it

Before the exile, the Tribes of Reuben, Gad, and half-Manasseh had together been settled in **GILEAD** and Bashan on the eastern banks of the Jordan in the Land of Israel. Later part of the Tribe of Simeon also settled there (1-Chronicles 4:42) alongside offshoots from other Israelite Tribes. This pattern of settlement was to be paralleled later by descendants of these same tribes in Scythia.

There were some Galatian groups (such as the Tectosaces and Gala) in the Hugie federation of Scythia. Most of the Galatians however had reached Gaul, Britain, and the west much earlier and remained there. In Scythia the Hugie (of Reuben) were adjacent to the Goths of Gad and to the Amyrgian-Sakae descendants of Machir who had been the leading element in half-Manasseh, east of the Jordan, in Israel. "GILEAD" was a name given to a good portion of the Land of Israel east of Jordan including that in which the Tribe of Reuben dwelt. Gilead was also the name of a son of Machir son of Manasseh. The Galaadi or Galatians received their name either from the Israelite region of Gilead or from the Israelite clan of Gilead son of Manasseh who dwelt in part of Gilead. This is worth emphasizing since it can cause confusion: "Gilead" was an important clan in the Tribe of Manasseh east of the Jordan but the name "Gilead" could also be applied to the whole Israelite area east of the Jordan in which settled Reuben, Gad, and the half-tribe of Manasseh.

The clan of **Gilead** comprised most of the Manasseh group that had been east of the Jordan in the Land of Israel and had neighbored Reuben who in turn had adjoined Simeon in the south. In Scythia the Samnitae of Simeon also neighbored the Hugie area. The name Hugie is derivable from that of Hagi, son of Gad, though most of the Hugie-Franks appear to have come from Reuben. The first son of Reuben was Hanoch (i.e. "Chanoch": חנוך, Genesis 48:9) and since "n" in both Hebrew and the Steppe dialects of Scythia appears to have been occasionally inserted and/or omitted for euphonic reasons in nomenclature maybe Hanoch and Hagi, though originally independent

146

entities, became confused with each other due to familial connexion, geographical proximity and historical community.

A Scythian people, the **Heniochi** (cf. **Hanochi of Reuben**), had been reported of in the Caucasus region. To the east of Scythia (in "Serica") the **RHABBANAEI**[10] of Reuben had bordered the Garinaei who are identifiable with Eri or "Geri" (עֵרִי) of Gad, the Damnae whose name elsewhere was pronounced like that of Dan, and the Aspacarae whose name is a form (as explained later) of Joseph.

In the Land of Ancient ISRAEL, the tribe of REUBEN is called "**Rahabbanai**" on Ptolemy's map of "Arabia". In very Ancient Times (long before the Northern Israelites being exiled) the Mari correspondence of Northern Syria on the Euphrates mentions the Rabeans (of Reuben) alongside a group from Benjamin (Banu/Maru Yaminas) and Gad (Bene Šimal and Zapunni). Manasseh was also recalled from this region and is referred to as "Manas" and as "Mentiu". Reuben in the Land of Israel east of the Jordan had adjoined half-Manasseh of Joseph and Gad. This is the same pattern as we later find in Serica east of Scythia. From Serica they moved westward as part of the Franks.

Reuben In Europe

In West Europe the Franks were divided into several groups of whom the main ones are assumed to have been the Ripuarian Franks, the Salian Franks, and the Chatti or Hessians[11]. The Ripuarian (i.e. "River-Bank") Franks were allegedly so called by the Romans since they were first known to them on the banks of the Rhine and in Latin "ripa" means river bank. The name is **also** given as "**Ribuari**" and this name

147

in Hebrew is **another form for REUBEN***. The ancient Greeks and Romans (as well as the Hebrews), when they came across a foreign name, were wont to interpret its meaning according to a similar sounding word in their own language. This was especially so. when the word in question was descriptively pertinent, as it was in the case of the "River-bank" (i.e. "Ripuari") Franks on the Rhine. "**Ribuari**" appears to have been the Franks own name for themselves. Reuben in Hebrew could also be rendered **REUBAR**! "**Ribuari**" means sons of Reuben which was the name of their ancestor. A shortened form of Reuben is "**Rubi**" and a people by that name were situated at one stage on the banks of the Rhine. They appear to have been Ribuari Franks.

In 276 CE[12] the Franks were reported as encroaching on the borders of Roman Gaul together with the Alamans. They were pushed back to their bases on the Rhine after which they began a process of peaceful infiltration receiving lands from the Romans in return for military services. Apart from the RIBUARI, the Franks included the Salian Franks and the Hessians. In the region of Holland, Salian Franks intermixed with Sigambri[13]. The Sigambri and Ambri had encountered Alexander the Great east of the Caspian[14] in Scythia and had also been reported from besides Nysia on the Indus[15]. The name *Sigambri* was another form used in Europe for *Sicambrian*

---

* See the Aramaic Translation of Onkelos to Genesis 29:32. In the Hebrew name "**Reuben**" (‏רְאוּבֵן:‎ pronounced something like "Ra-oo-ben"), "RA-OO" means "See" and "BEN" means "son", thus "Reu-ben" meant "See-a-son". "BAR" is Aramaic for "son" or rather a Hebrew synonym for "son" which is more common in Aramaic. Aramaic and Hebrew shared a common stock of word roots to some extent. "BAR" is (maybe) used for SON instead of the usual "ben" in the Hebrew Bible in Proverbs 31:2. See the Concordance of Iben-Shushan. At all events "bar" in Hebrew would be an accepted form for "son" (alongside the usual" Ben" meaning "son") similar to the Scottish "bairn." Also there is evidence that the Hebrew of part of the northern Israelites was influenced by Aramaic and this point holds true especially for the Tribes east of the Jordan, see "Ephraim" pp.238-239. Thus **REU-BAR** is another form for **REU-BEN**. In Semitic dialects "R" and "N" are often interchangeable so that the "N" in "BN" (BeN) becomes "R" in BR (BaR) both meaning "son".

and were represented (by Ptolemy) as the Scymbi-Scyths in the Hugie area of Scythia. They are associated with Secem, a clan of Manasseh. Part of the Sigambri in Scythia neighbored the Salei, who according to Pliny had been east of the Caspian on the Jaxartes River banks[16]. The Salei in Europe became the Salian Franks and these intermixed with the Sicambri and became identified with them. In Scythia they had also been associated with each other. The Salians[17] after merging with the Sicambri in Europe were also known as Sicambri. These, due to Hun pressure in the early 400s CE, overran Belgium and Northern France. At about the same time more Ripuarian Franks and Alamans entered Gaul from east of the Rhine where they had been centered in Westphalia. The Franks had sojourned in East- and in West- Phalia. The name "PHALIA"[18] wherein the Franks had been sojourning is derived from that of the **PHALUI**, descendants of the second son of Reuben (Genesis 26:9 Numbers 26:5). The Phalui or Falhi[19] (Franks) in Eastphalhia were known also as Cheruski and were partly absorbed by the Saxons. There were Saxon contingents who later settled in Gaul alongside the Franks. The Phalian Franks descended from Phalui while the "Hugo" Franks (Chauci) came from both Gad (Hagi) and Hanoch of Reuben. Hanoch was recalled earlier in the Heniochoi who had been in the Scythian area of the Caucasus on the eastern coast of the Black Sea (Pliny, N.H. 6;26). The Franks were also present in Germany and a region in West Germania is called "Franken" i.e. Franconia. Nevertheless, the general opinion concerning this part of Germany is that "The old population of former Hermunduri/Thuringians remained largely unchanged, while (a) Frankish elite was installed in the 6th/7th centuries" (Dirk).

The third son of Reuben, **Hetsroni**[*] (Chetsroni), is recalled in the Istaevones who were a division of the Germanic peoples enumerated by Tacitus and Pliny. They were said to comprise several tribes (Tacitus: "Germania" 2) but the only one

---

[*] Transliterated as "Hezron" in the KJ.

identified for sure were the SICAMBRI who amalgamated with the Salian Franks (Pliny, "Natural History" 4;4). The name Hetsron was to be connected to that of the Hessuari (Chattuari) who, together with the Chamavi, Bructeri, Amsivarians, and Sicambri, were in the northern sphere which the Franks later occupied and whose people became the HESSIAN Franks or Chatti[20]. The name HESSE may be derived from HUSHIM (Hus-im) son of Dan (Genesis 46:23) and at first the Franks were attributed a DANISH origin or association. The fourth son of Reuben, **Carmi**, is recalled in the CHARINI. The Charini are included in the Vandili group by Pliny together with Vandili, Burgundians, and Gutones. [*The Gutones were Goths descendants of Gad and past associates of Reuben*]. Groups of Vandili were to settle in France. Carmi is also a name associated with the Cimmerians. The Cimmerians were based for a time in southern Russia in the Crimea, which was named after them: *The Crimea is known locally as "KRIM"*. In addition Carmi gave his name to Carmania in Southern Iran wherein and besides which several other groups from both Gad (Gadophydres, Pasar-gadae, Gadrosia) and Reuben (Carmania, Parthia, the Astaveni from Hetsroni) were noticeable in earlier times.

In Scythia the HUGIE (Franks) appeared in the area associated with the Eastern Goths who were also called Tokharians or Togar and linked with Thogarma son of Gomer (Genesis 10:3). A similar name occurred in east Serica (as reported by Ptolemy) where the RHABBANAEI were neighbored by the Taguri and Thogara. The said names recall the THORINGI (Turingii, Thuringii, Thuringians) who marched alongside the RIBUARI Franks in Europe and became associated with them. They gave their name to Thuringia in Germany. The Ribuarian or "Ripuarian" Franks were known as RIBUARI[23] which word in Hebrew would have had the same meaning as Reuben just like the Rhabbanei of Serica were named after Reuben.

Reuben and Gog

The names for the sons of Reuben parallel those of important Frankish groups; Hanoch=Hugo; Phalui=Falhi; and Hetsron (Chetsron)=Istaevone & Hessuari (Chattuari), with the fourth son Carmi being represented by the Charini. All these groups were amongst the settlers of France. An important descendant of Reuben and apparently the founder of a clan (1-Chronicles 5:3) was called **GOG**. "GOG" is a name applicable to part of the Tribe of Reuben **as well as** being the name of a foreign northern king, *"the chief prince of Meshek and Tubal"*; *"Gog, land of Magog"* (Ezekiel 38:2-3). The Tribe of Reuben was intertwined to some extent with that of Gad whose name in Hebrew could be pronounced like the name for GOTH. Maybe the Reubenite clan of Gog in the Caucasian province of Gogarene (Iberia) and its Gothic-connection caused later authors to confuse the Goths and Scyths with Gog and Magog? In Tibetan literature the area of Serica (once populated by the Rhabbanei and other groups) was at a time referred to as "Gog". **Both** Gog and Magog and the GOTHS were identified in folklore with the Ten Tribes of Israel[24]. Gog and Magog in Biblical terms refers to the peoples of Russia and Asia. The confusion of Gog and Magog with the Ten Tribes derives from two causes: 1. The tendency of German Literature to view the Lost Ten Tribes as the future arch-enemy. 2. The Goths and Franks had emerged from Central Asia and this area was traditionally associated with both Gog and with the Ten Tribes[✖].

[✖] Ezekiel says: "SON OF MAN, SET THY FACE AGAINST GOG, THE LAND OF MAGOG, THE CHIEF PRINCE OF MESHECH AND TUBAL, AND PROPHESY AGAINST HIM, AND SAY:, THUS SAITH THE LORD GOD; BEHOLD, I AM AGAINST THEE, O GOG, THE CHIEF PRINCE OF MESHECH AND TUBAL" [EZEKIEL 38:2-3]

In Hebrew the word for "Chief Prince" is "Rosh" [i.e. head of] and this was taken by medieval non-Jewish Commentators to refer to Russia. The Russians themselves identified with the forces of Gog and Magog and took pride in it, as documented by Leon Poliakov in *The Arian Myth*.

"NOW THE SONS OF REUBEN THE FIRSTBORN OF ISRAEL (FOR HE WAS THE FIRSTBORN; BUT FORASMUCH AS HE DEFILED HIS FATHER'S BED, HIS BIRTHRIGHT WAS GIVEN UNTO THE SONS OF JOSEPH THE SON OF ISRAEL: AND THE GENEALOGY IS NOT TO BE RECKONED AFTER THE BIRTHRIGHT..... (1-CHRONICLES 5:1).

"THE SONS OF REUBEN THE FIRSTBORN OF ISRAEL WERE, HANOCH, AND PHALU, HEZRON, AND CARMI.

"THE SONS OF JOEL; SHEMAIAH HIS SON, GOG HIS SON, SHIMEI HIS SON,

"MICAH HIS SON, REAIA HIS SON, BAAL HIS SON,

"BEERAH HIS SON, WHOM TIGLATHPILNESER KING OF ASSYRIA CARRIED AWAY: HE WAS PRINCE OF THE REUBENITES.

(1-CHRONICLES 5:3-6).

Characteristics of Reuben: According to a Midrash (Numbers Rabah 2;5) the symbol of Reuben was Mandrakes. Reuben had found mandrakes in the field (Genesis 30:14) and brought them to his mother Leah. Leah used these mandrakes to "hire" the attentions of her husband away from Rachel. Mandrakes, traditionally, had aphrodisiac qualities. Reuben is recalled as once having acted irregularly with Bilhah, his father's concubine (Genesis 35:22). Rightly or wrongly the French historically have had an international reputation for romantic proclivities. The Mandrake is described as having a purple or white flower, perhaps this gave rise to the white lily (Fleur-de-lis) the traditional symbol of the French monarchy whose precedent is to be found on Judaean coins[26] of ca. 130 BCE The first Frankish kings, the Merovingians, had a sun cult[27] and the French king Louis XIV (considered the apotheosis of French Royalty) was known as "The Sun King". The rising sun is also a symbol associated with Reuben, according to popular traditional Jewish* sources. In Jewish synagogues the symbols of the twelve tribes serve as a frequently employed theme of decoration. More often than not Reuben is accorded the rising sun symbol.

Each Israelite tribe was represented by an animal[28] in addition to some other symbol. The symbols of different tribes were also interchangeable under certain circumstances and one tribe could use (on occasion) the sign normally reserved for the other (Song of Songs Rabah 4;7). The animal symbol of Reuben is unknown to the author but the Merovingian Franks did have a **BEAR** cult[29]. The Parthians too are compared to "BEARS" in the Talmud (Megilla 11a). The Parthians in Eastern Scythia took control of Persia. They were connected to the Goths in the east and were of Israelite origin to a significant degree. Part of the Tribe of Reuben had been important amongst them. France prior to the Franks was known as Gaul or Galia and its inhabitants were called Galli, which in popular Latin also means "rooster".

The French later used a rooster or **"cock"** as their national animal representation. A crowing-cock in Jewish and General folklore is connected with the sunrise which conforms with the "Sun" or "Rising-sun" symbol of Reuben. So far, Reuben and the clans of Reuben have been traced to entities who eventually settled mainly in France, such as the Ribuari Franks (also known as the "Rubi") and their kin. Even so, the prevailing modern opinion is that most of the French are descended from the ancient Gauls, Celts, Aquitaners, and others of Celtic culture. Only a small minority (it is claimed - maybe wrongly) actually come from the Franks, Goths, Vandals, Normans, Alamans, and the like. It is these latter bodies who, from Scythia, invaded the west via Scandinavia

---

* Popular Jewish representations of the Tribal Symbols in some cases represent Reuben by a symbol representing the sun, or the sunrise. The present author has as yet not ascertained the source for this tradition. A possible source is that in Hebrew and Aramaic a root meaning "SEE" ("HAMA": חמא) and a root for the sun (HAMA: חמה) are in effect identical.

and Germany. The Celtic-associated populace (who, it is said, fathered most of the French) was composed of indigenous tribes together with others, such as the Cimmerian-Galatae, who arrived from the east.

"GALATAE" is the name applied to the Gauls in Greek writings. They were called "Galli" by the Romans. Both "Galatae" and "Galli" are Hebrew nominations. "Galli" connotes both "Exiles" (as noted by Apartian) and "Galilaean". The name "Galatae" is rendered "**Galadi**" in some accounts and is a form of the Hebrew name "Gilead". In French translations of the Bible "Gilead" is written as "**Galaad**".

After having exiled the Ten Tribes of Israel, the Assyrians re-formed the former area of Gilead together with parts of the lands of Reuben and Gad into the Province of "Galazu" which is their version of "Gilead". Similarly, the later Seleucian-Syrian Greek monarchs named approximately the same region "Galaaditis". In the Book of Joshua it says that the Reubenites and Gadites and the half-tribe of Manasseh went unto the land of Gilead:

"AND THE CHILDREN OF REUBEN AND THE CHILDREN OF GAD AND THE HALF-TRIBE OF MANASSEH RETURNED, AND DEPARTED FROM THE CHILDREN OF ISRAEL OUT OF SHILOH, WHICH IS IN THE LAND OF CANAAN, TO GO UNTO THE COUNTRY OF GILEAD, TO THE LAND OF THEIR POSSESSION, WHEREOF THEY WERE POSSESSED..." (JOSHUA 22:9).

It follows from the above passage as well as from the Assyrian term "GALAZU" and the Seleucid "Galaaditis" that the name "Gilead" and its derivatives could be used to encompass all the lands of Reuben and Gad as well as that of "Gilead" proper within Manasseh. This inference is confirmed by existence until recently of a town in northern Syria south of the Euphrates named "Galaad", i.e. the name "Galaad" was found within the former territory of Reuben. The appellation "Galaadi" or "Gileadi" or "Galatae" would therefore also be applicable to the former inhabitants of the "Gilead" area in its more general sense, which included descendants of Reuben.

Since Frankish and other entities who settled in France bore names recalling Clans of Reuben and the character and positioning of France is applicable to Reuben, **the GALATAE of France were also most likely derived from that portion of GILEAD belonging to REUBEN**. A similar line of reasoning connects the Caledonians and Galedon of Britain to Gilead of Manasseh.

French Reuben in History

Some points of interest are that: The sons of Reuben were destined (Zohar, VaYechi, 551, Sulam Edition) in the Latter Days to wage war in the LAND OF ISRAEL against (or for) Jerusalem. It was the French "Franks" who led the Crusaders of Europe (1069-1270) in their attempts to conquer the Holy Land and Jerusalem. The French Emperor, Napoleon Bonaparte in 1799 offered to restore Palestine to the Jews. Whether Bonaparte had been genuine in his intention or not, it was the French together with the British who created the political climate which made possible the Balfour Declaration and ultimately the State of Israel. The British would probably not have issued the Balfour Declaration if it were not for French agreement in principle. French Gentile volunteers fought on the Jewish side in Israel's War of Independence (1948 -1949). France assisted the State of Israel in its nuclear program and armament in general in the early years after the Israeli Declaration of Independence. At a later stage the French showed that they could also be anti-Semitic and virulent supporters of the "Palestinians" who want to kill all the Jews. Reports suggest that in Europe support for armed intervention on behalf of the Palestinians and against the Jews in the year 2001 was led by France. This impression may be exaggerated but it is worth bearing in mind. France as a nation contains many non-Israelite elements who frequently obtain dominance. France today contains about 20% Muslims from North Africa, and many others who are descended from Italians, Germans, Poles and others. France like all European countries also contains elements from Edom. Esau (Essuvis) was worshipped as a god in Ancient Gaul. From the very beginning in Ancient Gaul the nobles treated their subjects almost as slaves and as belonging to another race. [In Britain on the other hand the natives had a reputation for assertiveness and egalitarian qualities.] The nobles of Gaul were admitted to the Roman Senate as equals and this may reflect a racial connection to the Romans. There were elements amongst the French who identified with the Germans. Vichy France in the Second World War exhibited pro-German tendencies but the Free French who fought on the side of the allies made a very good account of themselves. It was the Protestants of France who were the most Israelite in outlook and they went out of their way to rescue Jews from extermination. The attitude of the French Protestants may reflect their culture, their own experiences, or the influence of the Bible combined with their ancestry.

Leon Poliakov reports that in the Middle Ages: <<*The French bothered little about whether they were descended from Japheth or the Trojans. They were Christians. Moreover it was generally understood, at least among the learned, that the human race had once spoken a universal language which was current before the dispersion of Babel, and that this language was Hebrew. There was general agreement as to the place where humanity was cradled. It was Judaea, on the confines of the Holy Land*>>[30]. In its own way this passage just about sums up the spiritual attitude of the Israelite element in France: No open definite identification with the Israelites but a hazy notion of maybe having once spoken Hebrew before "Dispersion" (represented by Babel) and perhaps one day of returning.

For a short period the French once ruled over the country of Syria (1920-1928) and Syria is within the territorial expanse once belonging to the Tribe of Reuben. The French were traditionally also involved with Lebanon and were patrons and protectors of the Christian Lebanese population. Some of the Christians in Lebanon may even descend from French Crusaders.

According to the Book of Ezekiel (48:7) Reuben is destined to inherit its Tribal portion between Judah in the south and Ephraim in the north, i.e. in territory between the descendants of the Jews and of the British.

Tribal Names Show National Character

The name Reuben in Hebrew primarily means "See-a-son" (Rue-ben) though it also has connotations of increase ("Ribui") and plenitude.

Of the sons of Reuben, "**Hanoch**" means "Inauguration", or "Education"; "**Phalu**" means "Distinction"; "**Hetzron**" denotes "Dweller-of -the-Courtyard"; and "Carmi" is derivable from "Cerem" meaning "Vineyard".

All of the above names acquire an additional significance when considered in the light of French history and culture. The French tend to emphasize high-quality educational requirements and are big on ceremonial: both characteristics being represented by the Hebrew name "**Hanoch**". They prefer quality to quantity and in some fields really are the best in their area, i.e. "**Phallu**" = Distinction. The French like distinction and style. French fashion and French perfumes are known for attempts to achieve that little bit "extra" that makes for distinction. The French are famous both for their aristocrats and for their peasants and both types are implied in the Hebrew name "**Hetsron**" meaning courtyard-dweller. "**Carmi**" in Hebrew means "My Vineyard". France is known for its good wines and expert wine-makers. French wines are considered the best in the world. The French consume large amounts of wine and wine is a staple part of French diet. The export of wine and wine-products such as brandy is an import earner of foreign exchange for the French. The names of the sons of

157

Reuben were those of important elements in the early history of France. These names also describe important aspects of the French national character.

France in the Bible and Traditional Sources

In early Medieval and Modern Hebrew the country of France is called "Zarephath". Zarephath was originally a Phoenician town, "Zarephath which belongeth to Zidon" (1-Kings 17:9) in which Israelites also dwelt. Throughout ancient Gaul and especially on the northwest coast there are signs of Phoenician or Israelite settlement[31].

It may be that France received the name Zarephath for ethnic reasons due to some connection with the mixed Israelite-Phoenician center of Zarephath (Daat Sofrim). The name is also recalled in the Book of Obadiah and most of the Classical Commentators said that the intention was to France (Rashi, Radak, Daat Sofrim), or to the North in general (Nachmanides, Segfer HaGeulah), or (according to Abarbanel) France and England together.

Obadiah (1:20) says:

"AND THE CAPTIVITY OF THIS HOST OF THE CHILDREN OF ISRAEL SHALL POSSES THAT OF THE CANAANITES, EVEN UNTO ZAREPHATH; AND THE CAPTIVITY OF JERUSALEM, WHICH IS IN SEPHARAD, SHALL POSSESS THE CITIES OF THE SOUTH."

The above translation is from the King James (KJ) version. The Hebrew original of the first part of Obadiah 1:20 according to the Commentators may be translated as:

"THIS FIRST EXILE [OF THE LOST TEN TRIBES] WHO REACH FROM THE LAND OF CANAANITES [I.E. GERMANY AND HOLLAND] TO ZERAPHATH [FRANCE AND BRITAIN].."[32]

The Hebrew Bible both according to its simple meaning and in light of tradition may be understood to say that at least a portion of the Lost Ten Tribes will be in Zerapath meaning France or France and Britain together.

Historical Provinces of France

PEOPLES OF REUBEN

Reuben:

Rahabbanai in northeast "Syrian" Israel according to Ptolemy's Map;

Rhabbanai (east Scythia).

Ribuari (Franks),

Rubi (Franks),

CLANS OF REUBEN:

Chanoch = Chauci, Hugo (Franks, Saxons).

Palui (Phalui) = Falia (Phalia in Germany whence the Franks invaded Gaul)

Chetsroni = Chassuari (Franks), Istaevones (Sicambri-Franks).

Carmi = Carmania (in southern Iran), Crimea (Scythia), Carini (Franks in Gaul).

Gog (a clan of Reuben) = Gogarene (Iberia in Caucasus), Gog (state in Scythia north of Tibet), name of Goths and of the Lost Ten Tribes in popular traditions.

Nemuel - Nemetes of Gaul (?)

WEAPON ADORNMENT
PERTAINING TO FRANKISH
OR SAXON SETTLERS IN
NORTHERN FRANCE.
NOTE THE
STAR OF DAVID SYMBOL.

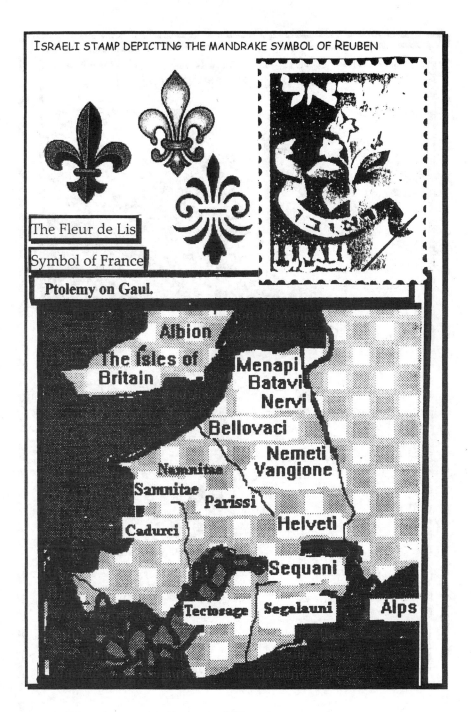

ISRAELI STAMP DEPICTING THE MANDRAKE SYMBOL OF REUBEN

The Fleur de Lis

Symbol of France

Ptolemy on Gaul.

Albion

The Isles of Britain

Menapi
Batavi
Nervi

Bellovaci

Nemeti
Vangione

Namnitae

Samnitae

Parissi

Cadurci

Helveti

Sequani

Tectosage   Segalauni   Alps

161

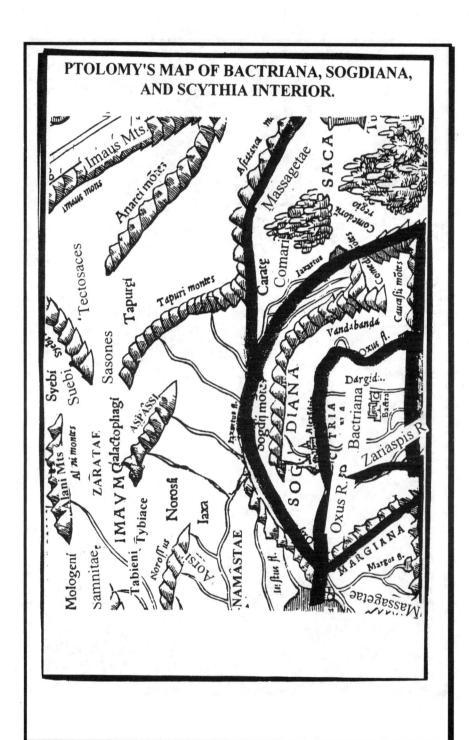

PTOLOMY'S MAP OF BACTRIANA, SOGDIANA, AND SCYTHIA INTERIOR.

9

Israel in the East According to Ptolemy

The chapters in this work based on the Geography of Ptolemy are meant to be accompaniments to the Maps of Ptolemy and to the Modern Maps showing the approximate locations of places mentioned by Ptolemy. These maps are illustrations and the text is an explanation of these illustrations. There may be repetitions of points made elsewhere in this work. If some of the passages lack appropriate references then they are probably repetitions of facts given in the appropriate chapters.

The following maps of Ptolemy relate mainly to the situation after the Scythians had been driven out of the Middle East and dislodged from Iran:

These maps depict **BACTRIANA, SOGDIANA,** and **SCYTHIA-INTERIOR.**

The following points should be noted:

Drangiana was a Scythian center also known as Sakastan. It was to the South of Hara, which in Ptolemy's terminology is referred to as **"ARIA".** Another name for Drangiana was Nimroz meaning "Nimrod". "Nimrod" represented the Assyrians and local tradition regarded the Sacae (Scythian) settlers of Drangiana as colonists of the Assyrians, as indeed they were. They were Israelites whom the Assyrians had re-settled on the fringes and border-areas of their Empire.

To the North and East of Drangiana and Hara were Bactriana and Sogdiana. To their east was **SACARUM REGIO** (Kingdom of the Sacae) which today is referred to as

Badakhshan. In this region were found the Massagetae and the Cimmerian-Comari other groups of whom were also further to the west besides the Caspian Sea.

EXPLANATION OF THE MAPS:
BACTRIANA, SOGDIANA, AND SCYTHIA INTERIOR

North of Aria was **MARGIANA** whose very name is cognate to that of Machir, son of Manasseh, as were the names of **MARACANDA**, the **MARYCAEI**, and MARACODRA in Bactria to the east of Margiana. In this general area were the Amyrigi-Scythae who became the Skati Maruka of Sweden, the Myrings of the Goths, and the Mercians of Saxon England.

In Margiana was a portion of the **MASSAGETAE**, also known as the Greater-Goths, and whose name may has been understood by others to represent the combination of Manasseh (Massa) and Gad (Goth-Getae). Besides the Massagetae were the **PARNI** or Aparni who joined with the Parthians. Their name is believed to be a version of Abar or "Iber" meaning Hebrew. "Iberia" in the Caucasus was further to the west. It was one of the places to which Israelites had been taken as well as being another Scythian locality.

The Parthians in a Sanskrit document are referred to as Kamrups meaning Cimmerians who on Ptolemy's Map are recalled in the **CHOMARI** of Bactriana and further to the east in the **COMARI of SACAR (SACARUM REGIO)** where too they are neighbored by another group of **MASSAGETAE**. It is apparent that, in both Margiana and in SACAR Cimmerians (i.e. Chomari and Comari) each neighbored separate sections of the Massagetae. The Massagetae were reported to bear the same type of weaponry as the Classical Cimmerians had done. Procopius, the Byzantine historian, in one passage identifies the Massagatae with the Cimmerians and in another with the Huns. In general, contemporary Roman observers identified the Massagatae with the Goths. The Indian Rigveda also recalls the Chamaru or Cimmerians on the Iranian plateau. The

164

Cimmerians first appeared on the fringes of Assyria. The Classical Cimmerians known from earlier history had migrated to the west and merged with the Galatians and Celts. They were associated with the CIMBRI whom Ptolemy locates in Jutland of Scandinavia and place-names testify to their presence all over the Scandinavian Peninsula which, at one stage, was ruled by the Goths and wherein Goths were to settle. The people referred to as Chomari, Comari, Kamrups, and Chamaru therefore represent an eastern branch of the original Cimmerians and were connected to the Parthian nation which later became prominent in this region.

BACTRIANA was named after the Bachrites (Numbers 26:35) from Becher, son of Ephraim. "The population of Bactria was largely Scythian"[1] and "The Bactrian Empire was founded by the Scythians"[2]. Steven COLLINS points out that Ephraim contained the clans of Bachrites, Eranites, and Tahanites (Numbers 26:35-36) and that amongst the Parthians the Eranians (Eranites of Ephraim), Dahanians (Tahanites of Ephraim) and Bactrians (from Becher of Ephraim) were present[3.] Becher of Ephraim also gave his name to Bukhara, later capital of neighboring Sogdiana. The city of Bukhara was also named SAMARKAND in honor of Samaria, former capital of Ten Tribed Israel. In Parthian Hyrcania there was a major city named Samariane. The Khazars were later present in this area and settlements named after Samaria were characteristic of them. The Boroctuari were also named after Becher. The Boroctuari participated in the Anglo-Saxon invasions of Britain, had been part of the forces of Attilla the Hun, and are considered as a Frankish group. The city of **"MENAPIA"** in Bactria recalls the Menappi of Britain, Ireland, and HOLLAND. A comparison of Roman and Chinese histories shows that the **TOCHARI** in Bactriana were synonymous with the Goths or Gu-ti The name is cognate with TOXANDRIA in Western Europe (Belgium and Holland) which was settled by Scythians and wherein Scythian and Sarmatian artifacts have been found.

Ptolemy's Map of Bactriana and Sogdiana

Ptolemy's Map of Scythia Interior

The **ZARIASPAE** may have come from the Zarhites, sons of Zerah of Judah (Numbers 26:20), similarly to the **IATII** over the border in Sogdiana, who gave rise to the Jutes.

In east Bactria, south of the Marycaei, were the **VARNI** known by the same name in Europe and also as Varini, and Warings. They were to be closely associated with the Angles and considered a Vandal Tribe. Herodotus recalled the **AEGLI** on the fringes of Bactria and the names Aegel and Angle in Europe were synonymous and interchangeable. "Aegel" in Hebrew means Bull-calf and in the Bible is a name applied to the northern ten tribes, especially to the leading tribe of EPHRAIM, Jeremiah 31:18. The Aegli mentioned by Herodotus are considered as identical to the **AUGALI** of Ptolemy in Sogdiana to the north of Bactria, besides the **IATII** and **TACORI**. The Iatii were also known as Yeda meaning Judah and in Europe became the Jutes who, together with Angles and Saxons, invaded Britain. The Thacori became the Thiringi who sojourned in Thyringia in Northern Germany which province for a time was an Angle centre.

The **CHORASMII** in Western Sogdiana gave their name to Chorasmia which nomination was used to encompass the entire region east of the Caspian Sea. Chorasmia was termed HAVILA in Medieval writings and was the traditional home of the Angles, Saxons, and Frissians of Holland. Neighboring Chorasmia was Sogdiana. The very name **SOGDIANA** is considered a form for THATAGUDES, who were a combination of Teutons (Thata-) and Goths (Gudes). The Thata came from Tahan (Numbers 26:35) and Tahath (1-Chronicles 7:20) of the Tribe of Ephraim, while the Goths, on the whole, came from Gad. In Europe Ptolemy reported the Teutons (Thata) besides the Angles and Saxons prior to their advance westward.

East of Sogdiana was the Kingdom of **SACAR** (Sacarum Regio) where the **COMARI** (Cimmerians) and **MASSAGETAE** (Goths from Manasseh and Gad) bordered the **GRINAEI SCYTHAE** who may have been descended from ERAN (ערן:

pronounceable as "Geran") from Ephraim (Numbers 26:36). The name SACAR may be a derivation of Issachar.

In Inner Scythia the **TECTOSACES** to the northeast were known as Volcae Tectosaces in Southwest Gaul. They were related to the Belgae of Northwest Gaul, Southern Britain, and Ireland. The **ASCOTACAE** became the Scotings among the Alamans of Switzerland and Alsace. The Germans called the Vikings "Askomen." This has been explained to mean "ash-men" after their wooden ships but (as in many other cases) this explanation may be a rationalization of an already existing appellation. Scandinavian mythology said that the first man was named "Ask". This root-name is derived from Isaac and is quite frequent in the Scythian area. The **ALANORSI** were a combination of Alans and Aorsi. The **SCYMBI** came from the Josephite clan (of Manasseh) of Shechem. They were also known as Sigambri in east Iran and Bactria and later in Gaul. The Sigambri (Sicambri) were also referred to as Syrakusae (i.e. Syrians of Cush east of the Caspian) in East Iran and in Europe. The **SASONES** and **SAXIANI** became the Saxons who in Britain were also known as "Saeson." The **GALA** were Galatians possibly from Gaul though originally they came from the Galilee in Israel. The **ASPASSI SCYTHAE** of Chorasmia were associated with the Parthians. Similar names in Iran and Afghanistan were rendered locally as "Isap" or Joseph. The **CACHAGE SCYTHAE** became the Chauci or Hocings in North Western Europe and the Cauci of Ireland. In Scythia they were part of the Huga and in Europe of the Franks who were also known as Hugo. The **TYBIACE** and **TYBIANI** became the Tubante Franks. The **SAGARUCE** were called Sagartoi by the Greeks and Assakarta by the Persians. Legend says they derived from the Tribe of Issachar. The **NAMASTAE** came from Namuel of Simeon as did the nearby **ZARATAE** come from the Zarhites (Numbers 26:13) of Simeon and the neighboring **SAMNITAE** who were named after Simeon. Similarly in Gaul the Samnites (of Simeon) bordered the

Nemnetes from Nemuel of Simeon. "Simuen" was an important ancestral figure in Celtic mythology. He was considered the son of "Isru" (i.e. of Israel) and an ancestor of the British.

In **Inner Scythia:** The **ASIOTAE** and **AORSI** were connected to the Alani Scythiae in the north who later moved west into Brittany of France, Switzerland, and Portugal. The **HYPERBOREI** Mountains remind us that the Hyperboreans were thought to dwell in Britain and Scandinavia. Hyperborean means "Northern Hebrew."

The **MACHETEGI** were named after Maaachah, wife of Machir, son of Manasseh (1-Chronicles 7:16). Maachah was also the name of a wife of Caleb of Judah (1-Chronicles 2:48) who too was related to Machir (1-Chr. 2:18-23). The important center of Abel-beth-Maachah ("Stone of the House of Maachah") was in the land of Naphtali: The city of Emain Macha in Northern Ireland has a name with the same meaning in Hebrew.

Also connected with Manasseh were the neighboring Scythian tribes of **MASSAEI, SUOBENI,** and **SYEBI.** These became the Western and Northern Suebi in Europe a portion of whom were the Samnites and in Scythia the **SAMNITAE** adjoined them. These groups correspond tot he western section of Sienbi mentioned in Chinese records. The Suebi in Europe were also known as Suevi and as Sweaf. They were linked with the Anglo-Saxons. A tribe of Suebi were the Vangiones some of whom served as mercenaries in the Roman siege of Jerusalem. After the fall of Jerusalem they took Jewish women captive. The offspring of this union were raised as Jews by their mothers and the resultant community was one of the first Jewish settlements in the region[4]. The ancestor of Hengist and Horsa, the brothers who lead one of the early principal waves of Saxon invaders of Britain, may have obtained his wife in the siege of Jerusalem[5].

Ptolemy's Map of Exterior Scythia and Serica

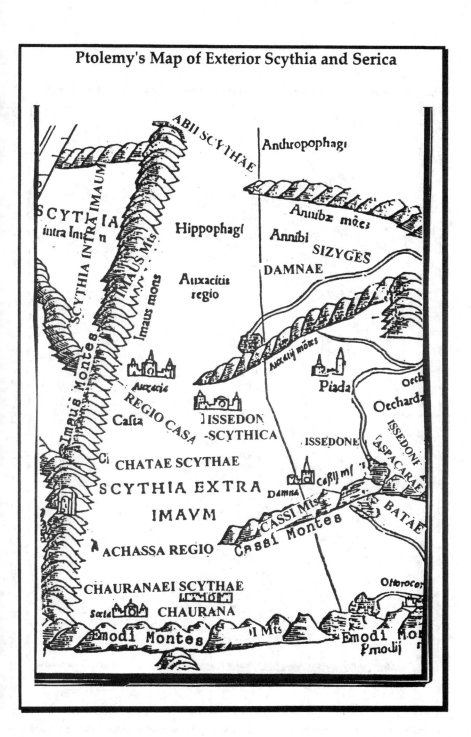

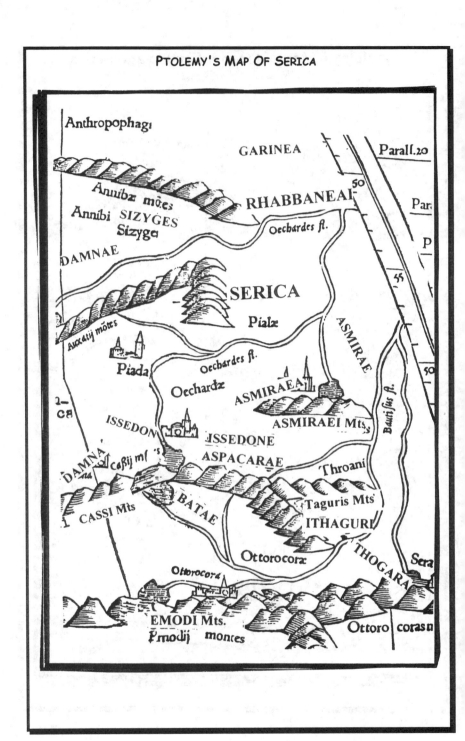

The name Hengest means stallion and the name Horsa means horse. The early Anglo-Saxon had some type of horse cult and burials of warriors with their horses and of horses in general were common. This was an inheritance from their Scythian past and the Steppe culture. The Israelites under Solomon (1-Kings 5:6) and later (Isaiah 2:7 31:1) kept a great many horses. The so-called "Arabian" horse may be a product of this period. Later the Assyrians in the Neo-Assyrian Era (after ca 700 BCE) and the exile of Israelites began to develop a cavalry corps using at first Israelite and Aramaean riders. When the Israelite-Scythians moved northward they introduced a horse-based culture into the region. Prior to the Scythians horses had been known in the Steppe region but their primary usage may have been for food. There was a close connection between the Scythians and Celts who were also known as proficient cavalry. Caesar comments that the early Britons relied heavily on chariots. After ca. 500 BCE the Celtic world was overtaken by the La Tene Culture. The initial bearers of this culture show some connection to the Altai Mountain Region in the far east of Scythia. Bede (731) traced the Picts of Scotland to Scythia and The Scottish Declaration of Independence (Arbroath) in the time of Robert the Bruce (1306-1329), stated that the Scots came originally from Scythia!

Exterior Scythia and Serica

Serica in Ptolemy's Geography was somewhere in the northeast of SIBERIA which region in the Scythian period was quite heavily populated. Adjoining Serica **was EXTERIOR SCYTHIA** (Scythia EXTRA IMAUM i.e. "Scythia Beyond the Imaus Mountains") which, together with Serica, may be considered one entity.

In the northeast of SERICA were the **GARINAEI** POSSIBLY DESCENDANTS OF ERI (pronounceable as "GERI") son of Gad.

Eri (Geri) may also be traced in the Greotingi-Goths and in the Grinae, reported by Jordanes as a tribe in Sweden. South of the Garinae were the **RHABBANAEI**, probable descendants of Reuben related to the Ribuari Franks of Western Europe.

To their west were the **SIZYGES** and **DAMNAE**. The Sizyges correspond to the Sigins reported by Strabo east of the Caspian and called Sigynnae by Herodotus who located a group of them in the Carpathian Mountains of Europe. According to Herodotus they dressed like the Medes and claimed to be a colony established by Media. The Israelites had been exiled to "The cities of the Medes" (2-Kings 17:6) and other places.

PIALAE, and **DAMNAE**: Claudius Ptolemy had the settlements of Piala and Damna located next to each other close to **AUZACIA** when mapping Serica An Arab source, Yakut says: "...Abraham was the father of Khazar...Horesm [i.e. Choresmia-Havila], and Peel"[6].

ALTHEIM has equated the Ephtalite Huns (also known as Nephtali and from the Israelite Tribe of Naphtali) with the Sigins. The Sigins on the basis of archaeological finds have likewise been identified as part of the Sequani who settled in southern and north Gaul. A group named the Scygs settled in Essex of Saxon England and this people (like other Anglo-Saxon contingents) may have migrated from Serica where the similarly named Szygs were reported.

-**We repeat, however, our findings indicate that most of Naphtali moved to Scandinavia especially to Norway. Scandinavian traditions trace their ancestors to the region by the Don River in Scythia and to Yeda northeast of the Caspian Sea. Yeda was Naphtalite territory.**

South of the Szygs in Serica were the **DAMNAE** and the settlement called **DAMNA**. The DAMNAE were named

"Dinlin" (or Dingling) in Chinese accounts and correspond to the DANGALAE reported by Pliny in Carmania alongside the Utii (Yautiya) from Judah and groups from GAD. The Damnae, therefore, are identifiable as DAN-of-the-Galilee in the Land of Israel. Similarly, Ptolemy recalled the Damnonii near the British River DON (DAN) and Damnone in Cornwall. Later the area of the Damnone in Cornwall together with that of Southern Wales was referred to as DANNONIA and as DEFENIA. In the Land of Israel the northern section of the Tribe of Dan (DAN-of-the-Galilee) had been situated in the region of DAPHNE which name recalls that of Welsh DEFENIA. In Serica the Damnae of Dan adjoined the Sizyges whom we have identified as from Naphtali and the Geographer Ortellius reported the tradition of Dan and Naphtali being together in this area close to the Gauths whom he said were the Lost Ten Tribes of Israel.

The name SERICA is derivable from Issachar. The kingdom of **ASMIREA** and **ASMIREA** city recall SHIMRON of Issachar (Genesis 46:13). The root "ASMIR" in Semitic dialects is interchangeable with SHOMER that forms the basis of the name Shimron, i.e. ASMIRAE is an acceptable translation of the name Shimron.

South of Asmiraea and the Asmiraei Mountains were the **TAGURI** AND THE **TAGURI MOUNTAINS**, the **TAGURI** people and **THOGARA**. In some editions of Ptolemy the Taguri are called Ithaguri. This resembles an Aramaic or other Semitic version of the name Issachar. Aramaic was spoken in the region east of the Caspian. The "Barbarians" who came westward received their Indo-European "Germanic" tongue from an external force.

West of the Tagurus Mountains were the **ASPACARAE** and **ASPACARAEA** which name is reminiscent of the Aspageni in Afghanistan whose appellation was understood to be a variation of the name JOSEPH.

The Tribes of Joseph were Ephraim and Manasseh. The **ISSEDONES** to the west of the **ASPACARAE** are generally considered a branch of the **ASII** or WUSUN also known as ASEIR in SCANDINAVIAN tradition and belonging to the Tribe of ASHER. The **BATAE** relate to the BATAVI in Holland considered by Tacitus as part of the CHATTI national group. Similarly, the **CHATAE SCYTHAE** and their kin paralleled the Chatti of Western Europe in this area. In EXTERIOR SCYTHIA (see on Map: **"SCYTHIA EXTRA IMAUM"**: i.e. "Scythia beyond the Imaus Mountains") to the east of Serica are the **ABII-SCYTHAE** from Job son of Issachar (Genesis 46:13) who became the Ubii of Holland. Further south was **ISSEDONE-SCYTHICA** of the Issedone (Wusun) entity beyond them to the south were the Kingdom of **CASIA**, the **CHATAE-SCYTHAE**, the Kingdom of **ACHASSA** and the **CASSI** Mountains. These entities relate to the CHATAE who appeared in Western Europe connected to both the Franks and Saxons and ultimately absorbed by them. The Batavi of Holland were one of their offshoots and these had been foreshadowed by the **BATAE** in Serica. The Batavi of Holland were renowned warriors and on old maps their name is given as "Bethayven" which is reminiscent of "Beth-Aven" another name for Beth-El and once a capital and cultural center of the Northern Kingdom of Israel (Joshua 7:2, Hosea 4:15 5:8 10:5). The CHATAE (of whom the Batavi were part) in Europe were also known as HESSI and descend from HUSHIM son of DAN (Genesis 46:23). South of **ACHASSA** (in "Outer Scythia" were the **Emodian Mountains** (the Altai) which the ancestors of the SAXONS, Angles, and Dutch Frisians had once been made guardians of, according to legend.

On Ptolemy's Map of Serica the distribution of identified groups before they moved to Northwest Europe in the Barbarian invasions shows some parallelism to the Tribal allocations in the Land of Israel. In the northeast were the **GARINAEI** (from Geri-Eri, of Gad) with **RHABBANAEI** (from Reuben) to their south. In the Land of Israel, Issachar had lain to the west of Gad and Reuben, and south of Dan. Likewise in

176

Serica DAN (i.e. **DAMNAE**) was to the north in Serica proper along with the Asmiraea and the Ithaguri and Thogar and the Tagurus Mountains to the south and east. The Damnae represent Dan as shown, Serica is Issachar, the Asmiraea have a name similar (in Semitic tongues) to that of Shimron, son of Issachar. The Ithaguri and Thogara have appellations that relate to Togarmah with whose group part of the Lost Tribes temporarily amalgamated. At the same time the "S" and "T" or "TH" were interchangeable in the Mesopotamian-Iranian area, for instance, Assyria became known as "Aturia" or "Athuria" and in Aramaic a "t" is often found where the Hebrew equivalent has "s". In other words, the names ITHAGURI and Thogara may be forms for Issachar. Similar names (Thacori, Tochari) were to be found in the general Chorasmian area where the SAGARUCE-SAKARAUKAE were predominant and also in Switzerland (Toygeni and Tigorini allies of Cimbrians, Teutons, and Ambrones) which country other factors relate to Issachar. Also near Serica in the north were the **ABII SCYTHAE** from Yob son of Issachar (Genesis 46:13) whose name was recalled in the Abus River of Celtic east Britain and in the "ABIS Maurunganie" as the West Saxons in England were referred to. In Serica the ABII-Scythae were neighbored by the **SIZYGES** who, amongst the English Saxons, became known as SCYGS and settled in Essex. The **ABIS MAURUNGANIE** were probably a combination between Issachar (Yob) and Machir of Manasseh whose land in Israel adjoined (or at least was close to) that of Issachar. YOB may also be found in the Tribe of UBII who settled in Holland.

[Genesis 49:19] GAD, A TROOP SHALL OVERCOME HIM: BUT HE SHALL OVERCOME AT THE LAST.

[Deuteronomy 33:20] AND OF GAD HE SAID, BLESSED BE HE THAT ENLARGETH GAD: HE DWELLETH AS A LION, AND TEARETH THE ARM WITH THE CROWN OF THE HEAD.

Sweden was founded when in about 800 CE the Svears (Suione) and Gotar (Goths) became independent from Denmark. The two entities had already united in the 500s CE. The Swedes derive mainly from the Tribe of Gad. The names of most Tribal groups that settled in Sweden are those of the sons of Gad. The Heruli, for instance, who settled in Sweden derived their name Areli son of Gad. "Areli" means "Lion of God". A lion was one of the symbols of Gad (Deuteronomy 34:20) and lions appear on the Swedish Coat of Arms. These lions are depicted as enclosed by a kind of tent. Another symbol of Gad was a group of tents.

10

THE TRIBE OF GAD PRONOUNCED "GOTH"

The Dispersion of Gad

The Tribe of Gad was exiled with Reuben and the half-tribe of Manasseh to Halah, Habor, the River of Gozan, and to Hara (!-Chronicles 5:26). Gad re-appeared as the **Guti** who were allied to the Saka and Gimiri (Cimiri) in Mesopotamia and the Zagros Mountain region. From this area the Guti split into known groups. One group went west to become the Geti of the Balkans. Ancient writers who lived at the time recognized that the Geti and the Goths were the same people. Another group of Goths was in the east, branching out from Hara in Eastern Iran. In the sphere surrounding the area of "Hara" the Gadites reappeared as the Pasar-**Gad**ae, in the name **Gad**rosia, in the **Gad**anopydres of Carmania; and in the Gu-te (Goths) whose name is sometimes mistakenly transliterated from Chinese records as "Yuehchi'". The Gu-te were known to the Western World as Massagetae. The Romans knew that the Massagetae were Goths though the term could also be applied to other peoples of the area. The name "Goth" itself means **GAD** and is another way of enunciating it in Hebrew while the Goths

179

actually in some cases referred to themselves by the term "Gad" or something close to it. The Goths are recorded as having called themselves "**GUDA**"[2] or "**GODO**"[3]. "**GAD**" is recognized as a root occurring in Gothic toponomy[4]; i.e. the root "GAD" in a place-name is accepted by historians as evidence indicating that that place was probably once connected with the Goths. Gadites were also known in Scotland (as "**Gad**eni") and Ireland as the "**Gaed**hals".

The Goths of Gad

Goths were to be found amongst the sundry northern tribes who invaded England with the Anglo-Saxons and a Saxon group was known as the GEDDINGAS.

The main body of Gad was that associated with the Goths and with the so-called "Nordic" peoples. Goths were to settle in many lands but numerically they probably remained concentrated in Scandinavia and Sweden (Gotaland and Gothia)[5] is the only place where today they can be distinguished as a specific people.

The sons of Gad (Genesis 46:16, Numbers 26:15-17) were Ziphion (Hebrew: Tsifion: צפיון), Haggi (Chaggi: חגי), Shuni (שוני), Ezbon (Etsbon: עצבון), Eri (Geri: ערי), Arodi (ערודי) and Areli (אראלי). **Ziphion** (Tsiphion) is recalled in the Thaifalli who were close allies of the Goths. From the east they came westward with the Hun invasion and apparently settled in France[6]. The name of the second son, **Haggi** is close to that of "Huga"[7] which name was applied to the Franks in the north. The Franks consisted mainly of clans from Reuben with supplements from others, especially Manasseh. Nevertheless, the two tribes, Gad and Reuben, had been together on the other side of the Jordan and were also exiled together so that groups from one were to be found in the domain of the other. In an area associated with the Goths in eastern Scythia. Ptolemy's Map of Central Scythia has a people north of the Jaxartes River named CACHAGE

Scythae and this name too derives from Hagi or "Chagi".[*]
Likewise, Chagi is found in the CHAUKI (Hocings)[8] who were
a Frisian nation whose lands were overtaken in about 200 CE
by Saxons coming west from Holstein. The Chauci were obliged
to leave their lands and become amalgamated mainly with the
Franks[9] though some were absorbed by the Saxons[10]. Tacitus[11]
describes the Chauci as the noblest of German tribes, *"So
constituted as to prefer to protect their vast domain by justice
alone...yet they are ready with arms, and if circumstances should
require with armies, men, and horses in abundance."* There was also
a people named Cauci in Celtic Ireland who were related to the
Chauci on the Continent. The Batavia who settled in Holland
were regarded as part of the Chauci. They form a contingent
from Gad amongst the Dutch population. Pliny included the
Chauci in the Ingueone group of "German" tribes together with
the Cimbri and Teutoni. The Ingueones relate to Yngvi[12]. In
mythology, Yngvi (of the Ingueone group) was a son of the god
Odin and an ancestor of the Swedish kings whose dynasty was
known as the Yinglings[13]. This association connects the
Ingueones (Chauci, Teutons, and Cimbri) with the Swedes. The
Cimbri were located by Ptolemy in Jutland where their name is
recalled in the modern places of Himmerland and
Himmersyssel[14]. [*The sounds "k", "c", "ch", and "h", interchange
in studies of that era, thus "Cimmer" or "Kimmer" becomes
"Himmer"*]. The name also occurs in Uppland Himbran
(Uppsala in Sweden), Hymber in South Norway, and Himbrin
and Himmerstein in Trondheim, also Norway. There is also
Krimisham in Sweden as well as quite a few place-names
containing the root-word "hammer" indicating a possible
Cimbrian association. Simon Grunau[15] (ca.1530) wrote that the
Swedish Isle of Gothland was formerly known as Cymbria and
that Goths had resettled it, in about 500 BCE, after being forced
out of Italy which they had previously invaded. He also said

---

[*] In Hebrew the "H" in "Haggi" (חגי) is the letter "het" which can be rendered as "h" or
as "ch" or even as "c" cf. Chaggi.

that the name Bruthenia was given once to Northern Prussia as a result of Gothic settlement. "Bruthenia" is probably a version of "Brith" a name that means "covenant" and that accompanied the Cimmerians to Britain. The Cimbrians were traditionally descended from the Cimmerians (Gimiri) of old. The triumvirate of Saka, Gimiri, and Guti (Goths) had been known since the Assyrian era. In some respects this threesome overlapped the two-and-a-half-Tribes who had settled east of the Jordan, i.e. the Cimmerians partly from Carmi of Reuben, the Amyrgio-Sakae from Machir of half-Manasseh and the Guti from Gad.

The ancient Guti were paralleled in Scandinavia by the Geats or Goths. The name "GUTI" itself in Scandinavia was used synonymously with Goth[16]. The Gimiri (Cimmri) became the Cimbri who descended from them and who were spread throughout Scandinavia with a historical connection with Denmark. The Cimbri were close allies of the Teutons. Ptolemy located the Teutons south of the Saxones and north of the (Aggiloi) Anglii. The Teutons were to be swept up in the Anglo-Saxon invasion of Britain. The name Teuton is cognate with "Teutarus" who according to legend was a Scythian and taught Hercules archery. The term "TEUTON" is connected to that of Tahan, son of Ephraim, son of Joseph. A similar form "TAHAT" (cf. Numbers 26:35, and "-Chronicles 7:20) was also known amongst the Tribe of Ephraim. "Tahan" and "Tahat" are considered to be related bodies[17]. The Saxons represent the SAKAE of old meaning the Scyths.

The sons of Gad were Ziphion and Haggi as well as Shuni, Ezbon, Eri, and Arodi, and Areli (Genesis 46:16). Haggi (Chaggi) and Eri (Geri) were represented in tribes of East Scythia who in the west became associated with the Goths and Suebians. Serica in Eastern Siberia was once the domain of the Eastern Suebi. This was prior to a drastic climatic change in that region. Also in Serica there dwelt a number of other groups who later reappeared in the west and who were of Israelite descent. One of these were the GARINAEI[18], descendants of ERI (pronounceable as "Geri") who reappeared as the GRANI of Sweden who were noticed by Jordanes[19]. The Greuthingi [also from "Eri" i.e. Geri: ערי] were a section of the Goths who intermingled with the Ostrogoths on the Black Sea coast. They are the same people as the GREOTINGI whom Jordanes[20] reported as being in Sweden. The Goths were traditionally considered to have come from Sweden. Modern research tends to the view that the initial base of the Goths was in Northern Poland but elite groups from Scandinavia settled amongst them and culturally influenced them.

Gothic History

Conventional accounts based on a combination of archaeology and the records of Jordanes say that the Goths appeared around 100 BCE by the Vistula River in what was once Prussia and now is part of Poland. From there they moved into the Ukraine and then along the shores of the Black Sea. They split into three sections known as the Gepids, Ostrogoths, and Visigoths. The Ostrogoths for a short period ruled over a large empire but were overtaken by the Huns and forced to join forces with them. This scenario is correct to a degree. The Goths were part of the Scythian forces. They were associated with the Massagatae east of the Caspian Sea. In the period 300 to 200 BCE a portion of them moved to Scandinavia. From Scandinavia and the Vistula region there was a movement backwards into Scythia linking up with elements that had remained in the east. With the Barabarian movements westward in the 400s CE offshoots from the Goths re-entered Scandinavia.

Were the Goths in Britain???

The Gadeni of Scotland may have been derived from Gad. The Goths had some type of connection with Scotland and some English authors named the Scottish "Ysgoths"[21] which connotes "Goths of the Island". Certain archaeologists believe that finds from the Viking ship Sutton Hoo indicate the presence of a Gothic element amongst the Anglo-Saxons. In 1404 Archbishop Johannes de Gabonifontibus (who had been in England) reported: *"Two small nations are living along and around the Black Sea; the Thats and a few Goths. The Goths claim to have descended from the Scots and speak like the English"*[22]. The Thats were a branch of the original Teutons. The Teutons had been in Northern Germany and Denmark and were absorbed by the Anglo-Saxons. A section of the Thats by the Black Sea shores of Southern Russia practiced Judaism and are known as "The Mountain Jews". These have been often traced to the Khazars who in turn were identified with the Lost Tribes of Israel.

The Sons of Gad

"AND THE SONS OF GAD; ZIPHION, AND HAGGI, SHUNI, AND EZBON, ERI, AND ARODI, AND ARELI" GENESIS 46:16.

"THE CHILDREN OF GAD AFTER THEIR FAMILIES; OF ZEPHON, THE FAMILY OF THE ZEPHONI: OF HAGGI, THE FAMILY OF THE HAGGI: OF SHUNI, THE FAMILY OF THE SHUNI:

"OF OZNI, THE FAMILY OF THE OZNI: OF ERI, THE FAMILY OF THE ERI:

"OF AROD, THE FAMILY OF THE ARODI: OF ARELI, THE FAMILY OF THE ARELI.

"THESE ARE THE FAMILIES OF THE CHILDREN OF GAD ACCORDING TO THOSE THAT WERE NUMBERED OF THEM, FORTY THOUSAND AND FIVE HUNDRED"

NUMBERS 26:15-18.

Dan and the Sons of Gad: The Shuni of Sweden

The DANS (DAN) who finally settled in Denmark formerly sojourned in **Sweden**[23] within which land the Tribe of Gad predominated. Sweden was formed when the kingdom of the Swedish-Goths (Gautland) united with that of the Svea[24]. The Svea were known to the Latins as Suiones. Tacitus mentions, (Germania 44) *"The states of the SUIONES right out in the sea. They are powerful not only in arms and men but also in fleets".* "SUIONES" (Svea) is similar to THE Hebrew **Shuni** the third son, whose name in Biblical times in the north was perhaps pronounceable as "SUONI" [*"S" for "SH" cf. Judges 12:6 "Siboleth" instead of "Shiboleth"; and "u" or "wu" before "o"*].

The union of Gad and Dan, who in Biblical times were close neighbors, was repeated in the **Gauti and Dauni** that, says Ptolemy, were on the Baltic coast.

The Goths were to dominate the region of Scythia, north of the Black Sea, and here river names, such as **Don**, **Dan**aper (Dnieper), **Dan**aster, and **Dan**ube, all bear witness to the presence of Dan. Strabo[25] says expressly that the DANUBE was known to have received its name from the Scyths[*]. The Aorsi (from north of the Caucasus) were neighbored by the UDINI[26] whose name is said to mean "The **DONS**". Amongst Scythian (and Gothic) clans the name **DAN** or compounds of it is considered typical[27].

Dan and the Sons of Gad: The Arodi and Areli of Norway and of Sweden

The **Arodi** and **Areli** of Gad were also once linked with Denmark of Dan. Denmark of the Danes was for a time ruled

---

[*] Some authorities connect these names (**Don**, **Dan**aper (Dnieper), **Dan**aster, and **Dan**ube) with an Iranian root meaning, "water". The fact remains however that the root had ethnic connotations.

by the Hread-Goths or Hrodgoths[28] who were either the same as, or at least related to, the HARUDI (Hardi). The Harudi from Denmark migrated to Hordaland[29] in Norway in the 200s and 300s CE. Also once in Denmark were the ERULI (Harules) who were expelled somewhere between 100-500 CE[30] and wandered extensively before finally returning to Scandinavia where some may have received part of their former patrimony in Denmark back while others (possibly the bulk) settled in Sweden[Δ]. The Herules are famous as a fierce, energetic, and knowledgeable people[31]. More than any other group they are considered to have been masters of the semi-secret Runic script. Runes in the early stages were especially associated with Gothic civilization that was reasonably cultured despite hostile and primitive surroundings. **RUNIC letters originated in the Middle East and are derived mostly from the ancient HEBREW script[♥].** Both the Harudi and Eruli (Harules) are related to sons of Gad, Harudi from the Arodi of Gad, and Eruli from Areli (Numbers 26:17)[☺].

[Δ] In the first edition of "The Tribes" it was stated that the Herules settled in Ostgoterland in Sweden. This information has since been contested. Mr. Orjan SVENSSON of Karlskrona in Sweden has written to me stating that the inhabitants of Blekinge in the south of Sweden have a tradition that they are descended from the Herules. In his opinion descendants of the Herules are more likely to be found in the south than in the east though he also says that no one really knows for sure in which part of Sweden the Herules settled. Mr. **Svensson** sent me an article (in Swedish) by Tommy WESTERBERG from which it appears that the Herules settled in Bleking and on the isle of Bornholm which is to the southeast of Sweden though it belongs to Denmark. The said article notes that the Herules (on their return to Scandinavia) included a definite eastern element that is traced to Armenia and the Caucasus. These in the opinion of Westerberg may also have been descendants of Jews or of other Israelites. Herules also settled at one stage in Holland and in other parts of Europe.

[♥] Dr. Kjell ARTUNS *"Runer"* (Oslo, Norway, 1994) proves in general that the Runes originated in the Middle East area. Dr. Kjell ARTUNS *and* Orjan SVENSSON, "De Blekin¸ska Runornas Hemlicheter" (Karslkrona, Sweden, 2001) have shown that the language of some of the runic inscriptions is Semitic; in some cases it is Hebrew and in others Aramaic or related dialects!!

[☺] It should be mentioned that in Hebrew the Arodi are referred to as "Ha-Arodi" (i.e. "The Arodi") and the Areli as "Ha-Areli" (i.e. "The Areli").

Ezbon (Etsbon) also Called Ozni

From the above it is apparent that the sons of Gad were represented in tribal groups which were part of, or somehow associated with, the Gothic nation. Most of these groups had representative settlers in Sweden: Ziphion was found in the Thaifali, who were Gothic-allies; Haggi appears in the Chauci and amongst the Hugi Franks and the Hocings of England, and the Yinglings of Sweden; Eri (Geri)♦ was represented by the Grani and Greotingi of Sweden and the Goths; Shuni (Suoni) by the Suiones of Sweden; Arodi by the Hreadgoths and Harudi; and Areli by the Eruli or Herules. The only son not accounted for so far is **Ezbon** (Etsbon) (Genesis 46:!6). "Etsbon" of Gad fathered the Hasdingas[32] who were a branch of the Vandals, marched together with the Goths[33] and shared the same dialect and customs. A branch of the Hasdingas participated in the Anglo-Saxon invasions of Britain where they were known as the Hastings[34].

Ezbon was also called **Ozni** (Numbers 26:16). His name is found in that of Osnabruch which is in West Germany but was once Frankish territory. The name "Etsbon" is recognizable in the Bastarnae and Hasdingas. The Bastarnae seem to have disappeared somewhere in France. The Bastarnae had been first reported as allied to the Goths and were referred to as

---

♦ The name ERI (Genesis 46:17) in Hebrew begins with an "AYIN" letter (ע). This letter may be described as a soft guttural and is sometimes transliterated as "H" as in "Hebrew" (Ivri: עברי), or some other vowel and at other times as a "G" as in "GAZA" for AZA (עזה). In the Caucasus area a similar sound receives a harsher emphasis and therefore the likelihood that the "AYIN" was pronounced as a "G" becomes more probable. Also some indications exist that the Asssyrians and Persians rendered Semitic words beginning with "AYIN" as if with an initial "G" sound. Thus "ERI" (ערי) may have been pronounced as "GERI". Names beginning with AYIN (such as ERI) and presumed to have been pronounced herein as beginning with "G" correspond with the suggested equivalents (e.g. "Eri" or "Geri" becoming "GRANI") due to additional factors apart from Nomenclature. cf. Isaac E. MOZESON "The Word," New York 1989 ("g" for "AYIN") on the words GARBLE, GAUZE, GIRL, GRAPHITE, etc.

"GALATIANS". The appellation "Galatian" comes from the Hebrew "Galaadi" (i.e. Gilead) which was the name of a grandson of Manasseh whose territory in the Land of Israel had intermerged with the territory of Gad. In another sense "GILEAD" and "Bashan" were names applied to the **COMBINED** territories east of the Jordan of half-Manasseh, Reuben, **and GAD**:

"AND THE CHILDREN OF REUBEN AND THE CHILDREN OF GAD AND THE HALF TRIBE OF MANASSEH RETURNED, AND DEPARTED FROM THE CHILDREN OF ISRAEL OUT OF SHILOH, WHICH IS IN THE LAND OF CANAAN, TO GO UNTO THE COUNTRY OF GILEAD, TO THE LAND OF THEIR POSSESSION, WHEREOF THEY WERE POSSESSED, ACCORDING TO THE WORD OF THE LORD BY THE HAND OF MOSES" (JOSHUA 22:9).

The Huguenots from Hugo or Haggi of Gad

The Huguenots are identified as the Calvinist Protestants of France though they probably existed before Calvin. Ruth **SHECTER**, an author and researcher at the Beer Sheva University in Israel proves that the Calvinists were basically Hebraic in character and mind-set especially when compared to neighboring peoples and religious groups. The Huguenots were persecuted and many of them fled to other lands. The name "Huguenot" is derived from that of a legendary king named Hugon or HUGO. The 11th edition of the Encyclopedia Britannica quotes from Henri Estienne (1566) who said that the Protestants at Tours used to assemble at night near the gate of King Hugo whom the people regarded as a spirit. A monk in a sermon said that the Protestants should be called Huguenots since like the spirit-king Hugo they only went out at night. They were therefore called "Huguenots" and the name became popular from 1560 onwards. "**HUGO**" WAS INDEED THE SOURCE OF THE NAME! Hugo is another form of the name Haggi son of Gad. The chief concentrations of Huguenots today in France are in Vendee in the west (once known as Pictavia), in the region of Paris, and in regions situated along the course of the Rhone River in the southeast. In the past Strasbourg in Alsace in the east was important. As mentioned the Huguenots were persecuted and suffered from massacres and expulsions. After 1685 about 400,000 Huguenots emigrated to Prussia, Holland, Britain, Switzerland, and North America. Among the Boer (Dutch-dominated) settlers of South Africa there were many of Huguenot origin.

The legend of King HUGO was known from the southeast area of France. The Huguenots displayed strong Israelite characteristics, appear to have been mainly of one ethnic cast, and came from areas in France where the Goths of Gad had once been present: The southeast of France was once called "Gothia" due to the Goths having ruled and settled there. Amongst the Goths in "Gothia" there had been movements to Judaize. The Goths themselves believed that they were descended from Israel. Jews from the region of Gothia were also called "Goth" and the terms "Jew" and "Goth" were used synonymously! The historian Arthur J. **ZUCKERMAN** ("A Jewish Princedom in Feudal France, 768-900", New York 1972) believed that Jews were referred to as "Goths" because they often came from the region of Narbonne which was also known as "Gothia". One opinion holds that many of the Goths in Southeast France and Spain at some early stage converted to Judaism! Much later, there were Jewish Marranos who became Huguenots. The Huguenots on the whole were a very positive and valuable element in French society. During the Second World War the Huguenots of France and the Calvinists of Holland probably more than any other group in Europe risked their lives to save Jews from extermination by the Germans.

Goths in Germany

Many Huguenots went to Berlin in the State of **Prussia** in **Mecklenburg**. This region had once been a Gothic center and from there many migrated to the USA. Between 1850 and 1890 approximately 146,000 (one out of every three) Mecklenburgers emigrated overseas, most going to the United States of America. The reason for leaving was dissatisfaction with the prevailing social order and conditions. The emigrants represented the remnants of the Goths of Israelite origin who were finally separating themselves out from their non-Israelite brethren. The same principle applies to the rest of Europe. In all seven million people left Germany alone. Some few people of Israelite origin may have remained and it is reported that in Berlin more Jews were given shelter than any other German city. Nevertheless the overwhelming majority of Hebrew ancestry had left the country.

Gad in Judaic Sources

Jacob (Israel) the patriarch prophesied of Gad, *"A troop overcame him: but he shall overcome at the last"* (Genesis 49:19). This Prophecy was perhaps exemplified when the Huns' hordes overcame the Goths and forced them to participate in the western invasions. On Attila's death a revolt by the Goths and their Gepid kin destroyed the Hun domination. The great commentator Don Isaac Abarbanel (on Genesis 49:19), after analyzing and weighing all the Biblical verses referring to Gad, came to (the inferred) conclusion that Gad would be numerous and divided into many groups which, nevertheless, would maintain some form of contact and be capable of concerted action. Historically, this concept did fit the Gothic peoples, though it is difficult to see what applicability it could possibly have today. "Goth" in Hebrew is another form for the name "GAD"[35]. According to the Zohar[36] the animal-symbol of the Tribe of Gad was the kid of a sheep or goat. This was based on the word for KID, "GADI", which is similar to Gad. Similarly the Goths of history are said to have had a GOAT as their symbolic-animal. The name "GAD" in Biblical Hebrew is also connected to the word for cutting and chopping as well as for groups or legions and also for deity (god)[36] . The Goths of

190

history interpreted their name to mean "People (Chosen) of God"[37]. **Popular traditions (such as that related by John Mandeville, 1499) identified the GOTHS of history with the LOST TEN TRIBES OF ISRAEL.**

Midrashic opinion holds that the tribes over the Jordan which included Gad, Reuben, and half Manasseh, were the first to be exiled and that they like the other tribes will be redeemed in the future.

Historically, Goths and Gothic clans and sub-tribes were shown as having been present in both the Scythian areas and in Scandinavia. From Scythia they disappeared but their descendants, as a recognizable entity, remain in Scandinavia. The migratory connection between Scythia and Scandinavia is reflected in the Mythology of Odin that relates how people from the Don River area in southern Russia migrated to Scandinavia.

The Tribe of Reuben had neighbored GAD and was exiled with it. Consequently, a certain overlapping may be noticed between groups identified as part of Gad and those seen to have come from Reuben. REUBEN appears to have been the dominating factor in the FRANK federations of West European history. Apart from Scandinavia, the second most important area of GOTHIC settlement was in southern France (Septimania) in the region surrounding the city of Narbonne, which province was known as "GOTHIA", and here too, the FRANKS (of Reuben) adjoined the Goths of Gad.

Peoples of Gad

Gad was a name for Goths and an identifying root in Gothic toponomy.

Gudos was also a name for the Goths.

Getae were a Gothic group in the Balkans and Scandinavia. In Scandinavia and elsewhere the name is just another form of Goth.

Guti was a name for the Goths both in Scandinavia and east of the Caspian though some modern historians incorrectly transliterate the name (from Chinese characters) as "Yueh-chi".

Guthones = Goths on Baltic coast.

Gautoi in Scandinavia.

Gadrosia in Iran.,

Pasar**gad**oi meant "Sons of Gad" in ancient Iran.

Thata**gydes** in ancient Afghanistan: "Thata-" represented the Teutons and "Gydes" the Goths.

Gadeni in Scotland.

Gaedhal in ancient Scotland and Ireland.

Geddingas were an Anglo-Saxon associated sub-tribe.

Clans of Gad

Ziphion: Thaifalli (Gothic allies from Scythia migrated to France),

Haggi (Chaggi): Chauci (Franks also known as "Hugo", and as "Hocing"). Yngling (Sweden), Cauci (Ireland).

Huguenots of France named after a legendary "Hugo" identifiable as "Haggi" of Gad.

Shuni (Suni): Suiones (Sweden).

Etsbon: Bastarnae (Gothic Galatian group moved to France), Astings, Hastings (Vandal group invaded England and Scotland).

Ozni: Osnabruch (Frankish Germany).

Eri (Geri): Grani (Sweden), Greotingi (Goths, Sweden).

Arodi (Ha-Arodi): Harudi (Norway), Hreadgoths (Scandinavia).

Areli (Ha-Eruli): Eruli (Herules) -associated with Goths, Sweden.

Guni: Chouni (Huns), see Guni of Naphtali (Egan -Denmark, Gugerni- Holland).

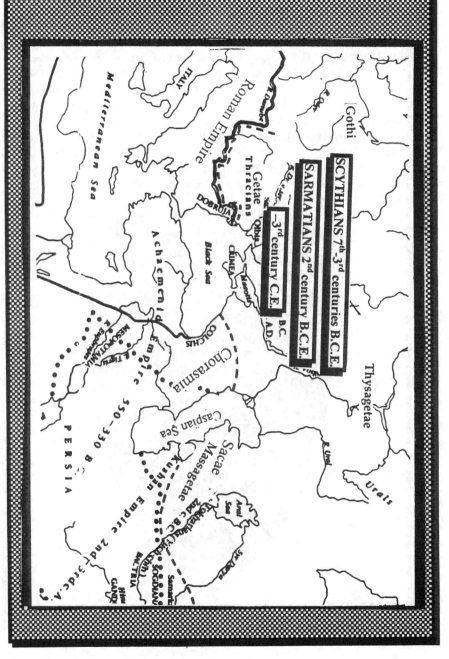

Scythians and Sarmatians 600s BCE to 200s CE
The Realm of the Goths

NAPHTALI = NORWAY

Norway was settled by groups (such as the Nephtalite Huns) who mainly descended from Naphtali. Elements from Benjamin, Gad, and other Tribes were also important. The Goths (from Gad) ruled over Norway for some time, as did the Swedes (who are also descended from Gad) after them. The symbol of Naphtali was a stag or deer and a deer was a symbol of Scandinavian (including Norwegian) royalty. The Norwegian coat of arms depicts a lion bearing an ax. A lion was one of the symbols of Gad (Deuteronomy 33; 20). Moses predicted that a blow from one of the weapons of Gad would be sufficient to sever arm with the head (Deuteronomy 33; 20) indicating the favored use of a striking ax-like weapon as compared with a thrusting pointed one. The ax or something like it was one of the major weapons of the ancient Cimmerians and of the Massagetae who were Goths east of the Caspian and with whom the Nephtalite Huns were affiliated.

Israeli stamp showing a camp of tents. This was
one of the traditional symbols of Gad.

LUXEMBOURG AND PART OF THE FLEMISH ARE OFFSHOOTS OF GAD

LUXEMBOURG

East Flanders in Belgium

196

The Two and a Half-Tribes of Reuben, Gad, and Half-Manasseh Reviewed

The Tribes of Gad, Reuben, and half the tribe of Manasseh had been given by Moses all the lands of Israel east of the Jordan River (Numbers 32:33). These tribes had also been exiled together, *"And he* [i.e. the king of Assyria] *carried them away, even the Reubenites, and the Gadites, and the half-Tribe of Manasseh, and brought them unto Hala, and Habor, and Hara, and to the river Gozan, unto this day"* (1-Chronicles 5:26). The half-Tribe of Manasseh had been dominated by the clans of Gilead and Machir (1-Chronicles 2:21-23). In their places of exile Gilead became the Galatians, also known as Galaadi and Giladon and Caledonian. Machir gave rise to the Sacae Amyrgioi in Scythia from whom emerged the Skati Meruka of Scandinavia and the Mercian Saxons of England.

Both Galatians and Myrcae (Mercians) were on occasion to be identified with Goths and the Galatians also had some kind of affinity to the Franks. The Goths came from Gad and the FRANKS from Reuben and their association went back to the period prior to their exile. The name GAD may be rendered alternatively as "GOTH" in Biblical Hebrew. The sons of GAD were Ziphion, Haggi, Shuni, Ezbon, Eri, Arodi, and Areli and these are all names associated with groups who belonged either to the Gothic or Frankish confederations, with the Gothic predominating. These peoples had, on the whole, previously been in Scythia where similarly named and similarly grouped entities were reported. They had also in Scythia, Scandinavia, and the Celtic west been associated with elements from Dan, part of who settled in Denmark. The symbol of the Goths is said to have been a goat and the Zohar says that a KID (lamb or goat) represented the Tribe of GAD.

REUBEN was found amongst the Franks who had, in part, once been in Scythia east of the Caspian where they were known as Hugie. At some stage they migrated eastward and the Frankish trail from the shores of the Black Sea to Pannonia

(South Central Europe) seems to have been widely recognized. Part of the Franks was probably also for a time in Scandinavia or its immediate neighborhood. The predominant section of the Franks was the Ripuarians or "RIBUARI", as they were originally known which name is a version of REUBEN son of Israel. The sons of Reuben were Hanoch, Phallu, and Hezron, and Carmi (Genesis 46:9). Hanoch, (like Haggi son of Gad) was later to be found amongst the Chauci and Hugo-Franks; Phallu became the Falian (Falhi) Franks; Hezron (Hetsron) was ancestor to the Hessuari-Franks and Carmi as Charini settled in Frankish France and had been part of the Cimmerian forces in the Crimea. The Cimmerians gave rise to Celtic groups such as the Galatians who also settled in France. The Goths and HUGIE (ancestors to the Franks) had been neighbors, allies and acknowledged relations of the Parthians in east Scythia. In the Talmud, the Parthians were called "PARSI" like the Persians whom they ruled. The Talmud symbolizes the "PARSI" (Persians or Parthians) by a bear (Megilla xi;a) and the Merovingian Franks had a bear cult. Both the Parthians and Merovingian-Franks were friendly to the JEWS. Some of the Parthian nobility converted to Judaism*. Justin says that the name Parthian means "exiles." The Parthians comprised a ruling dynasty (ther "Arsacids") ruling over a mixed group of peoples some of whom were Scythians. In Adiabene existed a

---

* The Parthians in general and especially their rulers were related (according to Chinese sources, say McGovern and Lozinski) to the Getae. Lozinski quotes Armenian records to the effect that the Parthian forcers included Nephtalites and Massagetae. **The Massagetae in effect were Goths** as attested by the Romans (WOLFRAM). The Parthian Empire came to an end in 226 CE. Steve COLLINS (p.330) links this event with the Gothic invasion (from the east) of Roman Balkan provinces in 256 CE i.e. the Goths left the Parthian Domain and invaded the west. Collins says that the Anglo-Saxons, etc., were all part of the Gothic forces. This is simplifying the matter but more or less correct to some degree. The Parthians were a Scythian people considered to be "exiles." De GOBINEAU records that the Arsacid ruling house of Parthia in its own time was ascribed Israelite origin. A similar point may be made concerning the Goths, see A. ANDERSON, I. KORKANER, John MANDEVILLE, and ORTELLIUS. The Parthian (Pahlevi) language was a mixture of Persian and Aramaic.

Scythian-Sacae Royal House ruling autonomously under the Parthians. This house converted to Judaism, helped save Jerusalem from famine and assisted the Jews against the Romans.

The ancient Gauls called themselves "Galli." In Hebrew this can also mean "exiles." In Latin the word connotes a rooster and so a rooster became the national symbol of the French. In Jewish and general tradition a rooster is associated with the sunrise and a rising sun was one of the symbols of Reuben.

The Two and a Half-Tribes of "Gilead and Bashan" Were First-Born Tribes!

The twelve sons of Israel gave rise to twelve tribes and were the children of four different mothers and the familial arrangements arising from that situation were to become reflected in the relationships between the different tribes. The two and a half-Tribes of Reuben, Gad, and half-Manasseh (which had occupied that part of the Land of Israel east of the Jordan) were all first-born tribes. Reuben was the firstborn of Israel (1-Chronicles 5: 11) being the eldest of all the Tribes and first son of Leah; Gad was the firstborn of Zilpah, Leah's handmaiden, while half-Manasseh east of the Jordan was dominated by *"Machir the firstborn of Manasseh the father of Gilead"* (Joshua 17:1): Manasseh being the firstborn of Joseph.

Judah in Gilead

Portions from this tribal grouping are traceable to the Middle East area and to Hara (Iran) while other sections were found in Serica and in Scythia proper and after that in Western Europe. The said distribution followed a more or less sequential order since the Israelite exiles came first to the north Mesopotamian and Iranian regions and from there went north into Scythia, after which they moved on into Western Europe. Parts of some of the other tribes (such as Dan, Simeon, Naphtali) were also noticed in places adjacent to those in which descendants of Reuben, Gad, and half Manasseh were found

199

and these continguencies often were similar to those which had prevailed previously before the exile. Part of **JUDAH** had been found in the eastern portion of Manasseh and came from Yair (Jair) the son of Segub, son of Hezron, son of Pharez, son of Judah, whose group had sixty cities amongst Gilead of Machir (1-Chronicles 2: 23) and may have included *"Judah upon Jordan toward sunrising"* (Joshua 19:34) to the east of Naphtali. Other bands from Judah were to be found both in Moab (1-Chronicles 4:22) which was to the south of Reuben and also in Reuben's land itself.♥ Judaeans were also together with a contingent from the Tribe of Dan in Cilicia (southeast Turkey) and these are probably the inhabitants of *"Hamath, which belonged to Judah"* (2-Kings 14:28) referred to in Scripture. In this northern area they would have adjoined the Tribes of Asher and Manasseh and possibly also of Gad. Nevertheless, most of Judah remained within its own territory in the south adjoining Benjamin and Simeon though, also from the south, a significant portion from Judah was taken by Sennacherib, the Assyrian king, into exile and these too were to be included amongst the exiled Northern Ten Tribes.✦

♥ Yehudah KIEL, "Sepher Divrei HaYamim" ("The Book of Chronicles") Jerusalem, 1986 pp.75ff. speaks of the intermingling of several of the Israelite Tribes. He comments on 1-Chronicles 4:7 ("The son of Helah Zereth" concerning the descendants of Judah) that the name "Zereth" also occurs in Joshua 13:19 as "Zarethshahar" in the territory of Reuben. KIEL suggests that part of the Judaean family of Zerath sons of Ashur (father of Tekoa) through his wife Helah settled in the territory of Reuben.

✦ LUCKENBILL quotes (in "The Annals of Sennacherib") the boast that Sennacherib took more than 200,000 people from Judah into exile cf. *"Sennacherib king of Assyria come up against all the fenced cities of Judah and took them"* (2-Kings 18:13), and only a remnant escaped the Assyrian Captivity (2-Kings 19:30). The Chronicle of Jerahmeel (a Jewish Medieval work, from ca.1100-1150 CE.) says that most of Judah and Simeon were exiled to beyond The Mountains of Darkness on the other side of the rivers of Ethiopia (Cush). Within Jerusalem, says the Chronicle, there remained only 130,000 from the Tribes of Judah and Benjamin (see GASTER p.183). This quoted version is probably exaggerating. It does however confirm the impression (also found in other sources, such as the Midrash Seder Olam and quoted by Don Isaac Abarbanel at the end of the Book of Kings) that a large portion of Judah also went into the Assyrian exile. These were lost together with the northern Lost Ten Tribes of Israel.

PTOLEMY:
ASIATIC SARMATIA-1

HYPERBOREI-SARMATAE

HYPERBOREI MOUNTAINS

SUARDENI

ASAEI

CHAENIDES

Tanais R.

Rha R.

NAVARIS

SIRACENI

SARMATIA·

·ASIATICA·

SCYMNITAE
AMAZONES

SURANI

ASTURICAN

SACANI

TUSCI

Udon R.

SANARAEI

C. Caucasis

GERRI

COLCHIDIS

IBERI

ALBANIAE

PTOLEMY: ASIATIC SARMATIA, version 2

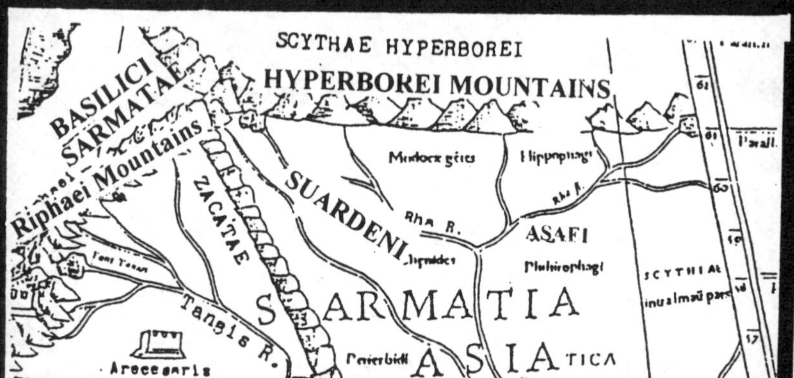

PTOLEMY EUROPEAN SARMATIA - 1

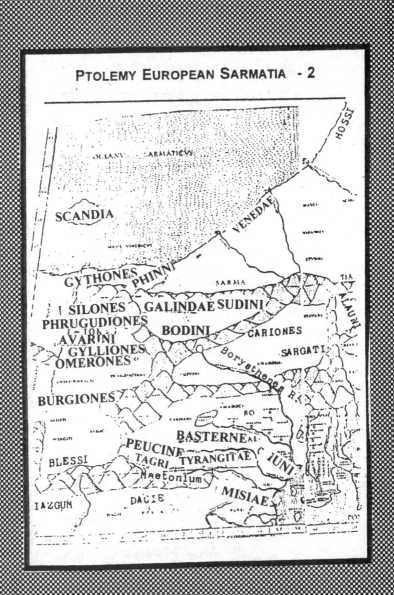
PTOLEMY EUROPEAN SARMATIA - 2

11

The Movement Westward:

Ptolemy On Asian
And European Sarmatia

King Arthur

Scott C. Littleton (*"Were Sarmatians the source of Arthurian legend"*, Archeological Journal, January/February 1997) recalls that in 175 CE the Roman Emperor Marcus Aurelius dispatched 5,500 Sarmatian Iazygs from the Danube region to garrison Hadrian's Wall in North Britain. In 184 CE Lucius Artorius Castus, commander of the Sarmatian conscripts stationed in Britain, led his troops to Gaul to quell a rebellion. When these auxiliary cataphracti (heavy cavalrymen) retired from duty they were settled near the Lancashire (in Northwest England) village of Ribchester, known in Roman times as Bremetennacum. In Professor Littleton's opinion it is from their culture that the Arthur legend originated along with the legend of the Holy Grail. According to the Encyclopedia Britannica, the Holy Grail is a round, wide vessel. French and Jewish scholars have traced the legends of King Arthur to Jewish legends concerning Moses and King David. The idea of the Holy Grail was derived from the breastplate of the High Priest that had been hidden away before the destruction of the First Temple. The breastplate was conducive to prophecy and one of its names was "Gorel" (whence we have "grail") meaning "lot". It was by means of the "Gorel" or Breastplate ("lot") that the Land of Israel had been divided amongst the Tribes (Joshua 19:1).

The Sarmatians

Who were the Sarmatians? Physically they were a group of people who looked somewhat like the previous rulers of Urartu. They dwelt besides the Scythians and eventually pushed them out to the west. Unlike the Royal Scythians and Sacae they intermarried freely with the local populace, while keeping them in a state of slavery. This slave population was of different origin but is sometimes confused with them as frequently happens in the history of this area. Whereas the Royal Scythians had been known as mounted archers the Sarmatians were heavily armored with lance and sword and their horses were also protected by armor. They were the forerunners of the mounted knights of Medieval Times. There was an overlap between the Sarmatians and Scythians and some groups of Scythian origin are classified by historians as "Sarmatian" due to cultural and geographical factors.

The Scythians had originally controlled much of the Eurasian region from the confines of China and reaching into Europe. The real Scythians were a minority ruling over others. They had eastern and western branches. Both parts of the Scythian people were known as Sacae but contemporary historians refer to the eastern section as Sacae and reserve the name Scythian for the western one. The Sacae in the east were culturally influenced by the same factors that affected the Sarmatians. The Sarmatians from the area north of the Caspian Sea began to push westward. Sarmatian pressure was one of the factors that forced the Western Scythians from north of the

Black Sea to push on into Europe. In Ptolemy's Geography the name Scythia is reserved for the eastern "Sacae" area whereas that part of Scythia north of the Black Sea is called Asiatic and European Sarmatia. Previously in the time of Herodotus (ca. 450 BCE) Sarmatia (especially the Asiatic section) had been known as "Scythia". This reflects the fact that in Ptolemy's time the Sarmatians had already pushed the western Scythians out of the region. Some later Roman records refer to Scandinavia, Holland, and Britain as Scythia. It may be that as the people moved westward so did the name of the area they dwelt in. All this may be confusing but don't worry. The most important point is tracing the migratory path of peoples of Israelite origin and for this purpose the Maps of Ptolemy are invaluable. The whole of the so-called "Sarmatian" area was later to be occupied by the Goths who together with the Sacae from the east were to be pushed westward by the Huns. The son of Elyahu of Vilna (one of the greatest and most revered Rabbinical authorities and Talmudic experts) wrote of a tradition that the Lost Ten Tribes went to Sarmatia. There was an Asiatic Sarmatia and a European Sarmatia. The River Don area had been included in the region of Sarmatia. The River Don was identified in Jewish tradition with the Sambation River on whose banks the Lost Ten Tribes had settled. The Sarmatians themselves as a people may descend from a portion of the northern Canaanites[☿]. The aristocracy of Poland identified themselves as Sarmatians and as distinct from the Polish masses. Portions of Poland were conquered by Prussia. The local rulers became Germanified and were allowed to retain their exalted status. At least 20 per cent (and maybe much more) of the Prussian aristocracy was of Polish (and ultimately of Sarmatian?) origin. **Sarmatians also settled in Hungary.**

[☿] Baruch Siger of Jerusalem identified the Sarmatians with the "Salmi" which was an Aramaic name for part of the Canaanites who dwelt in the region of Hamath in Northern Syria.

Asiatic Sarmatia

Asiatic Sarmatia in the Geography of Ptolemy was to the west of what he termed Scythia. The term "Sarmatia" was capable in local dialects of receiving several meanings one of which was "Syrians of Media." The Sarmatians were a definite people but the term "Sarmatian" could also encompass all those in the Sarmatian cultural region including the Eastern Sacae.

In Asiatic Sarmatia to the north were the **HYPERBOREAN MOUNTAINS** and to the south of these were the **ASAE**. These were a branch of the Aseir who migrated to Scandinavia. The **SUARDENI** were to be known in Sweden as the Suardenoi. They were descended from Sered son of Zebulon. The Suardeni of Sarmatia were related to the **SURANI** further south who became the Suareni of Holland. The Suardenoi of Sweden also later probably moved to the Netherlands which received a significant influx of peoples from Scandinavia. The **SIRACENI** descend from Issachar. The **UDONI RIVER** according to Pliny flowed through Udoni territory. Udoni means "The Dons," which is another way of referring to the Children of Dan.

The Assyrians had planted exiled Israelites to the south of this area in **COLCHIDIS**. Assyrian remains have been discovered in Ossetia north of the Caucasus. Some researchers (such as the late Immanuel Velikovsky) have been of the opinion that at one stage the whole of the Steppe area had been ruled by Assyrians. Diodorus Siculus writes that the Sarmatians were transplanted by the Assyrians from Media to the Steppe region. Pliny noted a people named Assyrianoi in the Crimea and the **ASTURICANI** have a name that could also mean Assyrian. The **ARBALI** may be named after Arbela which was a major center in the kingdom of Assyria.

The **SACANI** were a branch of the Sacae. The **TANAIS RIVER** was otherwise known as the Don and named after the Tribe of Dan. In early records the Don River is referred to as the Sambation and the personal name Sambation has been recorded from the Don River area. Jewish legend linked the Sambation with the Ten Lost Tribes of Israel. Scandinavian tradition said that their ancestors came from the Don River area as well as having been further east.

The **SCYMNITAE** descend from the clan of Shechem of Manasseh (Numbers 26:31). All of SARMATIA was to be dominated by the Goths before the Huns attacked them and forced other peoples to either join them or flee westward before them.

The **HENIOCHI** descend from the Hanochi clan of Reuben. The **ALBANIAE** were named after Lebanon as were Albion (Britain) and Alban (Scotland). The **IBERIAE** have a name meaning Hebrews and so too were the inhabitants of Britain named IBERNI for the same reason.

European Sarmatia

In European Sarmatia the **SALI** were in the north according to Ptolemy. These became the Salian Franks descendants of Shaul son of Simeon (Numbers 26:13). The Salian Franks in Europe merged with the Sicambri and became known by the Sicambrian name.

South of the Sali were the **AGATHYRSI** part of whom became the nucleus of the Khazar nation while another section crossed the seas to Scotland and became the leading element amongst the Picts.

The **AORSI** descend from the Israelite tribe of Asher. They are considered to have been a part of the WuSun of Central Asia and became the As of Scandinavia.

The **HOSSI** came from Hushim of Dan. Further south the **TANAITAE** were probably also known as Dani.

The **ALAUNI** were a branch of the Alans. They belong to the Aloni of Zebulon (Numbers 26:26).

The **SARGATI** relate to the Sagarti of the Middle East and Scythia. They descend from Issachar.

209

In the south were the **Cimmerian Promontory, Cimmerian Bosporus,** and the town of **Cimmeria.** All of these names testify to a Cimmerian presence at some stage.

The **CHUNI** are considered to have been an early offshoot of the Huns most of whom came westward much later. On the other hand there was Guni son of Naphtali and the Naphtalites are also referred to as "White Huns." The Huns of history have been identified with the Hsiung-nu and it may that the name "Hun" was later applied to them due to their association with the Guni of Naphtali and with the Naphtalites. Interchanges of names like this were very common in the Scythian area. Sometimes three or four entirely different peoples are registered under the same name.

The **VENEDAE** were to move into Germany and settle there en masse. They included the ANTES some of whom settled in the Ukraine while the rest also moved into Germany. The ANTES are the legendary "giants" of Scandinavian mythology. They were arch-enemies of the Aseir who settled for a while in Scandinavia but eventually became the forefathers to many in Northern England and Scotland.

The **PHINNI** came from Phuni of Issachar (Numbers 26:23) who settled both in Finland and in Switzerland.

The **GYTHONES** were Goths descendants of Gad.

The **SUDINI** were linked somehow to the Phoenician city of Sidon in Lebanon. The Tribe of Issachar conquered for a brief spell the city of Sidon though the Tribe of Asher encompassed the territory around it.

The **BASTARNAE** came from Etsbon (Genesis 46:16) son of Gad. Together with the **PEUCINI** they were termed Galatae though they marched with the Goths. Ultimately they settled in France.

The **BURGIONES** were Burgundians. The name is derived from the Hebrew "Beria-(g)h." This name ("Beriah") was given to a son of Asher (Genesis 46:17), a son of Ephraim (1-Chronicles 7:23), and a son of Benjamin (1-Chronicles 8:16).

Several groups appear to have been termed "Burgundian." The Varangians also derived their name from the Hebrew "Beria."

From **SCYTHIA** and **SARMATIA** most of these peoples were to move into Germany and Scandinavia and from there to Holland, France, Belgium, Switzerland, and the British Isles, as well as (in smaller numbers) other European states. In Roman times the term Scythia was applied to Scandinavia and Britain and it was said that the Scythians had been pushed up into those areas. On the other hand the "Barbarian" invaders of the west were also identified by the Romans as "Scythians" under different names. Conventional accounts regard these peoples as "Germanic" but this is a mistake due mainly to linguistic misunderstandings.

The Tribe of Gad became the Goths and Swedes, Reuben the Franks and Galatians of Gaul, Naphtali the Norwegians and Vikings, Zebulon the Dutch, Dan became the Danes, Simeon became the western Celts, Judah the Jews and Jutes, Benjamin the Belgae and Normans, Joseph became the Anglo-Saxons and groups associated with them as well as being found amongst the Celtic inhabitants of Britain.

[Genesis 49:21] NAPHTALI IS A HIND LET LOOSE: HE GIVETH GOODLY WORDS.

[Deuteronomy 33:23] AND OF NAPHTALI HE SAID, O NAPHTALI, SATISFIED WITH FAVOUR, AND FULL WITH THE BLESSING OF THE LORD: POSSESS THOU THE WEST AND THE SOUTH.

Israeli stamp showing the symbol of Nephtali

12

THE TRIBE OF NAPHTALI

"AND THE SONS OF NAPHTALI; JAHZEEL, AND GUNI, AND JEZER, AND SHILEM" (GENESIS 46; 24).

NAPHTALI IN THE MIDDLE EAST AND SCYTHIA:

Cadussi-Gaeli

The Tribes of Reuben, Gad, and Manasseh (from whom emerged most of the Gothic nations) on the east banks of the Jordan had been bordered by DAN and Naphtali who were to the west of them. NAPHTALI was to re-emerge under the same name **"Naphtali"** (sometimes incorrectly rendered as "EPHTHALI") in Scythia. The Naphtali were also known as Cadussi or "Kadassaye" in honor of Kadesh-Naphtali (Judges 4:6) which had been their former center in the Land of Israel. The Cadussi had first been recorded close to Mannae southwest of the Caspian Sea. The area was one of the major regions to which Northern Israelites had been transported by the Assyrians. The Apocryphal Book of Tobias mentions Israelite exiles from the Tribe of Naphtali in Ecbatana (Tobit 2:7) and Rages of Media (Tobit 5:6) both of which adjoined the Cadussii area. Pliny reported that the Cadussi termed themselves "Gaeli". The Cadussi-Gaeli were related to the Sacae Scythians according to Xenophon. [We identify the Sacae as ancestors of the Angles and Saxons who invaded Britain]. The Cadussi (or Kadussi) later moved northwards into Scythia east of the Ural mountains where they were also referred to as Naphtalites or Nephtalite Huns though some sources still referred to them as "Kadassaye" i.e. Cadussi. After a series of wars and migrations the Cadussi-Nephtalites (also known as "White Huns" and sundry other names) split up into several groups. The majority went westward and entered Scandinavia to form what later became the Danes and Norwegians. Another portion remained in Scythia to eventually merge with the Khazars who converted to Judaism.

The White Huns

The **"Naphtali"** were described by the Chinese as being of Gothic stock. The Naphtali were also known as Abdali, Ye-da, Ye-ta, Ephtha, Hua, Huones, White Huns, Thyssagetae, Little Goths, and other names. Some of the above names were actually those of subject peoples[1] with whom the Naphtalites became confused or those of peoples who occupied areas[2] associated with the Naphtalites shortly after the Naphtalites had moved out. Such confusion is frequent in Central Asian histories. The Naphtalites are also sometimes (wrongly) identified with the Kidarites[3] who were a Central Asian people of part-Arab origin whom the Assyrians had exiled.

The group identified with the Naphtalites by the Chinese are the same as the "Little-Guti"[4] as distinct from the "Great-Guti" who were the Massagetae. *"Guti" and "Goth" are different forms for the same name.* The "Little-Guti" or "Little-Goths" would have been rendered in the Gothic dialect of the Balkans as "Thyssagetae"[5]. A people called Thyssagetae were located by Herodotus in the north of Scythia in the Urals region (in present-day northeast Russia) neighboring the Iyrcae. The

IYRCAE (sometimes referred to as "Turcae") became forefathers to part of the Scandinavians and Finns of Finland. East of this area, the Cartographer Ortellius (Map of Tartaria) recorded a tradition concerning the Israelite Tribes of Dan and Naphtali. Ortelllius says that the Naphtalites were the same people who were called "White Huns". Procopius described the "White Huns" as a fair people and as entirely different from the Huns proper. East of the Naphtalites and Danes, Ortellius placed other Tribes of Israel in the approximate region of Serica on Ptolemy's Map. These other Hebrew Tribes, said Ortellius, were named "**GAUTHS**". "GAUTH" is a recognized form of the name Gaut or "Goth". The "GAUTHS" of Ortellius correspond to the Gu-te or Yueh-chi (i.e. "Great Goths") of Chinese records and to the Eastern Massagetae of Ptolemy. There were contemporary Roman Chroniclers who identified the Goths of the west with the Massagetae of the East[6]. One linguistic explanation of the name Massagetae is "Great Goths" as distinct from "Thyssagetae" or "Little Goths". Close to the Massagetae in the vicinity of Badakhshan and Tibet (where Chinese records present part of the Little-Guti as having been) local legends recorded the presence of the Israelite Tribes, Naphtali, Dan, Zebulon, and Asher.

Other Naphtalite Groups

A connection has been suggested (by Franz Altheim[7]) between the Naphtalites and a people known as "Sigins" or "Sigynnae". Strabo placed the Sigins east of the Caspian Sea and described their use of chariots drawn by swift shaggy horses. They were bordered by the Alans to their west. Herodotus (5:9) described the same people (calling them Sigynnae) and placed them in Europe north of the Danube. He mentions the same type of shaggy horse. The Sigins appear to have been scattered over great distances in the same way as the Alans were. Herodotus said that the dress of the Sigins was like that of the Medes and that they claimed to be colonists of the Medes. The exiled Israelites had been re-settled in "Cities of the Medes" (2-Kings 17:6). Archaeological findings[8] indicate that the Sigins were related to the Sequani who were located in east central Gaul and west of the Helvetti in Switzerland. Amongst the northern Belgae Caesar[9] mentions the Tribe of Segni. Similarly, Snorre said that SIGI (cf. Segni, Sigin, etc.) son of Odin received a kingdom in France. He may have been referring to a section of the Vandals who invaded France.

Chinese sources[10] indicate that a portion of the Naphtali ("Little Goths") were in Serica to the far east of Scythia. These were the SIZYGES (Sigini) mentioned by Ptolemy who were in proximity to the Damnae (of Dan), the Chatae Scythae, and the Achassa.

The "CHATAE SCYTHAE" and "ACHASSA" in Serica are reminiscent of the terms CHATTI and HESSE for a group of Franks in Western Europe. In Europe "CHATTI" and "HESSE" were considered different versions of the same name for the same people. A connection with **Hushim** (Hus-im) **of Dan** (Genesis 46:23) has been indicated: It should be remembered that Dan and Naphtali were full-brothers both sons of Israel from his concubine Bilhah and that the two brothers usually marched together. In England the Sycgs[11] were a group amongst the Saxons and settled in Essex. The Anglo-Saxon peoples had emerged from different areas of Scythia, including Serica. There was a connection between the SIZYGES of Serica East of Scythia, the SYCGS of England, the SIGINS of Europe, and the Naphtalite Huns.

The Naphtalites Move to Norway

The Chinese records say that that portion of the Naphtalites who had been to the north of China moved westward prior to 450 CE. They also say that another portion of the Little Goths (i.e. Naphtalites) had previously lived north of the Altai Mountains and were part of the "Great Goths" or Massagetae[12]. They are described as blue eyed and fair-haired.

Some of them had later come eastward towards the Great Wall of China where the Juan-juan (Avars? Huns?[13]) subjected them. They rebelled and also left for the west. The original, earlier NAPHTALITES and bulk of the Naphtalite nation who went westward and were since unheard of became the Vikings of Scandinavia, especially of **NORWAY**: Scandinavia in the 500's and 600's CE received an influx of settlers from the east[14]. This was shortly after the bulk of Naphtalites had embarked on their westward trek. In Norway during this period there was a rapid clearance of forests and the establishment of new settlements[15]. Examination of graveyards[16] revealed that the average height of the newcomers was taller than that of the previous inhabitants though culturally they may not have been much different. In Scythia, Naphtalites and Danites from DAN had been recorded together. At about this same time Denmark likewise received a large-scale immigration of people who had always regarded themselves as DANES, descendants of **"DAN the Great"**[17], meaning Dan of Israel. The wealth in quantity and quality of iron products in Scandinavia during this era of New Settlement[18] is outstanding, especially when compared to that known from the contemporary Franks and others in the south. The Naphtalites had departed from Serica and the area had been world-famous for its mineral resources and iron[19]. Metal working in the eastern Scythian region was associated with the ruling classes and the Sacae conquering peoples of Scythia, such as the Naphtalites and Khazars prior to their moving westward. In East Scythia and Serica, the working of metal has been ascribed to clans derived from, or attached somehow to, the Saka and Goths[20], with traits of shamanism reminiscent to the practices of Odin. Also names of products, such as "Solomon's swords"[21] as well as other factors[22] hint at Judaising tendencies such as are believed to have existed amongst the Naphtalites and which reached their logical conclusion in the conversion of the Khazars to whom the Naphtalites were related. The metallurgical activity of Serica and east Siberia seems to have ended fairly rapidly and may be directly traceable to the exodus of the Naphtalites. This metallurgical activity is taken up again almost without interruption in Scandinavia. Legends of Odin and Thor speak of the existence of kin and possessions in the east, in the lands of the "Turks", who have been identified as the Iyrcae neighbors of the Thyssagetae from Naphtali. The age was one of new found wealth and gold: <<The Migration Age was the great age of West Norway, with incredibly rich archaeological finds. In particular one cannot fail to note the amounts of gold. The gold that had been sparse, almost absent before that, now began to appear in large quantities>> (Keth). Eastern Scythia and Serica since the time of Herodotus had been famous as a source of gold. Scandinavian legend recorded their ancestors having been expelled from "**Yda**" in east Scythia. "Yda" or "**Yeda**" was one of the names that had been applied to the Naphtalites as well as being the name of an area east of the Caspian in which they had settled.

The art style of Scandinavia had always been similar to that of Scythia, especially the so called "Sarmatian" area east of the Caspian, but during the New Settlement era the impression is that "Sarmatian"[23] type jewelry henceforth was to be produced in Scandinavia as if it was a local cultural development. At the same time this style disappeared from the Sarmatian areas. The "Sarmatian" style had owed its origin and inherent dynamic development to the Sakae or Yeuchi-Goti (called "Tokharians" by Rostovtzieff[24]) of whom the Naphtalites were part. The migration of this style logically accompanied the movement of its originators.

The influx of population seems to have been continuous and by the 700's CE Scandinavia appears to have become overpopulated. Consequently, the excess "Vikings" of Sweden, Norway, and Denmark began their oversea excursions that led to settlement in Ireland, England, Scotland, France, and elsewhere. English historians formerly held the opinion that the

Vikings were coastal peoples who had been pushed out of Norway and Denmark by newcomers. This scenario fits the apparent migration of Naphtalites from the depths of Scythia reaching Norway at a late date.

The sons of Naphtali (Genesis 46:24) were: Jahzeel, Guni, Jezer, and Shillem. Jahzeel may be recalled in Zealand of Denmark. Culturally, the region of Zealand in Denmark had contacts with Zeeland in Holland up to the first century BCE after which the emphasis turned towards the Vandal Silingi area of Silesia[25]. In Danish Zealand itself are places known as Sjaelland, Silund, and Selund. These names are cognate to that of the Vandal-Silingi in Silesia and possibly derive from Shillem (Silem) son of Naphtali. Chieftains' graves[26] from the 200's CE in Silesia reveal pottery similar to that found in Danish Zealand, Fyne, Vendyssel (North Jutland) and from south Norway. Jezer, son of Naphtali, is connected to the Vraesan of Denmark. From the Danish isle of Fyne, the Vraesi are believed to have migrated en-masse to Britain[27]. Guni, son of Naphtali, is recalled in the Gugerni of Batavian-Holland and in the Egan of Denmark.

More on the "White Huns"

The Naphtalites were also known as the "White Huns". They were identified with the Huns with whom they associated though according to Procopius they did not mix with them. They also looked different from them: "They are the only ones among the Huns who have white bodies and countenances that are not ugly", says Procopius.

The term "Chouni" was recorded by Ptolemy north of the Black Sea. It is considered another form of the name Hun but actually may be more pertinent to the Naphtalites and derive from Guni son of Naphtali. S.G. OLSEN equated The CHUNI (Huns) with the Naphtalites who migrated to Scandinavia. "In Sweden today, the names Gunnar (masculine), Gunhild, and Gunn (feminine) are very popular and peculiar to

Scandinavia."[28]. The name "Hun" occurs in Swedish place names today. Examples given by Olsen[29] include: "Hunnehals" ("Neck of the Hun"), "Hunn", "Hunnamal", "Hunneberg" (Hun Mountain), "Hunnebostrand" ("The Beach of the Dwelling Place of the Huns" between Norway and Denmark), "Hunnerstad" ("Town of the Huns", two places with the same name), and "Huno" (Hun Island). In Norway there is "Hunndalen" ("The Valley of the Huns"). That the Huns or peoples associated with them once ruled over Scandinavia and settled in parts of it is a possibility that is frequently raised in Scandinavian archaeological and historical studies.

Norway Named after the Neuri

Olsen quotes Dalin, "Svea Rikes Historia (1747-1762) to the effect that Norway was named after the Neuri. According to Dalin Scandinavia was populated by the Scythian peoples "Vodini (Budini), Geloni, and Neuri. The Neuri were "a mixture of Scythians, Greeks, and Hebrews". Amongst the Neuri "were to be found remnants from the Ten Tribes of Israel whom Salmanassar, the king of Assyria, took captive from Canaan" [30]. The Neuri according to Dalin derived their name from "Nuori" which in the Lapp and Finnish tongues means "son" and originally came from the Hebrew "Naar" meaning "youth". In the Hebrew Bible the term "Naar" or "Naarim" (plural) is used for "youths in training" in the service of the King. Joseph was called a "naar" (Genesis 37:2); So were Moses (Exodos 2:6), Joshua (Exodus 33:11), David (1-Samuel 17:42), and Solomon (1-Chronicles 22:5). Israel in general is also referred to as a "naar": "WHEN ISRAEL WAS A CHILD [HEBREW: "NAAR"], THEN I LOVED HIM, AND CALLED MY SON OUT OF EGYPT". It may be a coincidence but the Norwegians were treated as "Naarim" for much of their history by Danish and Swedish rulers and by their own ruling class, i.e. not suppressed but as if they were in need of direction and from whom deference was expected and usually obtained.

The Symbols of Naphtali:

The Deer and the "Speakers". Odin and Thule.

[GENESIS 49:21] NAPHTALI IS A HIND [FEMALE DEER] LET LOOSE: HE GIVETH GOODLY WORDS.

A deer or stag was a popular symbol in Scandinavia.

The Naphtalites were linked with the Danes in the same way that Dan and Naphtali were the two sons of Bilhah maidservant of Rachel: The Danes and Naphtalites may be connected with the legend of Odin. Odin was a mythical leader of people who migrated from the Black Sea shores and the Don River estuary to Scandinavia and the West. Lars Ims reported:
<<Odin has been around a lot longer ....but maybe not as a warrior god. Thor and Tyr seems to be older warrior gods than Odin, even though they also may have had different functions at earlier stages of Norse or Germanic religion. I think it would be more fruitful to follow what we may call the thul-connection to understand Odin's early life. The Greek traveler Pytheas from Massilia [Marseilles in Southeast France] traveled along the coast of what is now known as Norway perhaps as far north as Bodo around 330 BC, and he called that land Thule, which a Norse scholars like Ottar Groenvik understands as "the land of the Thuls" or "the Thul land". If he is right, that would definitely connect Odin to an early stage of Norse religion, since Odin is both called "the old thul" and "the great thul" (Fimbulthul). The word means "speaker" in Old English, and Odin's pulpit or speaker's chair is referred to as "the chair of the thul" in Mnemonic lists of word synonyms are called thulur in Old Icelandic literature. From all this we might conclude that Odin as the thul is a cultic or religious speaker whose lore is knowledge such as runes and other intellectual skills. We may assume that in this early stage of his life, Odin is more a god of wisdom than anything else, and that he only later assumed the functions of other gods such as the martial aspect. Odin is after all not an active warrior in the myths. He himself only partakes in the

first and last battles of the world, when he initiates the Aesir-Vanir war by throwing his spear over the opposing army, and when he fights the Fenrir wolf and dies during Ragnarok. Thor, on the other hand, is always off somewhere in the east to fight the giants. Odin's main interest seems to lie in procuring knowledge at any cost, and this may reflect his earlier and perhaps truer self. .>>

Various interpretations have been given for the name of Odin: In the Caucasus area the name could mean The Dan and later Odin in Scandinavian Danish tradition was identified with Dan the Great ancestor of the Danes. Odin was explained by Isaac Mozeson ("The Word", 1989) to be a form of the Hebrew Adon meaning "lord" and one of the titles of Joseph (Genesis 44:30,33 translated as "lord").

Sometimes one name can have several meanings, or it can have one original meaning but receives additional meanings when it is interpreted according to the different language areas its bearer finds himself among. This is actually quite common. According to the above article by Lars Ims the concept of "Odin" is connected. with the acquisition of knowledge. We would suggest that the name "Odin" is derived from the Hebrew "Da" or "Yeda" meaning knowledge, knowing, make know. This root in different dialects could be pronounced as "don" or "Ydon" and confused with the proper name "Dan". We see from above that the name and personality of Odon were associated with knowledge. Norway was known as "Thule". P. Senstius (1931) suggested that Thule is a shortened form of Nafthali[31]. At all events we have located Naphthali in Norway. The above note says that not only Norway but also the people of Norway were called Thuls and that this word means Speaker. <<Odin is both called "the old thul" and "the great thul" (Fimbulthul). The word means "speaker" in Old English>>

<<The Greek traveler Pytheas from Massilia (Marseille) traveled along the coast of what is now known

222

as Norway perhaps as far north as Bodo around 330 BC, and he called that land Thule, which a Norse scholars like Ottar Groenvik understands as "the land of the Thuls" or "the Thul land".>>

Are these the goodly words that Naphtali speaks?

[Genesis 49:21] NAPHTALI IS A HIND LET LOOSE: HE GIVETH GOODLY WORDS.

Naphtali in the Light of Rabbinical Sources

The name Naphtali in Hebrew can connote "union" or "joining" or "wrestling".

AND BILHAH RACHEL'S MAID CONCEIVED AGAIN, AND BARE JACOB A SECOND SON.

AND RACHEL SAID, WITH GREAT WRESTLINGS HAVE I WRESTLED WITH MY SISTER, AND I HAVE PREVAILED: AND SHE CALLED HIS NAME NAPHTALI [Genesis 30:7-8].

Naphtali is the messenger and as such liable to be influenced (for better or for worse) by outside influences[32]. Reket (Tiberias by the sea of Galilee) was in the territory of Naphtali and it is in that region where according to tradition the future Messianic Kingdom of Israel will begin. The spies who brought back a bad report concerning the Land of Israel had been selected from all of the Tribes but those from the Tribes of Naphtali and Asher were the chief instigators[33].

The **Oslo Agreements** (1993-1996) and what led up to them and from them showed a lack of faith in the Israelite right to the land of Canaan. The people of Naphtali should repent. They were partly responsible for the Oslo betrayal that caused the death of many in Judah and much suffering and threatened all Israel with a diminution of sovereignty or worse over the Promised Land. Jews were forbidden to settle in Norway until 1851. Despite this, leading Norwegian thinkers were strongly sympathetic towards the Jewish people. Norway was also very pro-Israel and Zionistic up until the 1970s. Descendants of

Norwegians (and of Scandinavians in general) in the USA were amongst the strongest supporters of Israel.

The Blessing of Israel

According to UN reports Norway for several years running was considered to have the best standard of living in the world and is still in the running. Norwegian prosperity is based on farming, fishing, and petroleum resources. Norway has about 4,500,000 inhabitants.

Norwegian History

500 BC Bronze Age, agricultural tools, jewellery, glass, weapons. 500 BC - 800 AD Iron Age, iron ploughs and scythes.

800 AD - 1050 AD Viking Age, longships, trade and conquest, runic inscriptions, voyages of discovery, Leif Eiriksson discovers America. 900 AD Norway united into one kingdom.

1030 Christianity adopted in Norway.

1100 - 1200 Monarchy controls the church, slavery abolished.

1350 The Black Death reduces the population by almost two-thirds. 1380 - 1536 Union with Denmark through royal intermarriage.

1536-1814 Norway ruled by Denmark.

1814 Norway becomes independent. The Norwegian Constitution adopted, based on the American Declaration of Independence. 1814 - 1905 Union with Sweden.

1905 End of Union. Haakon VII crowned king.

1913 Norway is among the first in the world to grant women suffrage.

1940 - 1945 World War II, Norway occupied by Germany. Norwegian resistance was impressive but Nazi sympathizers (led by Quisling) were also present.

1970 Oil and gas deposits discovered off the Norwegian coast.

1993-1996 The Oslo Agreements: Norwegian diplomacy working with Israeli left wingers and freethinkers managed to arrange agreements with Palestinian terrorists that would give avowed Arab murderers autonomy and an armed presence in the territories of Judah and Samaria. Consequently many innocent Jews were killed or maimed in addition to which there were many Arab casualties that would have been avoided if it were not for the sin of Oslo. Partly as a result of the Oslo Agreements and what grew out of them anti-Semitism increased throughout the world, including in Norway.

The Three Divisions of Israel

The Israelite Tribes may be considered to be divided into three sections:

1. Those headed by the sons of Leah such as Judah from whom comes the Messiah son of David.

2. Those headed by the sons of Rachel from whom comes the Messiah son of Joseph.

3. Those headed by the sons of the handmaidens from whom come the Preparers of the Way such as Elijah from the Tribe of Gad[34].

The Israelite Tribe of Naphtali became the Nephtali-Huns (or "Hephtalites" as they are also called) who together with the Dani were once in east Scythia. From east Scythia the Naphtali migrated to Norway and the Danes to Denmark. This is proven by Scandinavian tradition, by tracing names, by demographic considerations, and by archaeological finds.

"THE RIVER WHICH SINCE THE END OF WORLD WAR-II MARKS THE BORDER BETWEEN NORWAY AND RUSSIA IS CALLED GRANSE JAKOBS ELV WHICH MEANS JACOB'S BORDER RIVER," -ORJAN SVENNSON

PEOPLES OF NAPHTALI

Naphtali

Kaddussi- Cadusians, related to the Sacae in Western Iran but later were found to the north. They were also known as Gaeli. The name derives Kadesh-Naphtali (Judges 4:6).

Naphtalite-Huns = Thyssagetae of east Scythia, =Sian Yueh-chi i.e. "Little Goths".

Thule (Norway).

Clans of Nephtali:

Jahzeel = Zeeland (Holland), Zealand (Denmark), Yssel (Scandinavia).

Guni = Egan (Norway), Gugerni (Holland), Chouni (Huni, Huns of Scandinavia etc.)

Jezer = Jassar (Alans); Vraesi (Denmark, emigrated en-masse to Britain).

Shillem = Sillingae (amongst the Vandals, Holland, and Scandinavia).

13

THE TRIBE OF DAN

"And the sons of Dan; Hushim" Genesis 46:23.

"These are the sons of Dan after their families: of Shuham, the family of the Shuhami. These are the families of Dan after their families" Numbers 26:42.

Character appraisals of Dan in tradition appear contradictory. One source (Talmud, Shabat 67) says that all the children of Dan were idolaters. It also says that Dan received the north side "whence darkness comes". A Midrash states that Samson the legendary judge hero had a Danite father and a mother from Judah whereas the future Messiah will have a father from Judah and a mother from Dan or from Naphtali (Genesis Rabah 98:13). Aholiab of the Tribe of Dan assisted Betzaleel of the Tribe of Judah in building the Tabernacle in the Wilderness (Exodus 31:2-6). Commentators said that this comes to show us that the future redemption requires the participation of all sections of the Israelite nation.

The mother of Dan was Bilhah (Genesis 30:6) who also bore Naphtali. Dan and Naphtali are often linked with each other. Bilhah was the maidservant of Rachel mother of

Benjamin and Joseph, and here too parallelisms are noticeable. The Tribe of Dan when it came out of Egypt with the rest of the Children of Israel was, after Judah, the most populous of Israelite Tribes with 62,700 males between the ages of 20 and 60 apart from women, children, and the elderly (Numbers 2:26).

The son of Dan was called "Hushim" (Genesis 46:23) who gave rise to the Danite clan known also as Shuhami (Numbers 26:43).

Eldad HaDani (ca.880 CE) quoted an old legend according to which the Tribe of Dan left the Land of Israel after the Ten Tribes separated themselves from Judah. The Northern Ten Tribes under Jeroboam ben Nebat warred against Judah in the south and so Dan rather than engage in a fratricidal struggle went into voluntary exile[1]. Jewish Rabbinical tradition said that: "In the period of the Judges there were wars and many were exiled among the nations of the world" (HaNatziv, Num.24;7).

"DAN SHALL JUDGE HIS PEOPLE, AS ONE OF THE TRIBES OF ISRAEL. DAN SHALL BE A SERPENT BY THE WAY, AN ADDER IN THE PATH, THAT BITES THE HORSE'S HEELS, SO THAT HIS RIDER SHALL FALL BACKWARD. I WAIT FOR THY SALVATION, O LORD" (GENESIS 49:16 - 17).

"AND OF DAN, HE SAID, DAN IS A LION'S WHELP THAT LEAPS FROM BASHAN" (DEUTERONOMY 33:22).

LESHEM-LAISH

The Book of Judges (chapter 18) relates how 600 men from Dan in the south went north and found a place named Laish whose inhabitants lived like Sidonian-Phoenicians. They conquered Laish, wiped out the inhabitants, and renamed the place Dan.

The Book of Joshua related a very similar account:
"AND THE COAST OF THE CHILDREN OF DAN WENT OUT [(TOO LITTLE)] FOR THEM: THEREFORE THE CHILDREN OF DAN WENT UP TO FIGHT AGAINST LESHEM, AND TOOK IT, AND SMOTE IT

228

WITH THE EDGE OF THE SWORD, AND POSSESSED IT, AND DWELT THEREIN, AND CALLED LESHEM, DAN, AFTER THE NAME OF DAN THEIR FATHER" (JOSHUA 19:47).

Both versions relate how the inheritance of the children of Dan in the south was either too small for them (Joshua ch.18) or how they had not taken possession of that which had been allocated to them (Judges ch.19). Both tell how the Danites went north seized a city, slew its inhabitants and re-settled it naming it after DAN their father. Nevertheless LESHEM and LAISH were two different places!

"Leshem" means a precious stone (maybe amber) whereas "Liash" means "a young lion". The place called Leshem and renamed Dan in the Book of Joshua was the site of DAN in Northern Galilee otherwise known as Daphne. On the other hand, LAISH which was also renamed DAN and is recalled in the Book of Judges (ch.19) was otherwise known as LUASH of the DANANU! LUASH belonged to Smal of Cilicia in modern Southeast Turkey. This region (of Liash-Dan) was known in ancient times as the Kingdom(s) of Smal of the Dananu and of Yadi and of Luash and Hamath. It encompassed the areas in Ptolemy's Map (of Arabia Deserta and Syria) depicting Chalybonitis, Cyrrestica, Commagena, Cilicia, and extending into Armenia Minor. To the east and southeast of this area were the territories of Bathanaei and the Kingdom of Bathanaea. Bathan is an Aramaic ("Syrian") pronunciation of BASHAN. Moses had blessed the Tribe of Dan: <<*Dan is a lion's whelp, he shall leap* **from Bashan**>> (Deuteronomy 33:22). The area of Luash (Liash) was part of Bashan. "LIASH" means young male lion and therefore connects with the expression "Dan is a lion's whelp", i.e. Dan is a young lion, a **"Liash"**, leaping forth from the Bashan: Luash-Liash is a geographical extension, a "leaping forward" from the area denoted as Bathan or Bashan. Near Luash was the entity of Yadi which was an enclave of Judaeans adjoining the Dananu of Smal and usually ruled by the same monarch. The Bible mentions Yair of Judah

(Deuteronomy 3:14) in the Bashan. Yair was connected both with Manasseh and with the Chelubie of Judah. The Chelubie are recalled in Chalybonitis which was to the Northwest of Bathanae (Bashan) on Ptolemy's Map. Yair was mentioned in Assyrian inscriptions as the IARI in the region of Chalybonitis and the surrounding area (including at times in Gauzanitis and elsewhere) raiding and waging wars on both sides of the Euphrates River[2]. Yadi was settled by the IARI of Judah and these were united with the Dananu i.e. Danites from Dan. The name Yair is often transliterated as "Jair" (Deuteronomy 3:14).

In both accounts (The Book of Joshua and The Book of Judges) the Danites conquered and re-settled a city which they renamed DAN "after the name of their forefather Dan" (Joshua 19:47 Judges 18:47). This may reflect a Tribal characteristic and some have interpreted the phrase "*Dan shall be a serpent by the way, an adder in the path*" (Genesis 49:16) as referring to a Tribal Trait of leaving their namesake everywhere along the path they went just as a snake leaves the trail of his crawling in the dust of the path, e.g. "Mahaneh Dan" (Judges 18:12), Dan, Dananu, Danaoi, Don, Daneister, Danaper, Danube, Denmark, Dana, Dannonia.. The king of Sma'al in the valley north of ASI (Orontes embouchement) on the edge of LUASH (LIASH) called himself "KING of the DANIM"[3]. The Danes (Dananu) also controlled the neighboring area of Cilicia and at one stage their capital was Adana by Tarsis of Cilicia and their suzerainty reached as far north as Karatepe in Central Turkey. A bi-lingual inscription of the Dananu found at Karatepe employs a Phoenician type of Hebrew and a version of Hittite. Thanks to this inscription the Dananu of Cilicia are identifiable with the people of Mopsus of Anatolia. Mopsus was also known as Moxus and is a variation of the name Moses. The northern portion of Dan is referred to variously as Dananu, Danau, Denye, Denyen, Danuna. They are identical with the Danaioi of Classical Greek writings. The Dananu ruled Cyprus which was named "Yadnana" ("Isle of the Dana") in their honor. Other sources indicate a strong Israelite influence in Cyprus at that time and later. Culturally Cyprus was very much a Phoenician island. This shows the possibility of an overlap between Dan and the Phoenicians.

Dan and Greece

The Tribe of Dan in the land of Israel were seafarers from an early stage:

"*Why did DAN remain in ships?*" (Judges 6:7) asked the Prophetess Deborah.

The Prophet Ezekiel linked Dan together with Javan (i.e. Ionia in west Anatolia or Greece in general) as trading with Phoenician Tyre:

"*Dan also and Javan going to and fro occupied in the fairs: bright iron, cassia, and calamus, were in thy market*" (Ezekiel 27:19).

The above verse is alternatively translatable (from the Hebrew) as saying:

"*Dan and Yavan from Uzzal were your sub- contracting intermediaries, they gave iron manufactured, alloyed, and in bars. They were amongst your guarantors*" (Ezekiel 27:19).

Cilicia was one source of iron and the Dananu were in Cilicia.

Danaus: Greek tradition related how Danaus after coming out of Egypt came with his daughters to Greece whereas his brothers went to Jerusalem. In Greece the daughters of Danaus intermarried with the local aristocracy and their children became rulers. In honor of Danaus the local Pelasgian Ionian Greeks renamed themselves DANAIOI by which term the early Greeks are often referred to by Homer.

"*Danaus, the father of fifty daughters on coming to Argos took up his abode in the city of Inarchos and throughout Hellas [i.e. Greece] he laid down the law that all people hitherto named Pelasgians were to be named Danaans*" (Strabo 5.2.40 quoting Euripides).

231

Diodorus Siculus (i;28;1 5): *"They say that those who set forth with Danaus, likewise from Egypt, settled what is practically the oldest city of Greece, Argos, and that the nations of the Colchi in Pontus and that of the Jews, which lies between Arabia and Syria, were founded as colonies by certain emigrants from their country"*

The early settlers of Greece and of Western Turkey (Ionia) included the Pelasgians. The Philistines are believed to have been of the same stock as the Greek Pelasgians and the term "PELAST" (meaning Philistine) in early Greek inscriptions is interchangeable for Pelasgian. The struggle of the Danites with the Philistines within the Land of Israel may be somehow connected with the coming of the Danaoi to Greece. There is an opinion that the Danaioi formed a peculiar military class amongst the Mycenean Greeks[4]. The Greek account may be understood as saying that a small number of DANITES came to Greece, intermarried with local rulers, gave their name to an early already present segment of the population, and not much more than that. Archaeologists now believe that an offshoot of the Hyksos, about the time when they were expelled from Egypt came to Greece, conquered it, and laid the basis for Mycenean civilization. They identify these Hyksos with the Danaioi of Greek tradition. This version also infers that the Danaioi were relatively few in numbers though qualitatively determinative[5]. The Hyksos were foreign rulers of Egypt who came from Canaan and in Egyptian tradition were expelled about the time when Scripture says the Exodus took place. In another work ("Lost Israelite identity" by Yair Davidy) we have identified a good portion of the Hyksos with Israelites.

Daphne and Mopsus

The Dananu of Cilicia were to be connected in Greek Mythology with a hero named Mopsus. Mopsus in turn was linked with Daphne and Apollo. The legendary Daphne was the supposed mother of Mopsus and she had established the colony of Colophon in Ionia. Ionia was in Western Anatolia (modern Turkey) opposite Greece. Most of Ionia belonged to Javan and the two names ("Yavan" and "Ionia") are essentially the same. To the east of Ionia was originally a Hittite Empire which was destined to be destroyed and ultimately replaced by Lydians and Phrygians and others. The time of destruction of the Hittite Empire was around that of the Dorian invasions of Greece, the Sea peoples' attacks on Egypt and maybe the destruction of Troy. Troy was to the southwest of Ionia. Troy overlooks the Hellespont (Dardanelles) where according to Saxo Grammaticus there once existed a settlement named Dan whence the Danites sailed to Scandinavia.

Apollo was originally a Hittite thunder god[6] who in Greek Mythology through Daphne fathered Mopsus[7]. From his base in Colophon (Ionia) Mopsus joined a group returning from the Trojan War. Mopsus founded colonies in Southern Anatolia (Aspendus) and in Cilicia[8]. Strabo (14;4;3) said that the Tribe of Mopsus invaded the eastern Mediterranean area and settled the coasts of Cilicia, Syria, and Phoenicia. Mopsus wandered about with his band of warriors, was famous for his riddles, and according to Xanthus died in Ashkelon of snakebite[9]. The Danite hero, Samson was also famous for his riddles (Judges 15:12), and gave his life apparently in Gaza (Judges 16:21) which like Ashkelon was a Philistine city. Samson's death was caused by his deliberately collapsing the two supporting pillars of the building he was in, in order to destroy its occupants at that moment. The movement of the Danites from the south to the north either took place in the time of Samson or shortly afterwards. The figure of Mopsus (Moxus) came to represent the founder of the Northern Danite entity. The name "Mopsus" is derived from that of Moses though Mospus was ascribed (in Greek accounts) the attributes of Sasmson. Mopsus died from a snake bite and in Talmudic tradition Samson's death was likened to that of a snake that bites the horse's heel in order to kill the rider but is himself crushed by the horse collapsing upon him.

"DAN SHALL BE A SERPENT BY THE WAY, AN ADDER IN THE PATH, THAT BITES THE HORSE'S HEELS, SO THAT HIS RIDER SHALL FALL BACKWARD" (GENESIS 49:17).

The Talmud (Jerushalemi Sotah 9;b-10;a) adduced additional reasons for likening Samson to a snake by the wayside which strengthen the similarity between Mopsus and Samson of Dan.

The Tribe of Dan as described in the Bible may also well be likened to a wandering group of warriors. The Northern Danites were the people of Mopsus who settled along the coasts of Syria, Phoenicia, and Cilicia and from one point of view these places are merely different parts of the Land of Israel. The mother of Mopsus was called Daphne and "Daphne" according to Josephus was the name given to a spot at the head reaches of the Jordan River on which the centre of DAN IN THE GALILEE was founded. It was on this spot that King Jeroboam ben Nebat set up one of his golden calves for the Ten Tribes to worship (1-Kings 12:29). The Geographical location of Dan (also known as "Daphne"!) in the Galilee contains a spring which is one of the sources of the River Jordan. Greece was conquered from the Myceneans by the Dorians who claimed to be remnants of the ancient Danaioi. The Heraclidae (Sons of Hercules) who led the Dorian invasion of Greece believed themselves descended from Hercules and a slave girl named JARDANUS (Herodotus 1;7). This name is derived from the Hebrew "Jordan". One Talmudic explanation of the name for the Jordan River was "Descend (Yored) from Dan".

The Dananu were at first centered in Smal to the east of Cilicia. In the 700s the center of the Dananu moved to Adana in Cilicia though Smal remained important. Dananu suzerainity stretched to the north in East Anatolia and reached at least to Karatepe[10] to the north of Cilicia. After the destruction of the Hittite Empire, small neo-Hittite states had arisen in Northern

Syria. They were of Hittite culture and influenced the Dananu. On the site of former Dananu center of Karatepe has been found a bi-lingual text using both a Hittite tongue and a form of Phoenician-Hebrew[11]. The King of Karatepe identifies himself as ruler of the Dananu and says he is descended from "the house of MPS". This appellation ("MPS") has been equated with the Greek rendition of MOPSUS. At all events, MOPSUS was considered a term of royalty in the Cilician area[12] and an important region (by the coast) was known as "Mopsopia".

"MOPSOS" appears also to have been a title given to the idol SANDON who was equated with Hercules and worshipped in Cilicia. The name Sandon is a dialectical version of Samson[13]. Legends concerning Hercules are based on identical themes to those in the story of Samson[14]. The Greeks said that Hercules was the great grandson of Perseus and Perseus was a descendant of Danaus of Greek Mythology. According to legend Hercules conquered the city of Jaffo in the Land of Israel and married Andromeda the daughter of the King of Ethiopia who then ruled there. Jaffo was the area originally bequeathed to the Tribe of Dan and which the Tribe of Dan unsuccessfully attempted to conquer and settle before directing their attentions elsewhere.

An Early Exile of Northern Dan?

Judges (chapter 17) says that when the Danites took Laish they took with them a graven image. This idol had formerly been in the house of Micah in the territory of Ephraim. It had been attended to by a Levite named Yehonathan who previously had promised their emissaries a successful mission. The Danites in their journey northward also took Yehonathan the Levite along with the idol and assorted appurtenances used in the idolatrous (or semi-idolatrous) cult. As recounted, the Danites conquered Laish, burnt it, and renamed it DAN after *"their father who was born to Israel"* (Judges 18:39).

"And the children of Dan set up the graven image; and Jonathan the son of Gershom, the son of Manasseh, he and his sons were priests to the tribe of Dan until the day of the captivity of the land" (Judges 18:40).

[In the Hebrew Bible the text indicates that Manasseh should be read as Moses. Only one letter (N) in the Hebrew text distinguishes between Manasseh and Moseh (Moses). The Hebrew text has the letter (N) in the name Manasseh (Judges 18:40) in an elevated position from the other letters in the word*. This is the only place in the Bible were the letters are consistently arranged in this way. The reason traditionally is in order to tell us that Yehonathan, the Levite Priest, was descended from Moses. The Dananu revered Mopsus (Moxus, Moses) as the founder of their nation.

Was there an early exile of Dan? We have seen above that different sources state that at least part of Dan left the land at an early date. What does Scripture say?

"AND THEY SET THEM UP MICAH'S GRAVEN IMAGE, WHICH HE MADE, ALL THE DAYS THAT THE HOUSE OF GOD WAS IN SHILOH" (JUDGES 18: 31).

Shiloh and the Tabernacle were destroyed by the Philistines in about 1000 BCE. The above verse seems to link the time of "**the captivity of the land**" (Judges 18:40) with the presence of the Tabernacle at Shiloh[15] (Judges 18: 31) i.e. until about 1000 BCE. The Hebrew original for "**captivity of the land**" is "Galut Ha-aretz" or literally, 'The Exile of the Country'. It follows that part of the Tribe of Dan may have been exiled already in ca.1000 BCE. Also in the south (around Jaffo) there appears to have been an early evacuation or exile of the Danites.

---

* Manasseh [מנשה] and Moseh [משה] (Moses). The Hebrew text has the letter (N) in the name Manasseh (Judges 18:40) an elevated position from the other letters in the word: [מ'שה] instead of [מנשה].

236

DAN IN THE GALILEE (Leshem)

The Tribe of Dan specialized in metallurgy. Aholiab (Exodus 31:6) and Hiram (2-Chronicles 2:3) who were expert artisans and metal workers both are came from the Tribe of Dan. Archaeological findings reveal the existence in Dan of the Galilee of a metal industry dating from the Time of Israelite Conquest (Late Bronze Age) to at least the 800s BCE. This industry specialized at first mainly in bronze and afterwards also in iron. Bronze is an alloy of copper and tin both of which in the Egyptian period were obtainable from the Sinai Peninsula. Other areas in Israel also supply copper as did Cilicia and the Caucasus area. Much of the tin (possibly the greater part) came from Britain. Herodotus (ca.450 BCE) gives the impression that all the tin of his time was produced in British Isles. An interruption in the supply of tin (making Bronze production most difficult) is believed to have induced the Iron Age in this area[16]. Iron was available from Cilicia and elsewhere. The Sea Peoples (with whom the Dananu were associated) were sophisticated copper smelters and workers[17].

Dan in the Galilee was destroyed in the 800s BCE by attacks from the Aramaean kingdoms to the north. Part of an inscription in Archaic Aramaic has been found on the site of Dan in the Galilee: From what can be understood from this inscription it may be inferred that the Aramaic (Syrian) monarch is stating that formerly the Israelites had been in the land of his father. Guided by the storm god Hadad (a form of Baal) he (i.e. the king of Syria) came against Israel and slew many including a King of Israel who was descended (he says) from the House of David. The Syrian king apparently laid waste to Dan. Dan in the Galilee is known to have been attacked by the Syrian monarch ben Hadad in 815 BCE and after that was unheard of.

Dan in Cyprus

The Egyptians counted the Dananu-Danites amongst the Peoples of the Sea. They connected the Dananu primarily with the areas north of the Orontes River[18] on the north Syrian coast, with Cilicia, and with CYPRUS[19], and according to Ed.Meier also with Crete[20]. These regions together with the Phoenician coast could all be called "Keftiu" by the Egyptians though this term was more often applied specifically to the isles. The Bible says that the Phillistines came from Caphtor which is believed to mean Cyprus. The Danites conquered CYPRUS and the Assyrians referred to the island as "YADNANA" meaning "Isle of the Dananu"[21]!

The Phoenicians mined tin in Cornwall and brought back walrus' tusk from Scandinavia[22]. The Dananu had had a Phoenician culture overlaid with Mycenean Greek and Anatolian influence.

North European Cyprus

The Assyrians in the time of Sargon (722-705) claimed to have conquered "Kaptara" (meaning Caphtor or Keftiu) and "Anaku" (The Land of Tin") which were in the Atlantic Ocean.

An Egyptian text mentioned a "Keftiu" in the far north where sea and sky meet[23]. Another Egyptian passage speaks of "Keft Heran" in connection with "Utur", the Great Sea[24] which can mean the Atlantic Ocean. An additional Egyptian source describes Keftiu and the Island in the midst of the sea as being the country farthest west known to Egypt[25] and the Egyptians did know of Britain and the North Sea coast. Keftiu is described as a tin importer[26], as a centre of metallurgical enterprise, the "home of the smith god"[27], and as an exporter of metal work. A land reachable only by sea yet not an island[28].

Bronze Age swords from Denmark have been found in Egypt. From the same period, amber from the Scandinavian ambit turned up on Crete. Things made out of Irish gold were found in excavations of ancient Crete and Philistine Gaza.

In Scandinavia during the Bronze Age there existed a highly developed civilization rich in metallurgical and gold products of a high standard which produced articles of furniture and implements similar to, or identical with, those known from contemporary Egypt, Phoenicia, and Mycenaean Greece. This civilization came to an end between 500 BCE and 400 BCE due to a sudden climatic change which was accompanied by upheavals and foreign invasions. The cultural standard of the populace quickly declined and the population of the region steadily dwindled[29]. Eventually Scandinavia would be re-populated by newcomers who emerged from Scythia.

Irish legends spoke of the Tribe of Dana (Tuatha De Danaan) who were renowned metallurgists, and scientifically adept. They arrived from the "northern isles" after some disaster[30], the only "northern isles" as far as Ireland is concerned are those of Scandinavia. The Tribe of Dana, said the Irish sources had originally come from the region of Mount Lebanon,[31] it had sojourned in Greece[32], been enslaved, fought with the "Phillistines", and then fled north after which it had come to Ireland. Welsh legends also spoke of the Children of Don who paralleled the Tribe of Dana.

Dan came to the north in two major waves. Shortly after the exile of the Ten Tribes Danites entered Scandinavia and from there they moved to the British Isles possibly after a sojourn in Western Gaul. These Danites were associated with the early "Megalithic" culture of the Atlantic West that was absorbed by Celtic Civilization. Much later another group of Danites emerged from Scythia, entered Scandinavia, and also moved westward to the British Isles.

Dan with Gad and Naphtali

The historical appearance of groups derived from Dan somehow linked with the Gothic forces was referred to in the chapter on Gad. Danites were also found together with the Naphtalites of Naphtali who were also described above.

Dan amongst the Celts. Dan in Wales, Ireland, Scotland, and Northern England

In Ancient Times in the Land of Israel the Tribe of Dan had been divided into several different sections. One section had been in the Northern Galilee (Joshua 19: 42) and neighbored Gad. The Damnae in Serica (east of Scythia), were also called "Dingling" and were linked to the "DANGALAI" whose name means "DAN-OF-GALILEE". They had been neighbors of the Goths (from Gad) of Gadrosia in Ancient Eastern Iran. The DAMNAE of Scythian Serica were named similarly to the DAMNONII of Scotland (who lived besides the northern River DON of Scotland) and the British DAMNONES of DANNONIA which was the name given to Devon and Cornwall[33]. DANNONIA was named after the Tribe of DAN. The Tribe of Dan was recalled in the Children of DON in Welsh legend and the Tribe of DANA who came to the British Isles (according to Irish tradition) from the Land of Israel via Greece and Scandinavia[34]. The area Damnonia in southern Britain was alternatively called Dannonia and "Defenia"[35]. The name "DEFENIA" is similar to that of DAPHNIA which was the former place of DAN in the Land of Northern Israel (Josephus, Wars 4;11), and is also a name associated by the Talmud (Jerus. San. ch.17, L.6,29,2, Num. Rab.16) with the Lost Ten Tribes. In Ireland (circa 500 CE) there were the Fir Domnan (People of Domnan) in the North-West (Connact). This area of Ireland (of the Fir Domnan) traditionally had previously belonged to the Tuatha De Danann. The name Tuatha De Danann means "People of Dan". Some Irish traditions distinguish between the Domnu (Dumnonii) and the Dana. The Domnu are linked with the Fomorians who came before the Dana and with the Fir Bolg who came afterwards. They also say that the Domnu came from the area Normandy in Gaul whereas the Dana came from further North. Since however Domnu is another form of Dan or Dana and they Domnonii and Dana were recorded as having occupied the same regions we may safely side with those accounts that identify the two peoples as one.

In Scotland the Damnonii (of Dan) adjoined the Gadeni (probably of Gad) and somewhat to the south (in Northern England) according to Ptolemy was the city of Danum which area was later to be occupied by Danes from Denmark. In this case we see the possibility of a group of Celtic culture descended from Dan who gave their name to the city of Danum being followed by Scandinavians who were also descended from Dan and settling in the same area. We have come across similar phenomena several times in this study.

Dan amongst the Vikings

Danes from Dan were recorded together with the Naphtali in Scythia. From Scythia the Danes (possibly moving via Sweden) conquered Denmark. The Danes and the Norwegians formed the Vikings who invaded England. The Danes settled in the northeast of England and the Norwegians in the northwest. They also conquered and settled in Ireland (especially in the east) and in parts of Scotland.

The Symbols of Dan Still Used Today!

Danes from the Israelite Tribe of Dan invaded Denmark at about the same time as the Naphtali moved in large numbers into Norway. The Tribe of Dan was represented by a snake (Genesis 49:17) or by a lion (Deut. 33:22). Other accepted symbols of Dan were a pair of scales[35], an eagle[36], and a dragon[37]. Many members of Dan settled in Denmark, in Ireland, in Wales, England, and the U.S.A. where 40-50 million people have Irish ancestry. The symbol of a snake was once worshipped in Ireland; a lion represents Denmark and

England, Wales has a dragon on its flag, and the U.S.A. has an eagle[*].

"Hushim" or "Shuham": The Son of Dan

The Son of DAN, **"Hushim"** (Genesis 46:23) was also called **"Shuham"** (Numbers 26:42). Hesse in north Germany represented Hushim. Shuham may be found in the "Suehani" who, according to Jordanes, were in Sweden like the Danes themselves are considered, perhaps, once to have been. It is noticeable that quite often the Tribes of Naphtali and Dan were interwoven and that both appear to have been present in the Scythian Naphtalite group. Another section of the Naphtali was known as Ye-da[38] or Ye-ta[39]. These terms are similar to variations on the name of Judah found in the North Mesopotamian area. In Assyrian, for instance, Judah was called "Yadi"[40] and later "Yetae"[41] and in the Caucasus "Yat"[42] meant Jew. Dan was recalled amongst the Naphtali. Dan colonized Denmark and his symbols are to be found in Ireland (a snake), in Wales (a dragon), in Denmark and England (a lion), and in the U.S.A. (an eagle, and scales). A people known as the Tribe of Dana in Irish tradition and as Don in Welsh were amongst the early settlers of Ireland and Britain and an analysis of the relevant traditions shows that they too represented a branch of the Israelite Tribe of Dan. A certain symbiosis existed between **Dan and Judah.** There was a tradition that the Jutes and Danes were descended from Judah and Dan of Israel and were brothers to the Angles[43].

---

[*] One of the symbols of Dan was a griffin (Abraham **EPSHTEIN**, "Kadmoniot HaYehudim; Braytot Atikot. Eldad Ha Dani," Jerusalem 1957). The Shepherd Kings "Hyksos" whom we identify with Israelites and who have been identified as the Danaoi founders of Greek Mycenean civilization incorporated the HYPERBOREAN Griffin as a regal symbol (Martin **BERNAL**, "Black Athena", Vol. II, pp. 42, 353, 375-388).
The Griffin is described as "a creature partly lion and part eagle. The griffins guarded the gold in the FAR NORTH...THE COUNTRY OF THE HYPERBOREANS..."
(Howe HARRER, "A Handbook of Classical Mythology", p. 110)

PEOPLES OF DAN

DAN: Don, Danaster, Danaper, Danube (all rivers associated with the Scyths).
Dangalai (Iran),
Danava (a Scythian Tribe),
Dana (from Lebanon-Israel to Ireland).
Don (Wales,)
Damnones (Scythia, Scotland, south-west Britain, also known as "**Dannonia**"),
Dumnonii – in Western Ireland, identified with the Tuatha de Danaan (Tribe of Dana).
Dani (Danes of Denmark).
SHUCHAM (Suham) = Suehan (Sweden), Suoumi (Finland, also associated with Simeon).
HUSHAM (Hussem) = Hesse (Franks in Germany).

Israeli Stamp showing the scales of justice, one of the symbols of Dan

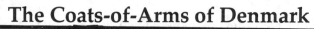

DAN: ICELAND

THE COAT OF ARMS OF ICELAND INCLUDES: A DRAGON, WHICH WAS ONE OF THE SYMBOLS OF DAN. A VULTURE, WHICH IN HEBREW IS GIVEN THE SAME NAME AS EAGLE, I.E. "NESHER", AND A "NESHER" WAS ANOTHER ONE OF THE SYMBOLS OF DAN. A BULL WHICH IS A SYMBOL OF JOSEPH; A GIANT, WHICH FIGURE MAY REPRESENT DAN AND SAMSON THE NATIONAL HERO OF DAN. ICELAND HISTORICALLY HAS BEEN ASSOCIATED WITH NORWAY AND DENMARK IN WHICH COUNTRIES (ESPECIALLY DENMARK) THE TRIBE OF DAN MADE A SIGNIFICANT CONTRIBUTION.

IRELAND (EIRE):

Ireland has a harp on its Coat of Arms. The harp is traditionally associated with King David of Judah and Israel. The father of Galileo Galilei (1564-1642) wrote that the Irish use a harp as a symbol since they believe they are descended from King David of Judah. We believe that Southern Ireland is dominated by segments of Dan and Simeon as well as non-Israelites. Descendants of both Joseph and Judah are also important.

14

JUDAH

""AND THE SONS OF JUDAH; ER, AND ONAN, AND SHELAH, AND
PHAREZ, AND ZARAH: BUT ER AND ONAN DIED IN THE LAND OF
CANAAN. AND THE SONS OF PHAREZ WERE HEZRON AND HAMUL"
GENESIS 46:12.

Why The Jews Are Judah?

Often in Scripture a distinction is made between Judah
and Israel. The Kingdom of Judah was the southernmost entity
and eventually included the Tribes of Judah, Benjamin, Levi, as
well remnants from the other Tribes. A portion of Judah was
taken into exile by the Assyrians along with the northern Ten
Tribes of Israel, Even so, in Biblical terminology, after the
Assyrian Exile, the name "JUDAH" refers almost
EXCLUSIVELY to the descendants of those Jews who kept their
identity. They were not exiled by the Assyrians but remained in
the Land of Judah until the Babylonians took them into
captivity. A portion returned under Ezra and Nehemiah and
re-established the Kingdom of Judah that was eventually
destroyed by the Romans. These (together with those who
joined them) comprise the entity of Judah in Scriptural terms.
"Judah" is linked with the expressions "Zion" and "Jerusalem".

Concerning Judah in the Last Days, Four Points were made by
Stephen Collins*:

---

* Stephen COLLINS, "Why the Jews are Judah", Brit-Am Truth, Issue no.6

1. Zephaniah chapter two predicted that Judah would inherit the coastal regions of "Palestine" including Ashdod, Ekron, Ashkelon, and all the coastland when they return from their captivity. This is what the State of Israel has done.

2. Zechariah chapter 14 supplements Zephaniah and explains how the Jews of Judah will dwell in Jerusalem and fight in defense of Jerusalem during this same period. "Judah" would be a militarily victorious nation in the Middle East.

3. Genesis 49 also predicted that Judah in the Last Days will be like an old lion (an old nation) and a young lion (a reborn entity) fighting nation in the End Times that casts terror on those around her. This fits the present State of Israel most of whose population are Jews amongst whom Judah is predominant.

4. Genesis 49 also shows how the reborn State of Israel set up by Judah will be agriculturally prosperous. The Jews in the present State of Israel have fulfilled all of the above conditions.

In addition:

During their time of Exile:

5. The Jews were persecuted by the Gentiles as it had been prophesied Judah would be: Zechariah 1:15, Zechariah 8:13, Isaiah ch.53, Isaiah 42:10, Psalm 44:22

6. The Jews kept the Law as it had been prophesied that Judah would: Psalms 60:9, 108:90 Genesis 49:10, Zechariah 8:23

7. The Jews keep the four fasts of mourning over the Destruction of the Second Temple as prophesied by Zechariah 8:19, i.e.

THE FAST OF THE FOURTH MONTH, -17th Tammuz

THE FAST OF THE FIFTH, - 9th of Av

AND THE FAST OF THE SEVENTH, - 3rd of Tishrei (Gedaliah)

AND THE FAST OF THE TENTH, - 10th Tebeth (Tevet).

Again concerning the End Times:

8. Isaiah predicted that the descendants of Judah would be known as Israel

HEAR YE THIS, O HOUSE OF JACOB, WHICH ARE CALLED BY THE NAME OF ISRAEL, AND ARE COME FORTH OUT OF THE WATERS OF JUDAH (Isaiah 48:1).

9. Micah 4:8 predicts that in the end times the beginning of the return "THE FIRST DOMINION" shall "TO THE DAUGHTER OF JERUSALEM" meaning descendants of Judah.

10. Judah would be recognized as Judah or Israel whereas the Lost Ten Tribes would not be so recognized until the end times:

[Genesis 49:10] THE SCEPTRE SHALL NOT DEPART FROM JUDAH, NOR A LAWGIVER FROM BETWEEN HIS FEET, UNTIL SHILOH COME; AND UNTO HIM SHALL THE GATHERING OF THE PEOPLE BE.

"SHILOH COME" usually explained to mean the Messiah who will rule in the End Times.

"THE SCEPTRE SHALL NOT DEPART FROM JUDAH":
Menasseh ben Israel explained the above as indicating that Judah shall always be recognizable as an Israelite Tribe.

The Messiah will enable individuals from the Lost Ten Tribes to know what Tribe they belong to. Until then they will not know or at least not be certain. Also until then Judah will keep the Law. See also Isaiah 49:21 in point 12 below.

11. Throughout the Bible and especially in the Prophetic works there are references to Judah that cannot and could not be fulfilled by anybody but the present day Jews. It was prophesied that Judah would suffer for being Jewish, keep the law, eventually be rewarded and recognized by his brother tribes and the world, and never depart from his basic truth. It was prophesied that the Ten Tribes would lose their identity and the opposite was said about Judah, i.e. it was not prophesied that Judah would be lost but it was prophesied that Joseph would be, and so he was.

12. Isaiah 49:21 describes Judah as being initially loath to accept the Lost Tribes and as having suffered alone and been persecuted and exiled from place to place alone. [Isaiah 49:21] THEN SHALT THOU SAY IN THINE HEART, WHO

HATH BEGOTTEN ME THESE, SEEING I HAVE LOST
MY CHILDREN, AND AM DESOLATE, A CAPTIVE,
AND REMOVING TO AND FRO? AND WHO HATH
BROUGHT UP THESE? BEHOLD, I WAS LEFT ALONE;
THESE, WHERE HAD THEY BEEN?
This description fits the Jews of today and no-one else

Jacob prophesied concerning the destiny of the Tribes
towards the End Times:
Judah would be recognized as Judah and Israel whereas the
Lost Ten Tribes would not be so recognized until the Messianic
Age or close to it:
[Genesis 49:1] AND JACOB CALLED UNTO HIS SONS, AND
SAID, GATHER YOURSELVES TOGETHER, THAT I MAY
TELL YOU THAT WHICH SHALL BEFALL YOU IN THE
LAST DAYS.
<<IN THE LAST DAYS>>: Even though this prophecy may
have some application in earlier times its main points will be
realized in the End Times.
Concerning Judah, Jacob foresaw:
[Genesis 49:8] JUDAH, THOU ART HE WHOM THY
BRETHREN SHALL PRAISE [Hebrew: yoducha:
"Acknowledge the righteousness of"] THY HAND SHALL BE
IN THE NECK OF THINE ENEMIES; THY FATHER'S
CHILDREN SHALL BOW DOWN BEFORE THEE.

In the last days the righteousness of the faith of Judah
will be acknowledged:
<<IN THOSE DAYS TEN MEN OUT OF ALL THE
LANGUAGES OF THE NATIONS, EVEN SHALL TAKE
HOLD OF THE SKIRT OF HIM THAT IS A JEW, SAYING, WE
WILL GO WITH YOU: FOR WE HAVE HEARD THAT GOD IS
WITH YOU>> (Zechariah 8:23).

Before he died Israel blessed his sons. He said unto Judah
"Yehudah Atah Yoduchah Acheecha" (Genesis 49:9). This is

translated in the KJ as "JUDAH, THOU ART HE WHOM THY BRETHREN SHALL PRAISE..." but actually in Hebrew the verse says: "Yehudah, you are he whom your brothers shall acknowledge the righteousness of": The key word "Yoducha" [translated in the KJ as "shall praise"] means "**acknowledge the righteousness of**" i.e. the brothers of Judah, the other tribes, the tribes that went into exile and lost their identity, that did not keep the law are destined to acknowledge that Judah had been in the right.

[Genesis 49:9] JUDAH IS A LION'S WHELP: FROM THE PREY, MY SON, THOU ART GONE UP: HE STOOPED DOWN, HE COUCHED AS A LION, AND AS AN OLD LION; WHO SHALL ROUSE HIM UP?

<<OLD LION>>: When Judah was a young nation it was formidable. In the centuries of Exile the Jews had to adapt to both appearing and actually being weak. It had been prophesied that Judah would retain his identity but for a long period of time be unable to defend himself but depend on others and the Will of Heaven:

[Hosea 1:7] BUT I WILL HAVE MERCY UPON THE HOUSE OF JUDAH, AND WILL SAVE THEM BY THE LORD THEIR GOD, AND WILL NOT SAVE THEM BY BOW, NOR BY SWORD, NOR BY BATTLE, BY HORSES, NOR BY HORSEMEN.

Here it was prophesied that Judah would lead a defenseless existence while in exile and be dependent entirely on the mercy of the Almighty and the grace of others.

This was necessary for survival. When you are outnumbered, and your women and children, old and infirm etc are in bondage you cannot afford to become a dead hero. Centuries of this situation takes its own price: They became "As sheep to the slaughter" (Psalm 44:22). Nevertheless, the potential is still there. Judah is still capable of surprising everybody. The present State of Israel has here and there demonstrated that the Jews have potential. An old lion is best not provoked and a young lion needs to be respected. Judah will yet take revenge from his oppressors (Isaiah 34:6).

[Genesis 49:10] THE SCEPTRE SHALL NOT DEPART FROM JUDAH, NOR A LAWGIVER FROM BETWEEN HIS FEET, UNTIL SHILOH COME; AND UNTO HIM SHALL THE GATHERING OF THE PEOPLE BE.
[Whether one says the Messiah has already come and will come again OR that he has still to appear, the above prophecy definitely speaks of what will happen in the End Times].
<<SHILOH COME>> The name "Shiloh" is usually explained to mean the Messiah.
<<THE PEOPLE>> In Hebrew "amim" meaning "peoples" in the plural.
Manasseh ben Israel* explained the above verse (in his book "Conciliator") as:
Judah shall always be recognizable as an Israelite Tribe, i.e. "THE SCEPTRE SHALL NOT DEPART FROM JUDAH".
<<SCEPTRE>>: Hebrew "Shevet" also meaning "Tribe", i.e. the Mark of being an Israelite Tribe will never depart from Judah but it will depart from the other tribes until the Messiah arrives. The Messiah will enable individuals and groups from the Lost Ten Tribes to know what Tribe they belong to. This is the "gathering of the peoples", i.e. NOR A LAWGIVER FROM BETWEEN HIS FEET, UNTIL SHILOH COME; AND UNTO HIM SHALL THE GATHERING OF THE PEOPLE[S] BE.

The Messiah will enable individuals from the Lost Ten Tribes to know what Tribe they belong to. He will enable the Israelites gather together with members of their own tribe with greater certainty. Until then they will not know or at least not be certain. Also until then Judah will keep the Law.

---

* Manasseh ben Israel (1604-1657) was a friend of Oliver Cromwell. He was also a friend of John Sadler who wrote a book identifying English traditional institutions with those of ancient Israel. Manasseh was the Chief Rabbi of Holland.

[Genesis 49:11] BINDING HIS FOAL UNTO THE VINE, AND HIS ASS'S COLT UNTO THE CHOICE VINE; HE WASHED HIS GARMENTS IN WINE, AND HIS CLOTHES IN THE BLOOD OF GRAPES:

The blood of grapes hints at the revenge Judah will take upon his enemies and tormentors (Isaiah 34:6).

[Genesis 49:12] HIS EYES SHALL BE RED WITH WINE, AND HIS TEETH WHITE WITH MILK.

This refers to spiritual fulfillment, military prowess, and material prosperity in the Messianic Era.

JUDAH AND EDOM

The Edomites were descended from Esau the twin brother of Jacob. Most of the Edomites were eventually to be found in Northern Syria, Mesopotamia, and later in Europe.* A small segment of the Edomites remained to the southeast of Judah and these were forcibly converted to Judaism in ca. 100 BCE (Josephus: "Antiquities of the Jews", Book XIII, Chapter IX, Item 1). It is not certain whether the Edomites received a full-fledged conversion or only a partial induction such as that given to captives and non-Israelite slaves who had not been freed*. According to Scripture the Edomites were to be allowed to enter the community of Israel after three generations (Deuteronomy 23:9). Full-fledged Converts were to be accepted and treated exactly the same as Israelites (Exodus 12:49). They were to be considered Israelites in the eyes of their fellow Israelites and in the eyes of the Almighty (Deuteronomy 10:18). If such people existed amongst Judah then in Biblical terms they would be considered part of "Judah". Different sources

---

* For details see "Ephraim. The Gentile Children of Israel", by Yair Davidi, 2001, chapter 8.

* Meaning that they were obligated not to desecrate the Shabbat or eat forbidden foods etc but were NOT burdened with positive injunctions. This was the status of a "Canaanite slave" who upon being freed automatically received the rights and obligations under the Law of a full-fledged Israelite. "Herod" was an Edomite and he is referred to in some sources as a "slave".

(e.g. a tradition quoted by Abarbanel, Jeremiah 31:5) suggest that the Edomites did not remain with Judah but returned to reunite with the general Gentile community. They had apparently not been numerous but rather a minority amongst Judah before leaving Judah altogether. They left no tradition of their own within Judah. Concerning their numbers or what eventually happened to them for the moment we cannot be certain one way or the other. If they did convert to Judaism in the full-fledged sense and some of them did remain then some Jews today may well be descended from them. They are still Jewish and part of Judah like all other converts. A Jew in Biblical terms is someone who is recognized as a Jew, who is bound by the Law, and is attached to Judah. At all events concerning the Edomites we are only speaking (at the most) of a minority amongst the general population. Most descendants of Esau remained amongst the Gentiles. In Jewish tradition the Gentile persecutors of the Jewish people were often identified as descended from Edom. Esau the forefather of Edom was worshipped as a god by certain Gentile peoples some of whom may be descended from him[1]. A portion of the Lost Ten Tribes when they went into Exile were delivered unto "Edom" by Philistine and Phoenician agents of the Assyrians (Amos 1:6, 9). Esau had been promised that he would inherit some of the most favored regions of the earth, become a warrior people, and constantly contest with Israel for world hegemony (Genesis

יהודה

254

27:38-40).* Esau plotted to murder Israel (Genesis 27:41)⁺. Today even though many Gentiles are descended from Israelites only Judah remains as openly identifiable as such. Judah is a link to the ancestral source through which all other Israelites will be enabled to return. Judah will be the initiating cause of the Lost Ten Tribes returning (Jeremiah 3:18). Enemies of Judah are enemies of Israel and enemies of the Almighty. Certain groups (e.g. Atheists, "Identity" freaks, Assimiliationists, Palestinians, etc) periodically attempt to ascribe the ancestry of the Jewish people to non-Israelite sources. Those making such attempts may in many (but not necessarily all) cases themselves be descended from one or other of the "displaced" peoples who have reason to hate Judah and Israel such as Ishmael, Edom, Canaan, or something similar. There is no other way the pathological compulsion that many of them exhibit to disqualify Judah can be explained. Such types need to repent of their treasonous ways. Otherwise they will be sorely confounded and should be kept away from.

---

*[Genesis 27:38] AND ESAU SAID UNTO HIS FATHER, HAST THOU BUT ONE BLESSING, MY FATHER? BLESS ME, EVEN ME ALSO, O MY FATHER. AND ESAU LIFTED UP HIS VOICE, AND WEPT.
[Genesis 27:39] AND ISAAC HIS FATHER ANSWERED AND SAID UNTO HIM, BEHOLD, THY DWELLING SHALL BE THE FATNESS OF THE EARTH, AND OF THE DEW OF HEAVEN FROM ABOVE;
[Genesis 27:40] AND BY THY SWORD SHALT THOU LIVE, AND SHALT SERVE THY BROTHER; AND IT SHALL COME TO PASS WHEN THOU SHALT HAVE THE DOMINION, THAT THOU SHALT BREAK HIS YOKE FROM OFF THY NECK.

⁺ [Genesis 27:41] AND ESAU HATED JACOB BECAUSE OF THE BLESSING WHEREWITH HIS FATHER BLESSED HIM: AND ESAU SAID IN HIS HEART, THE DAYS OF MOURNING FOR MY FATHER ARE AT HAND; THEN WILL I SLAY MY BROTHER JACOB.

THE LOSS AND KEEPING
OF IDENTITY PREDICTED

Throughout the Bible and especially in the Prophetic works there are references to Judah that cannot and could not be fulfilled by anybody but the present day Jews. The Ten Northern Tribes were taken into exile. It was prophesied that they would lose their identity (Isaiah 24:3, 49:21 Hosea 1:9. Jeremiah 3:6-7). It was NEVER prophesied that Judah would lose his identity but rather Judah is referred to as ALWAYS being recognizable as Judah. In their places of exile the Ten Tribes led by Ephraim are called upon to examine the past and return to their sources (Jeremiah 31:21). In the Last Days they will return and reunite with Judah (Ezekiel 37).

The Tribes of Judah, Benjamin, and Levi along with small portions of the other tribes were not exiled by the Assyrians. They retained their identity. In the Bible they are referred to collectively as "Judah" and sometimes as "Israel" (Ezra 2:2 2:59 2:70 3:1 etc, Ezekiel 2:3, 3:5 8:10 8:11 9:8 14:1, etc) since they were the only portion of the original twelve tribes of Israel that remained as an identifiable entity.

JUDAH AMONGST THE TEN TRIBES

Judah is the major tribe amongst the Jews. The Jews on the whole were not exiled by the Assyrians but very many were, as evidenced by inscriptions of Sennacherib, Biblical hints, and Midrashic sources. In addition enclaves of Jews from Judah had existed amongst the northern Ten Tribes and these were taken away with them. At other times bodies of exiled Judaeans may have merged with the Lost Tribes as autonomous groups.   Account should also be taken of numerous Jewish families and individuals who due to force or choice became assimilated amongst the Gentiles and whose descendants in one way or other eventually merged with the Northern Hebrews. Since we are dealing mainly with the Lost Ten Tribes it is pertinent to trace those groups from Judah who joined themselves to them. These entities became part of Israel in general and are not counted separately.

DAN AND JUDAH
Samson and the Jutes

In the Land of Israel the Tribe of Dan in the south bordered Ephraim, Benjamin, and Judah. The Danes had another section of their tribe in the northern Galilee surrounded by Asher, Naphtali, Gad, and the half-tribe of Manasseh. That portion of Manasseh adjoining Dan in the North on its eastern side was dominated by Gilead and within Gilead (who was the son of Machir son of Manasseh) was a band from JUDAH headed by YAIR ("Jair" in 1-Chronicles 2:18-23). Some of the Judaeans in Gilead of Machir are believed to have bordered Dan in the Galilee and to be those named "Judah upon Jordan toward the sunrising" in the Book of Joshua (19:34). Also farther north in Cilicia (southeastern Turkey) the Dananu of Dan and the Yadi of Judah adjoined each other. Thus, Dan and Judah were neighbors in both locations in the north as well as in the south of Israel. In Jewish tradition Judah and Dan are often juxtapositioned. **Samson** the superman hero came from the Tribe of Dan but his mother was from Judah[2]. Samson, in some respects, was considered a forerunner of the Messiah[3] who will come from Judah but his mother, according to the Midrash will be either of the Tribe of Dan or of Naphtali. A lion represented both Judah and Dan, though Dan has additional symbols such as the snake and dragon.

In Cilicia (southeast Turkey) there existed from ancient times an enclave of people named "Dananu" who were from Dan of Israel. The entity of the Dananu was known as "Smal" and adjoined YADI. Yadi was ruled over directly from JUDAH[4] in the south. The Bible tells us about:
THE REST OF THE ACTS OF JEROBOAM, AND ALL THAT HE DID, AND HIS MIGHT, HOW HE WARRED, AND HOW HE RECOVERED DAMASCUS, AND HAMATH, WHICH

257

BELONGED TO JUDAH, FOR ISRAEL, ARE THEY NOT WRITTEN IN THE BOOK OF THE CHRONICLES OF THE KINGS OF ISRAEL? [2-Kings 14:28].

"DAMASCUS, AND HAMATH, WHICH BELONGED TO JUDAH" are the territories of Yadi and Smal. "Damascus" did not mean the Damascus of today but rather an area further to the north[5]. At one stage Yadi and Smal were united. Biblical evidence (2-Kings 14:28, 2-Chronicles 3:4)[6] and the said toponomy shows that Judaeans had adjoined their Danite brothers in YADI of Cilicia. YADI was later called Yutae both names being forms of Judah. After the Ten Tribes had been exiled, the Yaati (Utii) were to be found in Carmania (southwest Iran) bordering the Dangalae whose name suggests "Dan-of-the Galilee". Similarly in Sogdiana east of the Caspian Sea the IATII (i.e. Yati of Judah) were recorded by Ptolemy neighboring the Augali (called "Aegli" by Herodotus) from whom descended the Angles. They were in Saka territory and the Saka (or SAXE as they were known) became the Saxons. Angles, Saxons, and Jutes were together in the invasion of England. A **Danish tradition**[7] relates that the DANES came from DAN of Israel and the JUTES (of Jutland in Denmark) from Judah. In Northern European dialects and in Latin, variations on the names JUTE (of Denmark) and JUDAEAN (Jew from Judah) are interchangeable.

In Europe, a group called the "Saxons Euthiones"[8] were recalled (in about 600 CE) as lying between Saxons and Danes in the north. These are believed to have been a section of Jutes[9] in the region of Frisia. This form of the name (i.e. "Euthiones" for Jutes) was also rendered as "Euthymachos"[10] who was illustrated on an ancient vase discovered in Italy. "Euthymachos" was depicted together with figures named "Toxamis" and "Kimerios". The said illustration is that of Scythians who at an early age began their incursions into Europe. The name "Kimmerios" means Cimmerian, and TOXAMIS is a variation of Toxaris who was a Scythian hero in

Classical Literature. Later, the region of Holland (where Pytheas reported the presence of Scyths from ca.300 BCE) was to be known as Toxandria and a Tribe of Belgae was to be named TOXANDRI.

JUDAH IN THE NORTH

Before the Assyrian Exile in ca. 730-720 BCE part of **JUDAH** had been found in the eastern portion of Manasseh and came from Yair (Jair) the son of Segub, son of Hezron, son of Pharez, son of Judah, whose group had sixty cities amongst Gilead of Machir (1-Chronicles 2:23). There was also *"Judah upon Jordan toward sunrising"* (Joshua 19:34) to the east of Naphtali. Other bands from Judah were to be found both in Moab (1-Chronicles 4:22) which was to the south of Reuben and also in the territory of Reuben's.[*] Judaeans were also together with a contingent from the Tribe of Dan in Cilicia (southeast Turkey) and these are the inhabitants of *"Hamath, which belonged to Judah"* (2-Kings 14:28) referred to in Scripture. In this northern area they would have adjoined the Tribes of Asher and Manasseh and possibly also of Gad. Together with the existence of Judaean enclaves around the peripheries of "Greater Israel" most of Judah remained within its own territory in the south adjoining Benjamin and Simeon. From the south, a significant portion from Judah was taken into exile by Sennacherib, the Assyrian king, and these too were to be included as part of the Lost Ten tribes. Luckenbill quotes (in "The Annals of Sennacherib") the boast that Sennacherib took more than 200,000 people from Judah into exile cf. *"Sennacherib king of Assyria come up against all the fenced cities of Judah and took*

---

[*] Yehudah KIEL, "Sepher Divrei HaYamim" ("The Book of Chronicles") Jerusalem, 1986 pp.75ff. speaks of the intermingling of several of the Israelite Tribes. He comments on 1-Chronicles 4:7 ("The son of Helah Zereth" concerning the descendants of Judah) that the name "Zereth" also occurs in Joshua 13:19 as "Zarethshahar" in the territory of Reuben. Kiel suggests that part of the Judaean family of Zerath sons of Ashur (father of Tekoa) through his wife Helah settled in the territory of Reuben.

them" (2-Kings 18:13). A remnant escaped the Assyrian Captivity and it was from this remainder that Judah in the Biblical sense was destined to re-emerge:
AND THE REMNANT THAT IS ESCAPED OF THE HOUSE OF JUDAH SHALL YET AGAIN TAKE ROOT DOWNWARD, AND BEAR FRUIT UPWARD.
FOR OUT OF JERUSALEM SHALL GO FORTH A REMNANT, AND THEY THAT ESCAPE OUT OF MOUNT ZION: THE ZEAL OF THE LORD OF HOSTS SHALL DO THIS.
[2-Kings 19:30-31].

The Chronicle of Jerahmeel (a Jewish Medieval work, from ca.1100-1150 CE) says that most of Judah and Simeon were exiled to beyond The Mountains of Darkness on the other side of the rivers of Ethiopia. The term "Ethiopia" is derived from Cush and could also refer to Central Asia or other areas. Within Jerusalem, says the Chronicle, there remained only 130,000 from the Tribes of Judah and Benjamin[11]. This quoted version is based on uncertified legend and is probably exaggerating. It does however confirm the impression (also found in other sources, such as the Midrash Seder Olam and quoted by Don Isaac Abarbanel at the end of the Book of Kings) that a large portion of Judah went into the Assyrian exile. These were lost together with the northern Lost Ten Tribes of Israel and are to be counted amongst them and as part of them.

Sons of Judah

"THE SONS OF JUDAH; ER AND ONAN, AND SHELAH...

"AND TAMAR HIS DAUGHTER-IN-LAW BARE HIM PHAREZ AND ZERAH. ALL THE SONS OF JUDAH WERE FIVE.

"THE SONS OF PHAREZ; HEZRON, AND HAMUL.

"AND THE SONS OF ZERAH; ZIMRI, AND ETHAN, AND HEMAN, AND CALCOL, AND DARA: FIVE OF THEM IN ALL.
(1 Chronicles 2; 3-6).

"AND AFTERWARDS HEZRON WENT IN TO THE DAUGHTER OF MACHIR THE FATHER OF GILEAD, WHOM HE MARRIED WHEN HE WAS THREESCORE YEARS OLD; AND SHE BARE HIM SEGUB.

"AND SEGUB BEGAT JAIR, WHO HAD THREE AND TWENTY CITIES IN THE LAND OF GILEAD"
(1- Chronicles 2; 21-22).

A son of Judah was **Shelah** who gave rise to the Shelanites (Numbers 26; 20). These Shelani (Selani) appeared in the region of Belgian-Toxandria as the SALIAN[12] Franks, who intermingled with the Sicambri and together with them invaded Gaul. Another son of Judah was **Pharez** who bore Hezron and Hamel. Pharez may be represented by the Frisians (or the FRISI descend in part from both Pharez of Judah and Peresh of Manasseh) within whose territory the Jutes and Saxons sojourned. There was also a tribe in Scandinavia named **Phiresi**, according to Ptolemy. **Hamel**, son of Pharez, is recalled in the German city of Hameln associated with the Chamaves[13] ("CHEME") who were part of the Frank union as were the Chessuari whose name resembles that of Hezron ("Chetzron" in Ashkenazic-Hebrew), the other son of Pharez. HAMEL was also represented by the **HAEMELE** tribal group amongst the Anglo-Saxon invaders of England. Pharez, Shelah, and Zerah (Zerach) were sons of Judah. Irish tradition said that descendants of Zerah of Judah were amongst Ireland's early settlers[14]. Calcol (1-Chronicles 2;5) is specifically mentioned[15] and Aitan the brother of Calcol is the name of an ancient Irish hero. In addition, an eponymous ancestor amongst the Scottish Gaels and ancient Irish was called "IAR"[16] which name equals YAIR (Jair) of JUDAH whose people is referred to in Assyrian inscriptions as the "Iari". YAIR (Jair) of JUDAH in the Land of Israel had been situated east of the Jordan amongst the clan of Machir from Manasseh (1-Chronicles 2:23). PERESH (1-Chronicles 7:16) from Manasseh has a name implying in Hebrew "Sanctified" or "Separated" which is the same meaning as "NEMEDE" in Gaelic[17]. Nemede was the legendary forefather of the Irish. The Iari (i.e. Yairi) of Ireland settled

261

amongst the **Nemedi** peoples the meaning of whose name links them to Manasseh, the same as the first Yair of Judah had settled amongst Manasseh. One Classical Irish source quoted by Geofrey Keating 1570-1646) says expressly that Jair (also known as Caei the Just) descended from Judah[18]. The symbol of Ireland (Eire) is a harp and a harp is traditionally associated with the House of David, king of Judah. The father of Gailileo Galilei wrote that the Irish use a harp as their symbol since they believe themselves to be descended from King David of Judah. In Ulster there also exists a tradition of a connection with Judah. The Jewish symbol known as "The Star of David" appears on the flag of Ulster.

THE RED HAND OF ULSTER

In addition to the descent from Jair, discussed above (Jair though born to Segub son of Hezron son of Pharez of Judah was actually counted with Menasseh), Calcol son of Zerah son of Judah was also recalled. Camden[19] (1551-1623) stated that Calcol of Judah sailed from Egypt to Spain (where the city of Zaragossa was named after Zerah[20]), and then on to Ireland where he founded Ulladh. "Ulladh" (i.e. Ulster) has actually a name similar (in some types of Hebrew pronunciation) to that of ELADAH of Ephraim (1-Chronicles 7:20).

Zerah was the brother of Pharez and both were born to Judah (son of Israel) from Tamar. In Celtic southwest Britain Ptolemy recorded the Tamarus River (there was also a Tamarus River in Northwest Spain). Zerah and Pharez were twins. The manner of their birth is described in the Bible.

"AND IT CAME TO PASS IN THE TIME OF HER TRAVAIL, THAT, BEHOLD, TWINS WERE IN HER WOMB.

"...WHEN SHE TRAVAILED, ... THE ONE PUT OUT HIS HAND: AND THE MIDWIFE TOOK AND BOUND UPON HIS HAND A SCARLET THREAD, SAYING, THIS CAME OUT FIRST.

"AND IT CAME TO PASS, AS HE DREW BACK HIS HAND, THAT BEHOLD, HIS BROTHER CAME OUT: AND...HIS NAME WAS CALLED PHAREZ.

"AND AFTERWARD CAME OUT HIS BROTHER, THAT HAD THE SCARLET THREAD UPON HIS HAND AND HIS NAME WAS CALLED ZARAH"
(Genesis 38:27-30).

A symbol of Northern Ireland (Ulster) is a scarlet hand superimposed upon the Star of David which universally is taken as representing the Tribe of Judah and appears upon the flag of the modern State of Israel.

Bennett states that, *"The ancient and traditional emblem of Ulster was and still is a Red Hand circled by a Scarlet Cord"*.[20]

The Star of David has twelve junctional-points and shows how the Tribes of Israel were encamped around the Tabernacle when they came out of Egypt. The red hand has been interpreted by some as representing the limb of an Irish ancestral hero whose hand was cut off. Others say that the hand represents Zarah of Judah father of Calcol who according to the legend quoted above sailed to Ireland and founded Uladh (i.e. Ulster).

From Ireland, the Scotts migrated to Scotland, and the Red Hand, *"appears in the Arms of several of the old families and in those of at least fourteen of the Clan Chiefs: Davidson, MacBain, MacNeil, MacNaughton, MacPherson, MacGillivray, MacDonald of Sleat, Clanranald, and Shaw of Rothiemurchus"*[21].

Nowadays many in Ulster identify with the State of Israel and frequently display the Israeli flag as opposed to the Irish Unionists who prefer the PLO one.

In addition to all the above numerous families throughout the British Isles have an uncertain tradition that they descend from Jews. Anti-Semites on the Continent (such as the previous Czar of Russia and Goebells in Germany) remarked on what they considered the 'Jewish" character of the British.

JUDAH: THE LAWGIVER
AND SUFFERING SERVANT

In Scripture the Jews are represented by the terms Jerusalem, Zion, or Judah. Judah, Reuben, and the Tribes of Joseph (Ephraim and Manasseh) all in their own way could claim a degree of pre-eminence:

"THE SONS OF REUBEN THE FIRSTBORN OF ISRAEL (FOR HE WAS THE FIRSTBORN; BUT, FOR AS MUCH AS HE DEFILED HIS FATHER'S BED, HIS BIRTHRIGHT WAS GIVEN UNTO THE SONS OF JOSEPH THE SON OF ISRAEL AND THE GENEALOGY IS NOT TO BE RECKONED AFTER THE BIRTHRIGHT.

"FOR JUDAH PREVAILED ABOVE HIS BRETHREN, AND OF HIM CAME THE CHIEF RULER; BUT THE BIRTHRIGHT WAS JOSEPH'S" (1-Chronicles 5:1 2).

From the above it is understandable that a certain balance of deference was to be expected from amongst the leading tribes and when this was not achieved tensions were to result. This factor contributed to tension between the northern tribes headed by Joseph and the southern domain of Judah and so ultimately the two parts split away from each other. The modern day Jews descend from Judah, Simeon, Benjamin, Levi, and some portions of the other tribes. Historically JUDAH was the leading tribe in the south and it was around him that portions of the other tribes gathered. In Biblical terminology JUDAH represents all of the southern entity whose descendants remained faithful to the Law.

"EPHRAIM COMPASSETH ME ABOUT WITH LIES, AND THE HOUSE OF ISRAEL WITH DECEIT: BUT JUDAH YET RULETH WITH GOD, AND IS FAITHFUL WITH THE SAINTS" (HOSEA 11:12).
"EPHRAIM IS THE STRENGTH OF MINE HEAD; JUDAH IS MY LAWGIVER" (Psalms 60:9, 108:90).

"THE SCEPTER SHALL NOT DEPART FROM JUDAH NOR A LAWGIVER FROM BETWEEN HIS FEET" (GENESIS 49:10).

In the last days the righteousness of the faith of Judah will be acknowledged:

"IN THOSE DAYS TEN MEN OUT OF ALL THE LANGUAGES OF THE
NATIONS, EVEN SHALL TAKE HOLD OF THE SKIRT OF HIM THAT IS
A JEW, SAYING, WE WILL GO WITH YOU: FOR WE HAVE HEARD
THAT GOD IS WITH YOU" (Zechariah 8:23).

Historically, the Jews of Judah were often senselessly
hated, persecuted, and despised. Isaiah had predicted this
situation:
"HE IS DESPISED AND REJECTED OF MEN: A MAN OF
SORROWS...HE WAS DESPISED AND WE ESTEEMED HIM NOT...HE
HATH BORNE OUR GRIEFS AND CARRIED OUR SORROWS YET WE
DID ESTEEM HIM STRICKEN, SMITTEN OF GOD AND AFFLICTED.
HE OPENED NOT HIS MOUTH, AS A LAMB TO THE SLAUGHTER...THE
lord HATH LAID UPON HIM THE INIQUITY OF US ALL"
(Isaiah ch.53).

The Jew is the servant of God and the witness to
Monotheism: "YE ARE MY WITNESSES AND MY SERVANT WHOM I HATH
CHOSEN. BEFORE ME THERE WAS NO GOD FORMED NEITHER SHALL THERE
BE AFTER ME" (ISAIAH 42; 10).

Because the Jew refused to acknowledge conventional
lies and deny the truth of the Biblical Promises and the Oneness
of God, he was persecuted: "FOR THY SAKE ARE WE KILLED ALL THE
DAY LONG; WE ARE COUNTED AS SHEEP FOR THE SLAUGHTER" (PSALM
44:22).

Hatred for the Jews is termed "Anti-Semitism" though
so called "Semitic" peoples (such as the Arabs) are often as
"Anti-Semitic" (i.e. Jew-hating) as any others. Anti-Semitism is a
form of mental sickness that amongst more intelligent sufferers
requires some modicum of rational justification. This
justification is provided by faults, real or imagined, which
reflect more on the haters than on the hated. Jewish behavior
and attitudes very often are of necessity formed by reaction to
the conditions imposed upon them in their host country. In any
event, if the Jew or his immediate ancestors had not been
faithful to the One True God he would not be now susceptible

to victimization. The Bible repeats this essential truth and warns the nations:

"HE WILL AVENGE THE BLOOD OF HIS SERVANTS"
(Deuteronomy 32:43).

"HE THAT TOUCHETH YOU, TOUCHETH THE APPLE OF HIS EYE"
(Zechariah 2:8):

also understandable as meaning *"He that touches you, touches the apple of* HIS [i.e. God's] *eye"*.

"I AM VERY SORE DISPLEASED WITH THE HEATHEN...FOR I WAS BUT A LITTLE DISPLEASED, AND THEY HELPED FORWARD THE AFFLICTION" (ZECHARIAH 1; 15).

"THE SONS ALSO OF THEM THAT AFFLICTED THEE SHALL COME BENDING UNTO THEE" (ISAIAH 60:14).

THE RIGHTEOUSNESS OF JUDAH TO BE ACKNOWLEDGED BY THE OTHER TRIBES!

When the Patriarch Israel was dying he blessed all of his sons. Concerning Judah he said:

"JUDAH YOU ARE HE WHOM THY BRETHREN SHALL ACKNOWLEDGE THE RIGHTEOUSNESS OF: YOUR HAND SHALL BE IN THE NECK OF YOUR ENEMIES; YOUR FATHER'S CHILDREN SHALL BOW DOWN TO YOU"
(Genesis 49:8).

The words "shall acknowledge the righteousness of" in Hebrew are "Yoducha" and are translated in the KING JAMES as "shall praise" but in this case our translation is the more literal one. The Hebrew expression "Yoducha" connotes "own up to you" or "acknowledge your righteousness after a disagreement"! The brothers of Judah will acknowledge his righteousness!!!!

Judah was destined to maintain the Law and as the Jewish people alone out of all the tribes) not to transgress the First and Second commandments. He was not to admit any

266

other God but the ONE GOD OF ISRAEL and not to accept any intermediaries between the ONE GOD and themselves. Judah was destined to suffer largely due to the faults of others (Isaiah 53:6) but in the end Judah will be rewarded and his oppressors punished. The persecutors of Judah will be forced to acknowledge their mistake: By harming Judah it was as if they had harmed the ONE GOD HIMSELF (Zechariah 2:8)!

The Jewish people are an entity in its own right with its own internal characteristics. The JEWS and many of the peoples who emerged from Western Europe are in a Biblical sense of the same stock and have a mutual destiny. The Lost Ten Tribes FROM THE NORTH COUNTRY, AND FROM THE COASTS OF THE EARTH (Jeremiah 31:8) are destined to re-unite with the Tribes of JUDAH: THEY SHALL BE NO MORE TWO NATIONS, NEITHER SHALL THEY BE DIVIDED INTO TWO KINGDOMS ANY MORE AT ALL (Ezekiel 37:22).

The unity of origin and destined future union of the Jews with the Lost Ten Tribes of necessity indicates a need for the two bodies even now to evidence certain empathy towards each other.

OFFSHOOTS OF JUDAH

Judah

Yadi (Cilicia in northwest Syria),

Yeda (in Scythia amongst the Nephtalite Huns),

Iutae (Bactria),

Jutes (Denmark),

Juthingi (Switzerland and Alsace).

JEWS (of Israel and of Diaspora),

Clans of Judah ("Yehudah"):

Zarah = Zaratae (Scythia)

Hesron = Chassuari (Franks).

Hamul = Hamlyn (Frankish Germany);

HAEMELE (Anglo-Saxon group).

Paretz (Pharetz) = Frisi (Friesland in north Holland, and in Anglo-Saxon Britain); Parissi (Parissi of Gaul, Parissi of Celtic Britain in York area; Parsi (Parthians in Iran), Phiresi in Scandinavia. [**Paretz of Judah** and **Paresh of Manasseh** intermixed and so the same identifications may hold for both groups].

Shayloni = Sali (Franks).

Carmi = See Carmi of Reuben (Carmania, Crimea, Carini).

Eitan = Eytan (an Irish ancestor in Irish Mythology).

Calcol = Calcol (an Irish ancestor according to Camden).

Calubi (Chalubi) = Chalybes of Scythian Caucasus and Calybes of Celtic Spain -both peoples were famed as metallurgists.

Darda = Ancestor of groups amongst Scandinavian Royalty.

Yair (Jair) = Iari of early Middle East and later Iari of Ireland and Scotland. See the book *Lost Israelite Identity* (1996) by Yair Davidy for more details.

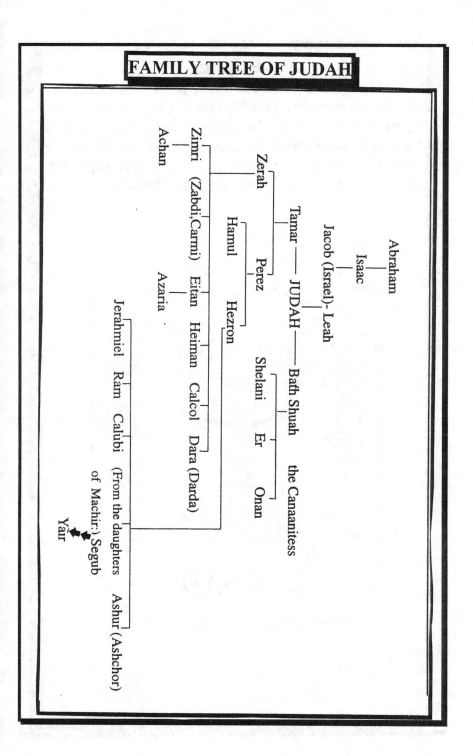

FAMILY TREE OF JUDAH

269

JUDAH

The State of Israel today uses a Menorah as its official symbol. The Menorah (Lev. 24; 4) and its lighting was part of the daily Temple service and thus represents the fulfillment of the Mosaic Law to which those of the Tribe of Judah amongst the Jews of today have alone remained faithful.

THE LION OF JUDAH

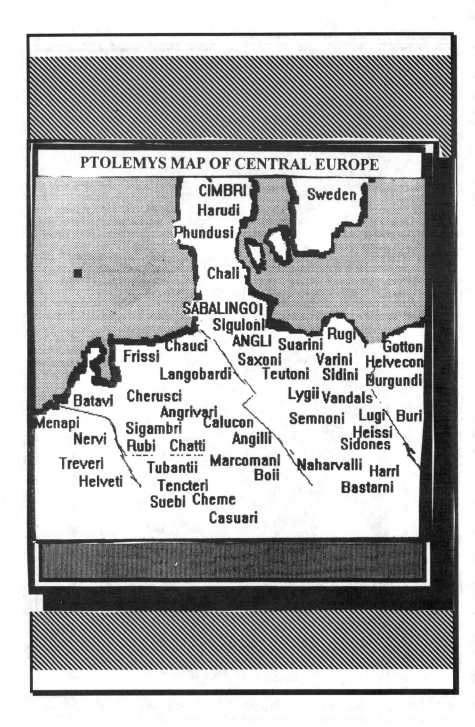

PTOLEMYS MAP OF CENTRAL EUROPE

15

PTOLEMY ON
NORTH CENTRAL EUROPE

Most of the peoples, like the Franks and the Anglo-Saxons, who invaded the west, sojourned for some time in Germany and Scandinavia before evacuating the German area. Ptolemy's Map of Germania reflects the situation that existed prior to the said peoples moving out and to the west and therefore is of historical significance and pertinent to the present study. In the Isle (i.e. Peninsula) of **SCANDIA** (which name is a corruption of Scathanavia or Scythia) were the **LEVONNI** from Levi, the **PHANONE** from Phuni (Phuah) of Issachar, the **PHIRESI** from Peresh (Pheresh) of Machir of Manasseh, and the **DAUCIONES** and **GUTAE**. The latter two were descendants of the Dacii and Getae who had migrated from the Balkans. In Jutland were the **CYMBRI** descendants of the Cimmerians, the Harudes (Eruds, **CHARUDES**) from Arodi of Gad, the **CHALI** from Jahleel (Yachlayl) of Zebulon and the SABALINGOI from Zebulon. The **SIGULONES** have a name reminiscent of the Hebrew, "Am-Segulah" (Deuteronomy 7:6) which was a name applied to Israel and meant "A Special People". It should be noted that apart from Ptolemy other sources give appellations of significance regarding this area. For the moment, it suffices to note that the Jutes have a name meaning Judah, the Danes one meaning DAN, the Goths (of

273

Sweden) one meaning GAD, and the Suiones (of Sweden) one close to Shuni, son of Gad.

In the east (in the region of Poland) the **GYTHONES** (Guthones) and **PHINNI** from Gad and from Phuni of Issachar were in European Sarmatia on the Baltic coast. This was the region of Baltic Amber. In Ancient Times amber was a very valued material and was considered to have magical qualities. It was more valuable than gold. Phoenician merchants had traded in amber from a very early period. Ashur-nasir-apal, The King of Assyria, in ca 883 BC sent his people to the Land of Amber   "where the seas wash copper-like amber ashore...". Ashur-nasir-apal in another inscription speaks of receiving "ivory from walrus tusk" apparently as tribute from the Phoenicians. The walrus is only found in far northern regions. The source of amber used by the Assyrians was along the Baltic source in the area later controlled by the Gothic Gythones. Besides them were the **OMANI** and **LUGI** of the Vandals who came from the Israelite Tribe of Asher. They were adjoined by the **SIDINI** whose name is reminiscent of the fact that in the Land of Israel the Tribe of Asher had bordered Sidon of Phoenicia. A similarly-named people, the **SIDONES**, were south of the Lugi. The **ELVAEONES** have a name cognate with Hilleuiones which people Pliny reported as populating Scandinavia. This name is connected to the Chalus River (says Chadwick[1]) to the west. The said appellations are similar to those such as Chalus, Hilvon, etc. associated with Halah[2] whereto Israelites were transported in the Middle East.

The city "**ASCAUCALIS**" was in the east by the **OMANI** and the city "**ASCALINGUM**" in the west by the **ANGRIVARI**. The root "Ask" is associated with Isaac and with the Scythes and Saxons.

The **SAXONES** gave their name to the conquerors of England; their name means "Sons-of-Isaac". The **TEUTONARII** come from Tahat of Ephraim. They were absorbed by the

Saxons and joined in the invasion of Britain. Previously they had marched with the **CIMBRI**. The appellation "Teuton" is sometimes misapplied to the Germans who are mostly unrelated to them.

The VIRUNI equal the Varni or Warings and were a Vandal group.

The **SEMNONES** have a name meaning Simeon and the **LACCOBARDI** (Lombards), to their south, originally came from Scandinavia and were also called Headobardi after Ohad, son of Simeon.

The **CALUCONES** came from Helek (Chelekh) son of Gilead from Manasseh. They were swept up (like the **CHERUSKI** and others) by the Franks and Saxons. The **Angili** and **ANGRIVARII** joined the Saxons in invading England. "Aegle" was a diminutive for Angle. In Hebrew "aegel" means bull-calf and a nickname for Ephraim.

The **CHEME** gave their name to Hamlyn and came from Hamul of Judah. They became part of the Franks as did the Casuari sons of Hezron (Chetsron) of Reuben. The **CHATE** had been recalled in the CHATAE SCYTHAE and the **TUBANTES** had previously been known as the Tybiace and Tabieni of Scythia. The **SUEVI** represent the SUEBI also known from Scythia and (in this case) descended from Joseph.

In the south, the **SUDINI** caused Switzerland at one stage to be known as "Sidon". In Biblical times Issachar, for a brief period, had conquered Sidon of Phoenicia.

Simeon

The Israeli stamp bears the coat-of-arms of Simeon that depicts the walled city of Schechem. This was the city that Simeon and Levi conquered (Genesis 34:25) when they slew all the males in revenge for the defilement of their sister, Dinah.

16

THE TRIBE OF SIMEON

"AND THE SONS OF SIMEON; JEMUEL, AND JAMIN, AND OHAD
AND JACHIN, AND ZOHAR, AND SHAUL THE SON OF A
CANAANITISH WOMAN"
(GENESIS 46:10).

THE SONS OF SIMEON AFTER THEIR FAMILIES: OF NEMUEL, THE
FAMILY OF THE NEMUELI: OF JAMIN, THE FAMILY OF THE
JAMINI: OF JACHIN THE FAMILY OF THE JACHINI.

"OF ZERAH, THE FAMILY OF ZARHI: OF SHAUL, THE FAMILY OF
THE SHAULI"
(Numbers 26:12-13).

"THE SONS OF SIMEON WERE NEMUEL, AND JAMIN, JARIB,
ZERAH, AND SHAUL"
(1-Chronicles 4:24).

The Tribe of Simeon was counted amongst the Lost Ten
Tribes even though the other Tribes were to the north of Judah
whereas Simeon was in the southern region. Simeon is spoken
of as having shared the fate of the Lost Ten Tribes who were
exiled and is counted amongst them (2-Chronicles 34:6).*
Before the Exile of the Ten Tribes, the Northern Kingdom of
Israel had had a degree of sovereignty over part of the area
south of Judah —meaning the territory of Simeon. There are

---

* "And so he did in the cities of Manasseh, and Ephraim, and Simeon, even unto
Naphtali, with their ruins [Hebrew: "Charvotayhem"] round about" (2-Chronicles 34:6).

277

hints in the Bible concerning this as well as archaeological evidence: In Kuntillet Ajrud much to the south of Judah in the Tribal Region of Simeon an inscription and illustration from Ancient Israelite times has been found. It depicts and mentions "Yahwah of Samaria and his Asherah". The inscription uses the dialect of Northern Israel*. Samaria was one of the capitals of Northern Israel and possibly its most important city. "Samaria" is a term applied to the Northern Kingdom of Israel in general in the same way as "Jerusalem" is sometimes used to represent all of Judah. The inscription therefore suggests the type of Northern Israelite religious practices in the Simeon area. These practices in those times would have been connected with some degree of political domination.

THE EXILE OF SIMEON
AMONGST THE TEN TRIBES

The Bible relates that the Assyrians after having attacked, conquered, destroyed and exiled all of the northern Lost Tribes also attacked the territory of Judah:

"Sennacherib king of Assyria come up against all the fenced cities of Judah and took them" (2-Kings 18:13).

In an inscription Sennacherib speaks of capturing forty-six fenced cities and of carrying away to Assyria 200,150 people from the region of Judah. Jewish tradition relates that due to Sennacherib capturing "all the fenced cities" a large portion of

---

* <<An interesting thing about Kuntillet Ajrud is the fact that there are no local wares to be found. All the pottery was imported -- the majority from the north, though some from the Jerusalem area (the big stuff, I think).
<<I have argued that the north may have pushed its way south down through the Shephelah [coastal plain]. Kuntillet Ajrud is architecturally nothing like other sites in the area, though there are similarities with some sites I'd call "Israelite" describing what we also call the northern kingdom ...The majority of the names were of the northern form and there is the mention of yhwh Smrn [of Samaria] (and yhwh tmn [of Teman in Edom?]). The drawings have been described as Phoenician influenced (as one would expect in the north). A clear Samarian presence so far from home would not be understandable to me without some control in the area as well.>> Ian Hutcheson.

the Kingdom of "Judah" including most of Simeon also went into the Assyrian exile. These were lost together with the northern Ten Tribes of Israel. The sources emphasize that those lost to Judah encompassed the overwhelming majority of the people of Simeon. On the other hand they who DID REMAIN belonged mostly to Judah, Benjamin, and Levi. In Biblical terminology the term "Judah" is always applied to those of Judah and the other Tribes who remained "Jewish" in the religious sense. Most of Simeon was exiled. Nevertheless, it should be emphasized that many from Simeon remained with Judah and are to be found amongst the present-day "Jews". All of the different traditions probably have some truth to them. Most of Simeon indeed were exiled and are to be counted as amongst the Lost Ten Tribes. The Midrash (Seder Olam) says that all of Simeon was taken away in Assyrian times by the King of "Cush". "Cush" could mean Ethiopia or another part of Africa but the name was also applied to a region of Elam in Persia as well as to the area east of the Caspian Sea. This last possibility is the one accepted by us in accordance with other evidence. From the regions of Iran and Central Asia elements from Simeon moved westward together with the rest of the Tribes of Israel. While still in the Land of Israel Simeon had been located on both the west and eastern sides of the River Jordan.

THE EXILE OF SIMEON FROM
EAST OF THE JORDAN

At the beginning Simeon had been largely encompassed by Judah (Joshua 19:1, 9 Judges 3:1). King Saul tried to separate Simeon out of Judah. Later in the time of King Hezekiah a portion of Simeon moved east of the Jordan and conquered lands of the Hamites and of the Edomites and settled there:
[1-Chronicles 4:38] THESE MENTIONED BY THEIR NAMES WERE PRINCES IN THEIR FAMILIES: AND THE HOUSE OF THEIR FATHERS INCREASED GREATLY.

[1-Chronicles 4:39] AND THEY WENT TO THE ENTRANCE OF GEDOR, EVEN UNTO THE EAST SIDE OF THE VALLEY, TO SEEK PASTURE FOR THEIR FLOCKS.

"Gedor" has been identified as a region south of Petra east of the Jordan called "Koodur" by the Arabs. Another opinion says that Gedor is an area of South Sinai[1]

[1-Chronicles 4:40] AND THEY FOUND FAT PASTURE AND GOOD, AND THE LAND WAS WIDE, AND QUIET, AND PEACEABLE; FOR THEY OF HAM HAD DWELT THERE OF OLD.

[1-Chronicles 4:41- AND THESE WRITTEN BY NAME CAME IN THE DAYS OF HEZEKIAH KING OF JUDAH, AND SMOTE THEIR TENTS, AND THE HABITATIONS [Hebrew: "Maunim"] THAT WERE FOUND THERE, AND DESTROYED THEM UTTERLY UNTO THIS DAY, AND DWELT IN THEIR ROOMS: BECAUSE THERE WAS PASTURE THERE FOR THEIR FLOCKS.

<<HABITATIONS [Hebrew: "Maunim"]>>: This should be translated as "Maonites" who were an Arab people (Judges 10:12) and traditional enemies of Israel.

[1-Chronicles 4:42] AND SOME OF THEM, EVEN OF THE SONS OF SIMEON, FIVE HUNDRED MEN, WENT TO MOUNT SEIR, HAVING FOR THEIR CAPTAINS PELATIAH, AND NEARIAH, AND REPHAIAH, AND UZZIEL, THE SONS OF ISHI.

[1-Chronicles 4:43] AND THEY SMOTE THE REST OF THE AMALEKITES THAT WERE ESCAPED, AND DWELT THERE UNTO THIS DAY.

The Book of Chronicles in the verses above, in effect tells us that there were two major movements of Simeon. One movement was to the Plains of Gedor to the south or to east of the Jordan. The second movement was initiated by 500 men under the sons of Ishi. Regarding the first movement we must assume that they too were exiled alongside of all the Israelites east of the Jordan.

The second movement was a continuation of the first. It involved "THE SONS OF ISHI": According to the Talmud (Baba Batra 123, 300-500 CE) "the sons of Ishi" were descended from Ishi who is listed later (1-Chronicles 5:23-26)* amongst the Princes of half Manasseh east of the Jordan who were taken into Exile by the Assyrians. The men of Simeon led by the sons of Ishi went northward to settle. They had placed themselves under the leadership of a Princely Family of the half-tribe of Manasseh. The father of this family was listed amongst the Princes of Manasseh who in the exile of the Northern Israelites were taken to "HALAH, AND HABOR, AND HARA, AND TO THE RIVER GOZAN" [1-Chronicles 5:26]. Rabbinical Tradition linked this movement of Manasseh-led Simeonites to the foundation of the Khazar nation.

Simeon amongst the Khazars

The Bible (1-Chronicles 4:42-43) tells us how five hundred men from Simeon under the leadership of the Sons of Ishi from half-Manasseh (Machir) went to Mount Seir, smote the Amalekites, and took possession of it. Mount Seir is conventionally considered to have been east of the Jordan River to the southeast of Judah in the Land of Edom. Nevertheless, there was another area in the far north in the region of Armenia

---

*[1-Chronicles 5:23] AND THE CHILDREN OF THE HALF TRIBE OF MANASSEH DWELT IN THE LAND: THEY INCREASED FROM BASHAN UNTO BAALHERMON AND SENIR, AND UNTO MOUNT HERMON. [1-Chronicles 5:24] AND THESE WERE THE HEADS OF THE HOUSE OF THEIR FATHERS, EVEN EPHER, AND ISHI, AND ELIEL, AND AZRIEL, AND JEREMIAH, AND HODAVIAH, AND JAHDIEL, MIGHTY MEN OF VALOUR, FAMOUS MEN, AND HEADS OF THE HOUSE OF THEIR FATHERS. [1-Chronicles 5:25] AND THEY TRANSGRESSED AGAINST THE GOD OF THEIR FATHERS, AND WENT A WHORING AFTER THE GODS OF THE PEOPLE OF THE LAND, WHOM GOD DESTROYED BEFORE THEM.
[1-Chronicles 5:26] AND THE GOD OF ISRAEL STIRRED UP THE SPIRIT OF PUL KING OF ASSYRIA, AND THE SPIRIT OF TILGATHPILNESER KING OF ASSYRIA, AND HE CARRIED THEM AWAY, EVEN THE REUBENITES, AND THE GADITES, AND THE HALF TRIBE OF MANASSEH, AND BROUGHT THEM UNTO HALAH, AND HABOR, AND HARA, AND TO THE RIVER GOZAN, UNTO THIS DAY.

which was also the domain of Edom and of Amalekites (*Josiphon*). Here too there was a region known as "Seir". It was in this area that a portion of the Lost Ten tribes were resettled after being exiled by the Assyrians[*].

[*Scripture speaks of only 500 men from Simeon taking part in this enterprise but it will be recalled that only 600 men from the Tribe of Dan were engaged in the capture of Laish (The Book of Judges, chapter 18) and from this small beginning a formidable entity arose. There were occasions in history when great conquests were achieved by small numbers, e.g. in 1532 Francisco Pizarro with 168 Spanish soldiers defeated an army of 80,000 and conquered the Inca Empire in Peru. Similarly Cortez conquered Mexico with a small number of men and this event that led to the wiping out of 95 per cent of the native population[2]. It may also be true that the real Khazars were never very numerous but despite their meager numbers had managed to control a significant kingdom.*]

Baschmakoff has proven that all early references to the Khazars show them to have emerged from Sacasene[3] which was in the north of what was then termed Armenia. Eldad HaDani (880 CE) said that the Khazars descended from the Tribe of Simeon and half-tribe of Manasseh. Eldad traced the Khazars to 1-Chronicles 4:42-43 that spoke of the 500 men from Simeon and Manasseh. Whether these 500 really did found the Khazar nation or not is largely irrelevant. The point is that Khazar traditions, early Jewish reports, and the writings of their Gentile neighbors all recall the belief that the Khazars were descended from Israelites Tribes with Manasseh and Simeon usually being mentioned[4].

---

[*] <<Armenia is sometimes identified in literature with the biblical Minni (Pal. Targ., 51:27, (based on onomatopoeic exegesis of Armenia = *Har*) "Mountain" *Minni*; similarly, Harmon (*ha-Harmonah*, Amos 4:3) is understood in the Targum to denote the region where the Ten Tribes lived "beyond the mountains of Armenia." Rashi identified Harmon with "the Mountains of Darkness," the term used by medieval Jews for the Caspian mountains, believed in the West to surround the kingdom of the Khazars (who were often taken for the Ten Lost Tribes) and to include the Caucasus.>> Abraham N. Poliak.

A Letter from King Joseph of Khazaria to Ibn Shaprut Hasdoi reports:

"Our forefathers told us that at the beginning they settled in a place name Mount Seir. My Lord [i.e. the person addressed] knows that Mount Seir is far away from the place of his residence. Our elders say that the Land of Chebar was called Mount Seir. However decrees [misfortunes] went out and from one calamity to another [so they moved until] they seized hold of the land they are now settled upon"[+].

Another document[5] dating from 950 CE is a letter from a Khazar personage that speaks of Jews who came to Khazaria and intermixed with the local population. They lost a clear recollection of their origins and abandoned most of their customs apart from the rite of circumcision. A descendant of these Jews became the head of the army. He decided, with the encouragement of his wife and advisors, to openly re-embrace Judaism. Consequently descendants of Jews and the local Khazars together converted. After that a great many Jews from neighboring lands moved to Khazaria. The letter speaks of a tradition that the native Khazars were also originally Israelites from the Tribe of Simeon.

Nearly all evidence from Jewish sources and from the west indicates that the Khazars were Hebrews and that their kingdom originated in the Caucasus neighborhood or close to it. Modern scholarship tends to trace Khazar origins to east of the Caspian Sea. This is based on interpretations of Chinese

---

[+] This letter is part of a correspondence that took place in the late 900s-1000 CE between King Joseph of Khazaria and Hasdoi Iben Shaprut of Spain. Internal evidence indicates that the document has been altered and edited but it is essentially genuine and has been referred to be other near contemporary sources

Avraham Harcavi published (1878) an alternative version of the letters in question taken from the collection of A. Firkovitch. This version is somewhat different and traces the Khazars to Togarmah son of Gomer of Japeth. Firkovitch however was a wealthy Karaite scholar who had ulterior motives and was a notorious forger. Tombstones with Israelite inscriptions (sometimes referred to in British-Israel Literature) in the Crimea are often forgeries produced under the patronage of Firkovitch and anything originating with him must be suspected.

documents that speak of a Kosa people in the east and later apply a similar (but not identical) term to the Khazars. The evidence tracing the Khazars to the east is actually quite uncertain and ambiguous. From an objective point of view it does seem that the Khazars had several power bases. Even if the Chinese sources are accepted as indicating an early Khazar presence in the east there is no actual contradiction. We to have concluded (from other sources) that Khazar entities or Israelite groups that eventually joined the Khazars were also to be find east of the Caspian Sea. In our analysis of the Maps of Ptolemy we found Tribal names relating to Simeon and Manasseh in the said area.

At all events, eventually the Khazar Empire was defeated and those Khazars who had converted to Judaism presumably were absorbed by the Jewish people. Apart from this there were groups from Simeon who remained attached to their fellow Israelites from the Lost Ten Tribes and moved to the west with them. Some went westward at an earlier date and became part of the "Celtic" culture. Others came later and were to be found amongst the so-called "Germanic" groups.

THE TRIBE OF SIMEON IN THE WEST

SIMEON has a name derivations of which were applied to Celtic ethnic groups. Ptolemy recalled the SIMENI on the east coast of Britain. The Welsh are called Semoni[6] in Welsh and Irish Literature. The Fir Bolg, of Irish Mythology, settled in Ireland and Britain and named Semuen[7] son of Isru (i.e. "Israel") as their ancestor. Ptolemy registers the Samnetes (of Simeon) in French Brittany. This area of France had cultural contacts with Wales and was to be settled in part by Celtic settlers from Britain. In Celtic Britain, according to Ptolemy the SIMENI were bordered by the Iduma River that is similarly named to Idumea or Edom part of whose lands had been conquered by the Tribe of Simeon, as we noticed, in the Land of Israel. South of the British Iduma River were the ICENI (Ikeni) people whose name resembles that of **Jachin** (Numbers 26:12) son of Simeon. In Phoenician-Hebrew "Yachin" would have been rendered something like "ICEN". Yachin is also recalled in the Euchatae recorded in Pliny (N.H. 6; 50) as beyond the Jaxartes River east of the Caspian. Pliny recorded similarly named groups such as the Auchatae (N.H. 6; 22) on the Lower Don and the Auchetae (N.H. 4; 22) in the northwest close to the Baltic. Euchatae, Auchatae, and Auchetae are all considered different sections of the one people[8] and their trend of direction seems to be from east to west. Herodotus says that the Auchetae were a major Scythian people. In the region of the Euchatae east of the Caspian were the Zaratae (from Zerah son of Simeon) and the Samnitae of Simeon.

The Euchatae themselves descended from Yachin of Simeon. Within this area popular Jewish tradition said that part of the Tribe of Simeon had settled together with other tribes and from here came a section of Khazars who were also believed to be descended from Simeon and Menasseh. The Euchatae are the same as the "EUCAE" who, together with other peoples from SAKAE[9] areas, were admitted to the Macedonian elite unit, "The Companion Guard" of Alexander the Great. The Anglo-Saxons had a tradition[10] of having served in Alexander's forces and the Eucae of Scythia equate the "Saxon EUCI"[11], who were reported in North Europe in about 540 CE. Pliny (N.H. 6;19) himself mentions the Euchatae of Scythia being called SAKA (which name is the source for "Saxon") though he says their original name (along with that of the other Scyths) was ARAMI which means SYRIAN. The term "Arami" (Syrian) was also applied to Israelites and to Judaean. The Hecani clan amongst the Anglo-Saxons came from Yachin of Simeon.

In Europe the Semnones (cf. Simeon) were a section of the Suebi with whom the Angli were federated. Ptolemy shows the Semnones bordering the Laccobardi (Lombards), Angles, and Viruni (Warings). The Lombards in Scandinavian

Literature have been identified as the HEADOBARDS[12] of old, whose name is reminiscent to that of **"OHAD"** (Genesis 26;10), son of Simeon. Similarly in South Central Italy (Campania) in ancient times dwelt the Samnites. These are considered to have originally been a Celtic people amongst whom settlers from the region of Sparta (Lacedaemonia) settled. The Samnites fought on the side of Carthage against Rome in the Second Punic War (218- 201 BCE). Consequently, <<He [the Roman leader, Sulla] did not rest satisfied until he had destroyed, or driven from Italy, every one who bore a Samnite name.>> (Strabo IV;11). Nevertheless, remnants of the Samnite people must have remained in Italy.

Of the other sons of Simeon, **Yamin** perhaps became the YOM Vikings of Scandinavia; **Shaul** became the Silures of South Wales, a fierce darkish people according to Tacitus and others; **Namuel** became the Nemeti who adjoined the Vangiones on the Rhine. According to the Jewish historian, Heinrich Graetz (1817-1891), the first Jewish community in Germany derived from descendants of Vangione mercenaries in the Roman army and captured Jewish maidens.

The national color of Simeon in Rabbinical tradition (Num. Rab 2;7) was green[*] and green is the national color of Ireland. The Green and white colors of the Tudor dynasty that originated in Wales form the background of the Welsh flag. In both Ireland and Wales the "Celtic" element contains a significant Simeon-portion. Simeon was found in Semuen, in the Semoni, Simeni, and Samnetes which names were all those of major groups amongst the Celts of Ireland, Wales, Britain, and Gaul. In addition, on the Continent prior to the Anglo-Saxon invasions, the Semnones (of Simeon) were a portion of the Suebi and belonged to the same group, says Tacitus, as the Angles. Yachin, son of Simeon, fathered the ICENI in Celtic

---

[*] In Classical Hebrew "Yerok" can mean either green or yellow since yellow is considered in Midrashic terminology to be a type of green. In Modern Hebrew the word is applied exclusively to the color green.

Britain and the Eucae amongst the Saxons. Zerah son of Simeon had neighbored (as "Zaratae") the Samnitae (of Simeon) in Scythia northeast of the Caspian. South of the Samnitae and Zaratae in Scythia were the Namastae descendants of Nemuel son of Simeon (Numbers 26:12 Nemuel is called Jemuel in Genesis 46:10). Other sons of Simeon were Jamin (the Yom-Vikings), Ohad (the Headobards-Lombards) and Shaul (the Silures of Wales). Judah had assimilated a good portion of Simeon and their descendants are to be found amongst the modern-day Jews. In Rabbinical tradition descendants of Simeon were prominent amongst schoolteachers, scribes, and indigents. Descendants of Simeon in Jewish tradition were considered often to be quick-tempered, strict of nature, vengeful, and to a degree prone to violence.

SIMEON ASSIMILATED IN PART
AMONGST JUDAH -

"AND JUDAH SAID UNTO SIMEON HIS BROTHER, COME UP WITH ME INTO MY LOT, THAT WE MAY FIGHT AGAINST THE CANAANITES; AND I LIKEWISE WILL GO UP WITH THEE INTO THY LOT. SO SIMEON WENT UP WITH HIM" Judges 1:3.

"AND THE SECOND LOT CAME FORTH TO SIMEON, FOR THE TRIBE OF THE CHILDREN OF SIMEON ACCORDING TO THEIR FAMILIES: AND THEIR INHERITANCE WAS WITHIN THE INHERITANCE OF THE CHILDREN OF JUDAH" Judges 19:1.

IRELAND

In Ireland settled the same peoples who reached other portions of the British Isles, though in different proportions Danites from the Tribe of Dana in pre-Celtic times and Danes from Denmark in the Viking era contributed their share from the tribe of Dan. The Nemedians who followed the DANA were connected to Peresh from Manasseh, Belah (Belgae) from Benjamin, and to Semuen (Simeon) son of Isru (Israel) who seems to have pre-dominated amongst them and also settled in Wales. The Milesians who followed the Nemedians were also known as Hiberi (Hebrews) and as Gaedhals possibly from Gad - though one of the names they gave to Ireland, -"ERIN" derives from Eran son of Ephraim. From this latter group came the Scotti who later settled in Scotland. Irish and Scottish tradition says explicitly that the Hiberi (Milesians, Gaedhals, Scotti) came out of Egypt with the Children of Israel[13] and once kept the Mosaic Law[14].

There are about 60 million people in the world today of Irish descent though only around three million live in Ireland itself. Most people of Irish origin live in the U.S.A. as well as being numerous in Australia and the United Kingdom. In the past, whole tribes from Ireland invaded and settled on the west coasts of Wales, England, and Scotland in the period when the Anglo-Saxons and kin were invading from the east. Throughout the centuries numerous waves of migration from Ireland to Britain have taken place parallel to the settlement of many people from Britain in Ireland itself. It may be that the various migratory movements represent a re-organization and re-amalgamation of hereditary tribal groups. The Irish of today as recognized in Ireland and America have characteristics applicable both to Dan and to Simeon. In the U.S.A. the Irish dominate much of the Police Force. They are officious and inclined to violence. Many lawyers and judges are of Irish descent. The Irish are usually not initiators but are conservative though there are exceptions. They tend to be religious, even superstitious, though this quality is mitigated by outbursts of profligacy. They can be poetical and mystical. They can also be hardy, tough, very brave and proficient warriors with a sense of fair play. They are known to drink alcohol, sometimes overduly. They are also often generous, good-natured, and seekers of justice. They exhibit qualities associated with Simeon

288

on the whole and with Dan upon occasion. Jacob prophesied concerning Simeon and Levi that, "Simeon and Levi are brothers, instruments of violence are their source of livelihood"* (Genesis 49:5). The expression "Simeon and Levi are brothers" is used in spite of the fact that all of the twelve brothers (including Simeon and Levi) were being spoken to at the time. This suggests that there was a characteristic-similarity between these two brothers that was less apparent amongst the others. It is an interesting phenomenon that, as stated above, in many parts of the U.S.A. many of the policemen are of Irish descent whereas in the State of Israel descendants of the Tribe of Levi appear to be disproportionately represented in the Police Force.

Dr Clifford Smyth of Belfast once proposed that the present conflict between the Protestants and Catholics over Ulster be explained by the descent of many today in Ireland from Simeon and of the British from Joseph. According to Rabbinical Biblical Commentary Simeon was the instigator of the plot against Joseph and that was why Joseph caused him to be temporarily incarcerated.

[Genesis 42:24] AND HE TURNED HIMSELF ABOUT FROM THEM, AND WEPT; AND RETURNED TO THEM AGAIN, AND COMMUNED WITH THEM, AND TOOK FROM THEM SIMEON, AND BOUND HIM BEFORE THEIR EYES.

This explanation suggests an on-going tension between Joseph and Simeon.

There is also an anti-Israelite non-Hebraic element amongst the Irish that upon occasion asserts itself strongly. Non-Israelites are to be found throughout the Israelite nations and in some cases they make their presence strongly felt.

---

* The KJ version says: "Simeon and Levi are brethren; instruments of cruelty are in their habitations" (Genesis 49:5). This translation is also consistent with the Hebrew though the one given above is closer to the original meaning.

Peoples of Simeon

Simeon: Amongst Jews, Khazars, Irish, Welsh, Italians

Samnites: Italy

Samnitae: Scythia

Samnetes: Brittany (France)

Semnones: Germany Angles

Semoni: Welsh

Simeni: Celtic Britain

Semuen: Britain and Ireland

Ohad: Lombards (Italy)

Zerah: Zaratae (Scythia)

Yachin: Iceni (Celtic Britain), Euchatae Auchatae, Auchetae (Scythia), Eucae (Scythia), Euci (Saxon Germany), Hecani (Anglo-Saxon),

Yamin: Yom Vikings

Shaul: Silures (Wales)

Namuel: Nemeti (Rhine region)

Symbols of Wales

NORTHERN IRELAND

Most of the tribes settled in, at some time or other the British Isles. Britain was essentially to be dominated by the tribes of Joseph. In Scotland Menasseh, Asher, and Gad were especially prominent. In Wales and Ireland Dan and Simeon are noticeable though elements of Manasseh, Judah, and Levi were also important. The official flag of Northern Ireland has a **Magen David** Star in its center which symbol is traditionally associated with Judah and the Jewish people. In ancient times Ulster was knoiwn as Uladah which is an alternative pronounciation for "Eladah" a clan of Ephraim (1-Chronicles 7:20). Most Presidents of the USA descend from the Scot-Irish of Ulster and most of them have been distantly related to each other.

THE ARMS OF THE GOVERNMENT OF

NORTHERN IRELAND

17

The Tribe of Levi

"And the sons of Levi; Gershon, Kohath, and Merari", Genesis 46:11.

LEVITES AND COHANS

The Levites were the priestly tribe to which Moses and Aharon belonged. From Aharon came the Priests or COHANS. Although they belong to the same Tribe Levites and Cohans are traditionally distinct from each other. The task of the Levites was primarily to teach though they also fulfilled roles in the formal administration and –policing of the Kingdom. They were to be supported from communal tithing and from small plots of their own land surrounding their own city-settlements that were scattered throughout the other Tribes of Israel. From this an important principle is to be learnt from the words of Maimonides:

<<Why did Levi not merit a [Tribal] Inheritance in the Land of Israel and its spoils [at the time of conquest] together with his brothers? The reason is he had been separated out to serve the LORD, to work for HIM, and to teach His ways, His righteous paths and His just judgments to the multitude, as it says, "THEY SHALL TEACH JACOB THY JUDGMENTS, AND ISRAEL THY LAW" [Deuteronomy 33:10]. For this reason they [the Levites] are absolved from regular requirements: They do not have to fight in wars like the rest of Israel. They do not inherit or bequeath to others through the force of their arms, rather they are the Armies of the Almighty, as it says, "BLESS, LORD, HIS

Prowess*" [Deuteronomy 33:11]. Levi was blessed and merited the offerings given to the Almighty, as it says, "I AM THY PART AND THINE INHERITANCE" [Numbers 18:20].>>

<< Not only those from the Tribe of Levi, but every human being throughout the world whose spirit has made him willing, and whose intellect has guided him, to set himself apart before the LORD, to minister unto Him and to serve Him with the purpose of knowing the LORD -- to walk honestly as God intended when He created him and to remove from himself the yoke of the many earthly affairs that human beings pursue. Such a person is holy to the highest degree! The Almighty becomes his portion and his inheritance for all eternity, and will grant him in this world whatever will suffice for his needs, even as He has done for the Kohanim and the Levites. Thus David, peace be upon him, said, "The LORD is my allotted portion and my share, You guide my destiny" [Psalm 16:5].>> Rambam (MAIMONIDES 1135 – 1204) Mishneh Torah, Book 7, Zeraim, the Laws of the Sabbatical and Jubilee Years 13:12-13.

Eventually, the overwhelming majority of Levites fled to Judah before the Ten Tribes were exiled.

"AND THE PRIESTS AND THE LEVITES THAT WERE IN ALL ISRAEL RESORTED TO HIM [REHOBOAM, KING OF JUDAH] OUT OF ALL THEIR COASTS.

"FOR THE LEVITES LEFT THEIR SUBURBS AND THEIR POSSESSION, AND CAME TO JUDAH AND JERUSALEM: FOR JEROBOAM AND HIS SONS HAD CAST THEM OFF FROM EXECUTING THE PRIEST'S OFFICE UNTO THE LORD"
2-Chronicles 11:13-14

Nevertheless, in one way or another groups and individuals from the Tribe of Levi did get mixed up with the Lost Ten Tribes.

LEVI AND SIMEON IN SCANDINAVIA, ITALY, AND AMONGST THE JEWS OF NORTH AFRICA and ASHKENAZ

---

* From the Hebrew "chailo" interpreted in the KJ as SUBSTANCE but "prowess" is the more correct especially in the present context.

Simeon and Levi were brothers, destined to be divided in Jacob, scattered in Israel (Genesis 49:7) and therefore were not to be concentrated in one specific area. The name LEVI recurs in family appellations such as Levison, and Lewis. Likewise a good portion of SIMEON was to be absorbed by Judah both before the Assyrian Exile and afterwards when the Khazars of Scythia (descendants of Simeon and Manasseh) re-converted en-masse to Judaism. Talmudic tradition relates that Simeon was to receive an especial blessing via his affiliation within the Tribe of Judah. Therefore, what applies to Judah in prophecy also has significance concerning the Tribe of Simeon. The Headobards-Lombards descend from Ohad son of Simeon. They were destined to migrate southward from the area of Scandinavia and ultimately conquer and settle the region of Northern Italy now called **LOMBARDY** which is famous for its capital of Milano.. LOMBARDY in ancient times had been known as "Gallia Transpadana" and its one-time inhabitants according to Pliny (N.H. 3; 17) had been called "Laevi" or "**Levi**" (sic.). Thus, the Simeon-Levi association may have been repeated when the Headobards (Ohad from Simeon) settled in the "Levi" neighborhood creating a Lombard-Laevi conjunction. As stated, the Lombards (Headobards) had emerged from Scandinavia and were closely associated with the Angles who later conquered England. Ptolemy reported a people named "Levonii" in Scandinavia. These too may also have had Levite connections and may have been part of the Lombards, since Ptolemy's report dates to the time when the Lombards were probably still within the Scandinavian area, at least in part. Levi, however, like Simeon, seems to have achieved his natural expression more easily through partnership to Judah to whose kingdom (2-Chronicles 13:9-11) many Levites fled. Most Levites appear today to be found scattered amongst all sections of the Jewish people and seem to be especially noticeable amongst certain sections of the North African Jewish communities. The Levites were attendants at the Temple Services and provided the choir. Quite a few outstanding Jewish musicians have been from the Tribe of Levi.

The "Sons of Moses"

The Children of Moses ("Sons of Moses") were a portion of the Levites. In Jewish folklore they are often depicted as a separate entity and linked with the whereabouts of the Lost Ten Tribes*.

"Arabian" Jewish Traditions from the early Christian Era said that the Sons of Moses along with the Lost Ten Tribes were to be found in Central Asia (where part of the Anglo-Saxons were still to be found at that stage) as well as in Gaul (France and its surroundings) and the British Isles. These traditions were almost lost apparently due to the Moslem extermination of Arabian Jews. A few Moslem-Jewish sources however did retain the skeleton of what was once known so that it is quite easy to reconstruct them*. These sources indicate that the location of members of the Lost Ten Tribes in Western areas at one stage had been common knowledge amongst learned Jews in the Middle East. Another point is that in Germany there existed a small group of people known as the Wends or Sorbs. The Sorbs are related to the Serbians and had a Slavic culture until they were overrun by the Germans. DNA

---

* Alternately, it has been proposed that the "Sons of Moses" were not necessarily from Moses at all but rather from Jethro the Midianite who attached himself to Israel because of Moses. It had been prophesied the descendants of Jethro (called "Kenites") would be exiled with the Ten Tribes and ultimately return with them:
<<AND HE LOOKED ON THE KENITES, AND TOOK UP HIS PARABLE, AND SAID, STRONG IS THY WELLINGPLACE, AND THOU PUTTEST THY NEST IN A ROCK.
<<NEVERTHELESS THE KENITE SHALL BE WASTED, UNTIL ASSHUR SHALL CARRY THEE AWAY CAPTIVE. [Numbers 24:21-22]
The Kenites here are those who were to convert together with Jethro and attach themselves to the Children of Israel. They always remained as a somewhat separate group. They were exiled by the Assyrians with the Ten Tribes. They are destined to return with them (Rashi).

* See "Ephraim. The Gentile Children of Israel", Yair Davidi, 2001, chapter two.

studies* indicate that there may be a connection between the Sorbs and the Levites. Similarly the Serbs in Serbia were preceded by the Tribe of Moesi (named after Moses?) of Celtic culture in the present region of Belgrade.

[Deuteronomy 33:8] AND OF LEVI HE SAID, LET THY THUMMIM AND THY URIM BE WITH THY HOLY ONE, WHOM THOU DIDST PROVE AT MASSAH, AND WITH WHOM THOU DIDST STRIVE AT THE WATERS OF MERIBAH;

[Deuteronomy 33:9] WHO SAID UNTO HIS FATHER AND TO HIS MOTHER, I HAVE NOT SEEN HIM; NEITHER DID HE ACKNOWLEDGE HIS BRETHREN, NOR KNEW HIS OWN CHILDREN: FOR THEY HAVE OBSERVED THY WORD, AND KEPT THY COVENANT.

[Deuteronomy 33:10] THEY SHALL TEACH JACOB THY JUDGMENTS, AND ISRAEL THY LAW: THEY SHALL PUT INCENSE BEFORE THEE, AND WHOLE BURNT SACRIFICE UPON THINE ALTAR.

[Deuteronomy 33:11] BLESS, LORD, HIS SUBSTANCE, AND ACCEPT THE WORK OF HIS HANDS; SMITE THROUGH THE LOINS OF THEM THAT RISE AGAINST HIM, AND OF THEM THAT HATE HIM, THAT THEY RISE NOT AGAIN.

---

* DNA studies are not necessarily as reliable as is generally assumed but they have some limited applicability and are worth taking note of. We attribute DNA to changes that take place to the subjects concerned for unknown reasons at unique time periods and are then inherited. At present scientists already admit that DNA changes of the same type can occur on a massive scale can take place after the death of the subject but not before even though they cannot adequately explain why:

<<Our analysis of 1000-year-old mitochondrial DNA from Vikings in England and elsewhere seemed to show that a third or more of them had Middle Eastern ancestry. What was going on? As it turns out, our findings have not led us to rewrite Viking history. Instead, they give exciting new insights into how DNA changes before and after death.....

<<It is almost 15 years since Svante P bo, the "guru" of ancient DNA analysis, showed that bases the "letters" of the genetic code can be modified to resemble one another after death, just as happens in some point mutations during life. .Proceedings of the National Academy of Sciences, vol 86, p 1939>>

Tom Gilbert, "Death and Destruction", New Scientist Magazine 31.5. 03 Scientists also admit that animals and humans can be infected (a type of environmental influence) by an intracellular parasite that effects changes in their mitochondrial DNA and these changes are then transmitted through heredity. See Nadjar Nitz, Antonio Teixeira "Cell" 23 July 2004, The Scientist July 23, 2004

Levi

The Israeli stamp depicts the High Priests breastplate that was worn during the Temple service and as an oracle. It is the symbol of Levi.

- 01: **Caledones (Caledonii)**
- 02: **Taexali**
- 03: **Carvetii**
- 04: **Venicones**
- 05: **Epidii**
- 06: **Damnonii**
- 07: **Novantae**
- 08: **Selgovae**
- 09: **Votadini**
- 10: **Brigantes**
- 11: **Parisi**
- 12: **Cornovii**
- 13: **Deceangli**
- 14: Ordovoices
- 15: **Corieltauvi**
- 16: **Iceni**
- 17: **Demetae**
- 18: **Catuvellauni**
- 19: **Silures**
- 20: **Dubunni**
- 21: **Dumnonii**
- 22: **Durotriges**
- 23: **Belgae**
- 24: **Atrebates**
- 25: **Regni**
- 26: **Cantiaci**
- 27: **Trinovantes**

British "Celtic" Tribes

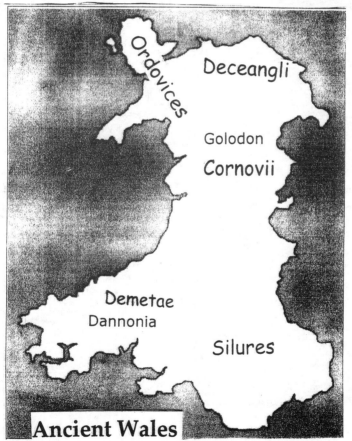

Ordovices

Deceangli

Golodon

Cornovii

Demetae

Dannonia

Silures

Ancient Wales

299

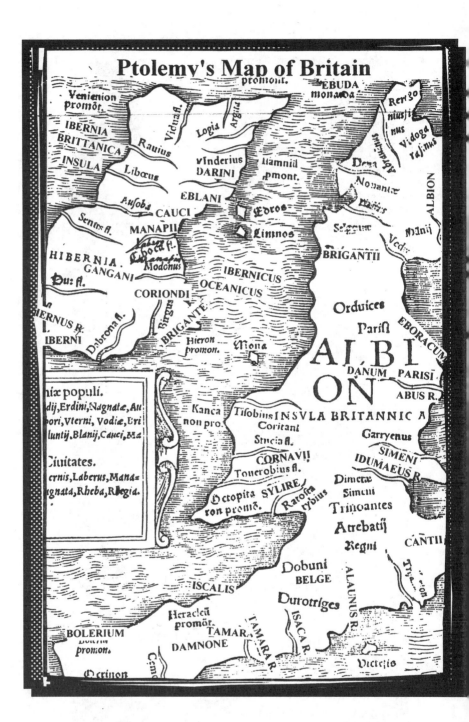

Ptolemy's Map of Britain

Ptolemy's Map of
SCOTLAND

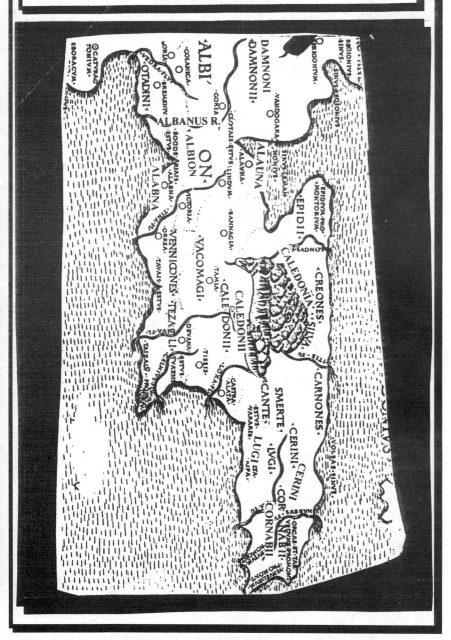

Ptolemy's Map of
IRELAND

OCEANUS HYPERBOREUS

ROBOGDI

DARNII

VOLUNTII

Boreum Pr.

ERIDINI · VENICNII

BLANII   ○ Eblana

NAGNATE

CAUCI

MANAPII   ○ Manapia

AUTEIRI

CORIONDI

GAGGANIE

BRIGANTES

Sinus R.

VELIBORI ○ Ivernis

OUTERNI VODIAE

IBERNI

18

Ancient Britain and Ireland

PTOLEMY ON THE BRITISH ISLES

There follows a brief analysis of Ptolemy's Maps of the British Isles and the situation as it developed after Ptolemy. There are separate maps Britain, Scotland, and Ireland. Ptolemy's Map of Britain shows the Tribal situation in the Celtic era but is not all-inclusive. Other groups not mentioned by Ptolemy are known to have been in Britain according to Roman and later Celtic accounts though at all events Ptolemy's description is, on the whole, the best available. The information on which these maps are based dates from before the Anglo-Saxon and Viking conquests. Our analysis will continue to include a description of the situation after the Anglo-Saxons and their associates had settled in Britain.

In Northeast **SCOTLAND** (Albion) Ptolemy placed the **LUGI**. The Lugi were also reported on the Continent near the Vistula River and, like the Lygi, are considered part of the Vandals or a Celtic people whom the Vandals absorbed. The Vandals were destined to settle in Northern England and Lowland Scotland and descend from Asher.

The **CALEDONII** relate to Gilead and the Galatae. **ALAUNA** reminds one that the name ALAN was to be found amongst the Celtic Scotch suggesting a connection with the Alans of Scythia who came from Elon, son of Zebulon. The presence of the **GADENI** near here is known from other sources. The Gadeni came from Gad.

The names **ALBA** and **ALBION** imply a relationship with Albania of the Caucasus from which area part of the Picts traditionally came. Alba" and "Albion" are also cognate with Lebanon. The Picts were in this part of Scotland and derived from the Agathyrsi, as did the Khazars. The **DON RIVER** of Scotland is in this region and there was another Don River to the south confluent with the Humber in Northern England and passing by the city of Danum. The Don Rivers are reminiscent of the Don River in Scythia and the Tribe of DAN.

The **DAMNONII** also relate to DAN, as explained in the chapter on Dan. The **BRIGANTES** came from BERIAH (Beria-g-h), son of Asher, and were also found in Switzerland and Southeast Ireland.

The **PARISI** came from Peresh son of Machir and part of Gilead, meaning the Galatae. They were centered about Eburacum (York City of Hebrews) and also were in Gaul where they gave their name to Paris, the capital city.

The **ABUS** River (i.e. the Humber) bears a name recalled in the Abi Scythae who came from Job, son of Issachar, near Scythian Serica

The **SIMENI** came from Simeon of Israel. They adjoined the Iceni of Yacin, son of Simeon, and on their border was the **IDUMAUS** River, just as in the Land of Israel Idumea (Edom) bordered the territory of Simeon and was in part conquered and settled by Simeonites. The **SYLIRES** (Silures) of Southern Wales came from Saul, son of Simeon. The **ALAUNUS** River in the south parallels the presence of **ALAUNA** town in the north.

The **ISACA** River was named after ISAAC, father of Israel, just as the Usk River in Silure territory of Southern Wales was named Isc and flowed by the town of **ISCA**.

The **TAMARUS** River in the south was named after TAMAR, a wife of Judah, and mother of Perez and Zerah, sons of Judah. The territory of Judah had adjoined that of Dan and the **DAMNONES** were also called Dannonians and Daunians and relate to Dan, as do the **DAMNONII** in Scotland and the Damnae of Scythian Serica.

In **IRELAND** existed a portion of **BRIGANTES** from Beriah of Asher; the **IBERNI** suggest Iberia in the Caucasus, a place of Israelite exile. The Scotch and Irish Gaels called themselves IBERI or Hiberi which name means HEBREW. All the inhabitants of the British Isles were known as Iberi meaning Hebrews. The **MANAPII** were recalled in the Menapii of Holland and Menapia of Bactria east of the Caspian Sea. The **CAUCI** were parallelled by the Chauki Franks in Europe and the Cachage Scythae of Scythia, descended from Hagi (Chagi) of Gad. Irish Mythology is replete with Hebrew sounding names and ancestral appellations similar to Israelite Tribal Clans. On the West Coast (Mayo region) Ptolemy located the Venicni who were related to the Venetes in Brittany (France) and the Galedoni in North Wales.

Additional Celtic-British associations with Biblical Patriarchs include Gebar of Manasseh: Gabraontovices, Gabraige, Gabair, Gabreta, Guberni, Gabran, Gabair, Girvii, etc.; Gomer = Mont-gomery, Gumeraeg, etc.; Eladah of Ephraim = Uladah (i.e. Ulster); Abel beth Maachah of Nephtali = Emain Macha of Ireland; Maachah of Manasseh = Machah of Ireland; Israel= Isru; Keren (i.e. Karnayim of East Manasseh) = The god Cernunnos and numerous tribal names especially in Scotland and West Britain bearing the root CRN; Oriel = The province of Oriel in Ireland.

BRITAIN AFTER THE TIME OF PTOLEMY AND THE SUBSEQUENT INVASIONS

The Picts were first reported after 280 CE. They were believed (like the Iberi-Scotts) to have arrived from Southern Scythia where they were known as the Agathyrsi or Akatziri whose remnants later formed the nucleus of the Khazar nation in Southern Russia. The Khazars were descended from Simeon and Manasseh as well as containing representatives of other tribes such as Judah, Ephraim, Naphtali and Asher. Vikings from Norway (from Naphtali) settled in areas of the Scottish Highlands as well as in Northwest England. Vikings from Denmark (Dan) settled in the Northeast of England and the east coast of Ireland.

The Angles and Vandals settled in Northumbria which in the wake of the later Viking invasions moved north into Lowland Scotland whilst losing ground in Northern England to the Scandinavian invaders. The Vandal element was represented by the Varin or Warings. These were akin to the Varangian Vikings and Varachan Khazars. The name WARING may be derived from that of Beriah*, son of Asher. They settled besides the Bryges or Brigantes who also were descended from Beriah (Numbers 26:44). In some records the name "Beragio" appears amongst the list of peoples invading Britain and this name too may be a form for Beriah and represent the Waring Vandals.

The Frissi from Frisia (Holland), according to Procopius, joined in the invasion with the Angles and settled in the former area of the Celtic Parissi in Northern England. In Hebrew both the names "Frissi" and "Parissi" may be derived from the one original "Peresh", son of Machir, son of Manasseh (1-Chronicles 7:16). This region was later approximately that wherein the Danish Vikings from Denmark settled. The Danes were descended from Dan, son of Israel, and were not far from the British Don River and the Celtic city of Danum, both of which related to an earlier branch of Dan's people in Britain.

Galedon in North Wales (also known as Gododdin and Votadini) represented a later group of Celtic culture related to the Caledonians of Scotland and also associated with the Isle of Wight. They included elements of the Venetii from Brittany in Gaul who had once achieved renown for their maritime

---

* In Hebrew "B" may be exchanged for "V" or "W", and the "-iah" in Beriah, has a guttural "ayin" rendered sometimes as "g" thus Beriah = "Veriah-(g)h", Varing, Waring

abilities and show traces of Phoenician culture. The Galedoni came from Gilead, son of Machir, son of Manasseh, and neighbored the Mercian Saxons, also from Machir. Norwegian Viking invaders were to settle to the Northwest of Mercia and derived from the Nephtalite Huns, descendants of Naphtali, who, from Scythia, had colonized Norway before re-settling in Britain. The clan of Davis was centered in North Wales having moved there from Southern Scotland.

The Mercians came basically from Machir of Menasseh whereas the Angles in Northumbria, to their north, and in Anglia, to their east, came from Ephraim.

South of the Mercians and Angles were the Saxons who had no relation to the people later known as "Saxons" in Germany. The Saxons of England often called themselves "Angles" or at least did not object to being subsumed under the Angle name. The whole country was later called "Angle-land" or "England" as it is called today. The diminutive of Angle was "Aegel" meaning "Bull-calf" in Hebrew and applied in the Bible as a diminutive for the Tribe of Ephraim. The Saxons were descended from the Sacae of Scythia, and their name means "Sons of Isaac". Abraham, the forefather of the Hebrew race, had been Divinely assured, *"In Isaac will your seed be called"* (Gen. 21:13). This may be understood as a promise that that portion of his seed which would most blatantly fulfill the worldly aspect of his hereditary mission would bear a name recalling his own, as the Anglo-SAXONS, "Sons of Isaac", indeed do!

Amongst the Saxons of Essex were the Scygs, possibly related to Naphtali, as explained in the text relating to the Tribal distribution in Serica, east of Scythia.

In the Southeast were the Jutes who, according to tradition, had initiated the final full-scale Anglo-Saxon invasion and conquest of England. The Jutes were somehow connected (according to archaeological finds and references in French texts) with the Franks, though they had arrived originally from

Jutland in Denmark. Danish tradition related that the Danes and Jutes and Angles were all of one family and that the Danes descended from Dan, son of Israel, and the Jutes from Judah. The very name "Jute" as well as various variations of it on the Continent, was synonymous with the appellation applied to a JEW who, on the whole, probably descended from the Tribe of Judah, though the Jews also included many from Benjamin, Simeon, Levi, Ephraim, and Manasseh (2-Chronicles 15:10), as well as elements from most of the other tribes. The Jews thus contain similar Tribal constituents to those Israelite groupings amongst the British peoples, though the relative proportions differ. Different historical and religious experience has profoundly emphasized the present day gulf of identity between both JUDAH and JOSEPH.

In the east a portion of the Angles settled East ANGLIA in the area formerly ascribed to the Simeni and Iceni of Simeon descent. On the Continent Tacitus reported the Angles as belonging to the SEMNONE group which name also connects with Simeon. Though the Angles are proven to primarily been descended from the Tribe of Ephraim son of Joseph, a section from the Tribe of Simeon may too have been attached to them.

[Genesis 49:27] BENJAMIN SHALL RAVIN AS A WOLF: IN THE MORNING HE SHALL DEVOUR THE PREY, AND AT NIGHT HE SHALL DIVIDE THE SPOIL.

[Deuteronomy 33:12] AND OF BENJAMIN HE SAID, THE BELOVED OF THE LORD SHALL DWELL IN SAFETY BY HIM; AND THE LORD SHALL COVER HIM ALL THE DAY LONG, AND HE SHALL DWELL BETWEEN HIS SHOULDERS.

FINLAND (SUOMI)
SIMEON, GAD, ISSACHAR

Finland is identified in this work as belonging mainly to the Tribes of Gad, Simeon, and especially Issachar. For many years, Finland was ruled by Sweden (Gad) and many Swedes remained in Finland. One of the symbols of Gad was a lion, while the Tribe of Simeon could be represented by a sword (in popular Jewish Art) presumably due to the "instruments of cruelty" (Gen.49:5 *Clei Hamas* = *"tools of violence"*) they were likened unto and their use (together with Levi) of the sword in massacring the inhabitants of Canaanite Schechem. Both the Sword (Simeon) and the Lion (Gad) are prominent on the Finnish Coat of Arms.

Belgium

Belgium is a Union between Walloons and Flemings. The Walloons descend from the ancient Belgae who derive from Benjamin son of Israel. The Flemings came from the Sicambri (of Shechem from Manasseh), from the Salian Franks (of Shaul son of Simeon) and from Franks in general who mainly belonged to Reuben, and also from Zebulon. The Flemings also contain a Dutch element that is dominated by Zebulon.

The Walloons descend from the ancient Belgae. The general quality of BELGIUM in this work has been attributed to Benjamin.

The shield of Belgium features lions. The LION is a symbol of Israel and especially of the Kingdom of Judah (with whom Benjamin was united) and connotes the Tribes of Israel in their unified state under the House of David.

The motto on the shield, "Union Fait La Force", means, "UNION GIVES STRENGTH".

19

BENJAMIN

"And the sons of Benjamin were Belah, and Becher, and Ashbel, Gera, and Naaman, Ehi, and Rosh, Muppim, and Huppim, and Ard" Genesis 46:21.

Benjamin in Israel

The Tribes of Judah and BENJAMIN together were to compose the main stock of the modern Jewish people. They were the Tribes that remained after the Ten Northern Tribes split away (-Kings 12:23, 2-Chronicles 11:1,3 Ezra 10:9, etc). Most of Benjamin in the Land of Israel was contained within the Kingdom of Judah of which Benjamin and Judah were the major tribes. Nevertheless a portion of Benjamin was also to be found within the area of the Northern Kingdom and these must have shared the fate of their fellow Israelites who were exiled by the Assyrians. Archaeological findings from the city of Mari on the Euphrates River in Northern Syria revealed inscriptions that spoke of the Banu-Yamina (Benjamin) people in that area[1]. [They also speak of Manasseh, Reuben, and the people of Yair, and of Hebrews in general in the same regions]. The Talmud (Zebachim 118.b) says that a strip of land extended from Benjamin into Ephraim and encompassed the Tabernacle in Shiloh. Shiloh is about in the center of the territory of Ephraim according to conventional understanding and would have been well within the region of the Northern Kingdom after its secession from Judah. Similarly, the Bible recalls people from Benjamin in the area of Ephraim or sometimes associates the

Mount of Ephraim with Benjaminites, e.g. Shiba son of Bichri (2- Samuel 20:21) a Benjaminite in "Mount Ephraim". E.Z. MELAMED[2] and Yehudah KIEL[3] concluded from Biblical references (1-Chr. 7:12 cf. 7:15) that Machir the son of Manasseh on the east bank of the Jordan took wives from Benjamin whose descendants may have induced other Benjaminites to settle amongst them. Later, the Tribesmen of Benjamin in turn took spouses from Jabesh-Gilead of Manasseh east of the Jordan (Judges ch. 21). It was Saul of Benjamin who rescued the inhabitants of Jabesh-Gilead from their enemies (1-Samuel ch.11). In the Book of Obadiah (1:19) it says that in the future, "Benjamin shall possess Gilead" and it is likely that this prophecy was based on some past association of Benjamin with that area[4]. At all events, part of the Tribe of Benjamin was also exiled along with the Ten others.

We have traced BENJAMIN to the NORMANS and to part of the BELGAE tribes.

THE NORMANS

The Normans had the same country of origin in North Germany as the Saxons according to Julian[5]. They were called Transalbingi or Nordalbingi[6] (i.e. "North-of-the-Elbe") like the Saxons had also been termed. These Norman-"Nordalbingi" were connected to the remnant of Angles and Saxons who were left behind when their compatriots invaded England or who for some reason returned from the invasion. The Normans moved into Scandinavia and dwelt in parts of Denmark and Norway before moving onwards. There were some Swedes[7] amongst the Normans though Norwegian sagas and English tradition[8] suggest that most of them came from Norway. Genealogies of Norman-descended nobles in England often trace them to early Norwegian kings and heroes. Place-names in Normandy (France) suggest links with Norway. Modern consensus[9], however, seems to be that the Normans came mainly from

Denmark. Wherever they came from, they had their own peculiarities and quickly developed their own national character and culture. They even may have had their own particular physical features being often presumed as appearing somewhat darker than the usual Scandinavian, tending even to dusky, and also as being tall and lanky though these impressions may be exaggerated. The point is, in the same way as other groups had earlier emerged from the midst of the Scandinavians as distinct recognizable entities, so the Normans may always have been a distinct people a hard core of which had maintained their own identity.

The Normans really became recognizable to the historian when in 860 CE a band of Vikings led By Rollo received the area afterwards called Normandy from the King of France. Those Vikings who settled in Normandy together with local inhabitants who intermarried with them and/or identified with them became known as the Normans. Dudo[10] (ca 960), himself a Norman, said that the Normans came from Danes descendants of the ancient (Greek) Danae and had reached the north via the Balkans and that their forefathers were the Dacae. There are Danish traditions that trace their ancestry back to Israel.

Within one or two generations of their first settlement the Normans were no longer recognizable as Scandinavian. They had changed their language[11], religion, and culture. They intermixed with the peoples of Brittany in France. These were Celts and Alans. The Alans had come from the Caucasus area at the time of Attilla the Hun and settled in Brittany. Their use of armored cavalry and tactics were to influence the Normans[12]. Those Alans who remained in the east were to confederate with the Khazars and to be identified with them. The Celts of Brittany (amongst whom first the Alans then the Normans settled) were to a degree descended from Celtic peoples of Britain and after conquering England the Normans would adopt the Celtic Arthurian legends as part of their own heritage[13]. In 1066 the Normans conquered England. Their total forces included many others who came over from France with them, and these comprised maybe a third or more of their total forces. The "Normans" eventually contributed about ten percent of England's total population[14] and it has been estimated that approximately twenty percent of the English population has a significant degree of Norman blood in them. In the course of time Normans also settled in Scotland, Wales, and Ireland. There was also an element of Edomites amongst the Normans. In ancient times Essus (Esuvius i.e. Esau)[15] had been considered an ancestor and worshipped by some of the Celtic people within whose area the Normans settled and with whom they intermixed. Most of these Celtic peoples were however probably of Israelite origin.

The English upper classes contain a significant number of Norman descendants. After about 1700 a large proportion (it is claimed) of the higher ranked aristocratic English families intermarried with Jews[16] at some stage or other. [-*This group has however proved itself of being on occasion as anti-Semitic as anybody else. Apart from revealing a non-fraternal instinct anti-Semitism is a disqualifying factor for other reasons. It is usually concomitant with selfishness and non-Israelite characteristics*]. The modern Jews descend from the two tribes of Benjamin and Judah, on the whole.   Amongst the Normans were many descendants of Benjamin and possibly also of Judah. We thus see a tendency for Benjamin to reconnect to Judah. The basic Norman stock may have come from Benjamin in addition to which the area of Normandy in France settled by them had previously belonged to the NAMNETES who derived their name from **Naaman**, a son of Benjamin. Since the "-etes" Namn<u>etes</u> is a suffix the names are in effect identical. There were also Benjaminites in part of Norway wherein part of the Normans had sojourned though most of Israelite Norway is descended from Naphtali and other tribes.

Benjamin, Judah, Levi, Simeon, and small numbers of most of the other tribes had remained together as Jews in the southern realm of Judah when the Assyrians exiled most of the Israelites in the Northern Kingdom of Israel. At the same time large numbers from the southern kingdom were also to be taken into exile by the Assyrians and in other ways were to be counted as part of the Lost Tribes of Israel. Amongst this last group was part of the Tribe of Benjamin which apparently became the basic stock of the so-called Norman nation. Jewish Medieval tradition said that the Tribe of Benjamin (or a small part of it) had gone into exile to the Balkan region of Rumania[17], or to the land of Germany[18], or to both. From the Balkans (Rumania) emerged the Dacae who were considered a branch of Sacae-Scythians. The Dacae were together with the Getae. From the Dacae came the Normans who were believed to have reached Scandinavia via Germany. The Dacae according to Lempriere were a western branch of the Sakae[19]. The wolf was a symbol of the Dacae[20] amongst the Getae. The Norman symbol is also said to have been a wolf. The Conquest of England by the Norman William the Conqueror was celebrated on the Bayeux Tapestry whose execution was overseen by his wife, Queen Matilda. It depicts a wolf on the standard of William. Godfroi de Bouillon (ca.1099), Crusader King of Jerusalem, claimed descent from Benjamin (Genesis 49:27)[21]. Old accounts say that the Franks had come from the former Saxon area of Maurunganie in North Germany below the place of the Normans. The first ruling house of the Franks was the Merovingians and recently it has been claimed that the Merovingian Franks were descended from Benjamin*

---

* See BAIGENT, LEIGH, & LINCOLN, "The Messianic Legacy", 1986, 1987 U.K.
The genealogist, Athol BLOOMER, however says, "The Merovingians are most likely from the Tribe of Dan. Their tradition of long hair and the name Samson among the Royal House would indicate descent from Samson and thus the Tribe of Dan".
Another claim (H. HOEH, "Compendium of World History", 1962, 1967 USA) is that they derived from a non-Davidic branch of Judah.

SONS OF BENJAMIN: BELGAE

In France the Normans settled south of the Seine River. North of the Seine in Caesar's time dwelt the Belgae and later many of the Sicambrian Franks were superimposed on them. The name **"Belah"** (Genesis 46:21: בֶּלַע), son of Benjamin, may alternatively be pronounced in Hebrew as **"Bela(g)h"** which ultimately in the plural would become something close to BELGAE. Place-names derived from the Hebrew "Belah" include "Balagea" and "Belginaea". These were recorded by Ptolemy east of the Jordan in the former Land of Israel. The Belgae were present in Northern Gaul and gave their name to Belgium. Tribes of Belgae were also found in Southern Britain, in Northern Wales, and in Ireland. Bela(g)h was a son of Benjamin as was **Muppim** who became the Belgian MENAPI, also found as ("MANAPII") in Southeast Ireland and in the region of MENAPIA in Bactria, east of the Caspian, as recorded by Ptolemy. **Ard**, son of Benjamin, is found in the Ardueni, likewise in Belgae lands. In this area of the Belgae were the Samara (Somme) river and the city of Samarbriva and the Sambre River all named after **SAMARIA**[22] synonym for Northern Israel prior to the exile of the Ten Tribes.

South of the Belgae in what later became "NORMANDY" (or just south of it in Brittany) were the NAMNETES who either descended from **Nemuel** (Numbers 26:12) of SIMEON or from **NAAMAN** (Genesis 46:21) son of BENJAMIN or from both. A similarly named people to the Namnetes were the Nemeti just east of the Belgae in North Gaul on the west bank of the Rhine. **Rosh**, son of Benjamin seems to be represented in the ROSS clan of Scotland.

Nemuel was the name of a patriarchal figure of both Reuben (Numbers 29:9) and Simeon (1 - Chr 4:24).

Bela-g-h (i.e. Bela) was a clan-head in both Benjamin (Genesis 46:21) and in Reuben (1-Chr. 5:8). On the whole Reuben became predominant in Gaul though in some areas both Simeon and Benjamin were still important so a certain overlapping of Tribal identities is to be expected.

Benjamin altogether had ten sons (Genesis 46:21): Belah, and Becher, and Ashbel, Gera, and Naaman, Ehi, and Rosh, Muppim, and Huppim, and Ard. Most of the present day descendants of Benjamin are probably to be found amongst the Jewish people, and to have shared the Jewish role in history. Benjamin became a major contributor to the Belgae peoples and possibly also the Normans who conquered England and part of France.

Benjamin together with Judah, Simeon, and Levi were to comprise most of the Jewish nation which also contains small numbers of the remaining tribes in the same way as these tribes, or rather the nations they now represent, contain Tribal elements from the major Tribes of the present day Jews.

Already, here and there in the present study more than one Israelite group has been equated with the same historical people due to a shared similarity of names and other factors. Naaman of Benjamin, for instance, as well as Nemuel of Simeon may both be identified with the Namnetes of Breton-Normandy in France. A few further examples of double-identification amongst Israelite descended ethnic units will be found in the following pages. This phenomenon will be seen as consistent with Biblical and Historical evidence and will be discussed later.

So far in this work, the Tribe of Reuben was identified as the Franks and the Celts of France; the Tribe of Gad was identified with the Goths, Naphtali as Norwegian-Vikings, Dan as the Dans, Simeon as mainly Western Celts, Judah as Jews and Jutes, and Benjamin as the Norman and Belgae. The following chapters of "The Tribes" continue the explanation of Tribal - identification and deals mainly with the peoples of Scandinavia, Scotland, Holland, Switzerland, and Finland. The relevant Tribes are Asher, Issachar and Zebulon.

Finally the Tribes of Joseph and the English-speaking peoples are considered at length.

317

THE FAMILY TREE OF BENJAMIN

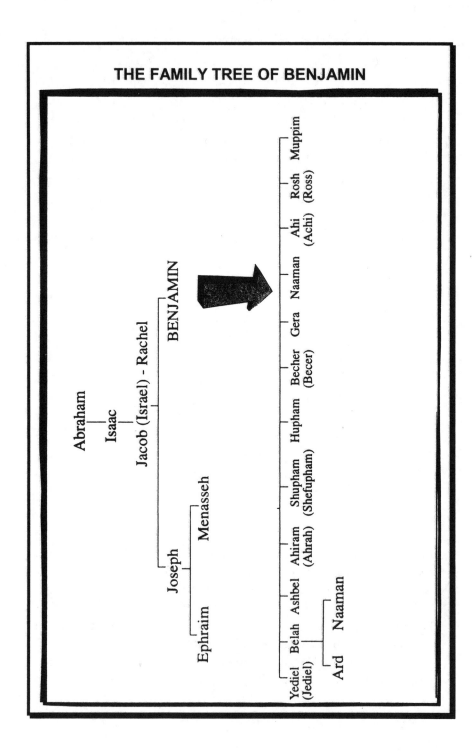

318

The Clans of Benjamin

Belah (Bela-g-h) = Belagae.

Becher = see Becher of Ephraim, similarity of name often presaged future combination.

Ashbel

Gera -

Naaman = Nemetae (north of Gaul), Namnete (in Brittania - Normandia possibly also from Nemuel of Simeon).

Ehi (Ahi).

Rosh = Rus (Vikings in Russia), Ross (Scotch Highlands).

Muppim = Menapi (in Ireland, Celtic Britain, and Belgium, and in Bactria east of the Caspian).

Huppim = Heath (in Anglo-Saxon England).

Ard = Ardueni (in Belgium).

20

THE TRIBE OF ASHER

"AND THE SONS OF ASHER; JIMNAH, AND ISHUAH, AND ISUI, AND BERIAH, AND SERAH THEIR SISTER" AND THE SONS OF BERIAH; HEBER, AND MALCHIEL" GENESIS 46:17.

THE VANDALS

Vandal-Isation?

Simplified descriptions of British History usually depict Britain as originally populated by "Celts", who were conquered by Anglo-Saxons, who in turn were conquered by Normans of Scandinavian origin. The actual details are far more complicated. The Normans included many native "Bretons" from Celtic Brittany in France and also many adventurers and mercenaries from various other parts of France were in the Norman forces. The Celts of Britain, according to some authorities, may not have been strictly speaking Celts at all. At all events they were not a homogeneous people but rather very disparate groups culturally and otherwise. Similarly, the Anglo-Saxon invaders actually consisted of numerous Scandinavian and Northern Tribes amongst whom the VANDALS were quite important.

The historian Procopius reported that the Vandals had come from the Sea of Azov area just north of the Black Sea by the River Don. The Vandals in the first century CE had been known as Lygians or Lugii. They had then been located by the

Upper Vistula River. They absorbed a Celtic group in the area who had previously had a highly developed "La Tene" type culture[1]. The Lygian-Vandal tribes were the Boreoi, the Omani, and the Heissi[2]. These names are similar to those of the sons of Asher (Jimnah, Ishuah, Isui, and Beriah) and several factors serve to equate Asher with the Vandals as well as with other entities. The sons of Asher were Jimnah, and Ishuah, and Isui, and Beriah, and Serah their sister: and the sons of Beriah; Heber and Malchiel (Genesis 46:17). The sons of Asher correspond to the Tribes of the Lygian Vandals; Jimnah became the Omani, Isui the Heissi, and Beriah the Boreoi. The Vandals may also be identified as the legendary VANES who had dwelt in Vanaland besides the Don River in Southern Scythia and then moved to Scandinavia. According to legend as recorded by Snorre Sturlassen (1179 – 1241), the Vanes had first warred and then amalgamated with the Aseir. The Aseir (singular, "As") like the Vanes were to become ancestors to part of the Scandinavians. "AS" in Phoenician Hebrew was a shortened form for ASHER[3], and Phoenician-Hebrew appears to have been the dialect employed by the Northern Ten Tribes prior to their exile[4]. The Aseir are also equated by scholars with the Ansis who become the ruling elite among the Goths[5]. The Royal family of the Ostrogoths were known as the Amal and "Amal" son of Helem (1-Chronicles 7:35) is recalled amongst the early forefathers of the tribe of Asher. Goths and Vandals spoke the same language and were considered different branches of the same people[6].

The Vandals had first appeared south of the Burgundians who in turn were south of the Goths on the Baltic coast, east of the Vistula. At that stage the Vandals were led by two leaders, named AMBRI and Assi[7]. The name "Ambri" is reminiscent of the Ambri who, with the Sicambri (Franks), encountered Alexander the Great in Bactria (Justin Book xii;ix) and later moved to Northern Europe whence in ca. 109-101 BCE they joined the Cimbri and Teutons in attacking Rome. Their name is recalled in Ambrum, Imbri, and Ymbre of Scandinavia[8]. They were descendants of Jimna (Yimna) son of Asher.

The name of the second leader of the Vandals was "ASSI" which is the same name as that of the people of "Assi" in Roman Chronicles. These were referred to in Chinese records as WUSUN[9]. They were recorded as having once conquered the Goths (Yueh-chi) in East Scythia. After that they then moved to the Don River region before migrating northward. They were also known as the Aseir (As). The Aseir were the people of Odin and migrated to Scandinavia.

BERIAH son of ASHER

Pliny (N.H. 4; 14) said that the VANDALS were a federation encompassing the Vandili, Varini, Goths, and Burgundians. The Burgundians were to settle in France and Switzerland and are associated with the Swedish isle of Bornholm[10]. The Burgundians descended from BERIAH son of ASHER whose name may also be pronounced as Beria(g)h or "Veriag"[*]. Similar appellations to Beria(g)h were "Barragos", "Varegu", and "Variag" which names were applied to the Vikings, especially those who penetrated Russia[11]. A related people were the Varachan Huns[12] who were a Tribal component amongst the Khazars in southern Russia. The Varins or "WARINGS" who came with the Angles and Saxons to Britain were to conquer the Celtic Brigantes. The Brigantes were also descended from Beriah. They were located in the northern areas of Roman Britain (i.e. North England), in Gaul, in east Switzerland and in southeast Ireland.

THE VANDALS BECOME "AFRICANS"

From the Vistula Region in present-day Eastern Poland the Vandals had moved south and for a time were subject to the Romans in Pannonia (Hungary). In the 400's CE the Vandals

---

[*] Since the " ah" of Beriah is a guttural "Ayin" (and can be pronounced like a "g") and "B" and V" interchange in Hebrew.

323

participated in the invasion of Roman Gaul and then penetrated Spain where Andalusia (Vandalusia) still bears their name. In 429 CE the Vandals, under their king Geiseric, crossed the Straits of Gibraltar into North Africa. From North Africa the Vandals raided and plundered the city of Rome (Italy) in 445 CE. A tradition states that in their raid on Rome the Vandals "liberated" treasures taken from the Temple in Jerusalem that the Romans had destroyed in 66 CE[13]. Some of the treasures were retaken by the Byzantines and may have been "liberated" again later by the Goths. The possibility also exists that some of the Temple treasures went with the Vandals to Ireland and then to Britain. The Byzantines in 533 CE crushed the last vestiges of the Vandal kingdom though most of the Vandals appear to have left the province of North Africa previously. At all events after their defeat, Procopius records that the entire Vandal nation took ship and sailed away. In the Vandal period North Africa via Spain had been invaded by other related groups such as the "Massagetae" (probably Nephtalites), Suebi, Franks, and others and these must have joined the Vandals and moved with them to Ireland and from there to Britain.

Geoffrey of Monmouth (History of the Kings of Britain", ca. 1136) reported that 160,000 "Africans" from Ireland joined the Saxons in invading Britain. These so called "Africans" were Vandals and kindred bands*

---

* Geoffrey of Monmouth: History of the Kings of Britain" Chapter 8.
<<Britain, in the flame of a civil war under king Careticus, is miserably wasted by the Saxons and Africans.

<<After Malgo succeeded Careticus, a lover of civil war, and hateful to God and to the Britons. The Saxons, discovering his fickle disposition, went to Ireland for GORMUND, KING OF THE AFRICANS, who had arrived there with a very great fleet, and had subdued that country. From thence, at their traitorous instigation, he sailed into Britain, which the perfidious Saxons in one part, in another the Britons by their continual wars among themselves were wholly laying waste. Entering therefore into alliance with the Saxons, he made war upon king Careticus, after several battles fought, drove him from city to city, till at length he forced him to Cirecester, and ther besieged him. Here Isembard, the nephew of Lewis, king of the Franks, came and made a league of amity with him, and out of respect to him renounced the Christian faith, on condition that he would assist him to gain the kingdom of Gaul from his uncle, by whom, he said, he was

Sons of Asher

The Vandal presence in Britain is also evidenced from other areas. The Romans after 277 CE had encouraged Alamans, Burgundians, and Vandals to settle in Britain and ultimately it is believed that these settlers assisted the Anglo-Saxons in invading Britain in the 450's. Bede (Ecclesiastical History book iv, ch.ix) mentions the Rugini amongst the Anglo-Saxon forces. The Rugini were a Vandal group. The Rugini on the continent

---

forcibly and unjustly expelled out of it. At last, after taking and burning the city, he had another fight with Careticus, and made him flee beyond the Severn into Wales. He then made an utter devastation of the country, set fire to the adjacent cities, and continued these outrages until he had almost burned up the whole surface of the island from one sea to the other; so that the tillage was everywhere destroyed, and a general destruction made of the husbandmen and clergy, with fire and sword. This terrible calamity caused the rest to flee whithersoever they had any hopes of safety.

Chapter 10
Loegria is again inhabited by the Saxons. The Britons, with their bishops, retire into Cornwall and Wales

<<But to return to history; when the inhuman tyrant, with many thousands of his AFRICANS, had made a devastation almost over the whole island, he yielded up the greater part of it, called Loegria [i.e. the area now known as England], to the Saxons, whose villainy had been the occasion of his arrival. Therefore the remainder of the Britons retired into the western parts of the kingdom, that is, Cornwall and Wales; from whence they continually made frequent and fierce irruptions upon the enemy...Many more went over in a great fleet to Armorican Britain [Brittany in Western France]..

<<The Saxons ... went unto Gormund, King of the Africans IN IRELAND, wherein, adventuring thither with a vast fleet, he had conquered the folk of the country. Thereupon, by the treachery of the Saxons, he sailed across with a hundred and sixty thousand Africans into Britain ... (and) laid waste, as has been said, well-nigh the whole island with his countless thousands of Africans>> (bk. xi, sect. 8, 10).

cf. GILBERT p.248: "As Vandal fleets of over 500 were not uncommon, the idea of a massive fleet able to evacuate the entire nation of some 160,000 people should not be discounted.... The disappearance of a King of Africa from Africa and the appearance at around the same date of a King of Africa in Ireland and Britain seems more than coincidental." (Adrian GILBERT, Alan WILSON, and Baram BLACKETT, "The Holy Kingdom", UK, 1998). We identified the "Africans" in Ireland with the Vandals before the work of Gilbert became known to us. Gilbert suggests that the Vandals from Ireland invaded England and are identifiable as the Mercians who dominated the West and Center. We, on the other hand, identify the Vandals with the Warings and company who settled in Northern England and Lowland Scotland.

were known to have been in the host of Attilla the Hun. The isle of Rugen in the Baltic is named after them and this isle was once a Vandal center[14]; there is also a Rogaland in Norway. [A small portion of this tribe settled temporarily in part of Austria[16]. They later moved out and today most Austrians belong to the Indo-Germanic and Slavonic elements that were "native" to Europe]. The names Rugini, Roga, and Rugen in connection with the Vandals derive from Rohgah son of Shomer son of Heber son of Beriah son of Asher (1-Chr. 7:30-34). Another group of Vandals were the Varini or Warings.

The VARINI had been allocated to the VANDALI group by Pliny together with Vandili, Goths, and Burgundians. The Varini in England were known as Warings and appear together with the Angles[16]. The royal clan of the Warings was the Billings. Also on the Continent, Angles and Warings were associated in the Province of Thuringia. The British Province of Brigantia was conquered by the Angles who contained a substantial Vandal and Varini component. The exact proportion of different peoples amongst the Anglo-Saxon invaders is unclear. East Anglia, for instance, was settled by Angles in the 450's but already in the 500's its kings were supposed to have come from Sweden[17] and presumably had brought Gothic or Swedish warriors with them.

Beriah [Beria(g)h], son of Asher, gave his name to the people of Bergio who were reported by Jordanes in Scandinavia, to the Varag-Huns among the Khazars, to the Variag or Varangian-Vikings, to the Warings, to the Burgundians, and to the Brigantes. The Brigantes were conquered by Angles and Vandal-Warings who occupied the area of Northumberland in Northern England. In Northumberland the native "Celtic" inhabitants quickly merged freely with the invaders.[18] This union had been preceded on the continent when the Vandals absorbed a Celtic entity in Poland. Later, when the Vikings invaded England the kingdom of Northumberland was "moved" somewhat northward into

Lowland Scotland and renamed "Bernicia" after its original Brigante inhabitants. Beriah, from whom the Brigantes and Burgundians descend, had two sons, Heber (Cheber) and Malchiel (Numbers 26:45). The name Heber is also pronounceable as "Cheber" and means friend or companion*. Heber of Asher gave rise to the Lygae and nearby Lugi which peoples formed the basis in Europe upon which the Vandal Federation built itself. The names Lygae and Lugi are derived from a root implying "Union" or "Alliance" e.g. Middle English "Ligg", modern "League". "HEBER" in Hebrew has the same meaning of "union" and "joining". Heber (of Asher) may also be recalled in the people named after "Caber". The appellation "CABER" occurs in an account of early British history, which states that Britain was first populated by the sons of Bruttus who, from Troy in Anatolia, reached Britain via Italy. Bruttus had three sons, Albion who received Scotland, Locris who took what later became known as England, and CABER who was given Wales[19]. We have identified Asher primarily with part of Scotland but Wales and Scotland had much in common. The Lowland Scots and the Northern Welsh to some degree overlap ethnically. The Northern Welsh are fair whereas those of the south are darker. Cheber (Heber) is also recalled in the Chabione Franks who, together with the Eruli (Ariel of Gad), are mentioned as invading Gaul in 289 CE.

THE ROYAL SCYTHS AND MALCHIEL

The second son of Beriah, son of Asher, was named Malchiel. "MALCHIEL" means "My King is God" and contains the element of royalty. It was the tendency for theonomic

---

* In 17th century English and later in Australian slang the word "Cobber" was used as synonymous with "mate" or friend and this word is believed to somehow been derived from the Hebrew "Chaber". One explanation regarding the origins of the word "Cobber" in English was that Jewish prospectors introduced it during the gold rushes in Australia but that does not explain how it came to be used in apparently the same sense in England somewhat earlier.

(references to God) parts of names to be dropped and in this case that would mean leaving the signification of "KING" alone. The Aseir whom we have seen to have belonged to the Tribe of Asher were reported both east of the Caspian and also in the region of the Don River. Similarly, the Royal Scythes are believed to have been in both areas since, east of the Caspian, they are equated with the Se-Wang (in Chinese) or (to westerners) "Sakaraukae"[20]. The Sakaraukae are also known as Saraucae. They were recalled east of the Caspian together with the Asii and were part of the Sacae forces. The name given them by the Chinese has the connotation of "Sacae-Kings", i.e. Royal Scythes[21]. The Royal Scythes by the Don River were known as Skuthae Basiloi and they migrated to Scandinavia which according to Pliny (Pliny N.H. 37;11) was known as "Basilia" and as "Scathinavia"[22] ("Scyth Land") after them. The Aseir who had also been in the Don River region together with the Vanes also believed went northwards to Scandinavia. It follows that the Royal Scythes had included part of the Tribe of Asher with the clan of Malchiel in its ranks.

ASHER AND SIDON

Regarding the Varini whom Pliny included amongst the Vandali peoples and who were closely associated with the Angles, it should be noticed that east of the Caspian Sea in Bactria they had been known as Varni and were then situated south of the Auglai (Angloi) who became the Angles and invaded England. From Bactria the Varni apparently moved firstly to the Carpathian region of Southeast Europe where they neighbored the Sidini and were referred to by Pliny as Varini. From the Carpathians the Varini advanced northward where Ptolemy again recorded them in Germany under the name Viruni besides the Saxones, Teutonarii, and Angilli. To their east were the Sidini who bordered the Vandal-Omani and Lugi, south of whom were a similarly named people called Sidones. Further east, by the Gothic-Guthones (Gythones) and Phinni,

328

were the Sudini. From the above it may be observed that groups associated with the Vandals whom we have identified with ASHER and especially with the Virini sub-section of the Vandals were several times found in the neighborhood of another people called Sidini, Sidone, or Sudini[+]. In the Land of Israel the Tribe of ASHER had received its territorial portion which encompassed the famous Phoenician city of Great Sidon (Joshua 19:28). Part of the Tribe of Asher appears to have participated in Phoenician "Sidonian" culture and mercantile activities and this fact together with geographical proximity in the past may explain the apparent "Sidonian" connexion, which was exemplified by the Sidini, Sidone, and Sudini accompaniment. In the LAND OF ISRAEL the Tribes of Asher, Issachar, and Zebulon had adjoined each other. This closeness was to be repeated in their places of exile[*].

[+] It may be objected that "SIDON" in Hebrew begins with the letter "Tsedeh" and may just as correctly be transcribed as "Z" or as "TS". Nevertheless, the form "SIDON" (with an "S") was that used by the Greeks and probably at a later stage by the Sidonians themselves.

[*] North of the Caucasus region were the Aorsi who were a branch of Aseir and belonged to the Tribe of Asher. Besides the Aorsi, and sometimes identified with them, were the Alans. Ptolemy also recalls the Alanorsi in the far north of Scythia. The Alanorsi are considered a combination of Alans and Aorsi. The Alans descended from Elon, son of Zebulon. In the same area north of the Caucasus besides the Aorsi were the Siraci from Issachar and, east of the Caspian, the Sacaraukae of Issachar were equated with the Royal Scyths from Malchiel of Asher. Later, in Switzerland were to settle the Burgundians from Beriah, son of Asher. The Burgundians had both fought with Attilla the Hun and also against him. In a list of peoples in the Hun forces, the Scirum-Burgundio are mentioned which suggested a combination from Issachar (Scirum) and Beria(g)h of Asher. The Burgundians came to dominate southeast France as well as settling in Switzerland. Together with the Burgundians in Geneva of Switzerland were settled a group of Alans, thus re-confirming the partnership of Asher and Alan (Elon), son of Zebulon. On the whole, Switzerland seems to have become dominated by clans from Issachar. The Tribe of Issachar are identifiable with the Assakarta of Iranian records who, by the Greeks, were termed Sagartoi and who appeared in areas which Jewish tradition associated with the Lost Tribe of Issachar. The Sagartoi are recognised as a Scythian group though they were also recorded amongst the Celtic settlers of Switzerland.

ASHER AND HIS BROTHER GAD.
THE SCOTCH AND THE JEWS

Despite the above reservation, an example of how family relationships were repeated historically may be seen in the case of Scotland. The Tribe of Asher was predominant in the north of England and in Scotland: Asher was found amongst the Brigantes, Vandals, Warrings, and Lyges. Gad was also found in Scotland and was represented by the Gaedhals and Gadeni and evidenced by a linguistic connection between Gaelic and Moeso-Gothic of the Goths, who also descended from Gad. Gad and Asher were both sons of Jacob by Zilpah, the hand-maiden of Leah. They were the only sons Zilpah had. The Scots according to their own tradition descended from the Scyths and the Goths were also regarded as a Scythian people. Herodotus said that amongst the Scyths the rearing of pigs was prohibited. The Scots had a similar prohibition that had existed from pre-Christian times. D.A. Mackenzie (1935) shows how the Scots also forbade other foods (such as eel) which the Mosaic Code prohibited[23], though there is no evidence that the Scots had ever been subject to Jewish influence in conventional histories. Certain similarities exist (or once existed) between the Scottish and Jewish peoples. The Scots were once noted for theological hairsplitting and philosophizing -like many Talmudically trained Jews. The Scots were sometimes thought by themselves and others to be a type of Jew or to contain Jewish elements[24]. The Scots (especially Lowlanders) are considered amongst the most intelligent people on earth and many scientific breakthroughs and important intellectual achievements are attributed to Scotsmen. -The Jews are in a similar position. Scottish individuals are amongst the wealthiest and most influential people in Britain; -the Jews in many continental-European countries once held a parallel status. Some modern Jews may descend from the Khazars whose national core derived from the Agathyrsi, a colony of whom had settled in Scotland.

The Vandals of Asher were to become an important constituent amongst the "Angle" forces in northern England. In this region other descendants of Asher had already settled in "Celtic" times prior to the Anglo-Saxon conquest. Similar phenomena have been noticed concerning other groups, many of whom settled in Britain.

In Ptolemy's Geography concerning the Map of Britain, Ptolemy refers to north Britain as "Albion" though other sources apply this same name to the whole country. "Albion" or the alternate "Alba" implies whiteness and may be seen as a Semitic word from the same root as the name "LEBANON" and having the same meaning[25]. Lebanon, in effect, was geographically a part of the Land of Israel and had been dominated by the Tribe of Asher though other tribes (such as Issachar and Dan) had also possessed footholds on the coast. In Celtic times the largest single ethnic entity in Britain were the Brigantes who were in the north. The Brigantes were descended from Beriah, son of Asher, and other groups in the north (such as the Lygi) also belonged to Asher, in addition to which groups from the Tribe of Dan were also present. The physical and climatic state of North Britain (especially Scotland) is similar to that of Lebanon (mountainous, rocky, cold, and misty) and other comparisons may be made. Similarly, "Albania" in the Caucasus became a Scythian region and was adjacent to places of Israelite re-settlement and may too have been named after the Land of Lebanon in the Homeland of Israel.

DESCENDANTS OF ASHER LOCATED

The Tribe of Asher thus appeared to have been strongly represented in the VANDAL nation. The Lygian-Vandal tribes corresponded in nomenclature with the sons of Asher: Boreoi equaled Beriah, the Omani came from Yimnah, and the Heissi equal "Isui", or "Ishuah" all sons of Asher. The Vandals had been represented in mythology by the VANE people of Vanaland. These were located besides the Don River. They were partners of the Aseir whose name is a form for "ASHER". The Aseir migrated to Scandinavia where too, the Vandals were recalled in the name Vendyssel. Yimnah, son of Asher, was to be found in the AMBRI who, from Bactria, moved northward where they were known as Ambrones and were partners to the Teutons and Cimbri. Beriah, son of Asher, was found in the Burgundians, in the Brigantes, in the Varangian-Vikings, in the Bergio of Scandinavia, and in the Varachan-Huns amongst the Khazars. The name Beriah may also be rendered as "BERIA(G)H".

Many Vandals entered Britain in the Anglo-Saxon invasions. The 160,000 "Africans" who, according to Geoffrey of Monmouth, came from Ireland were of Vandal and related Israelite Northern origin. The Angli conquerors of Northumbria were partnered by the Varini who were also a Vandal group as were the Rugini who participated in the Anglo-Saxon forces. The Varini were associable with the Sidoni, Sidini, or Seduni whose name is derived from the city of Phoenician SIDON which in Biblical times was encompassed by the territory of Asher. Heber (Cheber) son of Beriah son of Asher was represented by Caber who, according to tradition, settled Celtic Wales. Heber was also found in the Lugi-Ligi ("league" = union) of Vandal origin and too amongst the Chabiones who invaded Gaul together with the Eruli. The Eruli (Heruli) belonged to Arieli from the Tribe of Gad and according to Gibbon were classifiable as a Vandal sub-tribe. On the whole, Asher predominated in northern England and Lowland Scotland. A presence of Asher was also known in Scandinavia and Northern Europe. Some of those few Israelites who remained in Northern Germany and Poland and later migrated to America may have been descended from Asher.

THE CLANS OF ASHER

ASHER = Aseir (ancestors of Scandinavians, from Scythia).
Asii (Scythia),
Ansis (leading family of Goths, of Khazars and of Parthians.
Aorsi (Scythia),
Asianoi (Scythia, east of Caspian).

Clans of Asher:
Jimnah = Omanoi (Vandal group, Lowland Scotland, England).
Jesui = Heissi (Vandal group, Lowland Scotland, England).
Beriah (Beria-g-h) = Brigantes (Celtic-Britain, Ireland, Gaul, Switzerland); Brigands (branch of Brigantes); Brygges (Brigantes of Britain and of Phrygia in Anatolia, i.e. ancient Turkey); Boreoi (Vandal group); Barragos, Variag, Varangians (Vikings in Russia); Varachan (Khazar group in Russia of probable Viking extraction); Warings (Scandinavian group in Anglo-Saxon England).
Heber (Chever) = Caber (Wales), Chabiones (Franks), Ligi and Lygi [= Celtic groups absorbed by Vandals, both their names may derive form a word-root meaning "Union" (e.g. "league") which is also the meaning in Hebrew of the name "Heber"].
Malchiel ("Malchiel", i.e. "God is King") = Royal Scythes, Basiloi (Khazars), Basilia (Scandinavia), Sakaraukae (in east Scythia).
Amal (1-Chronicles 7:35, son of Helem of the tribe of Asher) =ruling family of Ostrogoths.

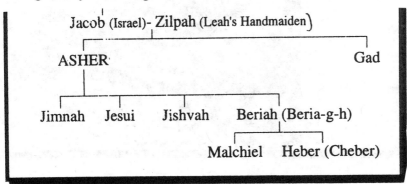

ASHER

An Israeli stamp depicts the traditional symbol of the Tribe of Asher. This was an olive tree. Asher was eventually to be found mainly in northern England and Scotland where they intermixed with descendants of Joseph. Asher was also important in Scandinavia. Moses bless Asher, "Let Asher be blessed with children: let him be acceptable to his brethren, and let him dip his foot in oil" (Deuteronomy 33;24). By "oil" it is understood that olive oil was intended. An American petroleum expert however understood it to mean petroleum and began to search off the north coast of Israel in the area adjacent to the former territory of Asher. Petrolem has been found in the North Sea area between Scotland and Norway. These are regions associated by us with Asher. Is this a coincidence?

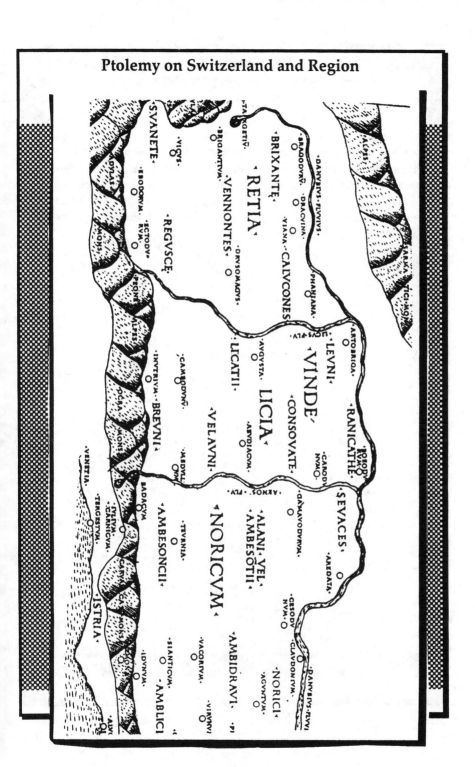

335

MAP OF SCANDINAVIA:
Finland, Sweden, Norway, and Denmark

Finland has been ascribed to the Tribes of Simeon and Issachar, with segments from GAD also being prominent. Sweden mainly derives from GAD with elements from Zebulon and others. Norway comes from Nephtali along with groups from Gad, Dan, Judah and Benjamin[10] (the Normans). The Danes of Denmark descend mainly from Dan though Israelite Judaeans, Gadites, Zebulonites, and others are also present.

Narvik

Trondheim
(Nidaros)

FINLAND

NORWAY

KARELIA

Olofsborg

SWEDEN

Åbo

Helsinki

Uppsala

Oslo

Sigtuna

Lyndanisse (1219)

Stockholm

ESTHONIA

Gothland (1361)

Kalmar

RUSSIA

Skåne (-1658)

DENMARK

Copenhagen

Nyborg

Ringsted

Bornholm

1920

Sl

21

THE TRIBE OF ISSACHAR

"OF THE SONS ISSACHAR AFTER THEIR FAMILIES; OF TOLA, THE FAMILY OF THE TOLAI: OF PUA, THE FAMILY OF THE PUNI:
"OF JASHUB, THE FAMILY OF THE JASHUBI: OF SHIMRON, THE FAMILY OF THE SHIMRONI:
"THESE ARE THE FAMILIES OF THE ISSACHAR ACCORDING TO THOSE THAT WERE NUMBERED OF THEM, THREESCORE AND FOUR THOUSAND AND THREE HUNDRED". Numbers 26:15-18.

"AND THE SONS OF ISSACHAR; TOLA, AND PHUVAH, AND JOB, AND SHIMRON" Genesis 46:13.

The Tribe of Issachar along with other Israelites had been re-settled by the Assyrians in the north, partly in the present-day Iranian area that was then known as Persia. The Sagartii were called "Asakarta" by the Persians. They were first reported of in the Zagros mountains of West Iran and appear to be identical with the Tribe of Issachar which tradition (recalled by Eldad HaDani 880 CE, and Benjamin of Tudelo ca. 1165) associated with that area. A similar group, the SAGARUCE, was recorded by Ptolemy on the east Caspian Sea shore. The

SAGARUCE have been equated with the Sakaraukae (or "Saraukae") who became the ruling tribe amongst the Amyrgian Scythians. The Sakaraukae have been considered as an eastern branch of the Royal Scyths[1] that, in the west, were centered around the Lower Don estuary in Southern Russia. The Sakaraukae together with the Amyrgian-Scythians and Goths were conquered by the Asii* who relate to the Aorsi. Both Aorsi and Siraci (i.e. Saraukae-Sakaraucae) were to be also found west of the Caspian Sea to the north of the Caucasus.

It will have been noticed that the same groups of peoples tended to appear in close proximity to each other even though separate portions of these nations were spread over wide areas. The Asii have been identified with the WUSUN of Chinese records and these in turn are equated with the Issedones of Ptolemy. The Issedones first emerged from the area of SERICA in east Siberia. This area was once more habitable than it may seem now and supported quite advanced civilizations and metallurgical industry[2]. The name **SERICA** itself may be an inverted form of Issachar -just as the terms "Siraci" and. "Saraukae" were applied to the Sakaraucae who did derive from Issachar.

In Serica (modern Siberia, east of Scythia) Ptolemy reported the Asmiraea who have a name similar (in Semitic tongues) to that of **Shimron**, son of Issachar. Ptolemy also placed the Ithaguri and Thogara in Serica and since the "S" and "T" or "TH" were interchangeable the names ITHAGURI* and Thogara are also be forms for Issachar[3]. Similar names (Thacori, Tochari) were to be found in the general Chorasmian area east of the Caspian Sea where the SAGARUCE-SAKARAUKAE

---

* The Goths in this area are also known to historians as Yueh-chi and Massagetae. The Amyrgian-Scyths were a branch of the Sacae-Scythians and are sometimes referred to simply as Sacae. The Asii were also known to Westerners as Asianoi and to the Chinese as WuSun. In relating the history of these peoples there is a tendency to use different terms for the same peoples depending upon what names were applied to them in the sources from which the relevant information is derived.

* In one edition of Ptolemy the Ithaguri are called "TAGURI".

(who also came from Issachar) were located. Later, in Switzerland appear the similarly named Toygeni and Tigorini allies of the Cimbrians. Near Serica in the north were the ABII Scythae from **YOB** son of Issachar (Genesis 46:13) whose name may be found in the Abus River of Celtic East Britain. The West Saxons in England were called "ABIS Maurunganie". In Serica the ABII Scythae were neighbored by the Sizyges who were associated with the Nephtali and amongst the English Saxons, became known as SCYGS and settled in Essex. The ABIS MAURUNGANIE of England were probably a combination between Issachar (Yob) and Machir of Manasseh. Another entity that may also have come from Yob of Issachar is the Tribe of UBII who settled in Holland.

Groups from Issachar were present amongst the Anglo-Saxons and company and also with the Celtic-Galatian grouping. The GALATIANS of Gaul were descended from Cimmerians and ISRAELITES who from Phrygia (Turkish Anatolia) came westward. Later the Galatians undertook expeditions to the east and a small group of Galatians re-settled in Phrygia in Turkey and their area was called "Galatia" after them. The Skirri (Skires) were a group amongst the GALATIANS in Galatia of Anatolia. The SKIRRI belonged to Issachar and (as "Skires") had once threatened Greek Olbia on the Black Sea coast and, together with their allies (the Bastarnae) had been termed GALATAE (i.e. Galatians) by the Greeks[4]. The Galatae belonged to Gilead of Machir in Manasseh of Israel and in the Land of Israel prior to the Assyrian Exile had neighbored Issachar who also had shared a border of sorts with GAD. Later the SKIRES (i.e. Skirri) of Issachar along with the Bastarnae[5] were reported on the North Sea shore as part of the Gothic (Gadite) forces. The Bastarnae were descended from Etsbon, son of Gad. Thus elements of Gad and Issachar were marching together. It should be noted that Galatian forces for some time were centered in the Switzerland area which region was destined to become the domain of Issachar. There are

339

traditional European legendary accounts[6] that claim that people from Sweden or Goths settled in Sweden and the people in question may actually have been the Skires of Issachar who had attached themselves to the Gothic forces.

Another son of Issachar was **PHUVAH** (Genesis 46:13) whose children were known as Phuni or **PUNI** (Numbers 26:23-24). "PUNI" was a name given to the Phoenicians amongst whom Israelite Tribes such as Zebulon and Asher were at some stages an important component. The major Phoenician cities were Tyre and Sidon. Sidon was conquered for a while by the Sakkala or Sakkara[7] who were one of the Sea Peoples and are proven to have been Israelites[8]. The Sakkara were from the Tribe of Issachar and the Phoenicians received their name from PUNI the son of Issachar. In Europe, an ethnic entity of similar name was quite widely scattered: In Ireland, one has the Fenni, in Jutland (Denmark) the Phundusi, in Scandinavia the Phanones, and the Finni who neighbored the Gotones on the Baltic coast and gave their name to Finland. In the area of Austria, Hungary, and its neighborhood once dwelt a Celtic people who gave the name Pannonia to the region before moving onward apparently to Switzerland. In Switzerland according to Ptolemy prior to the Alemannic occupation were the Vennontes people, the Peone Alps and Phaniana city. Job (Yob) son of Issachar was also called **JASHUB** (In Hebrew: "Yashub" pronounceable as "Yashuv") in Numbers 26:24. The Alamans who conquered Switzerland were considered part of the Suebi or Suevi and so seem to have also called themselves. The SUEBI in the west were divided into two distinct groups[9]: **(1)** The northern ones who were close culturally to the Frisians and Saxons and participated in the invasion of England; and **(2)** the southern section who settled in Switzerland. The Suebians had emerged from the Sienbi in Serica and Scythia and they were an amalgamation of different (though basically related) peoples. Forms of the name SUEBI applied to the northern group such as SWAEF and Svipdag, along with several other

340

factors, suggest a connection to JOSEPH, especially since prefixes such as "JO-" etc. were frequently dropped in the Scythian area. The southern group of Suebi, for similar reasons, may be said to descend from **Yashub** son of Issachar.

At all events, Issachar, as described in the Holy Books, was apposite to a good portion of the people of Switzerland as well as to some of the dwellers of Finland.

ISSACHAR AND FINLAND

In Finland were elements from Issachar and the southern Finnish province of Mikeli is reminiscent of **MICHAEL** (1-Chronicles 7:3) one of the heads of the Clans of Issachar. Two other minor sub-clans of Issachar, **Yahmay** (Jachmai) and Yivsam (Jibsom), brothers of Michael, may be recalled in the Finnish Provinces of Kym and Uusima*, both south of Mikeli in Finland. The Finns had a tradition that they were descended from the Lost Ten Tribes of Israel and their national hero, Marshall Mannerheim in a speech once expressly referred to them as "Sons of Issachar"*.

ISSACHAR AND SWITZERLAND

Issachar was described by the Patriarch Jacob (Genesis 49:14-15) as, *"A strong ass crouching down between two burdens. And he saw that rest was good; and bowed his shoulder to bear, and became a servant under tribute"*. Issachar was a "Strong ass

---

* It has been pointed out to the author that Uusimma in Finnish connotes "New Settlement" but even so the form of the name may have been adapted from an existing appellation as occurs very frequently in the etymology of place-names.

* "**Sons of Issachar**, stand and die, but let only scorched earth fall into the hands of the enemy," Richmond Norman STUART, "One of Isaac's Sons", *The Covenant Message* – September 1976, Johannesburg, South Africa.
Yair DAVIDIY, "Marshall Mannerheim Identified the Finns With Issachar!", Tribesman, issue no. 4, p. 19.

crouching down between two burdens". The Hebrew word for "two burdens" (Hebrew: *"Mishpatayim"*) may also be translated as meaning "Between the Walls", or "boundaries", and may well imply a land-locked, mountainous area. A group of Burgundians serving in the Hun forces of Attilla were called Skirio-Burgundio and some of the Burgundians settled in Switzerland. The name "Skirio" suggests Issachar and the Skirri-Skires of the Galatian and Gothic forces. So too, the son of Issachar, Phuvah of the Puni was recalled in the Vennontes, the Peones, and in Phanania of Switzerland. Yeshub, another son of Issachar, was recalled in the southern Suebi who also settled in Switzerland which country seems to have become dominated by groups from Issachar.

Issachar in Iran and Scythia was therefore recorded amongst the Asakarta-Sagartoi, in the Sagaruce, the Issatichae, in Serica, the Ithaguri, and in the Skires who were also known as Skirri. **Shimron**, son of Issachar has a name equal to that of the "Asmirae" in Sericae since "Asmirae" is a Semitic-alternative for "Shimron". **Yob**, son of Issachar, was recalled in peoples such as the "Abii" in Scythia and "Abis" in Saxon England, and "Ubii" in Holland. **Phuvah**, son of Issachar, headed a clan also known as the **PUNI** or Phuni who were to be found throughout Western Europe as Fenni (Ireland), Phundusi (Denmark), Phanones (Scandinavia), Finni (Baltic), and in Switzerland in the names Vennonte, Peone, and Phaniana. Jashub, son of Issachar, became that culturally and linguistically differentiated portion of the Suebi who settled Switzerland and Alsace and were either also known as "Alemanni" and "Alans" or were closely associated with them.

ISSACHAR IN PROPHECY

A famous Rabbinical Commentator, Don Isaac Abarbanel (1437-1508), in his commentary on Genesis, examined all the references in Scripture and Talmudic

Literature regarding the various Tribes and assembled a character description of each one.

Don Abarbanel said that Issachar loves rest. He is unwarlike and prefers to pay others to fight for him. He is a merchant by nature and lacks the "Monarchic" touch (i.e. he is a Republican) and many of his people are of a peasant's disposition and inclined to work the land. In addition, says the Don, from out of the sons of Issachar were also to emerge wise men with an aptitude for intellectual pursuits and of philosophical bent. A Talmudic source (Sifrei) says that only from the Tribes of Judah, Levi, and Issachar were destined to emerge Sages capable of determining what the Practical Application of the Law should be which implies Legalistic inclinations in both the theoretical and applicable spheres.

The above description fits Switzerland to an extent. Switzerland has traditionally been a republic and neutral, using its financial influence to ward off enemies and somehow making it worthwhile for others to respect its neutrality. On the other hand, the ancient Swiss (Helvetii) and their medieval descendants did, on occasion, exhibit militant prowess and Swiss mercenaries at one time were the most sought after in all Europe. So too, in Biblical times, contrary to the over stressed generalization of Don Isaac Abarbanel, Issachar did prove his prowess. *"The Princes of Issachar were with Deborah"* in the war against the northern Canaanites (Judges 5:15). In the time of David, people from Issachar were *"valiant men of might"*, *"chief men"*, and *"soldiers for war"* (1-Chronicles 7:2-5). Similarly, little **FINLAND** who also received settlers from Issachar, though LIKEWISE traditionally neutral and peacable did defeat the Russians single-handedly on the battlefield. Both the Swiss and the Finns are conceived internationally as peasant types with the habit of producing individuals of considerable intellect and of a contemplative-inclination. These attributes conform with those of ISSACHAR, as indicated in Biblical works. Issachar is conceived (in the Talmud) as being the intermediary between

343

Israel and foreigners and the Swiss are famous for their international connections and so in their own way, are the Finns. The legalistic bent ascribed to ISSACHAR is another Swiss national characteristic.

The Confederation of Switzerland in the modern sense was formed in 1291 when the Cantons of URI, Schwys, and Unterwalden banded together to protect themselves against the Austrians. Later, neighboring Cantons joined them. URI is a Biblical name. A master craftsman from the tribe of Judah was a son of URI:

"I have specially chosen Besalel son of URI, son of Hur, of the tribe of Judah. I have filled him with divine spirit, making him skillful and ingenious, expert in every craft, and a master of design.... for workmanship of every kind" (Exodus 31; 1-6).

The Swiss are also masterly artisans though pertaining to Issachar more than to Judah. Even so, both Issachar and Judah are full-brothers sons of Jacob from his wife, Leah.

The mother of Issachar was Leah, one of the four wives of Jacob. Leah conceived Issachar after hiring her husband away from Rachel, her sister and Jacob's more favored wife (Genesis 30:16-18). The name ISSACHAR in Hebrew connotes "reward" or "hire". Today, the Swiss are world famous for their banks which take a commission ("reward") for hiring out other people's money. Much of their fame as fighters the Swiss also earned by fighting for money.

In the Book of Chronicles (1-Chr. 12:32) is found the expression, *"And of the children of Issachar were men that had understanding of the times, to know what Israel ought to do"*. This was understood by the Sages (Talmud, Baba Kama 2b; Rash on Deuteronomy 33:18) to refer to expertise in astronomical subjects and in computing the calendar, which requires great skill and precision. Monthly divisions had to co-ordinate the lunar and solar cycles, agricultural and religious needs, and be compatible with chronological purposes. The characteristics and skills of Issachar were reflected in its symbols. ISSACHAR is represented by a donkey (Genesis 49:10) and also by the sun and stars, symbolizing the celestial movements the Sons of ISSACHAR were said to observe and be experts in. On an Israeli Stamp [*see illustration*] the arrangement of sun and stars used to represent Issachar bears the same form as the face of a clock might seem to*. An article in National Geographic (vol. 169, no.1 January 1986) is entitled, "Switzerland: The Clockwork Country." In a sense, the study of astronomy can be considered the study of "times". Switzerland is famous for its watches. "It works like a Swiss watch," means that it works well with reliability and precision. In one sense Swiss watches could be said to give "understanding of the times" to all the world. The characteristics for Issachar in Prophecy: mercantile, both plodding and intellectual, neutral but brave, legalistic, precise by nature and settled in a land-locked area, internationally-connected were all applicable to the inhabitants of Switzerland where many groups identified with Issachar indeed had settled. Finland too exhibits qualities pertinent to Issachar and Finland was also settled by part of the Tribe of Issachar as well as by other Israelites.

Lari Kemilainen gives the following insight into Finnish character:
<<Finland has been under providence for example in WW2, where we lost both fights against Russia, but managed to keep them out of our country and hold on to our independence and if you look at the sizes of armies, it's almost as amazing as existence of Israel today... Finland was also an important gateway for Russian Jews moving to Israel in 90's.
<<When it comes to the nature of Issachar, did you know that both Finns and Swiss have a history of mercenaries working for other countries? And I can't help but think of Sweden and Russia, our former invaders, as our "saddlebags". And in a survey done, say, 4 years ago, it was found that Finns in

---

* The resemblance of the Israeli stamp design symbolizing Issachar to the face of a clock was first brought to the author's attention by Mr. Aaron Minazzi of Milano, Italy; and Kiryat Arba, Israel.

general are very safety-oriented and don't want to risk what they've got: if you offer a Finn an option of getting thousand euros or a chance to get ten thousand with a 50-50 risk of getting nothing, Finns tend to take the thousand euros so they are sure to get even something. Watching "Who Wants To Be A Millionaire" isn't too interesting here, because very few people who do fine want to risk it and they opt out when they've gained "enough"...>>

Points of interest are: (1) It used to be believed that the Finns of Finland were related to groups in Eastern Russia. New research however indicates that they are just as equally genetically linked to peoples in Western Europe – as we have claimed. It is also claimed that the ancestors of the Finnish people were a very small group (maybe ca.2,000) who moved into Finland relatively recently. (2) In Switzerland German, French, and Italian are spoken as well (in the southeast) as a dialect named Romansch. Professor Luis BRUNNER (1981) demonstrated that Romansch evolved from an ancient language ("Rhaetic") that was similar to Akkadian. Akkadian was the language spoken by the Assyrians who exiled the northern Tribes of Israel. A strong Israelite presence in Switzerland appears certain but other non-Israelite elements were also present and often set the tone.

ישׁשׂכר

THE DESCENDANTS OF ISSACHAR

ISSACHAR = Assakar (Sagartoi - in Iran and Scythia), Sagaruce (Scythia), Sacaraukae (Scythia), Scirri (Galatians), Skirri (Gothic group), Serica (East of Scythia).

Tola = Tollund (Denmark), Thule (Norway).
Puvah (i.e. **Puni**) = Fenni (Ireland), Vannones (Switzerland), Peones (Swiss), Finni (Finland).
Job = Abii -Scythae (east Scythia), Abiis Maurunganie (Saxon group), Ubii (Holland)
Jashub = Suebi (Switzerland).
Shimroni = Asmirae (Scythia).
Yahmi (Yachmi) = Kym (Finland).
Yivsam (Jibsom) = Uusima (Finland).
Michael = Mikeli (Finland).

The symbol of Issachar is depicted on an Israeli stamp as the sun surrounded by stars in a form resembling the face of a clock.

MAP OF HOLLAND

All darkened areas are those below sea level; literally "on the shores of the sea".

The Port of Rotterdam handles more tonnage than any other port in the world.

KONINKRIJK DER NEDERLANDEN

22

The Tribe of Zebulon

"AND THE SONS OF ZEBULON; SERED, AND ELON, AND JAHLEEL" Genesis 46:14.

Moses grouped the two brothers Issachar and Zebulon together, saying, "Rejoice, Zebulun in thy going out; and Issachar in thy tents" (Deuteronomy 33:18). From this verse it was understood (Rashi) that Issachar and Zebulon had a symbiotic relationship, Issachar being involved in religious and scientific intellectual pursuits and Zebulon setting forth in ships to trade and, with his earnings, contributing to the support of Issachar. Other Rabbinical opinions (S.R. Hirsch) say that it merely implies that Issachar was more inclined towards working the land and less given to venture out. Groups of Zebulonite origin are often found in association with groups from Issachar. **Zebulon is identifiable with Holland.** The people of Alsace and Lorraine (in France) come from both Issachar and Zebulon and their region forms a bridge from Switzerland to Belgium and Holland.

The symbol of Holland was a ship in popular tradition[1] and a ship was the symbol of the former Dutch Republic. Many of the Boer (Afrikaans) population of the Republic of South Africa are of Dutch descent. A ship was also the symbol of Zebulon (Numbers Rabah 2;5). Zebulon, in Talmudic Literature, is pictured as a merchant seafarer, which description fits the Dutch. Rotterdam in Holland is the world's busiest port.

Moses blessed Zebulon: that he should "Suck of the abundance of the seas and of treasures hid in the sands" (Deuteronomy 33:19). Today both South Africa and Holland are on the seashores and a good portion of the earlier diamond wealth of South Africa was found in the "sands". Another important element in the population of both Holland and South Africa is a portion of Naphtali of whom it was said: "Possess thou the west and the south" (Deuteronomy 33:23); - being the west of England (settled by Vikings from Norway) as well as both Holland and Norway. The South meant both **South Africa** and **New Zealand**. South Africa was settled by British and Dutch, French Huguenots, and Germans and New Zealand by British of a particular type. There was an overlap of peoples between Scandinavia and the Netherlands. Zebulon, though dominant in Holland, is also represented by "Halland" of the southwest coast of Sweden, and by Hallin in Norway which names come from that of **Elon, son of Zebulon**, as does the name for Holland itself.

Only the Dutch dwell "on the shores of the Sea" since the Dutch descend from Zebulon!!

Jacob prophesied "Zebulon shall dwell at the haven of the sea and he shall be for an haven of ships; and his border shall be unto Sidon" (Genesis 49:13). Sidon (or "Zidon"), at one stage, was conquered by the "Sakkara" who were named after the Tribe of Issachar[☺] but whose forces in this case probably

---

[☺] Slouschz Nahum **SLOUSCHZ,**("Les Hebreo-Pheniciens. Introduction a ire des Origines de la Colonisation Hebraique dans les Pays Mediteranee," Paris 1909, p.61) mentions the conquest of SIDON by the Shakala about the time of Israelite expansion in the period of Judges. The Shakala were identical to the "SAKKARA" -"R" and "L" in Egyptian were represented by the same letter. "Sakkara" approximates to how the Egyptians may well have rendered the name ISSACHAR. The Sakkara, according to the Egyptians, came from the Land of Israel, were circumcised, were allied to other peoples with Israelite sounding names such as the Tulisha (Tola son of Issachar), the Daanau (Dan), Menesen (Menasseh), and so on, who also were centered in the Land of Israel. These peoples were called "Peoples of the Sea" and their Israelite identification is

comprised or at least included Zebulonites●. Prophecies concerning the tribes were applicable both within the Land of Israel and outside of it. In both cases, some degree of literal significance is to be expected. The expression concerning Zebulon, *"His border unto Zidon"* could be fulfilled in a number of ways®.

In the verse, <<ZEBULON SHALL DWELL AT THE HAVEN OF THE SEA AND HE SHALL BE FOR AN HAVEN OF SHIPS...>> Genesis 49:13: The expression, "dwell at the haven of the sea" according to the HEBREW original ("Hof-yamim") may be preferably translated as **"dwell on the SHORES of the Sea"**＊. The only nation in the world whose population is known for dwelling extensively on reclaimed sea-land, literally, "On the shores of the sea", is Holland. This description applies in some way or other to up to two-thirds of the Dutch people. Holland may also be recalled in the Book of Obadiah:

---

proven by the present author in the book **"Lost Israelite Identity"**. The Phoenicians received the name of "PUNI" which was also the name of a Issachar-clan: *"Of the sons of Issachar after their families: of Tola, the family of the Tolaites: of Pua, the family of the Punites"* i.e. (in Hebrew) *"PUNI"* (Numbers 26:23). All the Phoenician peoples were considered "Sidonians" by foreigners and the appellation may well have been applied to Israelites who lived in the "Sidon" area and at one stage in Sidon itself.

● Even so Issachar was also linkeable with Sidon: The Tribe of Issachar were destined to dominate Switzerland and a people named SEDUNI once dwelt in Celtic Switzerland (ca. Sion) and Switzerland in medieval times, was named "Sidon", BBL.

● "Sidon" (i.e. "Zidon") could be represented in any one of a number of ways. There were the people of "Sidone", scattered groups of whom seem to have usually accompanied Vandals from the Tribe of Asher which tribe had encompassed the original Phoenician City of Sidon. Switzerland was called "SIDON" in medieval times. The coast of northern Gaul (France and Belgium) had been partly settled by groups of Phoenician culture and possibly SIDONIANS were amongst them since Sidon and Tyre were the major Phoenician cities also all Phoenicians were called "SIDONIANS".

＊ Compare Kaplan's ("The Living Torah") translation, "on the seashores". "Hof-Yamin" in Modern Hebrew means "Seashores" and so most translators would understand the expression.

<<AND THE CAPTIVITY OF THIS HOST OF THE CHILDREN OF ISRAEL SHALL POSSESS THAT OF THE CANAANITES, EVEN UNTO ZAREPHATH>> Obadiah 1:20.

Rabbinical Commentators understood "Zarephath" to mean Gaul and the area to the north of it apparently including Holland. In the light of these explanations (Rashi, Nachmanides, Iben Ezra, Daat Sofrim, Abarbanel*) the verse should be understood to say:

<<AND THIS FIRST CAPTIVITY OF THE TEN TRIBES SHALL POSSESS THE REGION FROM THE CANAANITES OF GERMANY AND INCLUDING BRITAIN AND FRANCE AND THE NORTH>>

According to the Geneva Bible (1599) of Calvin:

<<By the Canaanites, the Jews mean the Dutchmen, and by Zarephath, France>>[2].

Near the Batavi of Southern Holland were the Cananefates whose name can be interpreted to mean "Union of Canaanites". The Land of Israel in the Bible is usually referred to as the "Land of Canaan".

The SABALINGOI were to the North of Holland and their name means "People of ZEBULON"!!!

Zebulon through the Alans and Alamans of Elon, son of Zebulon, merged with the Suebi from Jashub (pronounceable as "Ja-sueb", Numbers 26:24) of Issachar in Alsace and in Switzerland i.e. they bordered "Sidon", as Switzerland was referred to. Holland also runs into and borders the Northwest Block of Belgium. This area according to linguistic evidence was once settled by people from the Middle East and Turkish region who may have been related to the Sidonians of Phoenicia. In early Scythian times the name Zebulon was

---

* For a more complete discussion together with translation and consideration of the sources see Yair DAVIDI, "Ephraim. The Gentile Children of Israel", 2001, chapter seven.

recalled in ZABULISTAN which was to the south and southeast of Hara in the Iranian area.

The name of ZEBULON is also found in the **Sabalingoi** recalled by Ptolemy in South Jutland (Denmark) and Northern Frisia. The name SABALINGOI in Hebrew means **"People (Goi) - of - ZEBULON"** since in Northern dialects "Sabalin" and Zebulon would have been alternate pronunciations of the same name: The "Z" was replaced by "S"; and "goi" means people in Hebrew. The Sabalingoi were to the north of the Sigulones (whose name in Hebrew means "Chosen Ones") and of the Saxons and in turn, to the north of the Sabalingoi were the Chali sons of **Jahleel** [Yachlayl in Hebrew, and the **"Ya"** would have been dropped] (Genesis 46; 14). Jahleel was a son of Zebulon as was Sered and also **Elon**. From Jutland and Scandinavia there were several waves of migration into the area of nearby Holland especially into Frisia. The Sabalingoi and Chali moved to the Netherlands' region, or they were already in it. Ptolemy may in fact be interpreted as placing the Sabalingoi in Northern Frisia and thus in Holland or just on its borders. Pytheas (ca. 325 BCE) is reported as describing Holland as peopled by Skuthai (i.e. Scythians) meaning (probably) Frisians who, in the 300's and 200's BCE, are claimed to have begun absorbing the native Celts[3]. There followed several centuries in which the population fluctuated greatly. In about 200 CE the Franks invaded. Angles, Saxons, and Jutes from Jutland overran the land in 450-500 CE. Consequently, Frisians, together with others, participated in the Anglo-Saxon invasions. After ca.600 CE Frankish influence re-asserted itself. Roughly speaking, modern Holland has Frisians in the north, Saxons in the east, and Franks in the south. It also has important continents of French Huguenots, Sephardic and Ashkenazic Jews, Malays, Arabs, and Eurasians of mixed blood. In other words, the population is of mixed origins like the populations of most countries. This does not contradict the fact that a good proportion of the people (if not most) are descended from Israel or that amongst the Israelites a certain tribe has the ascendancy. Enough has been shown to prove that often groups of divergent backgrounds converging on one spot, are revealed as having originally the same tribal identity.

The **FRISIANS** are a people now concentrated in Northern Holland but once spread all along the coast from Scandinavia through Holland, Belgium, and into France. The Angles and Saxons before they, together with other northern peoples, invaded Britain in the 450s CE had sojourned (at least in part) for about 200 years in Holland especially in Frisia. Some of the Jutes had also been in Frisia. The Byzantine historian, Procopius (Gothic War vii; 20) said that the Frisians were an important element amongst the invaders of Britain.

The name of the Frisians is traceable to Peres son of Gilead of Manasseh but the actual inhabitants of present-day Frisia and Holland are identifiable on the whole more with Zebulon. In Biblical times, Tribes such as Zebulon, Issachar, and Asher were closely associated with Manasseh and it would seem that this linkage was repeated after their exile in areas of their re-settlement. At all events the identity of the Frisians must be closely linked with that of peoples who invaded and settled the British Isles.

Frisian-Legends Affirm Their Israelite Origins!

According to Frisian-legends* a certain King Adel was a descendant of **Shem** King Adel in India had three sons: Friso, Bruno, and Saxo. Legendary sources quoted by the historian Le Petit (1601) also mention Friso, Bruno, and Saxo and say too

---

* **Mr. Fred J. KOESLAG of Gouda, Holland,** sent me the following information that he obtained from a book ("Freische Mythen en Sagen" by J.P. WIESMA, 1973) about Old Frisian legends. This information supplements other sources such as that of Jean Francoise LE PETIT ("Le Grande Chronicle Ancienne et Moderne de Holland, Zeelande, Utrecht, Frise, Oversyseel; et de Groenungham", Dordrecht, 1601). The book of Le Petit is written in a dialect of Old French and a copy is to be found in the Rare Books section of the National Library in Jerusalem. Le Petit relates the history of peoples who settled in the Netherlands.

that they were descendants of Shem and lived in "India". The term "India", however, did not always mean the place known today as India but rather was more synonymous with "Cush" which term was sometimes applied to areas east of the Caspian Sea in present-day Central Asia and is the "Cush" (i.e. "Ethiopia") mentioned in Genesis 2:13. The Prophets Zephaniah (3:10) and Isaiah (10:10) said that "Cush" was one of the places to which the exiled Israelites would go. The Aramaic Translation renders "Cush" as "Hodu" (translated as **"India"**) but is referring to the region of Hara in eastern Iran and surrounding areas Similarly, Le Petit located the "India" he spoke of in a land by the Emodian Mountains which according to Ptolemy were in the area adjoining the Caspian and Aral Seas, **in east Scythia**, to the north of Afghanistan and India-proper. Tzvi Chasdoi related that in Jewish tradition the area east of the Caspian was known as "Cush"[4]. Jewish legends traced the Tribes of Zebulon and Naphtali to this area and placed other Israelite Tribes in the immediate vicinity. This is the area where Frisian legends say Friso, Saxo, and Bruno came from.

In this land east of the Caspian archaeologists have found the ruins of an extensive civilization whose inhabitants spoke Aramaic. Some of the Israelite Tribes had spoken Aramaic even before their exile and the language was used as an official tongue in the Assyrian Empire and is believed to have been the most commonly-used one. Phillip Lozinski (1953) believed that from this region east of the Caspian came the "Barbarian" peoples whom he suggests may have been at least partly Semitic[5]. They invaded Europe beginning from around the 200s CE. Additional evidence exists showing that the invaders must have come from Scythia and the region east of the Caspian. These invasions and migratory movements were often connected with activities of the Huns who themselves were a mixture of various peoples. The Huns from this vicinity caused other nations to flee westward. N.C. LUKMAN

("Skoldung und Skilfinge. Hunnen und Herulerkonige in Oostorlischer Uberliersering," Copenhagen 1943) showed how in Nordic Mythology the name Adel (meaning "Noble") was often used as a euphemism for Attila the Hun and for the Huns in general[6]. In the Frisian legends King Adel was the father of Friso, Bruno, and Saxo. Scientific Linguists have concluded that the Northern "Barbarians" who entered Europe had the later European aspects of their languages imposed upon them by an external force. They originally spoke both Hebrew and Aramaic.

The legends speak of these three brothers being descended from Shem and having been in Jerusalem at the time of its destruction by the Babylonians:

"In the time of the destruction of Jerusalem by Nebuchadnessar (586 B.C.), 3 brothers - Friso, Bruno, and Saxo with [their] wives, children, and relatives fled out of the country, encouraged to do so by announcements of the Prophets concerning the fall of the town".

In this legend Bruno represents the Angles who according to Ptolemy had at one stage been centered on the region of Brunswick in Eastern Germany. The Angles had also had a center in Angeln to the south of Denmark or else they moved to Angeln prior to the invasion of England. By placing Friso, Bruno, and Saxo in Jerusalem (which became representative of all Israel) before its capture the legend in effect infers that **the Frisians, Saxons, and Brunswickian-Angles were therefore originally Israelites or Jews.** The Venerable Bede also identified the Anglo-Saxons as the Chosen People.

F. KOESLAG points out that "In legends...events of several eras may be concentrated around famous historical figures - as you see with Charlemagne". The legend may therefore be taken as **reflecting a tradition that the three**

brothers were related to the Jews which is consistent with
their belonging to the Lost Ten Tribes who had been exiled
from their own lands in Israel at least 140 years before the
actual fall of Jerusalem. The legend contains the recognition
that the three brothers had left the Land of Israel (identified as
"Jerusalem" or the Land of the Jews) before Nebuchadnezzar of
Babylon captured it. The northern Israelites had indeed been
exiled prior to the Babylonian onslaught. The Lost Ten Tribes
had been re-settled in Assyria and in lands ruled by Assyria.
Another Frisian legend says that Albione and 32 sisters went
from Assyria by ship and landed in England which they called
Albion. After they landed, Brutus drove them out of the
country and re-named it Britain in his own honor. The Albioni
crossed the Sea and landed in Frisia where they intermixed
with the Saxons and returned together with them to conquer
the island. This legend may also serve as an indicator of
Israelite origins since the exiled Israelites had indeed been re-
settled in "Assyria" (or in Assyrian-controlled areas) before
asserting their independence and moving elsewhere

The legends relate how while still in "India" Friso
married Hilla daughter of Agathocles king of Thrace. They
were driven out of "India" and sailed to Greece where Friso
became a student of Plato (427-374 BCE) and then joined the
Army of Alexander the Great.

They Served With Alexander the Great
Historically it is known that: Alexander from Macedonia
and Greece advanced into Asia Minor (modern Turkey) and
from there continued into Persia, Bactria, the area east of the
Caspian Sea and Northwest India. In the east Alexander
reformed his army and took into his Special Forces mainly
peoples belonging to the Sacae-Scythian Tribes. From the Sacae
descend the Anglo-Saxons and company. A strong early
tradition existed in Europe that the Saxons had been soldiers in
Alexander's armies. This tradition was mentioned in the time of

357

Charlemagne King of the Franks (768-814 CE). Additional traditions and evidence connect the Anglo-Saxons with the ancient Sacae-Scythians some of whom really had been in Alexander's forces. Le Petit also says that the three brothers served under Alexander.

The legends state that via Asia Minor the people of Friso, Bruno, and Saxo came on a very large ship called "di Mannigfuald" (i.e. "The Multitude") to the west. Friso in 313 BCE landed in Friesland i.e. in Frisia. Bruno and Saxo (the brothers of Frisso) went eastward though Saxo (according to Le Petit) then returned to the west. Bruno founded the city of Brunswick in which area of Germany Ptolemy placed the Angloi thus identifying them with the people of Bruno. The Angloi (Angles) also moved northward to the regions bordering Denmark and from there they went to Britain some of them sojourning (like the Saxons) in Frisia on the way.

THE SONS OF ZEBULON

Zebulon was noticed in the Sabalingoi of Frisia; Yahleel in Chali of Jutland. **Sered**, son of Zebulon, appears in Ptolemy's map as the **SUARDENI** between the Don and Volga Rivers surrounded by Sarmatae, Siraceni (Issachar), Assaei (Asher) and others. They re-emerge as the Suardenoi in Sweden. The Suardenoi were the same people as the Continental Suardones, who were considered, together with Angles, and Longbards, Varini, Eudoses, and others, (Tacitus, Germania 40) as part of the Suebian confederation. At the end of the sixth century CE Venantius Fortunatus[7] mentioned Suebi, together with Frissi in the Netherland's area, and these Suebi, according to Zeuss, belonged to the Suarine tribe. "Suarine" and "**Suardone**" are alternative appellations for the same group. Sered son of Zebulon thus also was to be found in Holland.

ELON, son of Zebulon, was recalled in the names of Holland and Norway's Hallin, and the ALANS; also Halland in Sweden and the Swede associated tribe of Alands whose descendants are part of the population of modern Finland. At all events, Zebulon may well be considered to have gained ascendancy amongst the Dutch of Holland with their dykes and "SEA-SHORE" settlement. Elon became the "Alans" and "Alamans" who settled in Alsace, France. Contemporaries applied the two names (Alans and Alamans) to the both peoples quite indiscriminately. The "Alamanii" were named after "ALMAN" which was the Assyrian name for Holman ("Halah" in the Bible, 2-Kings 17:6) to which the exiled Israelites had been taken.

The Diamond Symbol of Zebulon and South Africa

Some additional points of interest concerning Zebulon and Holland are: The Stone of Zebulon (on the Chief Priest's Breastplate) was a diamond (Exodus Rabah 38;5). Today, South Africa produces most of the world's diamonds which, on the whole, are processed and traded with in Belgium. South Africa is dominated by the Boers who mainly descend from Dutch settlers and in Belgium the people of Flanders are considered to be of Dutch affiliation -at least in part.

The Tribal Occupations of Zebulon
Are Those of Present-Day Holland!!

The Tribe of Zebulon in the Land of Israel was occupied in the Purple Dye industry, in the making of White glass, and in Fishing (Numbers Rabah 13; 16). The Purple Dye was produced from a sea mollusk by a complicated chemical process and the dye then applied to textiles in a manner that also required expertise. Modern Holland is prominent in both the Chemical and Textile Industries and also in Metallurgy. The production of white glass uses what are considered metallurgical principles. Fishing also is important in the present day Dutch economy in which at least one quarter of the inhabited land has been reclaimed from the sea and another quarter or more is somehow dependent on protection from inundation:

359

"Zebulon shall dwell on the sea-shores
and his shore will be a haven for ships" (Gen.49:13). Rotterdam in Holland is the biggest port in the world. The Dutch people do dwell on the sea-shores and they are the only people who do.

Polders and Dykes of the Netherlands

According to an official governmental Dutch web-site about the Netherlands:

<<In 1986, the Netherlands proclaimed the new 12th province of Flevoland but they didn't carve out the province from already existing land nor did they annex the territory of their neighbors - Germany and Belgium. The Netherlands actually grew.

<<The Dutch and their ancestors have been working to hold back and reclaim land from the North Sea for over 2000 years. Over 2000 years ago, the Frisians who first settled the Netherlands began to build terpen, the first dykes to hold back the water.

<<In 1287 the terpen and dykes that held back the North Sea failed, and water flooded the country. A new bay, called Zuiderzee (South Sea) was created over former farmland. For the next few centuries, the Dutch worked to slowly push back the water of the Zuiderzee, building dykes and creating polders (the term used to describe any piece of land reclaimed from water). Once dykes are built, canals and pumps are used to drain the land and to keep it dry. From the 1200s, windmills had been used to pump excess water off the fertile soil; today most of the windmills have been replaced with electricity- and diesel-driven pumps.

<<Then, storms and floods of 1916 provided the impetus for the Dutch to start a major project to reclaim the Zuiderzee. From 1927 to 1932, a 30.5 km (19 mile) long dyke called Afsluitdijk (the Barrier Dyke) was built, turning the Zuiderzee into the IJsselmeer, a freshwater lake. (Much of the Netherlands is essentially a delta for the Rhine and other rivers.)

<<Further protective dykes and works were built, reclaiming the land of the IJsselmeer. The new land led to the creation of the new province of Flevoland from what had been sea and water for centuries. The collective North Sea Protective Works is one

of the Seven Wonders of the Modern World, according to the American Society of Civil Engineers.

<<Today, approximately 27 percent of the Netherlands is actually below sea level. This area is home to over 60 percent of the country's population of 15.8 million people. The Netherlands, which is approximately the size of the U.S. states Connecticut and Massachusetts combined, has an approximate average elevation of 11 meters (36 feet). The Netherlands ties Lemmefjord, Denmark for [the] claim to [be] the lowest point in Western Europe - Prince Alexander Polder lies at 23 feet (7 meters) below sea level.>>

The Dutch people do literally dwell on the shores of the sea. They are the only people who fit the description of Zebulon. Dutch ports serve as a haven (harboring-place) for ships more than those of any other country!! Peoples who settled in Holland bore names recalling those of Zebulon and the sons of Zebulon. The Sabalingoi had a name meaning "People of Zebulon. The present-age means of livelihood of the Dutch are parallel to those attributed to the Zebulonites in ancient times.

THE DESCENDANTS OF ZEBULON

Zebulon = Zabulistan (Afghanistan in Scythian times), Sabalingoi (Denmark, Holland).

Clans of Zebulon:

Sered = Suardinoi (Sweden), Suardone, Suarini (Holland).

Elon = Alan (Scyths, Khazar Jews), Aland (Sweden, Finland), Halin (Norway), Halland (Sweden), Holland (Netherlands).

Yahleel (Yachlayl) = Chali (Denmark and Holland).

> Original Seal (from 1579) of the union of seven provinces that formed the basis for the present Netherlands: It depicts a ship with a Bible on the prow and the shields of the seven provinces on the side. A ship was the symbol of Zebulon.

Israeli Stamp: Zebulon

The symbol of Zebulon was a ship and the original symbol of the Netherlands depicted a ship. Some may claim that our proofs based on national symbols and the like are nothing but quaint coincidences. This is only one aspect of our evidence but for that matter where else do such "coincidences" occur?

Map of Tribal Positioning:No.1 Israel
Compare With Map Of Tribal Positionings (Map no.2-Opposite). Maps Show A Similar Relative Positioning of the Tribes To Each Other Before And After Their Exile And Re-Settlement.

Dan

Asher

Gilead

Dan

Nephtali

Dan

Half Menasseah

Zebulon

Machir

Issachar

Gad

Menasseah

Ephraim

Dan

Reuben

Benjamin

Judah

Simeon

Simeon

(Propotions of map have been deliberatly adjusted for illustrative purposes)

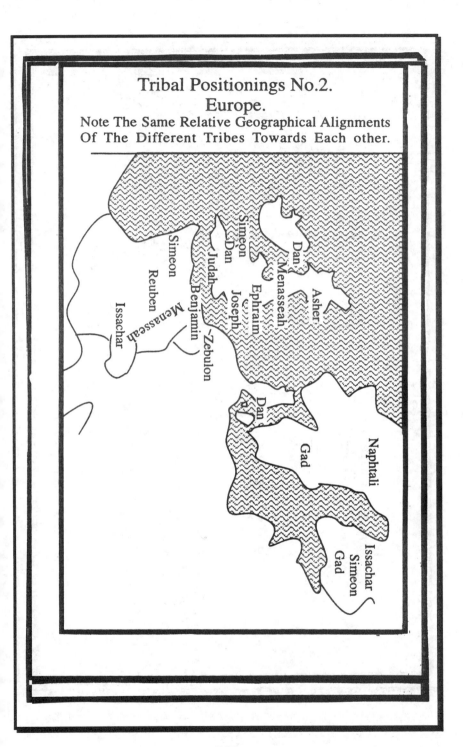

Tribal Positionings No.2.
Europe.
Note The Same Relative Geographical Alignments Of The Different Tribes Towards Each other.

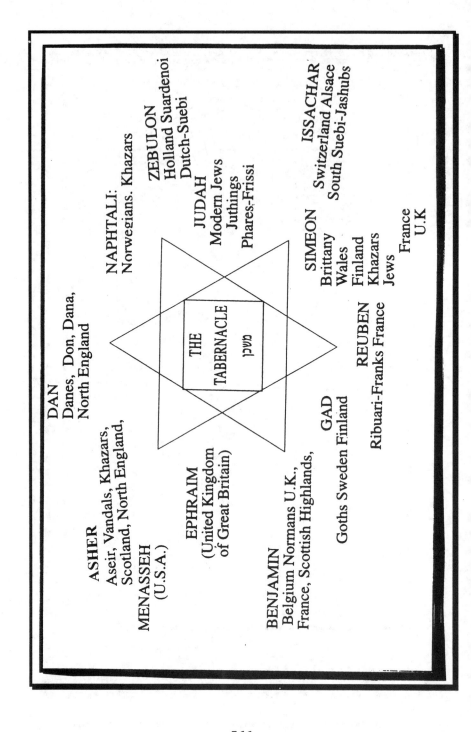

DAN
Danes, Don, Dana,
North England

NAPHTALI:
Norwegians. Khazars

ZEBULON
Holland Suardenoi
Dutch-Suebi

JUDAH
Modern Jews
Juthings
Phares-Frissi

ISSACHAR
Switzerland Alsace
South Suebi-Jashubs

SIMEON
Brittany
Wales
Finland
Khazars
Jews
France
U.K

THE
TABERNACLE
משכן

REUBEN
Ribuari-Franks France

GAD
Goths Sweden Finland

ASHER
Aseir, Vandals, Khazars,
Scotland, North England,

MENASSEH
(U.S.A.)

EPHRAIM
(United Kingdom
of Great Britain)

BENJAMIN
Belgium Normans U.K.,
France, Scottish Highlands,

23

THE ORDER OF ENCAMPMENT
IN THE WILDERNESS AND ITS
HISTORICAL SIGNIFICANCE
PARALLELISMS & SIMILARITIES

The present account concentrates on identifying Israelite Tribes and Tribal clans with groups who amalgamated with other entities to eventually form present day nationalities. Some aspects of the historical associations of the individual tribes and their equivalents are indicated in the order of encampment in the wilderness. The children of Israel when they came out of Egypt were destined to wander in the wilderness for forty years before entering the Promised Land of Israel. In the wilderness the Tribes were encamped in a specified order around the Tabernacle (Numbers chapter 2) and similarly on marching forward they were to proceed in the same order of march with the group belonging to Judah going first and that connected with Dan following behind at the end (Numbers ch. 10).   The camping arrangement divided the Twelve Tribes into four groups of three and these groupings have historical significance of their own. The camping alignment has some parallelism to the Familial order of Jacob and his wives (whose importance has already been briefly referred to) but not an exact one.

Judah, Issachar and Zebulon

Judah was to camp in the east together with **Issachar** and **Zebulon**. In history distinctly separate groups, both identified with Suebi though basically different, were to settle in Switzerland and Holland. The settlers in Switzerland were from Jashub son of Issachar whereas those identified as Suebi in Holland were actually Suardenoi from Sered son of Zebulon. Issachar was to dominate Switzerland, Zebulon -Holland; but groups from both Tribes were found in each country. Alsace was settled by the Alemanni whose name was often used synonymously with that of the Alans who in part settled in Switzerland and were named after **Elon** son of Zebulon whereas the Alemanni-proper were a branch of the Suebi and came from the **Jashubi (Suebi) of Issachar**. Amongst the Alemanni of Alsace were the **Juthones** whose name is reminiscent of that of the Jutes from Jutland of Denmark and both peoples descended from Judah. The Jutes at one stage had a center in the region of Holland amongst the Frisians part of whom may have come from Pharez son of Judah.

More on Alsace: Dreyfus

Alsace is on the border with Switzerland and lies between France and Germany. Alsace was considered a German speaking region though actually in Alsace and the region local dialects were used that nobody else could understand and that have not been studied properly. Alsace had been appropriated by France and was basically French in sentiment. Germany and France struggled for control of Alsace though most of the Alsatians considered themselves French. In 1870 the Prussians defeated France and took over Alsace which they ruled until 1918. Alsace was also an area in which many Jews had settled since Roman times. The Jews in Alsace were often not treated well though there were exceptions. Alfred Dreyfus was an officer of Jewish origin in the French Army in the 1890s. The family of Dreyfus came from Alsace. Dreyfus was suspected of spying for Germany so evidence was forged against him and he was convicted. The case then became the subject of contention between progressive and reactionary elements in France. Many people who considered themselves to be patriotic and conservative were against Dreyfus. There were however amongst the strongest defenders of Dreyfus many upright Conservative elements as well as many French Huguenot Protestants. Alsace had once been a Huguenot center and relationships between Jews and Huguenots were good ones.

Dreyfus knew his only crime was having been born a Jew. Because he was Jewish all the Anti-Semites condemned him. The Army also was against him. Dreyfus himself was fanatically pro-French and so was his family. New evidence came to light proving that Dreyfus was innocent and revealing the real culprit. The Army and the Establishment however at this stage had difficulty backing down and abandoned Dreyfus to serve his sentence. Eventually the innocence of Dreyfus was acknowledged though even today Jews are not really welcome in the French Army. The Germans later conquered France in the Second World War. They were assisted by traitors within France. In very many cases those who betrayed France were the physical and spiritual heirs of those who had falsely accused Dreyfus and been prominent in the attacks against him. The Dreyfus case inspired **Theodor Herzl** to found the Modern Zionist Movement. This helped lead to the creation of the State of Israel. **The Dreyfus case is important because it encapsulates several important "identity" concepts.** One section of the Israelite family cannot loyally assert itself at the expense of another. Any such attempt will cause the perpetrator to achieve the opposite of what he believes himself to want.

Reuben, Simeon and Gad

After the trio led by Judah, came that to the south headed by **Reuben**, who was encamped together with **Simeon** and **Gad.** Reuben was to become the Ribuari Franks who

369

gained control of France including the area of Brittany. In French Brittany were the **Samnites** from Simeon and the Namnites (from Namuel, son of Simeon) according to Ptolemy in ca. 120 CE. Much later, in the late 400's and 500's, the area of Brittany was to be conquered and populated by people from Wales and Celtic Britain who were being pushed out of Britain by the Anglo-Saxon advancements.

The peoples of Celtic Britain and Wales who re-populated Brittany also included descendants of Simeon. Simuen was the name of the Celtic-British forefather in Irish Literature which also referred to the Welsh as "Simeni", as we have seen. Ptolemy placed the SIMENI on the east coast of Britain in an area close to that of the ICENI whose name resembles a Phoenician rendition of the name Yachin, son of Simeon. The Silures of South Wales came from Shaul, son of SIMEON, son of Israel.

The Tribe of Gad gave rise to the Goths and the close relationship of the Goths and their offshoots with those of the Franks both in Scythia and in Western Europe have been referred to. This closeness was so great that sometimes it is difficult to distinguish between the two. An example was the **Chauci** (Hocings) of Hugo (Frank) association who was either descended from **Haggi** son of Gad **or** from **Henoch** son of Reuben, or a combination of both.

The Goths (of Gad) became the most important people in Sweden and also were influential in Finland. The Finns call themselves Suomi which name may originally have been a form for Simeon though later modified. The Finns once regarded themselves as descendants of the Lost Ten Tribes of Israel[1] as did the Khazars[2] who spoke a Finnish language[3] and in part are considered to have been a Gothic group[4]. From the above, Gad and Simeon were associated both in Finland and in Khazaria. The Goths also once had a kingdom in Southern France which became dominated by the Ribuari and other

Franks of Reuben and so Gad, Reuben, and Simeon were influential in the French kingdom.

Ephraim, Manasseh and Benjamin

The third trio described in the Book of Numbers (ch.2) in the Israelite encampment was to the west. This was composed of **Ephraim**, **Manasseh** and **Benjamin**, with Ephraim leading. Manasseh and Ephraim appear mainly to have been found amongst the Celtic-Galatians many of whom settled in Britain and also amongst the Anglo-Saxon hosts. Benjamin became the Normans who conquered the Anglo-Saxons and Celts of Britain and Ireland. A Jewish Rabbinical Commentator (the "Natziv" on Genesis 48:14) understood Ephraim's leadership to have been more spiritual, whereas Manasseh was to gain the material-lead. Indications are that Manasseh became the stronger element in the population of the U.S.A. (as will be considered) and Ephraim that of Britain, which conforms to the leadership distinction. Even so there must be very many from Ephraim in the USA which has become a center for all Israelite Tribes.

Dan, Asher and Naphtali

The last of the four groups of three among the Israelite Tribes in the wilderness was that to the north dominated by **DAN** who was together with **Asher** and **Naphtali**. Dan became the Danes and Naphtali became the Nephtali who migrated to Norway. Both Denmark and Norway produced the Vikings who invaded and settled in Northern England in an area previously belonging to the Angles and Varin (Vandals) and before them to the Brigantes. It has been shown that the Anglo-Brigantian inhabitants of Northern Britain were from the Tribe of Asher. The Aseir were considered ancestral gods by the Scandinavians including those of Norway and Denmark. Since the Aseir came from the Tribe of Asher the alliance of Dan, Naphtali, and Asher was retained and/or renewed both in Scandinavia and in northern England. Incidentally, in Celtic times the Children of Don from the Tribe of Dan had settled parts of Britain. Their presence in the north is indicated by the

Don River and the city of Danum (Doncaster). This was the **same area** which the Danes of Denmark were destined to occupy.

The above identifications show that the arrangement of the Camp was to some degree parallel to the future geographical positions of the Tribal descendants. What is more significant is that the triadic teams often reflected a destined close association.

The Colors of Israel

The above observations were based on the order of Israelite encamping around the Tabernacle in the Wilderness. The Tabernacle was constructed of wood and metals and various colored textiles. The overwhelming colors of the Tabernacle to an external viewer would have been red, blue, and white. Famous Commentators such as Nachmanides have noticed this fact. According to Rabbi S.R. Hirsch the relevant colors of Red, White, and Blue are the National colors of Israel. Most of the Israelite Nations employ these colors in their National Flags as brought to our attention by **Roger Waite** of Queensland, Australia, who made the following remark:

<<*One observation I've made about the nations which have Israel as their ancestor is that their national flags just about all have at least 2 out of the 3 tri-colours of red, white and blue much in the same way as the Arabs almost all have red, green, black and white in them. You may wish to include the following table ...*

> *Britain- red, white, blue*
> *America- red, white, blue*
> *France- red, white, blue*
> *Holland- red, white, blue*
> *Luxembourg- red, white, blue*
> *Denmark- red, white*
> *Norway- red, white, blue*
> *Sweden- blue, yellow*
> *Finland- blue, white*
> *Iceland- red, white, blue*

Belgium- red, yellow, black
Switzerland- red, white
Ireland- green, white, gold
South Africa- blue, white, gold
Israel- blue, white
Canada- red, white
Australia- red, white, blue
New Zealand- red, white, blue>>.

NAME SIMILARITIES

The Sages of the Talmud had the idea that a person's name reflected his innate qualities and even to some extent could influence his deeds and his fate. A similar notion is reflected in the Bible where Abram has his name changed (Genesis 17:4) to Abraham to reflect the blessing that he would become the father of many nations. Sari became SARAH (Genesis 17:15) since she was henceforth to become the mother of a son from whom would merge nations and kings of peoples, Jacob was re-named Israel for he had "Struggled with God and with men and had overcome" (Genesis 32:29).The name "Israel" (Genesis 35:10) was reaffirmed together with the blessing that Jacob-Israel would be fruitful and multiply, a nation and a company of nations would come out of him, Kings would emerge from his thighs, and the Land promised to his forefathers, Abraham and Isaac, would be given unto him and to his seed after him as long as they worshipped the One True God.

Israel had twelve sons and these sons became the Heads of Tribes and themselves had male offspring who became the heads of Tribal clans that were named after them. These clans amounted to about seventy in all. In addition, in several cases there occurred further sub-divisions of the Tribal clan-groupings and additional entities emerged who were named after later descendants of the Tribal Patriarchs. Here and there the names of certain clans in different tribes are identical or similar. In some cases similarity in name was further confused by geographical proximity in the Land of Israel itself or later in the course of the Tribal wanderings. It is suggested that the similarity in nomenclature had been pre-determined by Providence as indicative of a future merging or at least close association. Some examples of these similarities and identities are: Yair from the family of Peretz of Judah (1-Chronicles 2:22) settled in the territory of Machir of Manasseh with the prominent family of Peresh (1-Chronciles 7:16). Later the two names Peretz and Peresh were to be combined and reflected in the Parissi of France -Gaul and York -England and the Frissi of Northern Holland. Zerah (Numbers 26:13, 20) was a clan-name amongst both the Tribes of Judah (Numbers 26:13) and Simeon (Numbers 26:20). Judah (at least for a while) was destined (Joshua 19:1) to encompass the allocation of Simeon in the land of Israel and groups derived from Simeon (such as the Zaratae of East Scythia) are also found adjoining offshoots from Judah.

CARMI was a clan name amongst Reuben (Numbers 26; 6) as well as being that of a group in Judah (1-Chronicles 1:4). Also in both Reuben (Numbers 26:6) and Judah (Numbers 26:21) were found the two identically named Families of Hezron (Numbers 26:6, 21). Hezron of Reuben has been ascribed the Tribes of the Chassuari (Hetware) amongst the Franks but in this case as well as that of Carmi and its identifications there are indications that entities from Judah may also have been present. Likewise, BERIAH ("Beria-g-h") was found as a clan name in the Tribes of Asher (Numbers 26:45), of Ephraim (1-Chronicles 7:23), and of Benjamin (1-Chronicles 8:13). In the land of Israel a good portion from the Tribe of Asher actually settled (for a time) in the territory of Ephraim[5], while the lands of Ephraim and Benjamin not only were adjacent but according to some researchers seem to have intermerged. Similarly, groups identified with Beriah such as the Burgundians, Varangians, and Brigges-Brigantes are so located and had such a history that their familial connexion to the Lost Tribes is clear. Their belonging to Ephraim, Asher, or Benjamin is also fairly certain, though exactly to which of them is not always exactly determinable. The VARANGIANS, for instance, (also termed "BARAGGIO") contributed a group to the Khazar forces in southern Russia who later converted to JUDAISM. The Varangians also formed, for a short period, the conquering Swedish-connected ruling-elite of Russia in its formative years, and the Warings and "Bergio" contingents in the Anglo-Saxon forces that invaded and conquered England. A Russian Chronicle (The "Poviost") included under the term "Varangian" especially the inhabitants then of territories bordering on the Varaeger (Baltic) Sea, namely the Swedes, Norwegians, Angles, and Gothlanders[6].

The conversion of the Khazars to Judaism is compatible with their Varangian (Varachan) section belonging to the Tribe of Benjamin most of which had remained loyal to the House of David and shared the religious faith of Judah. The English WARING element is believed (like Bergio and the Brigges) to have located itself primarily in the North and to have overflowed into Lowland-Scotland and this area has been ascribed to Asher though bordering on the Joseph areas of Manasseh and EPHRAIM. Thus, the Varangians-Varager (etc.) entity belonged to Ephraim, Benjamin, or Asher.

Guni (Numbers 26:48) was an important clan in the Tribe of Naphtali which was close at one stage to the Tribe of Gad on the east bank of the Jordan. Amongst the Tribe of Gad there was also a group with ancestor named "Guni" (1-Chronicles 5:15). Guni has been identified as the Chuni, which from southern Scythia moved northward[7]. The name Chuni is, in effect, another name for Hun. The Huni in the east were originally part of the Sienbi but later the name was extended (possibly after conquest) to cover another much larger body originally named Hsiungnu and these became the Huns known to history in the west. The Nephtali were also known as Huns or "Nephtalite Huns" and the mention of Huns amongst the invaders of Britain and Scandinavia in the 400's CE and later, probably refers to the Nephtali or a portion of them. Numerous place names in southern Scandinavia (Sweden and Norway) such as Hunehals (Hun's-Neck), Hun, Hunnamala, Hunneberg, Huno, Hunnebostrand, Hunnestad (Hun town), Hunndalen (Hun Valley), etc.[7], testify to the presence of the Chuni from Guni. Since the Tribe of Naphtali largely settled in Norway, and the Tribe of Gad mainly in Sweden and both Gad and Norway contained groups named "Guni" then the presence of the Chuni (Huni) from Guni in both their countries is understandable. Guni was a clan name in both Gad and Nephtali.

Whilst still in Scythia, before moving north, the Nephtali had been loosely connected with the Guti-Goths of Gad and one of the appellations given to them was that of "Little Goths" (Sian Guti) translated as "Thyssa-Getae".

The Nephtali, Huni, the Sienbi and others, had also been part of a larger group called "The Ten Tribes" in Chinese Chronicles. They were possibly originally so named because they belonged to The Ten Tribes (1-Kings 11:31) who previously formed the Northern Kingdom of Israel taken captive by the Assyrians. Later the appellation was applied to a confederation of the Huns with which some Israelite Tribes were associated in the beginning. Such transferences of name were common in the area.

The involvement of the various cases could well be expanded upon but the point is obvious. Apparent contradictions where one entity is ascribed more than one identity, instead of negating each other and throwing doubt on the identification method, actually (upon closer examination) are seen to further confirm the validity of the given conclusions.

JOHN BULL

"End(s) Of The Earth".

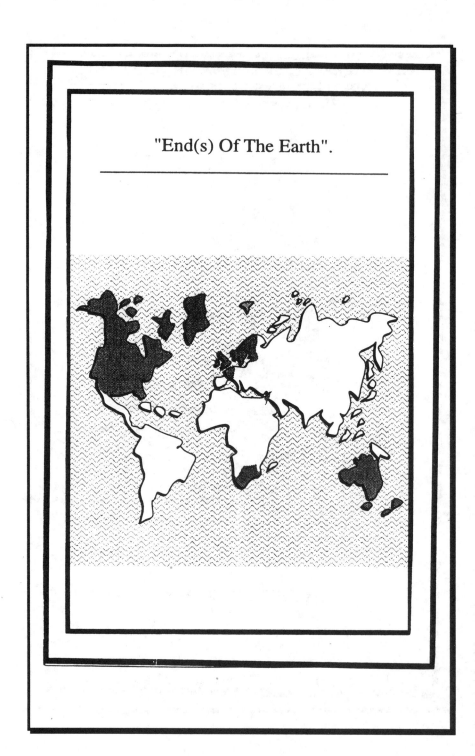

24

THE BLESSINGS
GENEAOLOGY OF THE BLESSINGS

Joseph

We have identified some of the North European peoples in general with the Hebrews. Specific groups have been equated with particular Israelite Tribes and Tribal clans. A deeper understanding of these matters is dependent to some extent on an understanding of the blessings and the manner of their fulfillment.

The Promised Blessings began with Abraham. He was the first Patriarch and to him was it promised to become, *"A great nation... and in you will all the families of the earth be blessed"* (Genesis 12:2-3). *"And I will make my covenant between me and thee, and will multiply thee exceedingly"* (Genesis 17:2). *"I will make nations of thee and kings shall come out of thee; And I will establish my covenant between me and thee and thy seed after thee in their generations for an everlasting covenant, to be a God unto thee, and to thy seed after thee"* (Genesis 17:6-7). Abraham begat Ishmael and Isaac. Ishmael traditionally was the forefather of many of the Arabs. Isaac received the covenant promise and to him devolved the promised blessings: *"My covenant will I establish with Isaac"* (Genesis 17:21); *"I will establish my covenant with him for an everlasting covenant, and with his seed after him"* (Genesis 17:19). God informed Abraham, *"In Isaac shall thy seed be called"* (Genesis 21:21).

Isaac begat the twins Esau and Jacob. Of Esau it was foretold, *"By thy sword shalt thou live, and shalt serve thy brother"* (Genesis 27:40). Esau became ancestor to the founder settlers of early Rome and to part of the German people (Megilla 6), as well as to part of the ruling elite[1] in Continental Europe. *"And Esau hated Jacob because of the Blessing where with his father blessed him"* (Genesis 27:41). The anti-Semitic so-called "Identity" scumbags are descended from Esau and from Canaanites. If it was not for these treacherous elements and their wicked agenda the truth of what we are saying in this work would have been more widely accepted and at the least seriously considered in many circles some time ago. They themselves are the servants of Satan and the seed of Darkness and Perdition.

Jacob received the Blessings promised to Abraham and to Isaac. The Children of Jacob were to become the Chosen People. Isaac blessed Jacob, *"God Almighty bless thee, and make thee fruitful and multiply thee, that thou mayest be a multitude of people; And give thee the blessing of ABRAHAM, to thee and to thy seed with thee"* (Genesis 28:2-3). Jacob was given the additional name ISRAEL, *"Thy name shall be called no more Jacob, But ISRAEL; for as a prince hast thou power with God and with men and hast prevailed"* (Genesis 32:8). *"Thy name is Jacob: thy name shall not be called any more Jacob, but Israel shall be thy name: and He called his name ISRAEL"* (Genesis 35:10). Jacob (Israel) had Twelve Sons, *"Now the sons of Jacob were twelve"* (Genesis 36:22).

The TWELVE SONS OF ISRAEL were Reuben, Simeon, Levi, Judah, Issachar, Zebulon, Joseph, Benjamin, Dan, Naphtali, Gad, and Asher. All the sons of Israel received a Blessing from their father, *"Everyone according to his blessing he blessed them"* (Genesis 49:28). In addition to the individual blessing given to each one there existed the Natural Right of Leadership and the Birthright. The Natural Right of Leadership was to involve Judah who provided the House of David and was to receive the task of Lawgiver. The Birthright, in effect, meant the reception of those same blessings given to all the Tribes but in greater quantity and intensity. It also indicated a natural right to a certain predominance -and a two-fold portion in the inheritance.

"Judah prevailed above his brethren, and of him (comes) the chief ruler; but the birthright was Joseph's" (1-Chronicles 5:1-2).

Jacob blessed Joseph, *"The blessings of thy father have prevailed above the blessings of my progenitors unto the utmost bound of the everlasting hills: they shall be on the head of JOSEPH, and on the crown of him that was separated from his brethren"* (Genesis 49:6). Joseph had two sons, Ephraim and Menasseh. Both Ephraim and Menasseh received the status of full Tribes in their own right. Jacob said: <<THY TWO SONS, EPHRAIM AND MANASSEH...ARE MINE; AS REUBEN AND SIMEON, THEY SHALL BE MINE.>> (Genesis 48:5) meaning that they should be counted as Tribes amongst the brothers of JOSEPH. Jacob blessed Ephraim and Menasseh, *"The Angel which redeemed me from all evil, bless the lads; and let my name be named on them, and the name of my fathers Abraham and Isaac; and let them grow into a multitude in the midst of the earth,"* (Genesis 48:16). *"And he blessed them that day, saying, In thee shall Israel bless saying, God make thee as Ephraim and as Menasseh: and he set Ephraim before Menasseh"* (Genesis 48:20).

The prevalence of Ephraim is repeated in Jeremiah (31:9), *"I am a father to Israel, and EPHRAIM is my firstborn"*. Nonetheless towards the end times (in our days) there was to be a stage in which Manasseh would be preeminent, as explained later.

The Promised Blessings were unconditional, *"By myself hath I sworn, saith the LORD...that in Blessing I will bless thee and in multiplying I will multiply thy seed"* (Genesis 28:15). *"God is not a man neither the son of man that he should repent...He hath blessed and I cannot reverse it"* (Numbers 23:19-20).

NATIONAL GOALS

The blessings were concomitant with a Divine Purpose. Of Abraham it was said, *"Abraham shall surely become a great and mighty nation, and all the nations of the earth shall be blessed in him. For I know him that he will command his children and his house after him, and they shall keep the way of the LORD to do justice and judgement; that the LORD may bring upon Abraham that which he hath spoken of him"* (Genesis 18:18-19).

The task of performing *"justice and judgement"* after becoming *"a great and mighty nation"* through which all the nations of the earth would be blessed devolved upon Joseph. Tens of millions (if not hundreds of millions) of people throughout the world have not starved to death or massacred each other only because the "Anglo-Saxon" nations saved them. The only real restraint on tyranny anywhere today is that exercised by these countries.

The quality of Empathic Consideration (Chesed) was associated with the Northern Kingdom in which the Tribe of Joseph was paramount. *"We have heard that the kings of the House of Israel are merciful kings"*, said servants of the King of Syria (1-Kings 20:31).

The prophet Amos condemned Judah for not keeping the Law, he also condemned "Israel", meaning the Ten Tribes, "because they sold the righteous for silver" (Amos 1:4-6). A great Rabbinical Authority (the "Natziv") explained that keeping the Law was the special forte of Judah and therefore it was expected of him. When he failed to fulfill the expectation he became liable. The Ten Tribes on the other hand, had never been noted as scripturally observant but they had been known for empathic consideration of others (Chesed). When, through selling the righteous for silver, their level of Social Justice fell and they too became liable.

In their place of exile and re-settlement it would seem that Social Justice is still expected from the Ten Tribes. *"Hate the evil and love the good, and establish judgement in the gate: it may be that the LORD God of Hosts will be gracious unto the remnant of JOSEPH"* (Amos 6:15).

Royal Arms of Scotland:
Note the Two Unicorns°.

I WANT YOU
FOR U.S. ARMY
NEAREST RECRUITING STATION

Israeli stamp depicts one of the symbols of Joseph. This was a sheaf of what. The Anglo-Saxons considered Sheaf Sceafing to be their ancestor. Sheaf was associated with a sheaf of wheat and named after one. Sheaf was also known as Beowulf and as Balder whose name is derived from the pagan god Baal. The northern Israelites had been exiled from their land for worshipping Baal and other idols (2-Kings 17; 16). Balder was killed when shot by an arrow. Joseph too had been a target for arrows, "The archers have surely grieved him, and shot at him, and hated him," (Genesis 49; 23).

JOSEPH – Canada

Canada, on the whole, belongs to the Domain of Joseph.

The motto means from "Sea to sea", and refers to the extent of Canada's area but the phrase itself is a quotation from the Bible where it is used three times, once (Amos 8;12-13) describing the future thirst for God's word amongst the exiled Ten Tribes before the Messianic era and twice (Zecharia 9;10 and Psalms 72;8) in connection with the Reign of the Messiah in the Future.

25

The Tribe of Manasseh
Joseph: Ephraim and Manasseh

Asap and Yasubi

The two sons of Joseph, Ephraim and Manasseh, were each considered separate tribes in their own right (Genesis 48:5). The figure of Joseph inspired the legend of Sceld Scefing (Sheafing) who was the mythological ancestor of the Anglo-Saxons and, in addition to Joseph, has aspects taken from the accounts of Moses and Noah after the fashion of synthetic mythologies. This person had been found as a child sleeping in an oarless boat which drifted into a harbor in the Land of the Angles before they crossed the Ocean to Britain. When he grew up he gave the people Laws and taught them agriculture. He was the ancestor of their leaders. Sceld had been named "Sheafing" due to the sheafs of wheat on which he slept in the oarless boat that brought him into the harbor on the North Sea shore[1]. In popular traditional Jewish art Joseph is also sometimes represented by a sheaf of wheat. The symbol of a sheaf of wheat for Joseph (or for one of his sons) derives from a. dream which Joseph related to his brothers, *"My sheaf arose your sheafs stood round about and made obeisance to my sheaf"* (Genesis 37:6-7)✝.

In Neo-Assyrian times Israelite groups from the Tribes of Joseph were discernable ("Yasubians"[2], "Yasubgallians"[3]) in the areas of Mannae and Media. Later, in the eastern Iranian area close to the Indus were the people of "Asapioi" who were also to be called "Isapoi" and "Ysufzi" meaning JOSEPH[4]. These names (like all those of Afghanistan –see Bellew) were later to be applied to other different peoples. The root "ASAP" in the Hebrew Scriptures is related to the birth of Joseph: *"And she* [i.e. Rachel] *conceived, and bare a son; and said God hath taken away* [in Hebrew: "ASAPH"] *my reproach: And she called his name Joseph"*, Genesis 30:23-24). The name Joseph in the Iranian-Afghan region was renderable as "Jo-asaph"[5] and at all events "ASAP" is a derivative in Semitic regions of Joseph[6]. Other Scythian peoples such as the Aspassi in Chorasmia and the Aspacarae (whose names bear the "ASP" root) in Serica were also descended from Joseph. The Aspacarae of Serica were identical to the Eastern-Sienbi or Suebi and in western Europe are sometimes referred to as SWEAF and represented by the eponymous figure of Svipdag. The Sweaf-Sienbi participated in the Anglo-Saxon invasions of Britain.

Sweaf and the root "Asap" were also linked with the Aspourgian Tribe near the mouth of the Don River in southern Russia. The Don River was identified by Jewish Chroniclers with the Sambation River. According to Talmudic tradition part of the Lost Ten Tribes had settled on the banks of the Sambation and beyond it. The Aspourgian settlement has been

---

✝ It should be noted that the Hebrew "Yoseph" in Assyrian would have been rendered "Yoshef" (with a "sh" instead of "s") and in Scythian areas the initial "Yo" sounds on names were often dropped and thus we have something like "sheaf." In Anglo-Saxon English the word "sheaf" means bundle of corn and is linked with the original story of Joseph and was one of his symbols.

In addition evidence links Sceld Sheafing with Targiteaus the legendary ancestor of the Scythians (mentioned by Herodotus) and with Aspourgos whom the Royal Scythians worshipped and who also was derived from the figure of JOSEPH son of Israel.

identified with the legendary Asgard home of the ancestral gods of the Scandinavians and Anglo-Saxons. Irma Haynman (Jerusalem, 1994) speaks of the military and religious organisation of the Aspourgians who revered a mythical "Aspourgos"[7]. There was also a Royal Scythian-Parthian dynasty named after Aspourgos. Ms. Haynman adduced evidence that the root "asp"[*] is derived from the same Semitic-root as the name of Joseph and that the figure of "Aspourgos" was regarded by his followers as identical with Biblical Joseph. The logical conclusion from this and from our own evidence is that they must indeed have been descended from Joseph.

MANASSEH

Julius Caesar (Gallic Wars 4;1) reported the Usipetes and Tencteri crossing the Rhine into Gaul in flight from the advancing Suebi. All three peoples relate to Joseph, the Tencteri via Tahan-Tachan, son of Ephraim, (Numbers 26;36) and "Usip" being a form of Joseph.

Tacitus ("Germania" 2) wrote concerning the "Germans" of his time, meaning largely Anglo-Saxon, Scandinavian, and Frankish groups who were ultimately to evacuate the geographical region of Germany. He wrote that they had a tradition of being descended from "Tuisto" and his son MANNUS father of the Herminiones, Ingaevones, and Istaevones. The name "MANNUS" apparently derives from the name Manasseh just as Shechem (Numbers 26:32), a clan of Gilead of Manasseh, is found in the Sicambri who were part of the Istaevones (sons of Mannus) and are the only known people from that group. Pliny (N.H. 4; 14;1) identified the Sicambri as Istaevones.

---

[*] Some researchers claimed in the past that the root "asp" was cognate with an Iranian word meaning "horse". Haynman shows that this derivation is unlikely or at least of secondary significance.

In Hebrew the "Sh" and "S" are interchangeable, the vowel "e" freely becomes "i". In Greek the " bri" of Sicambri is a known suffix, thus Shechem = Sicambri.

MACHIR THE SON OF MANASSEH

Machir was the son of Manasseh. Descendants of Machir were referred to as "haMachiri." Machir was the father of Gilead and ancestor to that portion of Manasseh (called "the half tribe of Manasseh", e.g. 1-Chr. 6:46) which settled on the east bank of the Jordan together with Reuben and Gad. MACHIR fathered the Amyrgian Scyths names for whom are recognised as permutations of the name Machir[8]. The Amyrgio Scuthae were first known east of the Caspian Sea in an area associated by Jewish tradition with the Tribe of Manasseh (Cochin Roll, Eldad HaDani). They were connected with, and neighbors to, the Massagetae whose name indicates the combination of Manasseh and Gad. Their area of Settlement contained locations, whose names bear witness to their presence: Margiana, Marycaei, Maruca.

SAMARIA OF ISRAEL

The city of Maruca in Sogdiana was later named "Samarkand", or "Camp of Samar", in remembrance of SAMARIA, the former capital of the northern Israelites in the territory of Manasseh and synonymous with it in prophecy[*]. Leonid S. CHEKIN (1989) recorded a host of ancient names in Scythia and the surroundings such as Sarmagana in Aria, Sama, Samarchan, Samarcam, Samarcha, and Samander one of the Khazar capitals. These places were mostly in areas associated with the Amyrgian Scythes. Chekin links them with the Khazars[9] whom legend says were descended from the Tribes of

---

[*] It has been objected that "Samaria" is rendered as "Shomron" in modern and Biblical Hebrew. Even so, "Samaria" is how its own inhabitants as well as the Phoenicians and others appear to have pronounced its name and how the name was rendered in contemporary translations.

Manasseh and Simeon. The names are based on the root SAMAR and may be traced to the North Israelite Phoenician-type pronunciation of Samaria (in the territory of Manasseh) the former capital of northern Israel.

SKATI MARIKA, i.e. SCYTHIANS (SKATI) from MARUKA

A group of Amyrgian Scythians in the time of Darius King of Persia (522-486 BCE) were reported as then dwelling on the Tigris banks. They were led by a chief Saku'ka and revolted against the Persian rulers. In a bi-lingual inscription these Amyrgians are called "Saka-Humuvashka" in Persian and "Gimirri Umurgah" in Babylonian[10]. "Gimirri" (in the Babylonian version) means either "Tribes" or "Cimmerians" or both since the Scyths and Cimmerians were originally one entity. The denomination Umerga (for Amyrgio) recurs in the "Umerugi"[11] of Saxon Germany who were probably a branch of the Mercian Saxons who in England were also known as Skati Marika[12], i.e. Scythians (Skati) from Maruka which was another name for Samarkand in Sogdiana east of the Caspian. It should be recalled that "Samarkand" means "Camp of Samar" and was named after "Samaria" in the Land of Israel. Similarly Saxons in West Holstein were called by the Geographer of Ravenna (700's CE) "Abis Maurungani" which indicates a connection with the Abii Scythae of northeast Scythia. In Europe the Amyrgioi of Scythia were also referred to as Mearings, Myrce, Myringas, Myrgingas, and Mercians. The Anglo-Saxon poet "Widsuth" spoke of the GUDMYRCE thus combining Goths ("Gud") with Mercians[13], as the Amyrgio of Europe are most commonly referred to. One of the titles of Theodoric the Ostrogothic Emperor was "Prince of the Maerings"[14]. In Saxon England the kingdom of Mercia encompassed a good portion of the country. Clans of the Mercians in England were Wigesta, Magonsaete, Nox, Oht gaga, Henrica, Unecinga, Hwicce, Gifel, Spale, and Grywe[15] (Thundy). The Magonsaete have a name that in Hebrew could mean "armor-bearers" (Magon-Saeti), Shupim

391

(=Spale) and Chupim (=Gifel) were clans of Machir (1-Chronicles 7:14-17). Other clans included Likhi and Aniam (=Unecinga).

GILEAD, SON of MACHIR and OTHER DESCENDANTS OF MANASSEH

The son of Machir was GILEAD (pronounceable as Gileath) from whom emerged the Galadon of northern Wales and the Galadi[16] -Galatians of Gaul and the Caledonians in Scotland. The sons of Gilead were Jeezer, Helek (Chelek), Asriel, Shechem, Shemida, and Hepher (Numbers 26:30). Helek was found amongst the Helvecones who became part of the Vandal-Lugi federation (Tacitus, "Germania" 43). The Vandals were involved in the Anglo-Saxon invasions of Britain, as were the Calucones who were also descendants of HELEK*. Ptolemy places the Calucones on the lower Elbe River between the Anglii, Cherusci, and Laccobardi-Lombards. ASRIEL (son of Gilead) gave his name to Isari in the Imodus Mountains east of the Caspian Sea from which area tradition (recorded by Le Petit) said that the Saxons, Frisians, and Brunswickian Angles emerged[17]. The Frisians (says Procopius, Gothic War viii; 20) were major participants in the Anglo-Saxon invasions and they descend from PERESH✦, son of Machir, by his Aramaean concubine Maacah (1-Chronicles 7:15-16). In East Frisia (Ost

---

* The name "Helek" in Hebrew begins with the letter "chet": (ח) which when transliterated into European tongues may take a "h", "c", or "ch" sound. The name means, "Portion".

✦ The Frisians of today appear to be dominated by descendants of the Tribe of Zebulon and the Sabalingoi [i.e. "people of Zebulon] were recorded in their area. It is our opinion however that those Frisians who participated in the Anglo-Saxon invasions belonged to the Tribe of Manasseh and were then sojourning in the Frisian region.
Also from Peresh came the Parissi of Gaul and the Partissi of north Celtic England from the region of York. In Hebrew "P" is interchangeable for "PH" or "F", thus Peresh became both Pariss and Friss.

Friesland) were the Chauki whom we have identified with Hagi of Gad and Gad settled besides the half-tribe of Manasseh. The Chauki were either also referred to as "Fransa-Masani" or "Cisa-Masani" or these were names of additional peoples in the Netherlands Chauki region[18]. According to our understanding of Ptolemy's Map of the former area of Manasseh east of the Jordan, as well as place-names in Spain and general Mediterranean usage,[19] "Masani" is a permutation of the appellation "Manasseh"! It follows that in the area of Frisia descendants of Manesseh had been present and these are those who invaded Britain. East Anglia is said to have received a substantial immigration from Frisia and these too contributed significantly to the early populating of America. ASRIEL (son of Gilead) gave a derivative of his name to Surrey, which was the southern portion of Saxon Mercia in England. SHECHEM, son of Gilead, became the Sicambri who were related to the Saxons and gave their name to the Salian Franks whom they conquered and partly merged with. The Sicambri had been known from East Iran and from Bactria. Other sections from the Clan of Secem (Shecem) were the Scymbi north of the Caspian in east Scythia and the Scymitae (whose name means "Tribe of Secem") on the Lower Volga River mentioned by Ptolemy in his description of "Asiatic Sarmatia". The Soumboi-Aggiloi (a branch of Angles), and the Soumboi-Laccobardi (Lombardi) all are associated with SHEMIDA from the family of Machir (1-Chron. 7:19). Likewise, "SAMIDES", in Celtic tradition was the ancestor of the Southern "Galli" in France who came from the Galilee of Israel. "Shemida" in Hebrew could be pronounced as Samida-g like the ancestral hero "SAEMDAG" in Scandinavian" mythology.

"JEEZER", son of Gilead, actually has a name more correctly transliterated from the Hebrew as AIEZER or "Ai-g-azar (איעזר) and he forefathered at least a portion of the people known as "Gazari", "Agathyrsi", or "KHAZARS" whom it was believed (according to the report of Eldad HaDani in ca.880 CE) had descended from the Tribes of Simeon and Manasseh and "Jeezer" (i.e. "Ai-g-azar") belonged to Gilead of Manasseh. The Agathyrsi-Khuzars were also associated with the Tribal leader AZRIEL (Gazriel) at the time of Assyrian Exile or close to it as discussed below. The clan of "Jeezer" (Aiezer, Aigazar) is considered the same as that of the "ABI-EZRI" (Judges 6:11) to which the Judge Gideon belonged. Gideon (Judges ch.7) with three hundred carefully picked men ambushed at night a vast host of Midianites and Amalekites who were oppressing Israel.

HEPHER was ancestor to the HAEFERINGAS who were a Saxon group whose name is recalled in the modern Havering east of London. In addition, HEPHER (son of Gilead) gave his name to the "Heafr" who were a Gothic element amongst the Anglo-Saxons[20].

THE DAUGHTERS OF ZELOPHEHAD

Zelophehad, son of Hepher, was famous for his daughters. Zelophehad (Numbers chapter 26) was one of the Israelites who came out of Egypt under the leadership of Moses and entered the Promised Land of Chanaan. Zelophehad died without male issue and his daughters received their own allocations within the Land of Israel. The daughters of Zelophehad gave their names to Clans belonging to Manasseh and to areas within the tribal apportionment of Manasseh (Joshua 17:3) [21]. This has been affirmed by archaeological evidence concerning the territory of Manasseh west of the Jordan River. The daughters were Mahlah, Noah, Hoglah, Milcah and Tirzah (Numbers ch.27, Joshua ch.17). NOAH also gave her name to the city of Nauaris on the Don River which in Jewish sources was known as the SAMBATION RIVER besides which, and beyond of, were said to be found the LOST TEN TRIBES OF ISRAEL. In the vicinity of Nauaris were the Scythian group named NEURI, first recorded by Herodotus. An 18th century History of Sweden (Dalin, "Svea-rikes Historika" 1747-62, volume 1, p.51), repeats the tradition that the NEURI were "REMNANTS OF THE TEN FAMILIES OF ISRAEL whom Salmanassar, the king of Assyria, took captive from Canaan." The source says that the Israelite Neuri, together with the Vodiver ("Holy People") and Gelones, migrated to Scandinavia[22]. The NERVI in northern Gaul also belonged to the Neuri as did the Naharvali who adjoined the Burgundions and Guttones (Goths) in west Scythia before they continued their movement westward. The Naharvalli were related to both the Angles and Vandals. The first part of their name "NAHAR" (Nahar-valli) in Hebrew literally means "RIVER". Regarding the other daughter of Zelophehad, HOGLAH (Choglah) has a name forms of which appeared amongst early Frankish leaders (e.g. Chocilarch); MILCAH's appelation denotes Royalty (MeLeC meaning "king", MaLCaH meaning "queen", in Hebrew) and is reminiscent of the Royal Scyths. The Sakaraucae in east Scythia have a name that can also be understood (in local dialects) to mean Royal Scythians. "Basil" is also a term connoting royalty and we have the Basili (i.e. Royal) group amongst the Khazars and the name "Basilia" applied to Scandinavia. The name MALCHIEL in Hebrew also is based on the Hebrew root "Malec" meaning king. Similar suggestions are therefore applicable concerning the clan of MALCHIEL in the Tribe of Asher that for a time was intertwined with the Tribes of Joseph and temporarily had sojourned in their territory. The name TIRZAH (daughter of Zelophehad) in Hebrew may more correctly be rendered "THIRTSA" and the "THYRSA-GETAE" (Pliny N.H. 4;12) have a name translatable as "Tirtzah-of-the-Goths". These Thyrsa-Getae of Scythia are otherwise known as the "Thyssagetae" (Little Goths) and were identifiably-associated with the Iyrcae (Turci of Scandinavia) and with the Nephtali.

YAIR of MACHIR??

An important element amongst the clans of Machir, son of Manasseh was that of YAIR (Jair in the KJ Bible) who was actually a descendant of Judah! Judah (1-Chronicles 2:5) begat

Pharez who begat Hezron. Later Hezron intermarried with Machir of Manasseh:

"And afterward Hezron went into the daughter of Machir the father of Gilead...and she bare him Segub.

"And Segub begat Jair, who had three and twenty cities in the land of Gilead."

"And he took [in addition to the twenty three cities of Gilead already in his possession] *Geshur, and Aram, with the towns of Jair from them, with Kenath and the towns thereof, threescore cities. All these belonged to the sons of MACHIR THE FATHER OF GILEAD"* (1-Chronicles 2:21-23).

It follows that Yair had intermarried with Machir and was counted as part of his clan even though paternally he was descended from Judah. The entity of Yair is identified with "Judah upon Jordan toward the sunrising" (Joshua 19; 34)[23] even though we know that the IARI of Yair were most powerful much further to the north. Judah of Yair in the north must have bordered Naphtali and Dan just as Dan in the south adjoined Judah[†].

Yair is recalled in Assyrian inscriptions as the IARI who fought on the Euphrates and even to the east of the Euphrates in the far north[24]. "IAR" was also the eponymous ancestor of groups in Scotland and Ireland[25].

PERESH

The Frisi and Parissi (of Northern England and of Gaul) were attributed the ancestry of Peresh son of Machir. The name PERESH means "Separated", or "Dedicated" (e.g. "Pharisee") and therefore has the same meaning as "NEMED" who was the legendary ancestor of early settlers in Ireland[26]. The names Peresh (of Machir) and Pheretz (of Judah) are similar and since descendants of both once lived in the same region, the Parissi

---

[†] It is also however possible that there were two clan heads named Yair in the portion of Manasseh, one being a descendant of Manasseh and the other originally from Judah but intermarried into the family of Machir.

and Frisi may also have contained Judaean elements. The Frisians came from Frisia in Northern Holland. A revised examination of Nordic tongues now regards the Frisian language to be similar to that of the Goths and the Mercian dialect of England to have been a form of Gothic[27]. This corresponds with our identification of the Goths with Gad, the Frisi with Paresh of Machir, and the Mercians with Machir of Manasseh. These groups had once been neighbors east of the Jordan. They had been exiled more or less together and had shared common historical experiences reflected in their language.

OTHER CLAN NAMES

Apart from the sons of Gilead listed above other clan names were extant amongst Manasseh east of the Jordan:

"AND THE CHILDREN OF THE HALF TRIBE OF MANASSEH DWELT IN THE LAND; THEY INCREASED FROM BASHAN UNTO BAAL HERMON AND SENIR, AND UNTO MOUNT HERMON.

"AND THESE WERE THE HEADS OF THE HOUSE OF THEIR FATHERS, EVEN EPHER, AND ISHI, AND ELIEL, AND AZRIEL, AND JEREMIAH, AND HODAVIAH, AND JAHDIEL, MIGHTY MEN OF VALOR, FAMOUS MEN, AND HEADS OF THE HOUSE OF THEIR FATHERS.

"AND THEY TRANSGRESSED AGAINST THE GOD OF THEIR FATHERS, AND WENT AWHORING AFTER THE GODS OF THE PEOPLE OF THE LAND, WHOM GOD DESTROYED BEFORE THEM.

"AND THE GOD OF ISRAEL STIRRED UP THE SPIRIT OF PUL KING OF ASSYRIA, AND THE SPIRIT OF TILGATH-PILNESER KING OF ASSYRIA, AND HE CARRIED THEM AWAY, EVEN THE REUBENITES, AND THE GADITES, AND THE HALF TRIBE OF MANASSEH, AND BROUGHT THEM UNTO HALAH, AND HABOR, AND HARA, AND TO THE RIVER GOZAN, UNTO THIS DAY"
1-Chronicles 5:24-26.

The above clan leaders at the time of the Assyrian exile (Epher, Ishi, Eliel, Azriel, Jeremiah, Hodaviah, and Jahdiel) seem to have given their names to groups considered in the present study. EPHER and JEREMIAH together were recalled in the Scandinavian Heartho-Raemes[28], Jeremiah also becoming known in the Raumar of Southeast Norway[29]. ISHI was recorded in North European Sarmatia as the HOSSI who adjoined a portion of the Agathyrsi (according to Ptolemy's Map) from whom came both the Picts[30] and the Khazars. The Khazars believed they were descended from both Manasseh and Simeon. We saw in the chapter on Simeon how the sons of Ishi of Manasseh (1-Chronicles 4:42) became the leaders of a group of Simeonites from whom emerged the Khazars. The Hossi and Agathyrsi in North Scythia were neighbored by the Sali (Shelah of Judah) who were later known in the west as the Salian Franks.

The Carbones and Careotae in far North European Sarmatia were placed besides the Hossi, Sali, and Agathyrsi. In Britain, Ptolemy located Carnones, Creones, Cerini, and Cornabii all in the north of Scotland in the Caledonni region and these apparently represent the Picts who called themselves Querves or Cruitingi or the like. These people all have names containing the root - "CRN" or "KRN" similarly - named groups were found in the rest of Britain. A horned-god named "Cernunnos" was widely worshipped amongst the British Celts reminding one that in Hebrew "KeReN" means horn. An area belonging to the ancient Israelites east of the Jordan was called "KARNAYIM" i.e. Horns and the Prophet Amos mentioned this area in connection with the Ten Tribes. After conquest the Assyrians re-named the province "Karnunu" just as they named the neighboring area of Gilead "Galazu". The Caledonni of Scotland came from Gilead of Manasseh. The Picts originally were effectually part of the Caledonni*. The Agathyrsi (i.e. Khazars) in the south of Scythia were attributed descent from Manasseh and Simeon.

The Agathyrsi are referred to as Acatziri, as GAZARI, and as Khazars which last two appellations derive from AZRIEL, one of the clan heads of Manasseh prior to the exile. The name AZRIEL (עַזְרִיאל) begins with an "ayin" (ע). The letter "ayin" though transliterated as "A " (in "A-zriel") could also be rendered in Assyrian and northern dialects as a "G" (e.g. "Aza" becomes "Gaza") or "K" and so one has "GAZARIA" (for AZRIEL) which is the name given in Medieval European documents to the Khazar region in the south[31]. The Khazars in Southern Russia were to convert to Judaism in which they were joined by a portion of the Alans also known as Gelons. The Gelons were one of the peoples believed to have migrated to Scandinavia. Similarly, a Roman writer mentioned the "Pictes Gelones"[32] in the general area of the Northern Agathyrsi in Scythia, and in Scotland there is evidence of an Alanic presence. The Scots themselves, like the Khazars, at one stage appear to have had Judaising tendencies.

From the above listed "heads of the house of their fathers", in eastern Manasseh, Epher was traced to the Scandinavian Heartho-Raemes, Jeremiah to Norway, Ishi to the Hossi and Azriel to the Khazars. From the remainder, ELIEL, may be recalled in the Hilleviones of Scandinavia (Pliny N.H. iv; 94-96) and the Elvaones by the Vistula in the region whence the Vandals and Anglo-Saxons advanced into Europe. The last clan leader to be located is HODAVIAH who gave his name to the EADWINE (in Hebrew, the two names may be pronounced similarly) who were related to both the Mercians and Lombards[33]. The Amyrgio-Scythae and the Mercians derived their names from permutations of MACHIR[34]. The Marcomani

---

* Today, the appellation "Picts" in modern historical works is applied to part of the aboriginal people in Scotland and this application may not be accurate.

of Germany also derived their name from Machir of Manasseh. Most of their descendants migrated to North America.

MACHIR AND AMERICA

An interesting fact is that THE NAME MACHIR IS ALSO RECALLED IN THAT OF AMERICA!

The Phoenicians are believed to have visited AMERICA and named it "The Great North Country"[35] and the Hebrew prophets predicted that in the end time the Lost Ten Tribes would return from the "North Country" (e.g. Isaiah 31;8) and they certainly were well acquainted with the Phoenicians. The Vikings attempted to settle in North America and named it "MARKLAND" which is believed to mean "Land of Darkness"[36]. Even so, Maruk (a permutation of Machir) and Mark (in "Markland") are not dissimilar. After the Vikings, the existence of America was realized by people in Britain including fishermen from the port of Bristol. Richard Ameryk, a Bristol merchant 1470's is now claimed to have maybe given America its name[37]. Ameryk was of Welsh ancestry and his family name originally was "Ap-Meryk", possibly denoting "Son of Machir". The more commonly accepted explanation is that the name "America" comes from that of the Explorer, Amerigo Vespucci (1451-1512) also called "America" and (after 1507) "America" is said to have been named in his honor. At all events, the name Amerigo or "America" is similar to medieval appellations (Aimerico, etc.[38]) for a Jewish Prince of Southern France whose proper Hebrew name (from which the Latinised appellations were derived) was MACHIR[39]. It follows that the name AMERICA may well be understood to mean "Land of Machir", son of Manasseh. The very name "Manasseh" in Hebrew (according to the Commentary of Rabbi Shimshon Raphael Hirsch*) can mean delegated responsible representation and

---

* This is explained at length in the book, "Ephraim," by Yair Davidy.

400

this is a fundamental aspect of the North American character. The USA was created when its early settlers declared "no taxation without representation" and fought against Britain for their Independence. America was named after Machir and Benyamin Turkia pointed out the "Machir" in Hebrew means "selling" and the principles of Captialism and Free Enterprise have also become part of the American character.

AMERICA TO BE REDEEMED FIRST?

The impression in the Bible (1-Chronicles 5:26) is that the Tribes of Reuben, Gad, and the half-Tribe of Manasseh were the first to be exiled. These groups had all been situated to the east of the Jordan River. A tradition says that the half-Tribe of Manasseh, which was east of the Jordan, are destined to be the first to be redeemed[*]. Descendants of Machir dominated in this area. Prophecies and traditions concerning Manasseh are applicable to the U.S.A. Britain, on the other hand, was to remain the province of EPHRAIM. Another portion of Manasseh appears to have remained in Germany and Central Europe whence it later moved en masse to America.

THE FRANKS IN LEGEND:
REUBEN AND MANASSEH

The Tribe of Reuben dwelt in that portion of Gilead adjacent to the half-tribe of Manasseh that appears to have inherited all the Bashan (Joshua chapter 13):
"AND THEIR COAST WAS FROM MAHANAIM, ALL BASHAN, ALL THE KINGDOMN OF OG KING OF BASHAN,

---

[*]   The Midrash (Perkei DeRabbi Eliezer, chi. 17; Yalkut Shimeoni, Psalms 60): <<God therefore said unto them, "I will give you a reward in the future for I am destined to gather in Israel from the Four Corners of the earth". **FIRST OF ALL HE WILL GATHER IN THE HALF-TRIBE OF MANASSEH!** This is written in Psalm (60:7): "Gilead is Mine, Mine is Manasseh", and after that He gathers in Ephraim, as it says, "Ephraim also is the strength of mine head" (Psalms 60:7)>>.

AND ALL THE TOWNS OF YAIR WHICH ARE IN BASHAN, THREESCORE CITIES" (Joshua 13: 30):

On the Map of Ptolemy titled "Arabia" the Bashan is recalled in the Bathanei. "Bathan" is an Aramaic form for Bashan. The Bathanei and Masani of Manasseh adjoin the Rahabeni meaning Reubeni. The Masani (of Manasseh) were later to be found in Frisia to the north of Holland. From Frisia they participated in the Anglo-Saxon invasion of Britain. On Ptolemy's Map to the Northeast of the Bathanei is a city called Daradar. Dardar is a term associated later with Troy. This association appear to be reflected in legends and in later historical developments.

According to tradition there were several movements from Troy and Scythia to the west. King Marcomir-I (442-412 BCE) led the Trojan Sicambri out of Scythia to a region by the Danube whence they were driven off by the Goths. They settled West Friesland (i.e. Frisia), Gelders, and Holland, and then part of France. Under King Priamus (384-358 BCE) the Sicambrian Franks began to speak the Saxon language. King Bassanus Magnus (286-250 BCE) conquered portions of West Germany and built Bassanburg (Aix-la-Chappelle) as his capital. [*In Northern Hebrew "Bassan" is synonymous with Bashan!*]. In the time of King Francus (39-11 BCE) the Sicambrians became known as Franks. The Franks split into east and west branches and it is uncertain whether the two were of one stock. The western branch were ruled by the Merovingian dynasty who wore their hair long and according to Athol Bloomer originated from the Tribe of Dan. The name Samson was common amongst them and Samson was a Judge of the Tribe of Dan who never cut his hair[+]. The Franks together with the Saxons and others also planted colonies in the east. The Sicambri were

---

[+] Michael BAIGENT, Richard LEIGH, & Henry LINCOLN, "Hold Blood, Holy Grail",.London 1982; N.Y. 1983, claimed that the Merovingians came from the Tribe of Benjamin.

named after Shecem of Manasseh. In West Germany to the south were the Marcomani who derived their name from Machir of Manasseh. We thus have in the West German area some of the Sicambri, Bassanburg named after the Bashan, and the Marcomani all of whom relate to Manasseh. These groups were never the majority in any region but in some areas their numbers were probably significant.

In proportion to where these groups were so too was there a later migration to North America.

THE ISRAELITE HOMING INSTINCT

Whole areas and family groups evacuated certain portions of Germany and moved en masse to America. It was an ethnic movement out of Germany motivated more by a migrating instinct than by economic or other factors. German officials themselves testified to this. So too, the migration from the British Isles to North America was one of specific social strata. It was also mainly from certain areas in all of which Manasseh had been dominant*.

A similar phenomenon may be noticed with the "Conversos" or Marranos of Spain. These were Jews who were forced to convert to Judaism. Some of them attempted to maintain some Jewish customs and were consequently persecuted by the Inquisition. Many of their descendants went to certain areas in South America. According to Mike Davis it has been estimated that as many as one quarter of all Spanish colonists in Mexico were Marranos/Anusim/New Christians all meaning "Conversos" of Jewish origin. Known Spanish Names of Conversos in many cases are now rare in Spain but common in Mexico and the USA. A similar study should be made concerning the Italians who migrated to the United States.

---

* Concerning the Migration of people from Germany and from the British Isles to North America and studies indicating that the migrants were of different Tribal and (in the case of Germany) national affinities from those who stayed behind see Yair DAVIDI, "Joseph. The Israelite destiny of America", Jerusalem, Israel, 2001, chapter nine.

403

THE DESCENDANTS OF MANASSEH

♦ **JOSEPH** = Yasubi, Yasubgalli (Zagros Mountains, east of Mesopotamia), Aspioi (Afghanistan), Ysufzi (Tribe of Joseph Afghanistan), Aspacarae (east of Caspian) Aspassi (Chorasmia, east of Caspian Sea), Usipetes (from Germany invaded Gaul at time of Caesar), Swaefi-Suabi from Germany to Holland and Switzerland), Suebi (equal Suabi), recalled by the same name in east Scythia.

♦ **Manasseh** = Mannus (legendary ancestor of tribes in Germany who moved to Gaul and Britain), Massagetae (east of the Caspia), identified with Goths).

♦ **Clans of Manasseh:**

♦ **Machir** = Maracanda, Maruka, Amyrgioi (all east of Caspian), Makran (southern Iran), Skati Marika (name given to Mercians, means "Scyths-from-Maruka" east of the Caspian), Mercia known on the continent as "Myringas", important element amongst Goths and Anglo-Saxons. Marcomanni.

♦ The name of MACHIR son of Manasseh became (after a simple letter permutation) the name "AMERICA" which therefore may be understood as meaning "Land of Machir".

♦ **Gilead** = Galatae (in Gaul), Galadi (name of Galatae), Giladon (in Wales), Caledonians (in Scotland).

♦ **Helek** = Heleucones (Germany to Britain), Calucones, (Germany to the west).

♦ **Asriel** = Isari (Emodian mountains in Scythia, legendary place of sojourn of the Angles, Saxons, and Frisians),. Aorsi (from west Scythia to Scandinavia), Surrey (Saxon England).

- **Schechem** (Secem) = Scymbi (east Scythia), Sigambri-Sicambri (Afghanistan, Bactria, from Germany to Gaul).
- **Shemida** = Soumboi Aggiloi (branch of Angles), Soumboi-Laggobardi (branch of Lombards), Samides (legendary ancestor of Gauls), Saemdag (Scandinavian Ancestral hero).
- **Hepher** = Hefr (nickname for Gothic warrior). Haeferingas (Middle Saxons in England).
- **Jeezer** (in Hebrew is pronounced like) **Aiezer (Ai-g-azar)** = Agathyrsi (became Khazars who converted to Judaism and Picts of Scotland).

Daughters of Zelophahad:

- **Tirtsah** (Thirtsah) = Thyrsagettae (name for Thysagettae of Scythia, migrated to Scandinavia).
- **Milcah** = Melicertii in Scythian Caucasus - Basiloi (Royal =MLC root in name Milcah) of Khazars, Scandinavia, and Royal Scyths.
- **Hoglah** = Frankish kings, e.g. Chocilarch.
- **Noah** = Neuri of Scythia to Scandinavia, Nervi of Celtic Gaul
- **Mahlah**

Additional Clan Names of Manasseh based on the Book of Chronicles:

- **Sheresh** (Seres) = Seres in Serica (East Scythia).
- **Peresh** (Peres) = Parissi (of Gaul and Britain), Frissi (of Holland and England), Phiressi (Scandinavia), Parsi (Parthians from east of the Caspian and in Iran).
- The name "Peresh" means "separated, sanctified" (cf. Pharisee) which is the same meaning as "Nemed" an ancestor in Irish mythology"). When pronounced with a

slightly different intonation the name also connotes "horseman" = SUS ["sus" means "horse" in Hebrew] = SUESSIONS, (Gaul), Sassi. There was a prince of the Tribe of Manasseh Gaddi the son of Susi (Numbers 13;11).

♦ **Epher** = Heartho-Raemes (Scandinavia).

♦ **Jeremiah** = Heartho-Raemes (Scandinavia), Raumar (Norway).

♦ **Ishi** = Hossi (Scythia, maybe part of Picts and Khazars).

♦ **Azriel (Gazriel)** = Gazaria (name of "Khazaria").

♦ **Eliel** = Hilleviones (Scandinavia), Elvaones (Vandals, Anglo-Saxons).

♦ **Hovadiah** (pronounceable as "Howadiah") = Eadwine (amongst Mercians of England and Lombards).

Mercian clans in England included Magonsaete, Nox, Ohtgaga, Henrica, Unecinga, Hwicce, Gifel, Spale, and Grywe (Thundy p.105). The **Magonsaete** have a name that in Hebrew could mean "armor-bearers" (Magon-Saeti). Other clans of Machir (1-Chronicles 7; 14-17) included Likhi and Aniam (=Unecinga)., Shupim =Spale of Mercia., Chupim =Gifel of Mercia.

FAMILY TREE OF MENASSEH

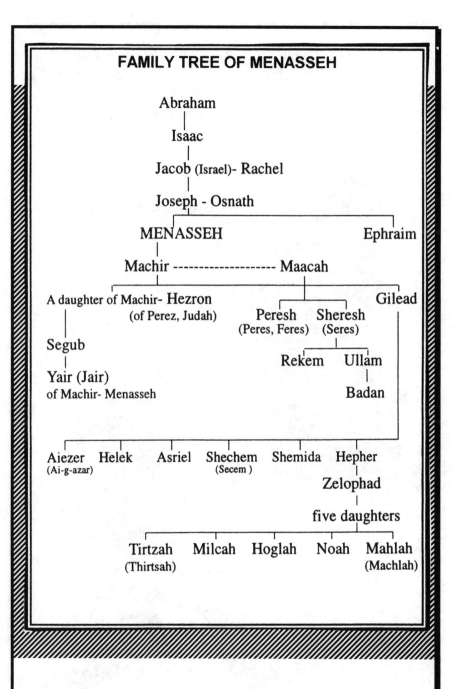

Abraham
|
Isaac
|
Jacob (Israel)- Rachel
|
Joseph - Osnath

MENASSEH   Ephraim
|
Machir -------------------- Maacah

A daughter of Machir- Hezron   Gilead
        (of Perez, Judah)   Peresh   Sheresh
                              (Peres, Feres) (Seres)

Segub   Rekem   Ullam
| |
Yair (Jair)   Badan
of Machir- Menasseh

Aiezer   Helek   Asriel   Shechem   Shemida   Hepher
(Ai-g-azar)   (Secem) |
                                              Zelophad
                                                  |
                                          five daughters

Tirtzah   Milcah   Hoglah   Noah   Mahlah
(Thirtsah)   (Machlah)

407

The USA was originally nicknamed "Brother Jonathan". Later this was changed to "Uncle Sam". The changeover ocurred in the period 1812-1850. Of the two figures below the first is a popular representastion of "Brother Jonathan" and the second of "Uncle Sam".

"Brother Jonathan"

"Uncle Sam"

JOSEPH: EPHRAIM .THE U.K

The United Kingdom of Great Britain and Northern Ireland has a lion and unicorn on its Royal Arms. A lion represents the Kingdom of David and Judah. Moses (Deut. 33;17) compared Joseph to a bull and to a unicorn. In the Blessing of Balaam the strength of all Israel is compared to that of a unicorn (Numbers 23;22). A Unicorn (Raem) was represented on the Standard of Menasseh and a bull on that of Ephraim, according to the Midrash (Numbers 2;7). The Standard of Scotland depicts two Unicorns.

The two Mottoes on the Coat of ARMS mean: "God and My Right" and "Shame be to he who evil thinks". This last expression is reminiscent of the fact that in Jewish tradition, the Evil Eye i.e. the power of suggestive malicious thought has no influence over the seed of Joseph (Berachot 10).

JOSEPH: AUSTRALIA

The majority of the population of Australia came from Britain and Ireland.

Australia means "Land of the South", and is called "Sinim" (Isaiah 49;12) in the Bible. "Sinim" is one of the places from which the descendants of the Lost Ten Tribes of Israel will return.

26

Ephraim Son of Joseph

The Tribe of Ephraim had been nicknamed "Bull-calf" since Joseph was likened unto a bull (Genesis 33:17) Jeremiah (31:18) called EPHRAIM an "Aegel" meaning "Young-Bull", in Hebrew. Herodotus (3;92) put the Aegles on the edge of Bactria and apparently these were the Augali whom Ptolemy much later positioned a bit further north in Sogdiana on the Banks of the Jaxartes River. This last region (i.e. Chorasmia) is also known as HAVILA. The Josephite Aspasi and Israelite connections of this area were recorded together with the tradition that the Saxons had once sojourned in Havila east of the Caspian Sea. Saxons and Angles in Northwest Europe were closely associated. The Angles and Saxons had once been located in the region between Southern Denmark and Havel in North Germany. "HAVEL" may well have been named after "Havila" in Chorasmia whence the Angles had come.

The resemblance between Havila and Havel is obvious, and there are other correspondences. The names AEGEL and Angle in Nordic dialects are interchangeable and it has been demonstrated that "Aegel" is the diminutive form for Angle*.

---

* The word "ANGLE" has two known meanings of potential importance to the present subject:

1. "Angle" means corner or edge in some European tongues including English. England was named after the Angles and Rabbi Manasseh ben Israel (ca.1640) of Holland is said to have remarked that the name for England in French, i.e. "Angleterre" literally means

411

A Polemical Diversion

So far, in this book evidence has been brought (and more follows) connecting the British, French, Dutch, Belgians, Irish, Scandinavians, and others with Israelites. All of the proofs are interconnected as emphasized elsewhere and each one reinforces the others. At the same time they are also independent and each one in its own right, once accepted, either proves in itself (or at least strongly indicates) that the West Europeans are of Hebrew descent.

How far can direct co-relations of names, mythology, art, and the rest be attributed to coincidence? Every fact deserves to be considered in context with other facts bearing on

---

"End of the Earth". The Lost Ten Tribes of Israel in Biblical Prophecy are frequently mentioned in connection with "the end of the earth" (e.g. Isaiah 49:6) and with "the END<u>S</u> of the earth" (Isaiah 41:9 in the plural since more nations than Britain are involved. This issue is expanded upon later.

2. An additional signification of "Angle" comes from the Aramaic Paraphrase of Psalms. There is a verse in the Book of Psalms 82:6) which reads: "I have said, Ye are gods; And all of you are children of the most High". The phrase "CHILDREN OF THE MOST HIGH" is translated in the Aramaic Paraphrase (attributed to Jonathan and considered inspired by the Talmud) as "ANGLII" which is plural for Angle. "Children of the Most High" corresponds to other epithets applied to this people, such as "Israel is my son, my firstborn" (Exodus 4:22), "Ephraim my dear son..." (Jeremiah 31:20). "I am a father to Israel and "Ephraim is my firstborn", (Jeremiah 31:9).

The significance of the words "ANGLI", and "Aegloi" may be so put: Ephraim was called an Aegel. Aegel is interchangeable with Angle. Anglii means, "Sons of the Most High." Ephraim is called "my son" - by the Most High, the Angles did dwell in an area associated with the Tribe of Joseph, the lands the Anglo Saxons dwell in today can be considered the "Ends of the earth" when viewed from the Land of Israel. The evidence presented in this book connects the Lost Ten Tribes of Israel with the Celts and Scythians and proves that they became the peoples of modern northwest Europe. Of these peoples, those of British descent became the most important historically and have had the most influence in the world, and for this consideration the USA and all other Anglo-Saxon nations can be grouped together with Britain. Groups from all of the Twelve Tribes of Israel were to congregate in Britain but of all groups the Angles and Saxons were the most determinative and had the most influence. This is appropriate to their identification as belonging to the Tribes of Joseph.

412

the same subject. Two names in two different places may well by chance be similar, ten or more names resembling each other from two different areas is less likely. When groups amongst the suggested "Originals" had the same relative positioning as those found amongst the "Derivatives" then the very high probability of some kind of connection between the two should be allowed for. We have hereby proceeded to show that the Ten Tribes of Lost Israelites when still in their Land before the exile were arranged in clans named after family heads. A good portion of them went to Scythia where the same clan names arranged in a very similar way relative to each other are to be traced [see the following discussion on Ptolemy in Section Two of this book]. From Scythia they eventually mostly reached Western Europe where the very same patterns of Tribal Nomenclature are immediately discernable. Even without the name comparisons the Historical Sources already exhibited make a very strong case in their own right and intellectual honesty would require the case for the names and that evidence adduced elsewhere to be considered together. An individual point in our argument, if for whatever reason it is to be dismissed, it falls alone; if it stands, it supports all the other proofs and is supported by them.

Havel and the Angles

As we mentioned,, the Angles were traceable to Northwest Europe where for a time they were centered in Havel and on Haithebu just south of Jutland: "HAVEL" in Hebrew Medieval Literature was a name for Chorasmia in Scythia east of the Caspian Sea. In the history of Le Petit the ancestors of the Frisians, Saxons, and Angles were traced to Havel meaning (according to the context) to Chorasmia. The Sacae had had part of their settlement in Chorasmia and the Augali (Aegli) had been situated nearby. From the Sacae descended the Saxons and the Angles came from the Aegli. The area of Havel (in Germany, by the Elbe River) was for a time a Saxon and Angle center and the name may derive from that once attached to Chorasmia (which had also been called "Havel") whence the Anglo-Saxons had come. Also connected to Chorasmia were the people called "CHERUSKI". The Cheruski appear to have first been reported from the region of Havel in Germany (Tacitus, "Germania" 36) or close to it. Later they moved further west and were associated with the Salian Franks after which the SAXONS advanced, conquered and absorbed them. The name "CHERUSKI" has been understood as meaning "People of CHORASMIA" in Slavonic[2]. B. Philip Lozinski states that the term "Chorasmia" was attached to the state of a particular people and that the name moved as the people shifted[3]. It should be remembered that the original and most proper application of the term "CHORASMIA" was, in effect, to the area just north of HARA in Eastern Iran. Hara was one of the places to which the exiled Ten Tribes of Israel had been transported (1-Chronicles 5:26).

Havel in Europe was to the south of Haithebu on the coast at the mouth of the River Elbe. Sceld Sheafing, according to legend, as a child drifted in an oarless boat into the port of Haithebu. When he grew up he gave laws and civilisation to the people of that area whence emerged the Saxons of whom Sceld is considered the ancestor[4]. His legend bears parallels to the lives of Joseph and Moses[5]. When first found Sceld had been sleeping on a sheaf of wheat. He is identified with "Skjold" of Scandinavian mythology. In honour of "Skjold" Denmark was once called Skedeland and the Danes "Skioldings". Sceld (Skjold) represents the "SCOLOTI" Scythians[6] who were descended from **SHUTELACH**, son of Ephraim. The son of Shutelach (Shutelah) was **BERED** (1-Chr. 7:20) who is recalled in a Gothic group named the Boradi[7], and in the Bardi Tribe of Sweden[8] and in the Celtic city "Bard-galli" (Bordeaux) in Southwest Gaul. In Nordic Mythology (as transcribed by Saxo Grammaticus ca.1240)[9], Skiold was the son of Lother, son of

414

Dan, son of Humble. Elsewhere Skiold (Skeld) is considered a son (or grandson) of Odin thus equating Odin with DAN (son of Humble) in the genealogy of Saxo. The name Odin may mean both "The Dan" and "Adon" (Lord) which was a title given to Joseph (Genesis 45;9)[10]. Both Joseph and Dan were sons of Jacob (Israel) one aspect of whose name connotes "Humility", and "Humble" (says Saxo) was the first Scandinavian Patriarch and father of DAN! An alternative Danish source (Vetus Chronicon Holsatiae) says expressly that the Danes, Jutes, Angles and Saxons were descendants of Israel. Saxo also says that Dan and ANGEL (of the Angles) were brothers.

Other Clans of Ephraim

In addition to Shutelah other clans of Ephraim were Becher, Tachan, and Eran (Numbers 26:35). **BECHER** was recalled in the neighboring regions of Bukhara and Bactria east of the Caspian Sea, which were the homes of the Aegloi or Angles (Augaloi in Ptolemy's Map) and of the Sacae-Saxons prior to their migrating to Europe. Becher was also recalled in the Boroctuari who participated in the Anglo-Saxon invasions according to Bede (ix), and in Gaul were also associated with the Franks[11]. These are identical with the BOGARI whom Nennius 800's CE) said were the sons of Neugione (ING) along with the Saxons, Wandal (Vandals), and Tarincga. Neugione (ING) represents the Ingueone group of peoples who, from Germany, moved westward. They had been located near the Baltic coast and comprised the Chauci, Cimbri, and Teutoni according to one account, and Sucambri, Teutons, and Chauci according to another[12], and also had a connection to the ruling Yngvi dynasty of Sweden[13]. The Teutons and Teutonarii were to be swept up in the Anglo-Saxon hosts moving westward. The name "Teuton" applied to the modern Germans is apparently a misnomer of very recent date and is historically misleading since this people did not remain (as far as can be determined) on German soil. The Teutons, in the Map of

Ptolemy, whilst in Germany were located just south of the Saxons. Together with the Cimbri they had once attacked (and almost defeated) Rome. The Teutons and Cimbri culturally and linguistically seem to have once been Celtic. The Teutons belonged to the Ephraimite clan of **TAHAN** (Tachan:תחן) which was either also called Tahat[14] (תחת) or else Tahat (1-Chronicles 7:20) was an important entity within Tahan (of Ephraim) in its own right. Tahan is recalled in the appellation: "Tehuni" which in the east was applied to the Scythian-Sacae[15], as a whole while in Greek mythology the Scythian archer "Teutarus"[16] (after Tahat) came to represent the Scythian as a whole. In Celtic-Gaul, Tahat may have been recalled in the god Teutas just as Tahan was recalled in the Tribal name of Teuton. The Teutons were allied to the Cimbrians, Ambrians, Tigorini, and Toygeni against the Romans. All these peoples had previously been recalled in Scythia. The Cimbrians, according to Classical historians, descended from the ancient Cimmerians; the Ambrones as "Ambri" together with Sigambrians had been recalled in the area of Bactria; the Tigorini as Tagora and Tokarian had also been found in Eastern Scythia. Tahan, son of Ephraim, may also have been connected to the Tabieni who neighboured the Joseph descended Aspassi in Chorasmia (near Bactria) and later in Europe were reported under the name of Tubantes together with Chatti and Chasuari. These last mentioned peoples in West Germany were absorbed by the Franks and Saxons and presumably moved westward with them. The name Tahan (Tachan) may also be recalled in that of the Tencteri who were allies of the Usipetes in Gaul. The name "Usipete" contains the root "USIP" which in some Middle Eastern dialects could be a construction from "JOSEPH".

A name linked to the Lost Ten Tribes, to peoples descended from Joseph in Scythia, and to the Saxons is that of "SASON". The Lost Ten Tribes had been exiled by the Assyrians to places which included the "Cities of the Medes", according to one source (2-Kings 17:6) and that of Elam (Isaiah 11:11),

416

according to another. Elam, Gutium, and Media were interchangeable terms to a certain extent. One of the discussions in the Talmud (Sanhedrin 94a) says that the Israelites were exiled to the "Mountains of Sloog" (i.e. "Snow") meaning the Caucasus as well as to "Afrikey", to Sus, to Sustair, and to Elymais. "Afrikey" was a center of the Medes either equal to Shushan in Elam or very close to it. Sus and Sustair were cities neighboring Shushan. "Elymais" ("Elymin") was in northern Elam, including or at least bordering on the area of Shushan. "Shushan" would have been rendered as Susan or Sason by some of the Northern Hebrews [cf. Judges 12:6: "Siboleth" instead of Shiboleth] and by the Assyrians who also switched "s" for "sh". The region of Northern Elam was one of Scythian and Cimmerian presence. After the Scythian movement northward into Scythia a people named SASONE were recorded by Ptolemy as having once been in East Scythia. In East Scythia the Sasones were to be found between the Tabieni (of Tahan from Ephraim son of Joseph), the Zaratae (of Zerah from Simeon), the Massaei (from Manasseh of Joseph), the Suobeni (from Joseph), and the Scymbi (from Shechem of Manasseh). In Northern Gaul a similarly named people, the Suessiones, were to be recorded, north of the Parissi, on the Isara (Oise) River. At the same time, place names[17] in GAUL such as Sasseignus, Sassenay, Sassiniacus, Sassen (Koblenz), are considered areas of early Saxon settlement. A people known as "SASSI" were either identical with a portion of the Saxons, "Or very closely connected to them", according to T.W. Shore (1906)[18]. In Welsh[19], the Saxons were called "Saesneg" and their language "Sassenach". The Sasones in Scythia had been situated in the Sacae area east of the Caspian. Archaeological findings[20]-indicate a historical connection between Elam and the Sacae. From the Sacae emerged the Anglo-Saxons who conquered England. The names Suesson, Sassenag, and Sason may well derive from the place names Sushan, Sus, and Sustair in Elam which was one of the places of Israelite exile. The Scythian

Sacae east of the Caspian Sea were culturally connected to Elam according to archaeological finds The Sacae-Scyths incidentally had a well known art style which was entirely Middle Eastern in type and had mainly originated in the Phoenician-Israelite area. This style remained discernible in later Anglo-Saxon art[*].

Regarding clans of Ephraim, Shutelah, Borad, Tahan, and Becher were considered above. There remains the clan of **ERAN** son of Shutelach who was the grandson of Ephraim. An area of Mannae to which the Lost Ten Tribes were exiled and which became a Scythian centre was known as Arran. There is a region named Arran in Scotland. Similarly, the island of Ireland received settlers of Hebraic and Scythian descent and Ireland was once named "ERIN". The names "Arran", "Erin", and "Eran" are not dissimilar.

Descendants from the Tribes of Joseph (Ephraim and Manasseh) seem to have been especially concentrated in the nations who settled the British Isles and, through them, amongst all English-speaking peoples of British origin. These peoples have played a unique role in history over and beyond that of the other Israelite nations as a whole. This historical record was appropriate to the character of their forefather, JOSEPH.

---

[*] An alternate or supplementary explanation for the above names as well as that of the "Sassi" section of Saxons may be understood from the commentary of Y. Kiel (Jerusalem 1986, in Hebrew) on the Book of Chronicles. Kiel says that Peresh, son of Machir, from the eastern half of the Tribe of Manasseh (1-Chr. 7;16) derived his name from "Parash" meaning Cavalryman or Cavalryhorse. Kiel says that a variation of the name may well have been Susi ("Horse" in Hebrew) e.g. Gadi son of SUSI, Prince of Manasseh in Numbers 13:11! In colloquial Hebrew, "Sasi" and "Susi" could easily have been variations of the one name. At the same time, it should be emphasized that "PERESH" is how the said name is actually rendered in the Bible and this name connotes "Separated" or "Dedicated" (e.g. "Pharisee") the same as the name "Nemede" who was an ancestral figure amongst the early Irish. The brother of Peresh was SHARESH (Sares) recalled in Serica (by Strabo) as the SERES.

418

THE TRIBES OF EPHRAIM AND MANASSEH: BRITAIN AND THE USA

Most of the entities identified as descended from the tribes of Joseph (Ephraim and Manasseh) are seen to have migrated to the British Isles. From Britain came many of the settlers of South Africa, New Zealand, Australia, and Canada, as well as of the U.S.A. Canada was to be populated mainly by immigrants from Britain and from France. The French-Canadians originated mainly in the Provinces of Normandy and Brittany. Normandy in France had been settled by the Normans from Scandinavia. The Normans later conquered England. They derived from Benjamin. Britanny in France had previously been populated by the Samnete (from Simeon) and was later occupied by "Celtic" refugees from Britain who gave it its name ("Brittany" after Britain) and who also comprised contingents from Simeon, such as the Simeni, Semoni, Iceni, and sons of Semuen.

The "British" colonizers of French "Brittany" were Celts who were fleeing from the Anglo-Saxons and their federates. Vikings from Norway and Denmark later attacked England, France and Ireland. The Vikings settled in Irish coastal cities, in northern England and in Normandy of France from which base they later conquered all of England. The Normans included a good proportion of Breton natives of Celtic origin some of whom had been Normanicized. The Normans adopted the native "British" cult figure of King Arthur. This Norman identification with Arthur may have had the conscious or subconscious effect of utilizing "British" Celtic sentiment against their previous Anglo-Saxon conquerors.

THE PROPORTION OF ENGLISH "CELTIC" ANCESTRY

At one stage it was widely supposed that the Anglo-Saxons must have exterminated most of the conquered Celts in England since very little signs of continued Celtic existence were found to remain[21]. Today historians have begun to reach the opposite conclusion. It has been claimed that the Anglo-Saxons constituted not more than one fifth of the inhabitants of England and that their presence was "meagre" in Wales, Scotland, and Ireland[22]. A recent study goes even further and states that the Anglo-Saxons were merely tens of thousands as against millions of indigenous inhabitants[23]. The truth is that the Anglo-Saxons also probably numbered in their millions and that they settled very heavily on the land, especially in the east and (IT USED TO BE THOUGHT) in the south, while driving most of the "Celtic" natives out to Brittany and to the west and assimilating the remainder. In the west, the descendants of Celts adopted Anglo-Saxon culture after the Anglo-Saxons conquered England and created several kingships, the largest of which was Mercia which, though in the center, derived much of its strength from the west. Regarding Mercia, it has been claimed: *"Many who called themselves Mercians were ethnically British [i.e "Celtic"], but now regarded themselves, and were regarded by others as Saxons"*[24].

WHAT DOES DNA SAY?
THREE SOURCES CONCERNING THE
RESULTS OF DNA STUDIES IN BRITAIN
FOLLOWED BY COMMENTARY

1. ANGLES, SAXONS, & FRISIANS
DOMINANT IN CENTRAL ENGLAND
Adapted from: "Y Chromosome Evidence for Anglo-Saxon Mass Migration" Michael E. Weale*,1, Deborah A. Weiss,1, Rolf F. Jager, Neil Bradman and Mark G. Thomas.

<<Today, the most hotly debated of all the British cultural transitions is the role of migration in the relatively sudden and drastic change from Romano-Britain to Anglo-Saxon Britain. This transition was once widely accepted as providing clear evidence for a mass migration from continental Europe and the

near-complete replacement of the indigenous population in England. Stories of migration are included in the writings of Gildas (ca. a.d. 540) and Bede (a.d. 731) and hinted at in Anglo-Saxon sagas, such as Beowulf. Archaeological evidence confirmed a rapid rise of continental culture in England and suggested a contemporaneous desertion of continental Germanic settlements. More recently, however, authors have questioned the evidence for large-scale immigration and continental emigration and emphasized the continuity of the Romano-British population in England. The sudden change to an Anglo-Saxon culture has been attributed instead to rapid acculturation and indigenous developments, with only a small number of Germanic immigrants (perhaps a male military elite) settling in Britain. The contribution of Anglo-Saxon immigration to the modern English gene pool thus remains uncertain.

<<The Central English towns were genetically very similar, whereas the two North Welsh towns differed significantly both from each other and from the Central English towns. When we compared our data with an additional 177 samples collected in Friesland and Norway, we found that the Central English and Frisian samples were statistically indistinguishable. Using novel population genetic models that incorporate both mass migration and continuous gene flow, we conclude that these striking patterns are best explained by a substantial migration of Anglo-Saxon Y chromosomes into Central England (contributing 50%100% to the gene pool at that time*) but not into North Wales.

<<Our results indicate the presence of a strong genetic barrier between Central England and North Wales and the virtual

---

* i.e. It could be anywhere from 50% to 100% depending on whether or not Angle, Saxon, or Frisian type input had been added previously or was to be added subsequently or is to attributed entirely to the time of invasion.

absence of a barrier between Central England and Friesland.

2. CELTS STILL PRESENT, FEMALES REMAIN
Adapted from: "Y chromosomes rewrite British history Anglo-Saxons' genetic stamp weaker than historians suspected" by HANNAH HOAG

<< "The Celts weren't pushed to the fringes of Scotland and Wales; a lot of them remained in England..." says study team member David Goldstein, of University College London. This is surprising: the Anglo-Saxons reputedly colonized southern England heavily.

<<The Anglo-Saxons and Danes left their mark in central and eastern England, and mainland Scotland, the survey says, and the biological traces of Norwegian invaders show up in the northern British Isles, including Orkney.

<<Similar studies, including one by the same team, have looked at differences in mitochondrial DNA, which we inherit from our mothers. They found little regional variation because females tended to move to their husbands.

<<The Y chromosomes of men from Wales and Ireland resemble those of the Basques.
<<References: Capelli, C. et al. A Y chromosome census of the British Isles. Current Biology, 13, 979 - 984, (2003). |Article| Nature News Service / Macmillan Magazines Ltd 2003

3. REGIONAL DIFFERENCES
Results stated on the BBC web-site:

North-East England:
<<England (and most of mainland Scotland) were a mixture of Angles, Saxons, Danish Vikings and Ancient Britons. The

highest percentage of DNA signatures from the invading groups (Angles, Saxons and Danish Vikings) was found in the North and East of England. Interestingly the place with the highest 'invader input' was York, a well-known Viking settlement site."

For South and West England:
<<Like in the North and East of England, a mixture of Angles, Saxons, Danish Vikings, and Ancient Britons were found in the South and West of England. But the percentage of DNA from the 'invaders' (Angles, Saxons and Danish Vikings) decreased as the test sites moved towards the south coast and Cornwall (the most Ancient Briton/Celtic part of England). It seems this part of the country has more genetic input from the Ancient Britons than the North and East of England. Curiously, mainland Scotland was not appreciably more Ancient Briton (Celtic) than southern England.

COMMENTARY:
a. THE DNA CONCLUSIONS
The conclusions say that Anglo-Saxons were dominant primarily in the center. Overall for England they say that about 50% of the MALE population remained Celtic and so did NEARLY ALL of the female. [Other studies however say that in the British Isles there is no effective difference between Celtic mtDNA (female) and that of the Anglo-Saxons and Scandinavians so this makes it hard to tell.] Anglo-Saxon input was important in Lowland Scotland and Celtic input in Southern England. The two areas were about the same regarding their Celtic/Anglo proportions.

b. THE DNA CONCLUSIONS IN THE LIGHT OF OUR RESEARCHES AND THE RESEARCHES OF OTHERS

If we place all of the "Germanic" invaders (Angles, Saxons, Jutes, Frisians, Vandals, etc) under the heading of "Anglo-Saxon" then the DNA results fit in with our general description. Regarding the Tribal Allocations the conclusions also accord with what we have stated remembering that both the "Celts" and "Anglo-Saxons" included elements from the different tribes with each tribe tending to converge and re-assemble together in the same areas.

b. APPLICABILITY OF THE CONCLUSIONS

We do not agree with DNA assumptions as presently accepted. DNA science says that mutational changes took place tens (or hundreds) of thousands of years in one male (Y chromosome) or female (mitochondria) ancestor and that from this ancestor all those who today have the same feature descend.

Our impression (based on DNA and general genetic writings) is that:

(1. The mutations could have taken place hundreds (not necessarily thousands or hundreds of thousands) of years ago.

(2. The changes could have affected large population groups all at once and not just one specific ancestor. People with the same type would not necessarily be related to each other (though there remains a chance they were) but rather that their ancestors had once been in the same area at the same time.

(3. After the changes do take place they become hereditary (until the next change) and therefore can be used to trace populations from one area to another.

For example it was stated that the DNA of most people in North and South Wales (two otherwise different areas) is the same as that of the Basques in Northwest Spain. The DNA assumption is that the Welsh and the Basques had the same ancestors. This may be so BUT according to our explanation the results merely mean that the ancestors of the Welsh and the ancestors of the Basques were once in the same region of Spain and later separated. Before separating they could still have been different peoples.

TRIBAL DIVISIONS WITH THE BRITISH ISLES

Regarding Israelite Tribal identifications, it was seen that from the SONS OF MANASSEH emerged entities prominent both amongst the Anglo-Saxon invaders: Manasseh = Mannus; Helek = Calucones & Heleucones; Asriel = Surrey; Machir = Mercians; Shechem = Sicambri; Shemida = Soumboi; Hepher = Hefer), as well as being found in "Celtic" spheres: Macha, Iar, Giladon, Gilaadi, Parissi -all groups connected to Machir, son of Manasseh, and his family such as Gilead, Maacha, Yair, Peresh. It seems that descendants of Manasseh were more important amongst the Celts who dominated in the west in addition to which those Anglo-Saxon entities who belonged to Manasseh (such as the Mercians) seem to have gravitated westward.

The descendants of Ephraim were paramount amongst the Anglo-Saxon invaders and seem to have been also present amongst the Celtic-British natives, for example descendants of Eran son of Ephraim were noted in Ireland and Scotland. The four sons of Ephraim (Shutelach, Eran, Becher, and Tahan) became peoples in the Anglo-Saxon host: Shutelach produced the Skioldings from Scandinavia; Eran -the Arri amongst the Saxons; Tahan -the Teutons whom the Angles absorbed in Europe before the invasion; Becher -the Boroctuari and Bogari who joined in the conquest. The Angles themselves were known as "Aegli" or "Bull-Calves" in Hebrew, a nickname in Scripture for Ephraim.

It follows from the above that a very rough approximate distinction may be made between the mainly Anglo-Saxon descendants of Ephraim in the south and east and the predominantly Celtic-British children of Manasseh in the west and in Scotland, Wales and Ireland.

The British Isles contained contingents from most of the Israelite tribes, apart from those of Ephraim and Manasseh. There were representatives of Benjamin (the Normans, and Belgae, and Menappi), Dan (Danes, Dana, Don), Naphtali (Norwegian-Vikings), Simeon (Semeni, Semoni, Iceni, Semuen, Semnoni, Silures), Judah (Jutes, Iari), Issachar (Fenni, Abis, Suebi, Scygs), Zebulon (Flemish), Gad (Gadeni, Gaedhals, Hastings), Asher (Vandals, Brigantes, Brygs, Caber), and probably others. Nevertheless, the Tribes of Joseph proved to be the prevailing constituent, Ephraim in the east and Manasseh in the west.

From the west of England and from Wales, Scotland, and Ireland the United States of America received approximately eighty-seven percent (sic. 87%) of its British immigrants in its formative period[25]. In other words, early American society was formed largely by groups from the Tribe of Manasseh. Even today, more than half the white population of the U.S.A. may trace its ancestry back to Britain and Ireland with the British side being slightly larger than that of Northern and Southern Irish origin. These people, descendants of Manasseh, still remain the determining factor in North America.

In an analysis of the national character of Great Britain and the U.S.A. it is apparent that the characteristics and symbols of Britain are pertinent to Ephraim and those of the U.S.A applicable to Manasseh. Some of these points were mentioned above and more follow. Thus, on both historical and psycho-symbolic levels the conclusions reached so far regarding Israelite Tribal identities are shown to be confirmed.

DESCENDANTS OF EPHRAIM

EPHRAIM the "Aegel" (Jeremiah 31:18), = Aegloi, Aggiloi, Angli (all names of Angles), Augali (north of Bactria.), Aegloi (Bactria).

Clans of Ephraim*

Shutelach = Sittones (Scandinavia), Sceald (Ancestor of the Anglo Saxons), Skioldings (Denmark).

Eran = Eirne (Ireland, Scotland), Irin (Ireland Arran, Mannae in Caucasus), Arri*, Hirri (Germany-Goths), Granni (Sweden), Garinae (east Scythia).

Becher = Bukhara (Bactria-Chorasmia), Boroctuari (invaders of Britain), Bogari (descendants of Ing of the Anglo-Saxons).

Tahan-Tahat (another name for Tahan?) = Teuton (Scandinavia), Teutarus (Scythian Representanive), Tencteri (Frankish groups). Tehuni (name for Scythians in east), Thatagydes (combination of Thata-Teutons and Gydes-Goths in Afghanistan and Sogdiana).

Bered = Boradi (Gothic group), Bardi (Sweden), Bordigali (Bordeaux -city of southwest Gaul).

Beriah = Portions of the Brigantae (Britain and Celtic Europe), Burgundians (France), Varangians (Vikings and Khazars), Warings (amongst Anglo-Saxons).

Zebed = Cobad (Denmark).

* Sources: Genesis ch.46 and Numbers 26 together with additional names from the Book of Chronicles which in some cases could represent the same entities under different appellations.

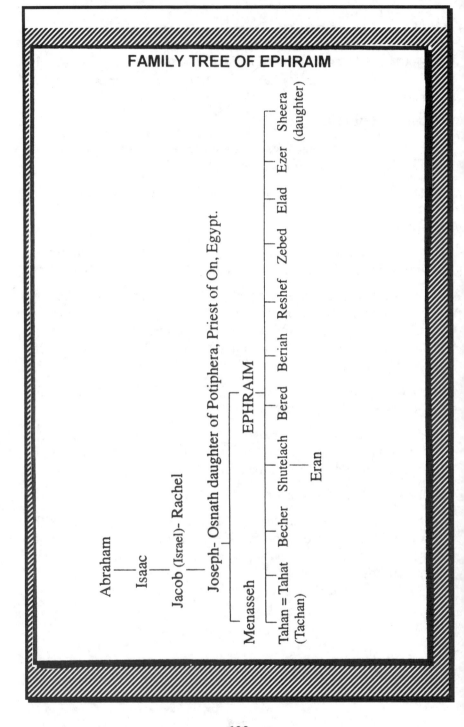

FAMILY TREE OF EPHRAIM

Abraham
Isaac
Jacob (Israel) – Rachel
Joseph – Osnath daughter of Potiphera, Priest of On, Egypt.
Menasseh
EPHRAIM
Tahan = Tahat (Tachan)
Becher
Shutelach
Bered
Beriah
Reshef
Zebed
Elad
Ezer
Sheera (daughter)
Eran

South Africa: Joseph-Naphtali-Zebulon

South Africa was colonized mainly by people of British and Dutch descent with others in addition to the presence of several different African nations. The white peoples are those who (in this case) belong to Israel. The Coat of Arms features a lion (from Joseph -Britain), and two deer (a springbox and oryx). The Deer was a symbol of Naphtali of whom it was prophesied that he would be greatly blessed and receive the "west and the south " (Deuteronomy 34:23).

JOSEPH: NEW ZEALAND

The Coat of Arms of New Zealand contain symbols from several Israelite Tribes: Stars, a sheep fleece, and a wheat sheaf recall Joseph as do the hammers representing the mining industry, "THE DEEP THAT CROUCHETH BENEATH", (Deut. 34;13). The ship was the symbol of Zebulon, and (according to one later popular concept) couid also be used to represent Asher, many of whose descendants settled in Scotland. New Zealand received many immigrants from Scotland and from Northern England and probably includes a high proportion of Naphtali's offspring as well as Asher's. On the whole New Zealand pertains to the Tribe of Joseph.

27

JOSEPH
AND LOST ISRAEL

The blessing to Abraham involved becoming "a great and mighty nation" in which all the nations of the earth would be blessed and which would do "justice and judgment" (Genesis 18:18-19). From the context it would seem that becoming mighty was a prerequisite to becoming a blessing to other nations and doing justice. The use of force and the possession of means enabling its use (if needed) were necessary to become a civilizing influence. Since the quality of Social Justice and mercy was special to Northern Israel so too does it follow that the necessary MIGHT and Greatness be theirs and these qualities were also promised to them.

The Ten Tribes are often referred to collectively as "Joseph" or "Ephraim". Joseph was sold as a slave into Egypt. He rose to become an effective ruler of the land and second only to Pharaoh (Genesis chapters 39-41, 41:41-44). As ruler of Egypt, Joseph saved much of the world from famine (Genesis 41:57) and changed the Egyptian economic and social order (Gen. 47:19-26). Joseph was unknown to his brothers at first and not identified by them (Gen. 42:8). They referred to him as *"The man, the lord of the country"* (Gen. 42:33). This situation had been necessary in order for Joseph to fulfill that task allocated him by Divine Providence, *"God meant it unto good, to bring to pass as it is this day, to save much people alive"* (Genesis 50:20). Similarly, the goal required of the Lost Tribes needed that their membership in Spiritual Israel (and therefore their obligations under the Mosaic Law) be temporarily suspended - as it were.

According to the Talmud the Lost Ten Tribes were legally classified as *"Gentiles to all extents and purposes"* (Yebamot 17a). This determination of status by Rabbinic Authority was preceded by Biblical indications:-

"Backsliding Israel had committed adultery, I had put her away and given her a bill of divorce" (Jeremiah 3:8). Likewise the Prophet Hosea, referring to the Lost Tribes of the Kingdom of Israel, echoed, *"Ye are not my people and I will not be your God,"* (Hosea 1:9).

At some time in the future this situation is destined to be changed and *"In the place where it was said unto them, Ye are not my people, there it shall be said unto them, YE ARE THE SONS OF THE LIVING GOD"* (Hosea 1:10).

JOSEPH AND THE LOST
TEN TRIBES IN THE BIBLE

Manasseh

The Tribe of Joseph with its two fold branches of Ephraim and Manasseh was shown through its family clan names to be mainly settled in the British Isles. Those Suebi who came from Joseph were among the invaders of England. Machir, son of Manasseh became the Mercian Saxons who established themselves on England's western side. Gilead, son of Machir, fathered the Scotch Caledonians the Galedon of Wales, and the smaller "Galatian" groups who preceded the Saxons on the Northwest continental coast and many of whom were swept up by them. Other sons of Machir and Gilad such as Helek, Semida, and Heapher were discernable as parts of the Anglo-Saxon invaders. The Frisians from Parash (Faras), son of Machir, also made significant contribution to the settlement of Anglo-Saxon England.

Ephraim

Ephraim likewise seems to have become known by his nickname of "Aegle" (i.e. Young Bull, Jeremiah 31:18) which was rendered as "ANGLE" in the north. Of the sons of Ephraim, Shutelach appears as Sceld-Sheafing who was the Saxons' legendary ancestor. Erin (pronouncable as "Gerin") was the Grinaei Scythae in the Sakae area from whence the Angles and Saxons came. Becher became the Borocteri whom Bede included amongst the Anglo-Saxon invaders of England. Tahan became the Teutons. The Teutons in ancient times were allied to the Danish Cimbri of British Khymree (Humber) connection. The TEUTONS were last reported on the Continent as neighboring Angles who presumably absorbed them in the westward push, as they had absorbed other groups in the region before, together with Jutes, Saxons, and others invading Britain.

Since the Sons of Joseph were concentrated in the British Isles it follows that those nations whose population is derived from British immigrants are also part of Joseph. Such Josephite nations are Great Britain, Canada, the United States of America, Australia, New Zealand, and South Africa. Analysis of Biblical and Talmudic sources concerning the Children of Joseph confirms the present identification.

Quite a few symbols were assigned to the Josephite Tribes and all of them are used today by nations descended from Joseph. The Zohar said that a lamb symbolized Joseph. Australia uses a merino sheep as an emblem. According to the Midrash, a BULL represented Ephraim but so too in a secondary sense was Simeon also symbolized by a bull (Zohar). The Celts, especially the Welsh, contained a large contingent

433

from Simeon and they historically have been irrevocably interspersed among the English. Thus "John Bull" of Ephraim in England and the Bull of Simeon were united. The connection of Ephraim and the bull was explained elsewhere but a brief recollection may be of use to the reader. Moses blessed Joseph (Deuteronomy 33:17) that his glory be like the FIRSTLING of his BULL (Hebrew: "Shor") and his horns as the horn(s) of Unicorns* In the prophets it was seen how the Northern Kingdom was several times referred to as an "AEGLAH" or female calf. Jeremiah states that, *"I have surely heard EPHRAIM bemoaning himself thus; Thou hast chastised me, and I was chastised, as a bullock unaccustomed to the yolk turn thou me, and I shall be turned; for thou art the LORD my God"* (31:18). The expression "a bullock unaccustomed to the yoke" can be rendered as "an untrained bull-calf". The word in Hebrew for "Bull-Calf" is Aegle (עגל} and "AEGLE" was a name applied to the Angli of old.

According to the Midrash (Numbers Rabah. 2;5) the symbol of Joseph was a picture representing Egypt. The Great Seal of America (shown on every Dollar bill) has a pyramid.

---

* Unicorn. The Hebrew word is "REEM". This beast has been identified as an oryx (a type of straight horned deer) and as a kind of auroch or wild bull now extinct. Midrashic sources apply the term "REEM" (Dr. Jehuda FELIKS, "The Animal World of the Bible," Tel Aviv 1962) to both the deer and bull. In profile the oryx appears as if it had but one horn. Assyrian illustrations apply the term "rimu" to the wild ox and thus REEM in the Bible may be considered apposite to Bull. Nevertheless, in Numbers 23:22 the word for "horns" is written as if it is singular though pronounced in the plural. [TOYAFATH: תועפת instead of תועפות]. This unusual usage hints that the expression of strength (Toyafoth translated here as "horns"), meaning the horns which are normally plural, in this case have become ONE The idea of a one horned bull is recalled in the Talmud (Hulin .ch.3) where it is said that the first man, Adam, sacrificed one.

The Greek Septuagint translated REEM as "One-Horned" or unicorn. Also the "Radak" (Rabbi David Kimchi) in Sefer HaShorashim said that Reem meant unicorn. Unicorns were depicted on Egyptian Walls in the Biblical Era and were popular themes in Assyrian heraldry. Saadia and Ibn Ezra also considered the "Reem" to be a unicorn as did Manasseh ben Israel. "This subject is discussed by Aryeh KAPLAN in the "Living Torah". A UNICORN appears on the British Coat of Arms. The UNICORN represents JOSEPH (Deut.33:17).

Egypt universally can be recognized only by the picture of a sphinx or one of a pyramid. Jacob said that Joseph *"is a fruitful bough, a fruitful bough by a well; whose BRANCHES run over the wall"* (Genesis 49:22). The USA is represented by an eagle bearing in its right claw a thirteen-leaved, thirteen-berried branch; in its left claw it has thirteen arrows. Jacob said *"The archers have surely grieved him and shot at him...But his bow abode in strength"* (Genesis 49:23). In the Last Days Ephraim will be the arrow in the bow fired by Judah against the sons of Javan (Zechariah 9:13). On the American coat of arms can be seen over the head of the eagle thirteen stars in a circle:- Joseph dreamt of stars representing his eleven brothers and the sun and moon bowing down to him (Genesis 37:9) i.e. thirteen heavenly bodies. On the chest of the eagle is a shield* whose upper half has thirteen bars. The number thirteen represents the original thirteen states of the USA but there are thirteen Tribes of Israel as enumerated in Ezekiel chapter 48 and as explained in Ezekiel 48:13, "JOSEPH SHALL HAVE TWO PORTIONS".

The Identification of the USA with Manasseh and Britain and her Daughters with Ephraim

The people of America in the early days of colonization came from all parts of Britain and later from all over the world. Today about fifty million citizens of the USA trace their ancestry to England, Wales, and Scotland and almost the same number to Ireland. In addition the USA has received many immigrants from Italy, Germany, Poland, Russia, and very many people of Jewish descent as well as Negroes, Mexicans, and others. It is highly improbable that all of these people are Israelites but many of them might be and it is the Israel character that determines the National Ethic. Maybe in the beginning many of the first settlers were from Manasseh. After

---

* "FEAR NOT, ABRAHAM, I AM THY SHIELD, AND THY EXCEEDING GREAT REWARDS" (Genesis 15:1).

the Declaration of Independence the Founding Fathers of America did consider giving the Mosaic Law constitutional[1] status and making Hebrew[2] the official language.

Most of the Tribe of Manasseh in existence today is to be found in the USA having been separated out from their Ephraimite brethren by Divine Providence. Case studies in Britain and Germany indicated that the migrants to North America came from specific regions or comprised distinct social groups that had always been differentiated from their neighbors. Descendants of Ephraim are also present in the USA and may constitute up to 30% of the total of Israelites. Nevertheless the dominant element is Manasseh.

OTHER SONS OF JOSEPH?

When Jacob blessed Joseph he said, *"Your two sons Ephraim and Manasseh ...are mine, as Reuben and Simeon, they shall be mine. And your offspring, which you beget after them, shall be yours and shall be called after the name of their brothers in their inheritance"* (Genesis 48:5-6).

In other words Jacob said that Ephraim and Manasseh would be the forefathers of separate tribes each in his own right. Other sons that would be born later to Joseph were to be attached to either Ephraim or Manasseh. It follows from this that Joseph had other sons who were absorbed amongst Ephraim and Manasseh. This was also the opinion of such commentators as Nachmanides and Iben Ezra*. Some of the people listed in the Bible (in the Book of Chronicles) as belonging to Ephraim and Manasseh may actually have been other sons of Joseph whom the Tribes of Ephraim and Manasseh later absorbed. [This would explain apparent anomalies between different sources.] It appears that most of the other sons of Joseph were absorbed amongst Manasseh and counted to Manasseh. Portions of

---

* Rashi however disagrees and says that Joseph only had tow sons, Ephraim and Manasseh.

Ephraim and of other tribes (such as Asher) were also apparently later assimilated amongst Manasseh.

Ephraim was younger than Manasseh yet he received a greater blessing than Manasseh.

Jacob blessed Ephraim and Manasseh, *"The Angel which redeemed me from all evil, bless the lads; and let my name be named on them, and the name of my fathers Abraham and Isaac; and let them grow into a multitude in the midst of the earth,"* (Genesis 48:16). *"And he blessed them that day, saying, In thee shall Israel bless saying, God make thee as Ephraim and as Manasseh: and he set Ephraim before Manasseh"* (Genesis 48:20).

The prevalence of Ephraim is repeated in Jeremiah (31:9), *"I am a father to Israel, and EPHRAIM is my firstborn"*.

The Promised Blessings were unconditional, *"By myself hath I sworn, saith the LORD...that in Blessing I will bless thee and in multiplying I will multiply thy seed..."* (Genesis 28:15). *"God is not a man neither the son of man that he should repent. He hath blessed and I cannot reverse it"* (Numbers 23:19-20).

In Biblical times Manasseh received an inheritance on both the east and west sides of the Jordan. Machir and Gilead dominated the eastern side. Economically it is considered to have possibly been as important as the whole of the West Side of the Jordan.

At that time the climate was different. There were forests and immense grasslands. The land has changed due to climatic change and ecological despoliation perpetrated by foreigners including the Romans, Turks, and Arabs. Destroy trees and vegetation coverage and you will heat up the earth, decrease precipitation and create a desert. With enough will and effort this process could be reversed and the region could be made to flourish and support a great many people in most congenial conditions. It is hinted that indeed that this is what will happen (Ezekiel 16:55, 2-Chronicles 7:14):

[Leviticus 26:42] THEN WILL I REMEMBER MY COVENANT WITH JACOB, AND ALSO MY COVENANT WITH ISAAC,

AND ALSO MY COVENANT WITH ABRAHAM WILL I REMEMBER; AND I WILL REMEMBER THE LAND.

The Northern Kingdom is often referred to as "Ephraim" since the Jeroboam the first king was from Ephraim and Ephraim was the most important tribe. In Prophecy "Ephraim" is often used as a general term for all the Ten Lost Tribes of Northern Israel.

Even so, the first capital of the Northern Kingdom was Samaria which is in the portion of Manasseh on the eastern side of the Jordan.

In the time of the judge Gideon (Judges ch.8) Ephraim fought a portion of Manasseh over the question of Tribal predominance. Ephraim lost. In the Biblical Pentateuch (i.e. the written "Torah" or Five Books of Moses) Manasseh is occasionally listed before Ephraim.

Jacob prophesied that (Genesis 48:19) Ephraim would be greater than Manasseh. The Commentary of the "NATZIV" Berlin ("Ha Emek Davar" on Genesis 48:14) analyzed the subject of Ephraim and Manasseh and after noting that in their camping orders Manasseh always preceded Ephraim and in tribal listings is always counted first he concluded that the relative greatness of Ephraim was primarily spiritual and that **in the Natural order of Things Manasseh would have precedence**. This description to some extent is applicable to the relative situations of Britain and the USA

The "NATZIV" Berlin ("Ha Emek Davar" Numbers 2:20: <Even though Ephraim was the chief standard [when the Israelites wandered in the Wilderness] this was because the nature of Providence in the Wilderness was miraculous. The power of Ephraim is greater regarding the miraculous aspect of existence. Concerning the regular way of the world however Manasseh is greater...

Numbers 13:11: "*Of the tribe of Joseph, of the tribe of Manasseh, Gaddi the son of Susi.*" The "NATZIV" Numbers 13:11 <...Since they now needed to act according to the laws of nature the main emphasis was now on Manasseh>.

Genesis 48:20 "*And he placed Ephraim before Manasseh.*" The "NATZIV": <In spiritual matters Ephraim had precedence...but in the ways of the world Manasseh was pre-eminent>.

The Tribes of Ephraim and Manasseh
Congregated in the British Isles.

The very name Aegel (diminutive of Angle) was a nickname for Ephraim and most of the Angles relate to Ephraim. Even so this equation is not an absolute one and exceptions exist, for instance a group of Angli (Soumboi-Aggiloi) was tentatively identified with Shemida of Manasseh and Frisians (from Paresh of Manasseh) also settled in Anglia. All of the Saxon peoples in Britain were quite content to refer to themselves as "Angles" or 'English". Most of Joseph was somewhere in Britain with offshoots in Holland, France, and elsewhere.

The early settlers of the USA came from Britain, therefore they were probably from Joseph. The "Egyptian picture" and other symbols of Joseph belong to the USA; "John Bull", sign of Ephraim, represents the United Kingdom of Great Britain. Areas of Britain in which clans from Manasseh are known to have been predominant produced a disproportionate number of the early settlers of North America. The Unicorn on the British Coat of Arms originally came from Scotland and many of the early settlers of America came from Scotland and North England. The Unicorn is a symbol of Manasseh. Other evidence strengthens the impression that characteristics of Manasseh are found in the USA and those of EPHRAIM in Britain. Indications in Prophecy (Amos 9:9 Isaiah 66:20-22) are that Tribal identities influence an individual's destiny and therefore people of Manasseh's tribe may somehow have been led to congregate in the USA.

Manasseh to be Greater than Ephraim?

When Jacob blessed the two sons of Joseph (Genesis 48) he set Ephraim before Manasseh and said that EPHRAIM would become a multitude of nations. Of Manasseh he said, *"He also shall become a people, and he also shall be great"* (Genesis 48:19-20). From these verses it could be understood that Ephraim would be several nations such as the United KINGDOM, Australia, Canada, New Zealand, and South Africa) whereas Manasseh would be one, albeit a great one. The expression applied to Manasseh "HE ALSO SHALL BECOME A PEOPLE and he also shall be great" could imply that Manasseh would become a people and be great ("also") AFTER Ephraim had already established himself. Manasseh was placed to the right of Jacob and Ephraim to the left. Jacob crossed his hands placing left hand on the head of Manasseh and the right hand on that of Ephraim. A Rabbinical Commentator, Tzvi Elimelech SHAPIRA of Dinov 1784-1840 known after his book as the "Bnei Yissachar") points out that Manasseh remained to the right of Jacob since he represented his essence. [Hence we have the nickname "Yank" meaning Jacob for Americans] whereas Ephraim represented the essence of Joseph. Manasseh, says this commentary, received the blessing with the left and slower hand to indicate that his coming to greatness would be chronologically later[3]. As shown above the very name "America" is derived from a permutation of the name "Machir" who was the first-born son of Manasseh.

In Hebrew the name "Ephraim" connotes an aristocratic-type of social organization such as exists in Britain. On the other hand "Manasseh" may be taken to mean responsible delegated representation* such as that expounded in the Constitution of the USA and to which many Americans credit almost religious significance. Jacob prophesied that Ephraim

---

* "Ephraim" by Yair Davidi where a linguistic analysis of the name "Manasseh" is given based on the Commentary of S.R. Hirsch to Genesis 41:51-52.

would be greater than Manasseh (Genesis 48:19). The Commentary of the "NATZIV" Berlin ("Ha Emek Davar" on Genesis 48:14) analyzed the subject of Ephraim and Manasseh and after noting that in their camping orders Manasseh always preceded Ephraim and in tribal listings is always counted first (in the Pentateuch) he concluded that the relative greatness of Ephraim was primarily spiritual and that in the Natural order of Things Manasseh would have precedence. This description to some extent is applicable to the relative situations of Britain and the USA.

JOSEPH RULES!!
"THE FULLNESS OF THE NATIONS"

In Genesis 48:19 it says about Ephraim, "His seed shall become a multitude of nations" or in Hebrew "Maloe [=fullness] HaGoyim [=the nations]." The King James version translates Genesis 48:19: "his [i.e. Ephraim's] seed shall become a multitude of nations". In this case the translation accords with the opinion of at least one major Rabbinical Commentator, i.e. with Abraham Iben Ezra (1084-1164). The Hebrew words translated as "a multitude of nations" are "Malo-HaGoiim", "Malo" means fullness and "HaGoiim" means nations, i.e. "his seed will be fullness of nations". What does this mean? Iben Ezra who combined a rational-spiritual and literal approach said it meant: "many peoples will come out of him", i.e. "a multitude of nations" just like the King James later rendered it. Onkelos (1st century CE) translated the words into Aramaic as "Banohi yihon Shalitin beAmmaia", i.e. "his sons shall be rulers over peoples", or "rulers over the peoples". Remember literally the verse says "his seed will be fullness of nations": The Midrash Rabah (97;7) takes an illustrative approach. The Midrash which is quoted by Rashi says that the fame or renown of his seed will be all over the world, fill up the world, as it was in the time of Joshua who caused the sun to stand still (Joshua 10:13). The rationalistic Rav Saadia Gaon said it means his seed will be full-fledged nations. Rabbi David Kinchi said the meaning is "world-filling nations". The Aramaic Paraphrase of Yehonathan ben Uzziel which stresses legendary sources says it means his seed will be famous or great among the nations. Taking all the above into cognizance we have a tendency to emphasize an interaction with the nations. The Hebrew can actually also be translated as "his seed will be involved with the fullness of the nations, the nations will need him to complete themselves, they cannot give expression to themselves without him, he will rule over them!!" This agrees with Onkelos. Onkelos translated the Torah (Pentateuch) into Aramaic. Onkelos worked under the guidance of Rabbi Eliezer and Rabbi Joshua (Megilla 3a). He is considered to have been inspired. The translation of Onkelos at one stage was required weekly reading for every religious Jew and in some communities still is. We have proven from historical sources that many descendants from Ephraim migrated to Britain and some of these later passed over to America. Onkelos translated the expression as meaning that the seed of Ephraim would rule over the peoples, and they did and through America to a degree they still do.

ENDS OF THE EARTH

Moses (Deuteronomy 33) prophesied concerning Joseph, (33:13): *"And of Joseph he said, Blessed of the LORD be his land (for the precious things of heaven, for the dew, and for the deep that croucheth beneath, And for the precious fruits...And for the chief things of the ancient mountains of the everlasting hills...of the earth and fullness thereof...the good will of HIM that dwelt in the bush.. His glory is like the firstling of his BULL, and his horns, are like the horn of a unicorn with them he shall push the people together unto the ends of the earth: and they are the ten thousands of Ephraim, and they are the thousands of Manasseh".*

In this (and other) blessings Joseph was promised agricultural bounty, mineral resources, favorable climate; He was associated with a people being pushed together unto the ends of the earth.

"Ends of the EARTH" when considered from the Land of Israel means the continents of America and Australia and the geographical extremities of South Africa and Northwest Europe. The very name of England ("Angleterre" in French) can be understood as meaning "Corner of the Land", i.e. Angle-Land, or "End of the Earth". The prophet Isaiah appears several times to have located the Lost Tribes of Israel in the "Ends of the Earth" e.g *"But thou Israel, my servant Jacob whom I have chosen, the seed of Abraham my friend...Whom I have strengthened (taken) from the ENDS OF THE EARTH and called thee from the CHIEF [i.e. best+] parts hereof"* (Isaiah 41:8-9).

A similar reference to World's ends is found in another passage: *"I will say to the north, Give up; and to the south, Keep not*

+ The King James Translation instead of "chief parts" has "chief men." This interpretation, if correct, is reflecting a most unusual employment of Hebrew expression for if men were meant the Bible would indicate it more explicitly. The Hebrew "ATZILAYAH" means "chiefs of" or "nobility of" and to the author's mind is qualifying which of the Earth's ends would belong to Israel, -obviously the best and most noble ones. The Hebrew word ("Atzil") is related to the Nordic "Aedil" meaning noble. It also connotes "reserved" and in a sense all the areas settled by the sons of Joseph had been "reserved" for them since previously they were sparsely occupied. Areas in which we have traced the Lost Ten Tribes to have settled are qualitatively the best regions of the earth. Climate and Geography influence the characteristics of the inhabitants. They are not the only factor but they are important. The Geography of Scandinavia, Holland, France, Britain, North America, South Africa, Australia and New Zealand, and the State of Israel has determined something in the National Personality of the people involved. It is the interaction of the people with the Land that is important.

The author once came across a book of instruction for professional Jewish Orthodox Scribes. These people have the very exacting task of exactly transcribing certain Scriptural passages onto parchment. Most of this parchment is derived from calve skins. The book of instruction was also a guide of professional advice. It was stated that North America and Argentina are the two main sources for calfskin. It was also stated that different geographic regions have intrinsic properties of their own and that something about North America rendered calve skin from there superior. The Talmud was quoted to the effect that different regions give rise to different types of people and that some areas are better in certain respects than others. Regions in which the Lost Ten Tribes settled are the best in the world.

443

back; bring my sons from far, and my daughters from the ENDS OF THE EARTH" (Isaiah 43:6).

"A LIGHT TO THE GENTILES"

An expression leading into other subjects of equal relevance is given in Isaiah 49:5-13: *"Though Israel be not gathered...to raise up the TRIBES OF JACOB, and to restore the preserved of Israel: I will also give thee for a light to the Gentiles, that thou mayest be my salvation unto the END OF THE EARTH"*. The phrase "End of the Earth" is associated with The Tribes of Jacob who need to be gathered. It also uses the expression "a light to the Gentiles." This is reminiscent of the fact that despite all the mistakes, corruption, and evil that the Anglo-Saxon nations may have done, they have, nevertheless, on the WHOLE, been a civilizing influence amongst the Gentiles. Modern "Western" concepts of human rights and innate dignity and so on are due to them more than to anybody else. To the extent that the Humanism of modern civilization is attributable to non-Anglo-Saxon elements then these too are usually from nationalities identified in this book as containing a significant proportion of Israelites. French, Scandinavians, Swiss, Dutch, and Jews, with the Anglo-Saxons are responsible for most of what good exists in the world today.

The quoted passage from Isaiah (49:5-13) continues: *"..I will preserve thee, and give thee for a covenant of the people* [i.e. a "BRIT-AM" in Hebrew], *to establish the earth, to cause to inherit the desolate heritages; That thou may say to the prisoners, Go forth...Behold these shall come from afar: and lo, these from the north and from the west; and these from the land of SINIM. For the LORD hath comforted his people.."*

The expression "Raise up the Tribes of Jacob" and "BRIT-AM" meaning Covenant of the people, is reminiscent of Britain, the Commonwealth, and the UNION-JACK (cf. Jacob) which in Hebrew would be rendered as Covenant of Jacob. The USA in

Modern Hebrew is called "Artsot-HaBRIT" meaning literally "Lands of the Covenant".

The term used by Isaiah (49:8-13): "A COVENANT OF THE PEOPLE" is also found in Isaiah 42;6 where the words are: *"And give thee for a COVENANT OF THE PEOPLE, for a light to the Gentiles, to open the blind eyes, to bring out the prisoners from the prison, them that sit in darkness out of the prison house"*. Here a Covenant of the People is associated with the freeing of prisoners. Also in the previously-quoted passage concerning "Brit-Am" (i.e. "Covenant of the People" in Hebrew) the release of prisoners was mentioned ("...say to the prisoners, go forth") together with inheriting desolate heritages and a return from afar from the north and the west and from the land of Sinim.

The whole passage can be understood as referring to the Latter Days but it also bears an intermediate sense of surprising historical applicability.

"BRITTANIA"

A Covenant of the People has a similar meaning to Commonwealth of Britain, or Commonwealth of Nations of the British Empire and also to the concept of a People's Covenant in North American thought. The Hebrew Bible's Original Words for "COVENANT OF THE PEOPLE" are "BRIT-AM". "Brit" means covenant and "am" means people [*"Ish" incidentally does mean "man", or "belonging to the same", as the suffix "-ish" in English, and "Brit-ish" means "Man of the Covenant" or "Belonging to the Covenant"*]. In Hebrew Brit-am in the northern dialects and in later spoken Hebrew would have become "Brit-aN" the final "m" being pronounced as "N". Not only that but on the British side the name for Britain itself in old documents was sometimes rendered by the English as "Britammia".

The "Brit-am" of Isaiah related to the "inheritance of waste heritages" and to the establishment of a land together with the freeing of prisoners. When Britain first began to colonize America she sent prisoners to serve their sentence there at the end of which they received lands and became settlers. After the American Revolution the same system was applied to Australia. Both North America and Australia were very much underpopulated and could have been termed "WASTE Heritages". The prisoners sent to Australia were let out of ship hulks, literally released from the darkness. America is north and west of the Land of Israel - Isaiah's standard of reference. "SINIM" is understood as meaning "Land of the South" according to the Jewish Commentators (e.g. the Aramaic Paraphrase and Rashi) and the name AUSTRALIA is derived from the Latin for "South land". The standard Latin (Vulgate) translation of the Bible translates "Sinim" as "AUSTRALIS". A complementary (but NOT contradictory) meaning to the verses in Isaiah 42 and 49 which speak of a "BRIT-AM" freeing the prisoners and causing the CHOSEN to come from the ends of the earth to inherit the "WASTED HERITAGES" is that of Great Britain having delivered the Jews from European oppression and enabled them to return to the Land of Israel. This point holds well despite British ambivalence and wavering. It is however problematic the British intermediate leadership at first having been willing encouragers of the Zionist enterprise and later to a degree ambivalent towards it. Nevertheless, almost against their will at some level they acquiesced. The British public was always supportive of Zionism and so were the greatest leaders of Britain, such as Winston Churchill.

The Biblical proofs so far cited should be understood as forming a composite picture which taken together gives the following: The Lost Israelites, especially Joseph, were destined to enjoy a wealth of physical resources; to be situated at the "ends of the earth"; to be a moderating and civilizing influence on humanity; to be a covenant of People which could mean a "Commonwealth", a "Brittamia." A passage of Isaiah (ch.49) is understandable as describing the early colonization by freed convicts of the "Heritages" of North America and the "South

Land" meaning Australia and/or the desolate land of "Palestine" and British encouraged Jewish Zionism.

MONARCHS

If these passages as explained are accepted then obviously it means that the "Anglo-Saxon" (i.e. of British descent) peoples are the Lost Tribes of Israel according to the Bible. A few more Biblical pieces of evidence will be presented which also prove the Anglo Saxon case. Regarding the European "Continental" Israelites, some independent proofs were previously adduced for each Tribe, for instance, Zebulon dwelling on the seashores was shown as attributable to Holland. Further evidence will be referred to and this is in addition to the Tribal proofs so far brought throughout the present work. An interesting curiosity is the presence of hereditary monarchs in most of the European-Israelite countries in Sweden, Norway, Denmark, Holland, Luxembourg, and Great Britain. These are almost the only stable monarchical lines remaining in the world. An hereditary monarch is regarded as a blessing.

Abraham was blessed, *"I will make nations of thee, and kings shall come out of thee"* (Genesis 17:6). Jacob was blessed, *"Be fruitful and multiply; a nation and a company of nations shall be of thee, and kings shall come out of thy loins"* (Genesis 35:11). Note that "A nation and a company of nations" could mean the USA and British Commonwealth.

The blessings were IRREVERSIBLE. They could not be annulled for reason of the promise given to Abraham, *"By myself hath I sworn saith the Lord...That in blessing I will bless thee and in multiplying I will multiply thy seed as the stars of heaven, and as the sand which is upon the sea shore; and thy seed shall possess the Gate of his enemies"* (Genesis 22:16-17).

Again the irrevocability of the promises was repeated to Jacob.

447

[Genesis 28:14] I AM THE LORD GOD OF ABRAHAM THY FATHER, AND THE GOD OF ISAAC: THE LAND WHEREON THOU LIEST, TO THEE WILL I GIVE IT, AND TO THY SEED; [Genesis 28:14] AND THY SEED SHALL BE AS THE DUST OF THE EARTH, AND THOU SHALT SPREAD ABROAD TO THE WEST, AND TO THE EAST, AND TO THE NORTH, AND TO THE SOUTH: AND IN THEE AND IN THY SEED SHALL ALL THE FAMILIES OF THE EARTH BE BLESSED. [Genesis 28:15] AND, BEHOLD, I AM WITH THEE, AND WILL KEEP THEE IN ALL PLACES WHITHER THOU GOEST, AND WILL BRING THEE AGAIN INTO THIS LAND; FOR I WILL NOT LEAVE THEE, UNTIL I HAVE DONE THAT WHICH I HAVE SPOKEN TO THEE OF.

This aspect of the blessings was confirmed by Bilam, *"God is NOT A MAN, that he should lie; neither THE SON OF MAN that he should repent; hath he said, and shall he not do it? or hath he spoken and shall he not make it good?....He hath blessed and I cannot reverse it. He hath not beheld iniquity in Jacob, neither hath he seen perverseness in Israel: the Lord his God is with him, and the shout of a king is among them"* (Numbers 23:19-21).

Regarding Monarchs, Sarah, wife of Abraham the patriarch, was blessed that she (Genesis 17:16) should become a mother of nations and that "Kings of people shall be of her". Which verse implies several kings over different peoples (all of whom are descendants of Sarah) contemporaneously with each other in the same way that in the Continental Israelite nations nearly all has each its own monarch today.

Abraham begat Isaac and Ishmael but the covenant was established only with Isaac (Genesis 17:19). Isaac in turn begat Jacob (Israel) and Esau but only Israel received the Blessings of Abraham (Genesis 28:4). Israel begat twelve sons from whom came the twelve Tribes of Israel and all of them received a portion of the blessings (Genesis 49:28) but the predominant Birthright equivalent of primogeniture went to Joseph. *"Judah prevailed above his brethren, and of him came the chief ruler but the birthright was Joseph's"* (1-Chronicles 5:2).

Joseph had two sons Ephraim and Manasseh, both became individual tribes in their own right. Of the two Ephraim was the preeminent (Genesis 48:19) as reflected in the Book of Jeremiah (31:9): *"For I am a father to Israel, and Ephraim is my firstborn"*.

GILEAD OF MANASSEH
CALEDONIA

Votadini

Selgovae

Novantae

Golodin

Brigantes

MANASSEH

PERESH (Menasseh)

Parisi

GILEAD

ANGLES

Golodin

Ordovices

MERCIA
(=Machir)

Coritani

SIMEON

Iceni

AEGELI= EPHRAIM

Trinovantes

Demetae

SIMEON
Silures

MENASSEH

Dobunni

Belgae

SAXONS

Cantiaci

Dumnonii

Durotriges

U.S.A: The United States of America

The official symbols of the U.S.A (as seen on a Dollar Bill) are used on the Great Seal which has a Shield and a Pyramid. The Shield of the USA contains the motto: *"Out of many, one"* (E Pluribus Unum). It has 13 Stars and a Shield with 13 stripes and an eagle holding 13 arrows and a 13 leafed olive branch. There were 13 Tribes of Israel. Stars featured in a dream of Joseph son of Israel and were preminiscent of his future greatness. Archery and a bow were connected with the blessing of Joseph given to him by his father Israel (Genesis 50:22-23). An eagle was one of the symbols of Dan while the Tribe of Asher was represented by the olive tree. The reverse side of the Great Seal of the USA (as depicted in the Dollar bill) shows a pyramid, and a single-eye said to suggest the eye of Providence. A PYRAMID is also a typical representation of Egypt and according to Jewish tradition (Num. Rab. 2;5) the Tribe of Joseph had A picture of Egypt for their Tribal Standard. When you see a pyramid you think of Egypt. The USA has a large and mixed population but it includes a large number from the Tribes of Israel, and the Tribe of Joseph especially the portion of Manasseh seems to be paramount.

453

THE CHOSEN PEOPLES

Isles of the Sea. The North Country. The Richest and Best Places. Coastlands of the earth. Seafarers. Ends of the Earth (Geographical Extremities) with ISRAELAND in the center .Mineral Resources. Agricultural Plenty. Sheep. Cattle. Corn. Wine. Gold. Military Prowess. World Power and Authority. A "POLICEMAN" of the Globe. A Colonizer of "Waste" Places. An enabler of Jewish Re-settlement in Israel. A World Example ("Light to the Gentiles"). A Confederation "Brit-am" of Peoples). Union Jack (i.e. covenant of Jacob-Israel) John Bull: Joseph -a young bull, "GATE OF YOUR ENEMIES": Strategic Points and Passes. "Heights of the Earth".

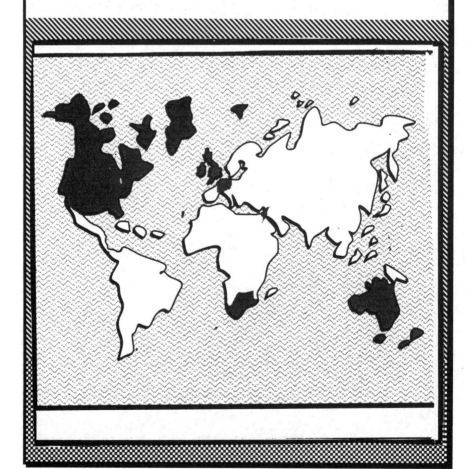

28

THE BLESSINGS IN STATISTICS

The Blessings of Israelite Nations on a World Scale
What is an "Israelite" Nation?

Brit-Am identifies the Lost Ten Tribes of Israel with groups that historically came to dominate the following nations: Britain, Ireland, the USA, Canada, Australia, New Zealand, South Africa (until recently), Switzerland, France, Belgium, Luxembourg, Netherlands (Holland), Denmark, Norway, Iceland, Sweden, Finland. All together there are 17 nations but five of these (Britain, Canada, Australia, New Zealand, South Africa) could be considered as the one entity of "Ephraim" whereas Luxembourg and Iceland could be considered too small to count on an international scale and should perhaps be subsumed under neighboring entities. That leaves us with 11 entities and with the State of Israel we therefore have 12 parallel to the 12 tribes of Israel. We do not say that everyone in the said nations is of Israelite descent. Descendants of Lost Israelites are to be found all over the world especially in Europe. We do however say that in the named nations are to be found a substantial percentage of Israelites (possibly a majority in some cases) and also that Israelite characteristics were strongly apparent in the formation of the national character and in the developmental history. These countries may therefore for the purposes of comparison be considered as "Israelite".

The Blessings to Israel

Part of the identifying characteristics of Israel was that they should be physically and materially blessed especially towards the End Times. The latest UN statistics shown below demonstrate as to how the blessings have been fulfilled. These statistics do not necessarily take into account factors that may be more important than those that are considered, e.g. an invigorating climate, personal self-respect, stable family life, etc should also be considerations in determining the quality of life. Anyway, for what they are worth here are the statistics:

Most Livable Countries: UN Human Development Index, 2002

The Human Development Index (HDI), published annually by the UN, ranks nations according to their citizens' quality of life rather than strictly by a nation's traditional economic figures. The criteria for calculating rankings include life expectancy, educational attainment, and adjusted real income.

"Most Livable" Countries, 2002			
1.	Norway	14.	Denmark
2.	Sweden	15.	Austria
3.	Canada	16.	Luxembourg
4.	Belgium	17.	Germany
5.	Australia	18.	Ireland
6.	United States	19.	New Zealand
7.	Iceland	20.	Italy

8.	Netherlands	21.	Spain
9.	Japan	22.	Israel
10.	Finland	23.	Hong Kong
11.	Switzerland	24.	Greece
12.	France	25.	Singapore
13.	United Kingdom		

Source: Human Development Report, 2002, United Nations; www.undp.org/hdr2002 .

Brit-Am Comment: From the above table we see that concerning the "Most Livable Countries" the top 8 were Israelite, then came Japan, then five more Israelite countries, then Austria (no.15), followed by Luxembourg (no.16), Germany (no.17), Ireland (18), New Zealand (19), Italy, Spain, and Israel. South Africa we can disregard for the moment due to the present crisis and domination by non-Israelite elements. The State of Israel is an exception due to the inclusion of Arabs and other factors. Taking the Jewish population of Israel alone then it too would be comparable to the other Israelite nations. On the whole we can say that Israelite Nations top the list and that all Israelite nations are in the top 20.

LOWEST INFANT MORTALITY RATE:[2] 2001 (deaths per 1,000 births)		
(1)	Sweden	3.4
(2)	Iceland	3.5
(3)	Singapore	3.6
(4)	Finland	3.8
	Japan	3.8
(6)	Norway	3.9
(7)	Andorra	4.1
(8)	Netherlands	4.3
(9)	Austria	4.4

	France	4.4
	Switzerland	4.4
HIGHEST LIFE EXPECTANCY (in years): 2001		
(1)	Andorra	83.5
(2)	San Marino	81.3
(3)	Japan	80.9
(4)	Singapore	80.3
(5)	Australia	80.0
(6)	Switzerland	79.9
(7)	Sweden	79.8
(8)	Canada	79.7
	Iceland	79.7
(10)	Italy	79.2

Brit-Am Comment: Israelite Nations had eight places out of the top eleven (I am not sure about Andorra?) regarding the Lowest Infant Mortality Rate. Concerning Life Expectancy Israelite nations held six places in the top ten but Andorra, San Marino, maybe Singapore and Iceland are rather small and exceptional. Also different mortality rates exist for males and females. Israeli males for instance have the second highest (after Japan) life expectancy in the world but females have less so this reduces the overall average.

THE RICHEST AND THE POOREST
(Source supplied by Craig White)
Bild Online published on July 10 a list of the richest and the poorest countries, based on the average personal income, life expectancy and education of each country's citizens. It is interesting that most of the richest countries belong to the lost tribes of the house of Israel. We realize, of course that this list is somewhat arbitrary, based on the three factors chosen on which

the list was based. Strictly focusing on the economy, for example, the list would of course look differently. Still, according to the list, the 20 richest countries are, in this order:

(1) Norway	(4) Australia	(7) USA	(10) Switzerland
(2) Iceland	(5) Netherlands	(8) Canada	(11) Denmark
(3) Sweden	(6) Belgium	(9) Japan	(12) Ireland
(13) Great Britain	(15) Luxembourg	(17) France	(19) Spain
(14) Finland	(16) Austria	(18) Germany	(20) New Zealand

Brit-Am Comment: Esau was also blessed. Evidently also derived from UN figures the Bild List more or less confirms what was said above: Israelite nations took the top eight places then came Japan (9), then 6 more Israelite nations, then Austria (16), then France (17), Germany, Spain, and New Zealand (20). Disregarding South Africa and the State of Israel the remaining 16 Israelite nations were all in the top twenty. Even regarding non-Israelite nations they too may contain Israelite elements and also constituents from Esau (Edom). Esau was also blessed with a promised material prosperity: [Genesis 27:39] AND ISAAC HIS FATHER ANSWERED AND SAID UNTO HIM, BEHOLD, THY DWELLING SHALL BE THE FATNESS OF THE EARTH, AND OF THE DEW OF HEAVEN FROM ABOVE. Esau was blessed and his blessing has been fulfilled in the peoples of Germany, Austria, Italy, and Spain all of whose ruling elites include descendants of Edom.

The USA in the World Economy[1]

[All the following figures are in $Billion: World Bank-Little data Book-03].

The US has the largest and most technologically powerful economy in the world, with a per capita GDP (Gross Domestic Product) of $37,800.

In 2001, the World GDP was $31,121 billion. The USA had 10,065 which was almost one-third of the total. The USA produced more than all the countries of the EU together, who with 25 countries (EUROPEAN UNION) had 8,269. JAPAN had 4,141.

The next 8 countries were China: 1,159. Canada: 694. Mexico: 618. Brazil: 503. India: 477. Korea: 422. Australia: 369. Russia: 310. Even including Russia, the European Economic Union would still have remained far behind the US. Russia has 140 million inhabitants, but its GDP was equal to that of the Australia with only 19 million inhabitants!

Source: Free World Academy Home Page

The USA in the World

<<The United States is the world's greatest economic power in terms of gross national product (GNP) and is among the greatest powers in terms of GNP per capita. The nation's wealth is partly a reflection of its valuable natural resources. With only 5 % of the world's population, the United States produces nearly one-fifth of the world's output of coal, copper, and crude petroleum. The agricultural area produces nearly one-half of the world's corn (maize); nearly one-fifth of its beef, pork, mutton, and lamb; and more than one-tenth of its wheat. The United States owes its economic position more to its highly developed industry, than to its natural resources or agricultural output.

<<The American economy produces and Americans consume more than any other economy in the world. It also plays a pivotal role in a global economy, where the economies of all nations have to various degrees become interdependent. **Source: Map Zones Country's Profile Home Page**

The US Dollar an International Currency

The dollar is an international currency. Most bank reserves around the world are in dollars. The price of oil and other raw materials is fixed in dollar. This means the USA can consume (to a great though ultimately limited degree) even more than it produces since dollars it puts out "disappear" in international trading and saving.

Gates of Your Enemies.
US Military Strength Around the World

<<According to a Department of Defense publication, "Active Duty Military Personnel Strengths by Regional Area and by Country," the United States has troops in 135 countries. This means that the United States has troops in 70 percent of the countries of the world. To this list could be added regions like the Indian Ocean territory of Diego Garcia, Gibraltar, and the Atlantic Ocean island of St. Helena, all still controlled by Great Britain, but not considered sovereign countries. Greenland is also home to U.S. troops, but is technically part of Denmark. Troops in two other regions, Kosovo and Hong Kong, might also be included here, but the DODs "Personnel Strengths" document includes U.S. troops in Kosovo under Serbia and U.S. troops in Hong Kong under China.

<<Possessions of the United States like Guam, Johnston Atoll, Puerto Rico, the Trust Territory of the Pacific Islands, and the Virgin Islands are likewise home to U.S. troops. Guam has over 3,200.

<<Regular troop strength ranges from a low of 1 in Malawi to a high of 74,796 in Germany. At the time the most recent "Personnel Strengths" was released by the government

(September 30, 2003), there were 183,002 troops deployed to Iraq, an unspecified number of which came from U.S. forces in Germany and Italy. The total number of troops deployed abroad as of that date was 252,764, not including U.S. troops in Iraq from the United States. Total military personnel on September 30, 2003, was 1,434,377. This means that 17.6 percent of U.S. military forces were deployed on foreign soil, and certainly over 25 percent if U.S. troops in Iraq from the United States were included.

<<The U. S. global empire is an empire that Alexander the Great, Caesar Augustus, Genghis Khan, Suleiman the Magnificent, Justinian, and King George V would be proud of.
Source: The U.S. Global Empire by Laurence M. VANCE, March 16, 2004

International Statistics Confirm

Our Conclusions!

We may conclude by saying that international statistics confirm Brit-Am beliefs. Israelite nations are the most blessed nations and amongst the Israelite nations that of Joseph is the most blessed of all. It may be objected that we identify, not only the USA, but all the "Anglo" nations as Joseph: The other nations though high up on the ladder are not in the same league as the USA. We would answer that the USA embodies Manasseh who was destined to achieve his greatness after that of Ephraim. The British Empire and Commonwealth in their hey day reached greater heights in many ways even than the USA has achieved at present. They represent Ephraim and they still maintain a respectable presence with their own potential and uniqueness alongside that of the US who is Manasseh.

<<The British Empire, which in the early decades of the 20th century covered nearly 30 million square kilometers with a population of 400-500 million people (roughly a quarter of the world's population), was the most extensive area under a single country's rule in history.>>
The American Encyclopedia

From Bob Davis:
<<You may have underestimated the numbers of countries that were part of the British Empire. This is the list (They are almost all now voluntarily part of the Commonwealth which is still lead by the Queen): Antigua and Barbuda, Australia, The Bahamas, Bangladesh Barbados, Belize, Botswana, British Virgin Islands, Brunei, Darussalam, Cameroon, Canada, Cyprus, Dominica, Fiji Islands, Gambia,
Ghana, Grenada, Guyana, India, Jamaica, Kenya, Kiribati, Lesotho, Malawi, Malaysia, Maldives, Malta,
Mauritius, Mozambique, Namibia, Nauru, New
Zealand, Nigeria, Pakistan, Papua, New Guinea, St Lucia, St Kitts and Nevis, St Vincent and the
Grenadines, Samoa, Seychelles, Sierra
Leone, Singapore, Solomon Islands, South Africa, Sri Lanka, Swaziland, Tonga, Trinidad and
Tobago, Tuvalu, Uganda, United Kingdom, United Republic of Tanzania, Vanuatu, Zambia. Under "Lost or given back" you should add America and Ireland. However, if you consider the countries that were invaded by the British army throughout history, and then returned promptly for whatever reason, you would need to include all of North Africa, The Middle East, the Near East, most of Europe, Afghanistan (3 times so far) and even Peking! >>

From Biblical, Historical, and all other perspectives the USA and Britain together with all other related nations must encompass within their populations the lost Ten Tribes of Israel. There is no other possible conclusion.

Another Version of "John Bull"

$$29$$

WHAT DOES IT ALL MATTER ANYWAY?

The Tribes of Israel are traceable primarily to peoples living in the present day countries of Canada, the U.S.A., the U.K., Ireland, Australia, New Zealand, South Africa, Finland, Sweden, Norway, Denmark, Holland, Belgium, France, Switzerland, and Israel. Peoples of non-Israelite ancestry are also present within these nations and make negative, neutral, and positive contributions of their own to the common ethos. As stated Israelites were scattered throughout many nations but the concern here has been with the apparent majority appearing in discernable concentration and in identifiable units.

It may be asked: What significance is there to an Israelite identity? What difference does it really make, anyway? Why bother to study questions concerning the remote past when there are no answers even to the immediate future?

The answer is that it makes a lot of difference and has importance not only in understanding what has been but also regarding what should be done. When a person realizes who he is and where he and those around him came from then his own task in life becomes clearer. God created all things and He left a message in Scripture applicable to all mankind but primarily directed to His Chosen People of Israel! If this message pertains strongly to you then you should be made aware of it. God wants His people to know who they are and to do His will accordingly. The requirement of Hebrew Tribal self-awareness from ALL of Israel is for their own sakes and to fulfill the purpose of all creation. There is a principle that in the Time of the Messiah everyone will know to which Tribe he belongs to and receive an inheritance in his Tribal territory. This means that knowing your Tribe is the way things should be. Each tribe has its own unique task and every person has his role to play within his Tribal framework. God spoke in the Bible to the people of Israel. If you are an Israelite you should want to hear what is being said to you.

What Do Others Say On The Subject?

The significance of an Israelite identity is that connected to the question of heredity and ancestral heritage both considerations being part of the aggregate of reasons justifying the present study. This work has revealed new possibilities for research to ultimately confirm all of the truth contained herein. The aim of all learning should be to arrive at the truth and at an understanding of reality from beginning to end to whatever extent is possible. The origin of individual nations explains much of their subsequent destiny.

Whatever has been said in this work has been said by others (in a more guarded way) on an academic level! There are acknowledged researchers who believe on linguistic grounds, for example, that a substrate amongst the peoples of Britain and Ireland may have come from the Middle East. Others see the probability that the "Barbarian" invaders of Europe at least in part emerged from Scythia and may have had "Semitic" origins. Someone else in effect says that the Scythians worshipped Joseph and considered him their ancestor. Another proves that the Scythians first emerged from the Middle East and so on. When one takes all of these and similar opinions into consideration and sorts out available findings the obvious conclusion should be that put forward in this present work.

Some authorities have made attempts of their own in other directions to open up new vistas of information. Immanuel Velikovsky wrote a series of works attempting to revise Ancient Chronology. He claimed that this planet had been the recipient of frequent Catastrophes caused by cosmic collisions. As a result of these planetary disturbances whole life forms had been wiped out and human civilizations several times disrupted. Whatever Science ultimately makes of Velikovsky's overall views, some of his ideas have already been proven correct and others have been contested and seem doubtful. Either way, his books provide a wealth of information and proofs concerning such matters as the lack of acceptable evidence to justify the Theory of Evolution and raising serious questions in regard to scientific dating and historical reconstruction. His revision of ancient chronology has not been accepted but the points he raised and others along the same lines have led to more modest (though significant) proposals receiving a hearing.

Martin Bernal ("Black Athena. The Afro-Asiatic Roots of Classical Civilisation", volume 1, London 1987) and other scholars have recently revived an old school of thought claiming that Classical Greek Civilization was originated and sustained from Egypt and the coastal West Semitic regions. Bernal devotes much of his first volume to demonstrating how historians discarded this notion-in the past due to unconscious as well as conscious ideologically motivated prejudice against the East and against Jews. Preconceived notions automatically adopted as axiomatic facts led otherwise great scholars to make serious errors of judgment. The point is that what one sees is sometimes determined by what one expects to find and that what is viewed may not be taken cognizance of until drawn consciously to the attention of the viewer.

467

It is worthwhile making a quotation from Alfred North Whitehead that Velikovsky used in connection to his own work but we will apply it perhaps to our own present one:

"If you have had your attention directed to the novelties of thought in your own lifetime, you will have observed that almost all new ideas have a certain aspect of foolishness when they are first produced"[9].

"The Tribes" has broken new ground in an old field and therefore has something of a pioneering character with all its strengths and weaknesses. We hope that the truth of our claims will be owned up to despite whatever faults this book may otherwise have.

ISRAELITE HERITAGE
AND RACIALISM

The Almighty created all mankind and everyone has free will to do right or wrong within the limitations imposed upon him by his surroundings and circumstance. Every person ideally should endeavor to do the best he can as well as he can with what he has which includes his inherited traits as well as his acquired ones. What applies to individuals is even more applicable to groups of common ancestry in which the communal effort re-enforces and empowers all of its members. In the same way as propensities for music and the like are often inherited so too are tribal traits for better or for worse. This does not mean that any group has the right to feel itself racially or otherwise somehow "superior" to any other or to be prejudiced against those who are not family members. By the individual and his group or sub-tribe understanding to what Tribal unit within the overall Israelite framework they belong or are attached to so will they be enabled to consciously contribute in the desired direction.

On the International level, this is a changing world, in which the same or similar forces and alignments periodically re-appear. It would help all concerned to be conscious of their ultimate familial connections as indicated in the BIBLE and what their interests should therefore be. More specifically, the Western peoples should know that the Jewish hold upon all of the Land of Israel is most desirable from the viewpoint of Scripture and is for the good of everybody. Also that as Israelites all Tribal members (especially those pertaining to the northern group headed by JOSEPH) have an obligation (beyond the duty incumbent on every human being) to do right and to regulate the affairs of humanity in a positive direction. It would pay us all to read the Bible more frequently and to strive for a deeper understanding.

CONCLUSION

The Lost Ten Tribes according to Prophecy were to be found in the Isles of the Sea, on the coastlands of the earth, at the ends of the world or geographical extremities measured from the Land of Israel, they were to be in "many waters", a "Brit-am", a confederation of nations, in the "north country", a sea-faring people, connected with Tarshish, meaning the Atlantic Ocean expanse, they were to have colonies overseas and were destined to return from the ends of the earth amongst which the "Land of Sinim", meaning Australia, was to be included. "Kings of nations" or hereditary monarchs were to be found amongst them. The above criteria were all fulfilled in certain European nations including Britain, along with North America, Australia, New Zealand and South Africa. The relevant West European nations such as France, Holland, Belgium, Denmark, Norway, Switzerland, Sweden, and Finland have certain values in common, their national psychologies are not so different from each other and when compared with the rest of the world some degree of common ancestry amongst these peoples seems plausible. The nations identified by the present book as being those of the Northern Hebrews are the only ones in the world apart from the Jews who have seriously worked for the betterment of mankind and for the principles of human dignity. It may be said that great men have arisen out of many nations and good decent individuals are to be found everywhere. This is true BUT only in the said Israelite peoples has the striving for good and justice managed to take a genuine national collective expression over recognizably significant periods of time in which positive results out-weighed negative ones. In most of these Israelite nations the most fruitful periods of their history, from an ideological point of view, were those in which the Hebrew Bible (i.e. the "Old Testament") was learnt and respected by very many families.

Historically the Assyrians had exiled the Northern Israelites from the Land of Israel. The Israelites become part of the Scythian Cimmerian and Gothic hosts and ultimately settled in Western Europe and the British Isles. To some extent specific Hebrew Tribes and even Tribal Clans are identifiable with historical groups who settled in the Northwest European area. Thus, the historical account is compatible with Biblical Prophecy and both conform to the cultural and ethnic reality of the world today. It should be emphasized that exactly what percentage of Israelite blood is actually present in the racial heritage of the said peoples today is unknown BUT IT WOULD APPEAR TO BE SIGNIFICANT! In addition, it also would seem certain that wherever else members of the Lost Ten Tribes of Israel may be, the overwhelming majority of them are to be found within these nations. The purpose of this book was to indicate sources of evidence proving the above points and to provide an over all framework for the stated case. This task has been (at least partly) achieved. What the practical conclusions will be remains to be seen. What the conclusions SHOULD BE is a theme for other works, though the prophet Ezekiel did foresee (Ezekiel 37:16-28) *"Judah, and. the children of Israel his companions"* being re-united with Joseph (represented by the stick of Ephraim) and *"ALL the house of Israel his companions"*.

[The Preacher (Ecclesiastes) 12:13-14] LET US HEAR THE CONCLUSION OF THE WHOLE MATTER: FEAR GOD, AND KEEP HIS COMMANDMENTS: FOR THIS IS THE WHOLE DUTY OF MAN. FOR GOD SHALL BRING EVERY WORK INTO JUDGMENT, WITH EVERY SECRET THING, WHETHER IT BE GOOD, OR WHETHER IT BE EVIL.

BRIT-AM LIST OF BIBLICAL PROOFS

[A group of peoples must be located that fit ALL of the criteria]

A. GEOGRAPHY

1. Ends of the Earth: Isaiah 24:16, 26:15, 41:8-9 43:6 49:6
2. Isles Isaiah 24:15 49:6 60:9 Jeremiah 31: 9-10
3. Thighs, Peninsulas, and Coasts: Jeremiah 31:8
4. Tarshish (Atlantic Ocean Area) Isaiah 60:9
5. Western Location: Isaiah 24:14, Hosea 1:10
6. Located to the Northwest of the Land of Israel: Isaiah 49:12
7. In the "North" Land: Jeremiah 3:18 31: 6-10
8. Australia ("Land of Sinim" Computer Codes) Isaiah 49:8
9. Best Places (Atziliyah) Isaiah 41: 9
10. Fires in the Isles referring to Celtic Britain Isaiah 24:15
11: Zarephath, meaning France and Britain, Obadiah 1:20
12. Dolmens showing Pathway of Migration Jeremiah 31:21
13. Many Waters (Several Oceans) Numbers 24:7

B. RECOGNIZABLE SYMBOLS

14. Bald-Headed Eagle (symbol of USA) Micah 1:16
15. Lion and Unicorn (Symbol of Britain) Numbers 24:7-9

C. HISTORICAL BEHAVIOR

16. Cyrus: Messiah son of Joseph (see "Joseph") Isaiah 44:28
17. Rule Over OTHER Peoples: Genesis 27:29 48:19 "A MULTITUDE OF NATIONS" (Hebrew: "Malo HaGoyim" i.e. Complete the Peoples, Onkelos: = Rule over the nations), Psalms 47:3
18. Brit-Am Isaiah 42:6 49:8 Covenant of the People
19. Seafarers Isaiah 42:10
20. Be the Dominant World Power Numbers 24:7-9 Micah 5:7-9
21. Military Power: Deuteronomy 33:27 33:29 Jer. 51:20-21

22. The "police-man" (battle-ax) of the Almighty Zechariah 10:7

23. Defeat Edom (Germany and Europe) Ez. 25:14 Obad. 1:18

24. Light for the Gentiles Genesis 12:2-3, 18:18-19, 22:18 24:4 Isaiah 42:1 42:6 Amos 6:15

25: Alcoholic Drunkards Isaiah 28:1, 3

D. SITUATION

14. Separate from Judah: Isaiah 11:12-13 49:21

15. Not known to Judah: Isaiah 49:13-14, 21. Hosea 1:7

16. Christianity: Hosea 2:8, 2:13, 2:16 11:12 Jeremiah 31:6

17. Gomer: Linkage with European nations: Hosea chapter one

E. BLESSINGS

18. Numerous: Genesis 15:5, 22:17, 24:60, 32:12, Numbers 23:10, Isaiah 10:22, 24:16, 26:15 Hos.1:10

19. Agricultural Plenty: Gen 27:28 49:25 Deut 33:13-16 Hoshea 2:8

20. Mineral Resources Genesis 49:25 Deuteronomy 33:13, 15

21. GATE(s) OF YOUR ENEMIES (International Strategic Points) Genesis 22:17 24:60

22, 23, 24. Cush (India), Egypt, Chains in Slaves from Africa to be taken overseas to homeland: Isa. 44:28 also Isa 43:3 45:14

25. Ruled by Sons of David Jeremiah 33:22, 26

26. Headed by Kings Genesis 17:6, 16, 35:11

G. ANCESTRAL NAMES IN GENERAL

27. The name Hebrew (Western Celts were "Iberi"): Genesis 14:13 39:17 40:15 1:12 43:32 Jonah 1:9

28. Isaac: (Genesis 21:12 48:16). Scythians, Zohak, Ishkuza, Sacasson, Saxon.

29. Jacob: Isaiah 49:6 Tribes of Jacob: Union Jack, Yankee,

30. John "Bull (nickname for Britain): Deut 33:17 Jeremiah 31:18 "Aegel" (Angle) was a nickname for Ephraim

31-101. Seventy Tribal and Clan Names still used

H. NATIONAL CHARACTERISTICS

102. Nobility Principle associated with Ephraim (UK) Jer. 31:20

103. Representative Democracy associated with Manasseh (USA) Genesis 41:51

104. The name "America" from Machir firstborn of Manasseh. USA the major Capitalist nation and "Machir" denotes Principle of Sale.

105. Zebulon on the shores of the Sea (Gen 49:13) Sabulingoi (People of Zebulon) in Holland who do literally dwell on the sea-shores.

106. Numerous Other Proofs in Scritpure and Related Sources.

Ending

CONCLUDING WORDS

How This Book Came To Be Written

The family of the author, for some generations, had demonstrated an interest in the notion that the British (or at least part of them) were descended from the LOST TEN TRIBES OF ISRAEL. The author, at an early age (in Australia) came across literature concerning the Lost Israelites and their West European identity. Later, additional works in this subject were obtained. It should be mentioned that the said writings were of varying standard and outlook and definitely were not homogeneous in their approach, or in their reliability. An attempt was made to independently establish the veracity (or lack of it) of the general idea but no conclusive results were then obtained and the whole subject was dropped and more or less forgotten.

Eventually, the author moved to Israel and immersed himself in his own concerns as well as in Judaic studies. Certain passages in Rabbinical sources (such as Rashi's Commentary on the Book of Obadiah, Nachmanides "Book of Redemption", etc.), together with the simple sense of the Hebrew Bible, features of contemporary events, and other factors caused an arousal in the author for the NEED TO ANSWER THE BRITISH ISRAELITE IDENTITY QUESTION, ONE WAY OR THE OTHER. At the same time, circumstances of a private nature enabled the dedication of considerable time and energy needed to conduct the necessary research, most of which was done in the National Library in Jerusalem. Hundreds, if not thousands, of works dealing with topics pertinent to the question were perused. The conclusions reached are revealed in completed manuscripts (one of which has become the present volume) as well as in much material which, hopefully, will be made available in future works. –In addition we have published the books *Ephraim. The Gentile Children of Israel* by Yair Davidy (Jerusalem, Israel, 1995, Yair Davidi 2001) and *Lost Israelite Identity. The Hebrew Ancestry of Celtic races* by Yair Davidy, 1996; *Joseph. The Israelite Destiny of America* by Yair Davidi 2001; *Biblical Truth. The Lost Ten tribes of Israel in the West According to the Book of Genesis* by Yair Davidiy 2002; and *Origin. You Too Are From Israel. You Too Are the People* by Yair Davidiy 2002. These works deal with additional aspects of this same subject and bring more proofs and discussion. There also were published articles of great interest and invaluable information in the magazine *Tribesman* and its successor *Brit-Am Truth*.

Sources For "The Tribes"

Biblical Commentators for some time have realized that Family and Clan denominations in the Bible represented historical entities frequently recalled in place names within the Land of Israel and sometimes also in the countries surrounding it. Parallels between familial alignments of the Patriarchs and the Wandering Israelites and between latter Settlement patterns had been noticed. It is only logical that after re-settlement in the places of exile these same patterns may have repeated themselves. A wealth of information had already proven (in the author's mind) the exiled Israelites to have become identifiable as, or with, the Cimmerians, Scyths, and Goths, and these had become ancestors to many amongst the present day Northwest European peoples and their overseas kin. Other researchers had already made observations each in his own field which taken together prepared the way for the relevant investigation. Charles FORSTER, "The Monuments, with a New Key For the Recovery of the Lost Tribes," London 1859, identified Israelite

Tribes (such as Manasseh) in the East Scythian region by comparing Jewish traditions concerning the LOST ISRAELITES with the Maps of Ptolemy. The Cambridge Ancient History in one passage was understood to confirm ethnic connections by comparing the names of Tribes on Ptolemy's Maps of two different areas. Colonel J. GARNIER, "The Ten Tribes From The Captivity Until Now", London, quoted Camden, who in turn quoted Cissner, that the Scythian tribes, after they came to Europe, retained the same vicinity (or relative position) they formerly held in Asia. This indicated a possibility that was checked and found to be applicable throughout history. In the case of the Lost Tribes of Israel the principal held right back to Biblical times. P. SENSTIUS "Die Stamme der Israeliten und Germanen," 1931, Leipzig, identified Israelite Tribal clans with Tribes of the "Germanic" nations (or rather of the "Barbaric" nations who invaded Europe from Scythia via Germany) and many of his equations, after examination were found to be acceptable sometimes for different reasons than the ones he gave. Senstius identified Israelite clans with "Germanic" Tribes whom he considered to be ancestors to the German Nation Historically, most of the said Tribes whose identification WAS ACCEPTED BY US did not remain in Germany but moved out. Those Israelites who did stay in Germany later emigrated en masse to the USA and elsewhere. This migration was a specific one entailing whole religious groups, social classes, villages, and even localities with the adjacent neighborhoods and groups remaining almost untouched -as expanded upon in *Joseph. The Israelite Destiny of America* by Yair Davidi 2001.

It remained to continue research concerning the Scythian, German, and West European tribes. It was necessary to affirm the Israelite identity of individual groups. Israelite Tribes and Tribal Clans in the Land of Israel were traced, after exile to Mesopotamia, Iran, and Scythia. The path led from there to Central Europe and thence to the north and west. Once most of the work had been done the co-relations were seen to be obvious and formed part of a pattern working to set rules with almost scientific predictability. Since the publication of the First Edition of **"The Tribes"** new information has been constantly coming to light and so far all of it has tended to confirm the conclusions arrived at. This is as it should be. Some ideas have had to be slightly revised but the over-all trend has been to strengthen and further clarify previous conclusions.

Edmund Burke: "The only thing necessary for the triumph of evil is for good men to do nothing."

Arthur Schopenhauer, "All truth passes through three stages: First it is ridiculed.

Second, it is violently opposed.

Third, it is accepted as being self-evident."

Acknowledgements

A lot of people helped us produce this work. There were those who assisted us financially. Others gave us spiritual and moral support and comradely encouragement. There is no point in listing all those who helped us since that would imply that the assistance of those listed was more important than that of those not mentioned and this is not necessarily the case.

Nevertheless we would like to especially thank Eddy Chumney, Rabbi Bret Oxman, Rabbi Avraham Feld, Israel Feld, Yosef Dayan, Colbert Bryan, Betty Mattheson Rhodes, Chaim Hyman, Shmuel Ben-Yaacov, Clifford Smyth, Oriel Davidiy, and numerous others including all those subscribed to the Brit-Am e-mail list whose friendship, opinions, and knowledgeable input help vitalise the whole Brit-Am movement. Brit-Am is an organization open to all whose aim is to encourage research and awareness into the Israelite origins of many Western Peoples and also to work towards an Ultimate Reconciliation between Judah and Joseph. If you are interested please contact us at:
Yair Davidiy, Brit-Am, POB 595, Jerusalem 91004, Israel
britam@netvison.net.il
http://www.britam.org

References to

"The Tribes"

Prologue: References

1. LUCKENBILL "Annals of Sennacherib" (p.126) quotes from an inscription of the Assyrian king; see also 2-Kings 18:13, and Midrash Seder Olam. 2. Concerning the completeness of the exile of the Northern Kingdom of Israel (Samaria) see: Kathleen KENYON, "Royal Cities of the Old Testament", London, 1971. Nadav NA'AMAN, "Population Changes in Palestine Following Assyrian Deportation" (Hebrew) in Cathedra, Jerusalem, no.54, December 1989. Sources quoted by Na'aman include: V. Fritz, "Kinnerat, Vorbericht uber die Auegraben auf dem Tell el Oremeem, see Genesaret in den Jahren" 1982 1985 ZDPV, 102. W.G. DEVER "Abel-Beth Ma'acah: North Gateway of Ancient Israel", in L.T. Geraty & L.G. Herr (eds.) "The Archaeology of Jordan and Other Studies", Barrier Springs USA 1986, pp.215-221. Bustenay ODED, "Mass Deportations and Deportees in the Neo-Assyrian Empire," Weisbaden, Germany, 1979, p.22 tries to maintain that very few Israelites were actually exiled. His evidence, however, consists in substance of one or two Hebrew inscriptions of doubtful date which MAY (**or may not**) belong to the

period after the Israelite exile to Assyria. This paucity of remains even tentatively ascribable to northern Israelites after 720 BCE actually proves the completeness of exile.

2. The Midrash Yalkut Shimeoni on 2-Kings 18; 236, indicates that one eighth (i.e. 12%) of the Northern Israelites were not taken into exile by the Assyrians. Another Midrashic source (Eliyahu Zuta 2; 1) says that some of the Israelites who were not exiled intermarried with the Samaritans. M. BROSHI is quoted in BIBLICAL ARCHAEOLOGOICAL REVIEW vol.1, no.3 1975, p.22ff, as stating that about the time of the Assyrian invasions the area of Jerusalem was suddenly increased, indicating that refugees from the north fled to the south. These survivors, however, must HAVE ACCOUNTED ONLY FOR A VERY SMALL PORTION OF THE TOTAL. NACHMANIDES (Ramban) in the Book of Redemption (Safer HaGeulah) quotes a Midrash to the effect that about 20% of the Israelites who returned with Ezra were from tribes OTHER THAN Judah, Benjamin, and Levi.

3. Isaac E. Mozeson, "The Word," New York 1989, p.13 "Aberration".

4. Eva FOGELMAN, "Consience and Courage. Rescuers of Jews During the Holocaust", chapter 15, NY, 1994.

5. A.J.P. TAYLOR, "English History 1914-1945", Oxford 1965, p.420 quoted by B. WASSERSTEIN, "Britain and the Jews of Europe 1939-1945" ch.1, n.7. Taylor is one of the few British historians who was once somewhat sympathetic or "objective" towards Germany. In this case, concerning British public opinion, he is unlikely to have been mistaken.

6. See for instance Arthur D. MORSE, "While 6 Million Died. A Chronicle of American Apathy" by 1967, 1968. see also David S. WYMAN, "The Abandonment of the Jews" by 1985. For a contrary opinion consider the following from William D. RUBINSTEIN, "The Myth of Rescue: Why the Democracies Could Not Have Saved More Jews From The Nazis", 1997, p. x:
"The argument of *The Myth of Rescue* is that no Jew who perished during the Nazi Holocaust could have been saved by any action which the Nazis could have taken at the time, given what was actually known about the Holocaust, what was *actually proposed* at the time and what was realistically possible. If there are any exceptions at all to this statement, their numbers

may be measured in the dozens or hundreds rather than some higher figure. *All* of the many studies which criticize the Allies (and the Jewish communities of the democracies) for having failed to rescue Jews during the holocaust are inaccurate and misleading, their arguments illogical and ahistorical." Rubinstein points out that the Nazis were implacably determined to destroy the Jews and nothing much could have been done to stop them. Rubinstein has a point of view that should be considered along with the other factors. On some points he may be mistaken but on the whole he appears to be historically correct. The depth of the German and East European determination to wipe out the Jewish race is not sufficiently realized. Some of the claimed possibilities for saving Jews were in practice non-existent. Bombing the concentration camps if it had have been possible and if it had have been done may have even speeded up the extermination process!

-cf. Robert PAYNE, "The Life & Death of Adolf Hitler", USA, 1973, p.470: "One day in 1942 Hitler told Himmler that it was not enough for the Jews simply to die; they must die in agony. What was the best way to prolong their agony? Himmler turned the problem over to his advisors who concluded that a slow, agonizing death could be brought about by placing Jewish prisoners in freight cars with dehydrated calcium oxide - quicklime -, which produced excruciating burns. The advisors estimated that it would take four days for the prisoners to die, and for that time the freight cars could be left standing on some forgotten siding. It was not necessary to send people to the extermination camps: the freight cars were all that was needed. Finally, it was decided that the freight cars should be used in addition to the extermination camps".

Albert SPEER, "Inside the Third Reich", New York, 1971, p.391:

"Yet hatred of the Jews was Hitler's central conviction: sometimes it even seems to me that everything else was merely camouflage for this real motivating factor...Hitler was even prepared to risk his plans of conquest for the sake of that mania for extermination...I can still recall the astonishment with which I read the final sentence of his testament. In the midst of an apocalyptic doom it attempted to commit us all to a miserable hatred of the Jews."

7. Ralph GIORDANO, "Wenn Hitler den Krieg gewonten hatte", 1988, (quotes from official Nazi German documents as sources Schumann/Hass); Hamburg. Leon POLIAKOV, "History of Anti-Semitism", volume 2.

8. For examples of British concern for the "natives" at the expense of their own people see C.E. CARRINGTON "The British Overseas", Cambridge UK, 1950, throughout.

9. Christopher SYKES, "Orde Wingate," 1959, UK, p.117 quotes from Morris Marguiles, "The American Zionist".

10. Ephraim KARSH, "Fabricating Israeli History. The 'New Historians'", USA, 1997.

11. Connor Cruise O'BRIEN, "The Siege. The Saga of Israel and Zionism", USA, 1986, p.306

Chapter One: References

1. Plutarch on Marius; Diodorus Siculus (32;4-7); Strabo (7), Stephen Byzantius. Homer locates the Cimmerians in Britain as does a Greek poem ascribed to Orpheus (ca.500 BCE).

2. W.E. FILMER, "Our Scythian Ancestors," an undated yet impressive eight page pamphlet printed in Kent, UK. Reprinted in the magazine "Brit-Am Truth" no.8, CAH 3 (Cambridge Ancient History volume 3, "The Assyrian Empire". Edited by Bury, Cook, and Adcock. Cambridge 1954) p.182, CHI ("The Cambridge History of Iran", volume 2. "The Median and Achaemenian Periods" Edited by Ilya Gershevitch. UK 1968) p.97

3. Askold I. IVANTCHIK, "Les Cimmeriens au Proche-Orient", Switzerland, 1993. W.E. FILMER (ibid), CAH-3 (ibid) p.53

4. CHI (ibid) p.97

5. Ernest E. HERZFELD, from Posthumous Papers edited by G. Walser, "The Persian Empire. Studies in Geography and Ethnography of the Ancient Near East," Wiesbaden 1968, p.327. M.A. DANDAMAYEB, "Data of the Babylonian Documents From the Sixth Centuries to the Fifth Centuries B.C. on the Sakas", in J. HARMATTA, editor of "Prolegomena. In the Sources

on the History of Pre-Islamic Asia," Budapest 1979, p.96.

6. See "Lost Israelite Identity" by Yair DAVIDY (1996) Appendix One to Section One, p.95 ff., for full details and explanation of the term Amuru, see IVANTCHIK (ibid).

7. Richard N. FRYE, "The Heritage of Persia," USA 1963, p.95.

8. CHI (ibid) vol.2 p.102.

9. Herodotus 1;103-104.

10. T. SULIMERSKI, "Scythian Antiquities in Western Asia. The Appearance of the Assyrians", in "Artibus Asiae vol. xvii, Ascona, vol. 17, Switzerland 1954, p.282 ff.

11. CAH 3 p.293.

12. Encyclopedia Judaica, "Josiah".

13. Avi YONAH (ibid)

14. CAH-3 p.145, p.295.

15. Allen H. GODBEY, "The Lost Tribes a Myth. Suggestions Towards Rewriting Hebrew History," USA, 1930, pp.108-109.

16. Franz ALTHEIM, "Alexander Und Asien", Germany 1953, p.13, Mary BOYCE, "A History of Zoroastrianism" Leiden/Koln, 1975, p.195.

17. Josef HOROVITZ, "Hebrew Iranian Synchronism," Bombay 1931, p.12ff.

18. Gherardo GNOLLI, "Zoroaster's Time and Homeland. A Study on the Origins of Mazdaism," Naples, Italy 1980, p.96.

19. HOROWITZ (ibid) p.12ff.

20. Encyclopedia Brittanica, 1966, "Assyria and Babylonia".

21. Encyclopedia Brittanica, 1966, "Assyria and Babylonia". G. RAWLINSON (on HERODOTUS) vol.4, p.414, Diodorus Siculus 2;24-26.

22. See "Lost israelite Identity" by Yair Davidy, 1996, 84-86. See also M. ROSTOVTZEFF, "The Animal Style in South Russia and China," New York 1973. M. ROSTOVTZEFF, "Iranians and Greeks in South Russia," Oxford 1922. Maurits Nanning VAN LOON, "Urartian Art. Its Distinctive Traits in the Light of New Excavations", Istanbul, 1966.

23. Amos HOCHAM, "Sefer Yishayahu" (The Book of Isaiah) vol.1, Jerusalem 1984, pp.7, 10.

24. Adolphe NEUBAUER, "La Géographie De Talmud," Paris 1868. Adolph REINACH, "Noe Sangariou. Etude

Sur le Deluge en Phrygie et le Syncretisme Judeo-Phrygien," Paris 1913.
25. Bustenay ODED, "Mass Deportations and Deportees in the Neo-Assyrian Empire," Weisbaden, Germany 1979, p.52 ff., Moshe ELAT, "Economic Relations in the Lands of the Bible ca. 1000-539 b.c." (Hebrew), Jerusalem, Israel 1977, p.8
26. Encyclopedia Biblica, "Mesopotamia"
27. ODED (ibid) p.52 ff.
28. Stephanie DALLEY, "Foreign Chariotry and Cavalry in the armies of Tiglathpileser-iii and Sargon-ii", Iraq, vol.xlvii, 1985, UK, p.31
29. DALLEY (ibid) p.31
30. R.D. BARNETT "The Siege of Lachish", Israel Exploration Journal [IEJ], vol.8 Jerusalem, Israel, 1958. For more details and discussion of these matters see "Lost Israelite Identity" by Yair DAVIDY (1996) chapter two.

Chapter Two: References

1. "LEMPRIERE'S Classical Dictionary," 1788 (Reprinted 1984 London), "Sacae".
2. H. M. CHADWICK "The Origin of the English Nation" Cambridge 1924, p.256.
3. G. RAWLINSON: The History of Herodotus (ca.430 BCE) translated and Annotated by G. Rawlinson, London 1858, vol.3 p.219 (Herodotus).
4. Pliny 37;11, J. SVENNUNG, "Scandinavia und Scandia," Lund 1963p.66.
5. Kaspar ZEUSS, "Die Deutschen und Die Nachbarstamme," Germany 1835, Heidelberg 1925, p.157.
6. M. MALLET, "Northern Antiquities of the Ancient Scandinavians," translated by Bishop Percy, London 1882.
7. B. Philip LOZINSKY, "The Original Homeland of the Parthians,", 1953, The Hague, Netherlands, p.26.
8. W. Montgomery MCGOVERN, "The Early Empires of Central Asia", USA 1939, p.94.
9. ibid.
10. James H. GAUL "Observations of the Bronze Age in the Yenissei Valley, Siberia," Studies in the Anthropology of Oceania and Asia, USA in honour of R.B. DIXON, 1943, p.179.
11. B. BRUGSCH, "Brugsch's Egypt Under the Pharoahs", trans. by P. Smith. London 1881, vol.1 p.269, p.354.

12. ibid
13. Alessandra NIBBI, "Canaan and Canaanite in Ancient Egypt," by, 1989, UK. See the article in *Tribesman*, issue no.3, 1999.
14. Allen H. GODBEY, "The Lost Tribes a Myth. Suggestions Towards Rewriting Hebrew History," USA 1930, p.83. A.H. SAYCE, "The Races of the Old Testament," London 1925, p.74. Jean VERCOUTTER, "L'Egypte et le Monde Egeen Prehellenique," France 1956, p.219. For color illustrations see Nina M. DAVIES, "Ancient Egyptian Paintings" USA 1936, Plate xxiv, Plate xlii.
15. Rabbi Avigdor MILLER, "A Nation is Born", Parshat *Beshelach*, Exodus 15; 27
16. Isaac E. MOZESON, "The Word," New York 1989, p.17 "Albino".
16. Israel HALPERIN, "Atlas Etz Haim", (Hebrew), 1985, vol.2 ;2

Chapter Three: References

1. Hans KUHN, "Grenzen vor und Fruhgeschichtler Ortsnamen," Darmstadt 1963.
2. C.M. WELLS, "The German Policy of Augustus," Oxford 1972 p.16. Rolf HACHMANN, "The Germanic Peoples", trans. J. Hogarth, London 1971, p.71.
3. Malcolm TODD, "The Northern Barbarians," London 1975 p.46.
4. J.B. BURY, "The Invasion of Europe by the Barbarians", New York 1967 p.6, TODD (ibid) p.56,
5. W.E. FILMER, "Our Scythian Ancestors," an eight page pamphlet printed in Kent,United Kingdom, reprinted in the magazine, "Brit-Am Truth", issue no. 8, 2004
6. W. McGOVERN, Montgomery, "The Early Empires of Central Asia," New York, USA 1939, p.247,
7. Bernard S. BACHRACH, "A History of the Alans in the West", USA ,1973 p.59, p.6,
8. The Venerable Bede, Ecclesiastical History, bk.v, ch. ix, T.W. SHORE, "Origins of the Anglo-Saxon Race," London 1906, p.79, p.292.
9. Tacitus, "Germania", 44. Gwyn JONES, "A History of the Vikings," Oxford, New York 1984, p.43. Hans HILDEBRAND, "Scandinavian Art," London, 1883, p.78.
10. E.H. MINNS, "Scythians and Greeks," New York 1965, p.10,
11. Mats PHILIP, "Birka at the Silkroad, 1997, in a detailed article on the Internet, also briefly mentioned by

Kevin Alan BROOK, "The Jews of Kazaria", USA, 1999, p.101.

12. PHILIP (ibid). JONES, Gwyn. "A History of the Vikings," Oxford, New York 1984.
13. Mary GARRISON in "Hen and Innes (eds.) "Uses of the Past in the Early Middle Ages."
14. F.L. BORCHARDT, "German Antiquity in Renaissance Myth", 1971 London and USA
15. D.M. WILSON, "The Anglo Saxons," London, 1960, p.140, M. ROSTOVTZEFF, "The Animal Style in South Russia and China," New York 1973. M. ROSTOVTZEFF, "Iranians and Greeks in South Russia," Oxford 1922. Books on the History of Jewelry, on Anglo-Saxon art, etc.
16. Herwig WOLFRAM, "History of the Goths," Germany 1979, tran. T.J. Dunlop, USA 1988.
17. B. Philip LOZINSKI,. "The Original Homeland of the Parthians," 1953, The Hague, Netherlands.
18. WOLFRAM (ibid) p.11.
19. CAH Cambridge Ancient History vol.2, p.37.
20. Hans Joachim DIESNER, "The Great Migrations", Leipzig 1978, translated by C.S.V. Salt, 1982, London.
21. Palle LAURING, "Land of the Tollund Man," New York 1958, p.101.
22. Wolfram (ibid) p.11.
23. These groups are usually attributed to the former "Gothic kingdoms at the Black Sea" that in effect could encompass most of the Scythian peoples (WOLFRAM note 138), or to the Huns and their allies that also included peoples of Israelite descent. A more detailed explanation of this whole process and additional references will be given in a work in preparation by the present author. Sources quoted in connection with the above include: Berthold SCHMIDT, "Hermunduren –Angel– Warnen- Thueringer-Franken-Sachsen" in Studien zur Sachsenforschung, No. 13, 1999. Bodo ANKE, 'Studien zur Reiternomadischen Kultur' p. 71, p. 131
24. H.M. CHADWICK, "The Origin of the English Nation," Cambridge, 1924, pp.92-93.
25. Lozinski (ibid) quotes from Russian archaeological journals. David A. LAW, "The Ten Lost Tribes of Israel", USA, 1991, p.8 quotes from I.N. Vinikov, "O Yazyke Pis'mennikh Pamyatnikov Iz Nisy (Uzhnoi

Turkmenistan)," Vestik Drenei Istorii, 3 (1954), 113-128.

26. Dr. Kjell ARTUNS, "Runer" (Oslo, Norway, 1994). This work traces the origins of runic-script back to the Middle East, to regions such as Cyprus, Anatolia, and ancient Canaan and Israel.

27. Orjan SVENSSON, "Belinges aldsta kanda rununskrifter", Karlskrona, Sweden, 1998. Orjan SVENSSON, "De Blekinska Runornas Hemligheter", Karlskrona, Sweden, 2001.

28. T. Blodgett, "Tracing the Dispersion", 1994, quotes from Izvestia o Chozarach i Russkich, as quoted and translated by Joseph C. Littke in Utah Genealogical and Historical Magazine, Jan. 1934, pp. 7-8.

Chapter Four. References

1. 2-Kings 17:6.
2. 1-Chronicles 5;26.
3. Talmud Sanhedrin 94a.
4. Talmud Kiddushin 72a, "Ginzak" (Radbaz), Ezra 8;17 "Casiphia".
5. Numbers Rabah (Midrash) 16;15.
6. Amos 4:3: Targum Yehonathan.
7. Numbers Rabah 16;15.
8. Talmud Sanhedrin 94a.
9. Strabo 16;1;1: "Aturia" = Assyria.
10. Ptolemy.
11. James DARMESTETTER, "The Zend Avesta", Oxford, 1895, p.5.
12. W. DRUMMOND, "Origins or Remarks on the Origin of Several Empires, States, and Countries" volumes I, II, 1824 London, p.299.
13. LE STRANGE, "The Geographical Part of the Nuzhat Al Qulub composed by Hamd Mustawfi of Qazwin in 740 (1340)," Translated by G. Le Strange, London 1919, p.212.
14. LE STRANGE (ibid) p.43, Moshe ELAT, "Economic Relations in the Lands of the Bible ca. 1000 539 b.c." (Hebrew), Jerusalem, Israel 1977, p.123.
15. Diodorus Siculus 11;6. G. RAWLINSON, G. Translation and Commentary to the 'History of Herodotus,' 1858, London, vol.4, Essay 1, p.128.
16. Georgina HERRMAN, "Lapis lazuli: The Early Phases of Its Trade", Iraq, vol.30, 1968, pp.21. Richard N. FRYE, "The Heritage of Persia," USA 1963, p.69.

17. Colonel Sir Thomas HOLDICH, "The Gates of India. Being an Historical Narrative", London, 1910, p.126, Le Comte de GOBINEAU. "Histoire Des Perses", Paris 1869, vol.i, p.128.
18. Dr. Hermann BRUNNHOFER, "Iran unt Turan," Leipzig, 1889 p.125, on Rigveda vii; 96;1, Purochottam hal BHARGAVA, "India in the Vedic Age", Lucknow, India, 1956 p.2.
19. M. ROSTOVTZEFF, "The Animal Style in South Russia and China," New York 1973, p.129, HOLDICH (ibid) p.53. Allen H. GODBEY, "The Lost Tribes a Myth. Suggestions Towards Rewriting Hebrew History," Durham, USA 1930, p.320.
20. H.W. BELLEW, "An Inquiry into the Ethnography of Afghanistan" Original edition, London 1891, p.197,
21. BELLEW (ibid) p.128.
22. J.W. MCCRINDLE, "Ancient India as Described by Ptolemy," London 1885, p.156.
23. BELLEW (ibid) p.197.
24. Encyclopedia of Islam vol.1 p.28ff., "Afghanistan".
25. Encyclopedia of Islam vol.1 p.28ff., "Afghanistan". Bellew p.197 ff.
26. BELLEW (ibid) p.197 ff, Arnold FLETCHER, "Afghanistan. Highway of Conquest," London 1965, p.11.
27. W. Montgomery MCGOVERN, "The Early Empires of Central Asia," New York, USA, 1939.
28. Gherardo GNOLI,. "Zoroaster's Time and Homeland. A Study on the Origins of Mazdaism," Naples, Italy 1980.
29. Professor Benoy Kumar SARKAR. "The Positive Background of Hindu Sociology," Allahabad 1914, p.22 ff.
30. SARKAR (ibid) p.22 ff., B. Philip LOZINSKI, "The Original Homeland of the Parthians,". Originally a paper read in Washington 1953. The Hague, Netherlands, p. 2.
31. SARKAR (ibid) p.22 ff.
32. Strabo 16;11, Talmud Kiddushin 72b.
33. Louis David LEVINE, "Contributions to the Historical Geography of the Zagros in the Neo Assyrian Period," Michigan, USA 1969, p.108.
34. LEVINE (ibid) p.108.
35. D.D. LUCKENBILL, "The Annals of Sennacherib," Chicago 1924, 2 ch.4 col.1 s.66.
36. Ptolemy's Map.

37. Xenophon.
38. Encyclopedia Judaica, "Sambation".
39. Jewish Encyclopedia, "Chazars";
40. W. SCHULZE, Wilhelm, "Samstag" in Zeitschrift Fur Zvergleichende Sprachforschungun, vol.xxxiii (1895), p.379 n.1. Sambation: Tanais (=Don).
41. Irma HAYNMAN, "The Syncretic Creed of Hellenized Jews From Tanais (Northern Black Sea Region). "Proceedings of the Eleventh World Congress of Jewish Studies; Division B: The History of the Jewish People; Volume 1, Second Temple Period To Modern Times. Jerusalem 1994, World Union of Jewish Studies.
42. Abraham POLAK, "KAZARIA" ("Chuzaria" Hebrew), Tel Aviv 1951.
43. Talmud, Kiddushin 72b.
44. Encyclopedia Brittanica (1955) "Assyria & Babylon".
45. Zevi KASDOI (Chasdoi), "The Tribes of Jacob and the Preserved of Israel", (Hebrew), Haifa 1928. p.8ff.
46. Adolphe NEUBAUER, "La Geographie De Talmud," Paris 1868, "Ten Tribes".
47. Strabo 11.2.8.
48. CAH 3 p.183. CHI vol.2 p.97.
49. M.A. DANDAMAYEB, "Data of the Babylonian Documents From the Sixth Centuries to the Fifth Centuries B.C. on the Sakas", in J. HARMATTA, editor of "Prolegomena. In the Sources on the History of Pre Islamic Asia," Budapest 1979, p.127.
50. KASDOI (ibid) p.8ff, Eberhard SCHRADER, "The Cuneiform Inscriptions and the Old Testament", London 1888, p.267.
51. Talmud Babli, Kiddushin 72a Radbaz.
52. Franz ALTHEIM, "GDH" "Geschichte Der Hunnen," Berlin 1962, vol.2, p.10ff.
53. Encyclopedia Judaica, "Exile. Assyrian".
54. Kiddushin 72a.
55. DANDAMAYEB, p.101.
56. ST. LANGDON in "Zeitschrift Fur Assyriologie", Berlin and Leipzig 1929, Strasbourg 1909, p.214 ff.
57. St. Langdon (ibid.), Guti and Subartu".
58. Rabbi Aryeh KAPLAN, "The Living Torah. The Five Books of Moses," Translation and Commentary, New York 1981, on Deuteronomy 26:5.
59. A.T. OLMSTEAD, "History of the Persian Empire", USA, 1948, p.245: Jewish mercenaries serving in Egypt in Persian employ referred to as "ARAMI".

Chapter Five: References

1. J.W. McCRINDLE, "Ancient India as Described by Ptolemy," London 1885, p.289: Ptolemy came to his conclusions from data of different sources and different dates. Encyclopedia Britannica (1955): "Ptolemy".
2. B. Philip LOZINSKI,. "The Original Homeland of the Parthians," The Hague, Netherlands, p.26.
3. "What Spake Zarathustra?" by Yair Davidiy
4. Allen H. GODBEY, "The Lost Tribes a Myth. Suggestions towards Rewriting Hebrew History," USA, 1930, p.335, quotes Periplous.
4. W. Montgomery McGOVERN, "The Early Empires of Central Asia," New York, USA 1939, p. 477.
5. Gherardo GNOLI, "Zoroaster's Time and Homeland. A Study on the Origins of Mazdaism," Naples, Italy 1980, p.149. Le Comte DE GOBINEAU, "Histoire Des Perses", Paris 1869, vol. i, p.169.
6. I. BEN-ZVI, "The Exiled and the Redeemed", London 1958, p.67ff.
7. Eldad, story 2 (in Abraham EPSTEIN, "Kadmoniot HaYehudim; Braytot Atikot. Eldad Ha Dani," Jerusalem 1957, note 9.
8. BARTHOLD, "Barthold's Iran," –a translation from the Russian by G.K. Nariman, Bombay, India.
9. H.W. BELLEW, "An Inquiry into the Ethnography of Afghanistan" Original edition, London 1891, p.55.
10. BELLEW (ibid) p.4
11. BELLEW (ibid) p.4, DE GOBINEAU (ibid) vol..i, p.195.
12. DE GOBINEAU vol..i, pp.125, 193
13. Eldad (ibid) story 1.
14. Eldad (ibid) story 5.
15. DE GOBINEAU (ibid).
16. McGOVERN (ibid) p.405.
17. Franz ALTHEIM, ("GDH") "Geschichte Der Hunnen", Berlin, 1962, vol. 2, p.10ff.
18. Amos 4:3 according to the Aramaic in Targum Yehonatan.
19. H.C. RAWLINSON, India and the Western World", UK, 1926, p.36.
20. McGOVERN (ibid) p.406ff. Rene GROUSSET, "The Empire of the Steppes", 1939, USA 1970, p.67. Cambridge Ancient History volume 3 (CAH 3) p.36.
21. D.J. Wiseman in D.W. THOMAS, editor, "Documents from Old Testament Times," New York 1961, p.56.

22. GODBEY (ibid) p.310.
23. James H. GAUL, "Observations of the Bronze Age in the Yenissei Valley, Siberia," Studies in the Anthropology of Oceania and Asia, USA in honour of R.B. Dixon ,1943, p.179.
24. Ortellius "Theatrum Orbis". Map of "Tartaria".
25. Richard N. FRYE, "The Heritage of Persia," USA 1963, p.67.
26. M. MALLET, "Introduction a l'Histoire de Danemarc," Copenhagen 1755, p.6.
27. G. RAWLINSON (on Herodotus) vol.3, p.214 n. A, says that Massegetae stands for Massa (Greater) Goths and that "Thessagetae" stands for Lesser Goths, i.e. the "Little Goths" of Chinese records.
28. McGOVERN (ibid) p.476.
29. GODBEY (ibid) p.17ff.
30. Eldad, story 5 as reported by Epstein (ibid)).
31. LOZINSKI (ibid) p.71.
32. Zevi KASDOI, "The Tribes of Jacob and the Preserved of Israel" (Hebrew), Haifa 1928, p.10. Charles FORSTER, "The Monuments, with a New Key for the Recovery of the Lost Tribes," London 1859, p.308. GODBEY (ibid) p.343.

Chapter Six: References

1. Amos HACHAM on Sefer Yeshayahu ("The Book of Isaiah", in Hebrew, Daat Mikra) 11;11.
2. Samuel BOCHARTUS, (Bochart). "Geographia Sacra; seu Phaleg et Canaan", Frankfort 1681, 1692, ch.5.
3. Herodotus 4; 45.
4. Targum Yerushalemi on Genesis 10;3.
5. Megilla 6b.
6. Genesis Rabah 86; 3.
7. Negaim 2;11, Maimonides on Negaim, Aruch HaShalem "Germani".
8. Talmud, Megilla 6b.
9. Le Comte de GOBINEAU. "Histoire Des Perses", Paris 1869, p.615
10. B. Philip LOZINSKI, "The Original Homeland of the Parthians," 1953, The Hague, Netherlands.
11. Steven M. COLLINS, "Parthia. The Forgotten Ancient Superpower and its Role in Biblical History", USA, 2003, p.17. Steven M. COLLINS, 'The "Lost" Ten Tribes of Israel...Found, USA, 1992, ch.8.
12. Dr. R. PAUL, "The Life of Alfred the Great", UK, 1889, p.333.

Chapter Seven: References

1. Jewish Encyclopedia, "Chazars".
2. Fritz MEZGER, "Angelsachsische Volker und Landernamen," Berlin, 1921, p.12. Mezger brings sources indicating that the Myringas in Europe had been called Skati-Maruka (i.e. Scyths from Maruka, Amyrgioi), and from the Myringas evolved the Mercian Saxons. Myringas were also present amongst the Gothic forces.
3. Bede, Ecclesiastical History bk.v, ch.ix. Recently it has been disputed as to whether Bede really did mean to say that these people had participated in the invasions of Britain or rather that they (in the time of Bede) were in the lands where the invaders had come from. At all events it would seem from the language he used that such was indeed his intention.
4. Ptolemy, T.W. SHORE, "Origins of the Anglo Saxon Race," London, 1906, p.36.
5. Dr. Hermann BRUNNHOFER, "Iran unt Turan," Leipzig, 1889, p.242.
6. Garnier p.60 quotes Sharon Turner v.1, p.130 whose source was the "Vetus Chronicon Holsatae".
7. Rashi, Rashi (Rabbi Shlomoh ben Yitzhak 1040-1105) on Isaiah 27;10 where he also quotes Jeremiah 31:[17]18.
8. F.R. KLAEBER, "Beowulf," USA 1922, p.xlii. Gwyn JONES, "A History of the Vikings," UK, USA, 1984, p.38.
9. NED, "A New English Dictionary on Historical Principles," Oxford 1901. Miles TAYLOR, "John Bull and the Iconography. Public Opinion in England c. 1712-1929 in "Past and Present" no.134, February 1992.
10. J.W. McCRINDLE, "Ancient India as Described by Megasthenes and Arrian," ca. 1885 reprinted in Calcutta, India 1960, p.183, Curtius 1b.viii, cap.10,11. ROOKE, "Translation of 'Arrian's History of Alexander's Expedition'", 1814. Prefix with Mr. Le Clerc's Criticism upon Quintius Curtius, p.xxxvii. Pliny 6;6. Apollonius in Ramesh C. MAJUNDAR, "The Classical Accounts of India," Calcutta, 1960, p.385.
12. Diodorus Siculus 3;66. Homeric Hymns in Dora ASKOWITZ, "The Toleration and Persecution of the Jews in the Roman Empire", New York, 1915, p.79.
13. Michael C. ASTOUR, "Hellenosemitica. An Ethnic And Cultural Study In West Semitic Influences on Mycenean Greece", Leiden 1967, also traces Bachus to the Hebrew "Bacuth".

14. B. Philip LOZINSKI, "The Original Homeland of the Parthians", 1953, Netherlands p.43 ff.
15. LOZINSKI, (ibid) p.15.
16. McCrindle (ibid) p.110, quotes Lassen.
17. McCrindle (ibid).
18. Justin, Book xii;ix.
19. E. BLOCHET, "Les Germaniques Sujets de Darius", in Revue d'Assyriologie Orientals", Tome xxi, Volume no.4, Paris. 1924, p.157ff.
20. I. TARDY, "The Caucasian Peoples and Their Neighbours in 1404", Acta Orientalia 32:1978, p.90
21. BLOCHET (ibid) p. 157ff
22. Victor STARCKE, "Denmark in World History," 1946, trans. 1962, 1968, USA, p.57.
23. J. N. L. MYRES, "The English Settlements" (USA 1986) p.77. Moshe ELAT, "Economic Relations in the Lands of the Bible ca. 1000-539 b.c." (Hebrew), Jerusalem , Israel 1977, p.123 ff.
24. G. RAWLINSON on Herodotus vol.4. Essay 1, p.181. Colonel Sir Thomas HOLDICH, "The Gates of India. Being an Historical Narrative", London, 1910, p. 236, MCCRINDLE (ibid) p.300. Allen H. GODBEY, "The Lost Tribes a Myth. Suggestions Towards Rewriting Hebrew History," USA 1930, p.17.
26. GODBEY (ibid) p.17.
27. GODBEY (ibid) p.17.
28. GODBEY p.343.
29. Charles FORSTER, "The Monuments, with a New Key for the Recovery of the Lost Tribes," London 1859, p.308. Franz ALTHEIM, "Geschichte Der Hunnen" ["GDH"] Berlin 1962, vol.1, p.188 places the Naphtalites in that region.
30. ALTHEIM (ibid).
31. Johanna Engelberta VAN LOHUIZEN de Leeuw, "The 'Scythian' Period," Leiden 1949, p.38.
32. Nachum SLOUSCHZ,. "Ba Eyay Ha Yam," (Hebrew). New York 1919, p.48.
33. Moran in W. F. ALBRIGHT, "The Bible and the Ancient Near East," "Essays in Honour of William Foxwell Albright," edited by G.E. Wright, New York 1961, p.54ff.
34. "Yingling Saga" Snorre.
35. "Yingling Saga" Snorre
36. Bernard S. BACHRACH, "A History of the Alans in the West", USA 1973. W. Montgomery MCGOVERN, "The Early Empires of Central Asia," USA 1939, p.247

Chapter Eight: References

1. Encyclopedia Judaica, "Babiru, "Habiru".
2. Roger GRAND, "Recherches Sur L'Origine Des Francs," Paris 1965, p.410
3. R. GRAND (ibid) p.12.
4. R. GRAND (ibid) p.1.
5. R. GRAND (ibid) p.1, Victor STARCKE, "Denmark in World History," 1946, trans. 1962, 1968 USA., p.83.
6. GRAND (ibid) p.38, F.L. BORCHARDT, "German Antiquity in Renaissance Myth," 1971, London and U.S.A, p.198ff., p.165.
7. H.M. CHADWICK, "The Origin of the English Nation" Cambridge 1924, p.91 n.2
8. GRAND (ibid) p.146.
9. Diodorus Siculus 16; 32 .
10. Ptolemy.
11. Hans Joachim DIESNER,. "The Great Migrations", Leipzig 1978, translated 1982, London, p.135.
12. GRAND (ibid) p.58.
13. GRAND (ibid) p.33.
14. Justin Bk.xii;ix
15. J.W. McCRINDLE, "Ancient India as Described by Megasthenes and Arrian," ca/ 1880s, reprinted Calcutta, India 1960, p.110.
16. Raymond COLE, "The Migrations of Israel", Eugene, Oregon, USA 1980.
17. GRAND (ibid) p.58.
18. R. PRIEBSCH and W.E. COLLINSON, "The German Language," London ca. 1936, p.43.
19. GRAND (ibid) p.38ff., p.58
23. ALTHEIM-1, Franz. ALTHEIM, "GDH". "Geschichte Der Hunnen". Berlin 1962, vol.i p.54 .
24. ORTELLIUS, "Tartaria". A. ANDERSON, "Alexander's Gate, Gog and Magog and the Enclosed Nations" Cambridge, Massachusetts, USA 1932, p.72ff; Dr Adolphe A. NEUBAUER, "Where Are the Ten Tribes Now?" in Jewish Quarterly Review (JQR) no.1, London iii, 1889. Sir John MANDEVILLE, "Travels", 1st printed ca. 1499, London 1903, ch.xxix .
26. BLL. Michael BAIGENT, Richard LEIGH, & Henry LINCOLN. "Hold Blood, Holy Grail", London 1982, N.Y, 1983
27. BLL. (ibid)
28. Song of Songs Rabah 4;7 .
29. BLL (ibid) p.238ff.

30. Leon POLIAKOV, *"The Aryan Myth"*, London 1974, p. 20.
31. Frederic DE ROUGEMONT, "L'Age de Bronze, ou Les Semites en Occident", Paris, 1866.
32. Yair DAVIDIY, "Ephraim" ch.7. Yair DAVIDIY, "Origin" pp.94, 95

Chapter Nine: References

1. Henry RAWLINSON, "Bactria" p.12 quoting Justin, see Steven Collins, ~The "Lost" Ten Tribes Of Israel...Found!~, Oregon, USA, 1995, p.210
2. (ibid)
3. (ibid)
4. GRAETZ, History of the Jews, iii, 40f.
5. J. Huston McCULLOCH: "The Franks Casket, an 8th century Anglo-Saxon Box... My hunch is that Hengist was claimed to be descended...possibly via one of the Judean slave women depicted in the scene...and perhaps the Jutes ...many of the captives from Jerusalem were thrust onto the German border by the Romans as an expendable buffer population, at approximately the right time for such an ancestry. (Horst & Hengist are also claimed by Bede and the Anglo-Saxon Chronicle to be descended, 6 or so generations back, from Wotan (Anglo-Saxon Chronicle) or someone named Wotan (Bede). But one has many ancestors."
6. I. BEN-ZVI, "The Exiled and the Redeemed", London 1958

Chapter Ten: References

1. B. Philip LOZINSKI, "The Original Homeland of the Parthians," 1953, Netherlands.
2. T.W. SHORE, "Origins of the Anglo Saxon Race," London 1906, p.29.
3. Isidore of Seville, "History of the GODOS, Vandals, Sueves".
4. BLOCHET, E. "Les Germaniques Sujets de Darius". in Revue D'Assyriologie Orientals". Tome xxi, Volume no.4, Paris 1924, p.159.
5. Gwyn JONES, "A History of the Vikings," Oxford, New York 1984, p.43.
6. O.M. DALTON, Introduction to "The History of the Franks by Gregory of Tours". volume I, London 1927, p.172.

References to Pages 180-190

7. GRAND Roger, "Recherches Sur L'Origine Des Francs," Paris 1965, p.146, Beowulf v. 2195 "Hugo".
8. SHORE (ibid) p.12.
9. PRIEBSCH, & COLLINSON. R. Priebsch and W.E. Collinson, "The German Language," London ca. 1936, p.43.
10. SHORE (ibid) p.77.
11. Tacitus, "Germania" 35.
12. Kaspar ZEUSS, "Die Deutschen und Die Nachbarstamme," Heidelberg, 1835, 1925. p.59ff, p.28ff.
13. (ibid)
14. Gudmund SHUTTE, "The Problem of the Hraid Goths" in APS, vol. Viii, 1933 34 Copenhagen p.94ff.
15. F.L. BORCHARDT, "German Antiquity in Renaissance Myth", 1971 London and USA p.157.
16. Herwig WOLFRAM,. "History of the Goths," Germany 1979, USA 1988, p.20.
17. Y. KIEL "Sefer Divrei HaYamim", Daat Mikra, Jerusalem, p.2.
18. Ptolemy.
19. JORDANES.
20. (ibid)
21. LA Tour D'AUVERGNE, "Origines Gauloises", Hamburg, 1801 (1796) p. 284
22. I. TARDY, "The Caucasian Peoples and Their Neighbours in 1404", Acta Orientalia 32:1978 p. 90
23. H.M. CHADWICK, "The Origin of the English Nation" Cambridge 1924, p.130.
24. Jones (ibid) p.43, Hans HILDEBRAND,. "Scandinavian Art," London 1883, p.78.
25. Strabo 7;65.
26. Pliny N.H. 6;13.
27. Gherardo GNOLI, "Zoroaster's Time and Homeland. A Study on the Origins of Mazdaism," Naples, Italy 1980, p.113.
28. F.R. KLAEBER, "Beowulf," USA 1922, p.144.
29. Victor STARCKE, "Denmark in World History,". 1946, 1962, 1968 USA p.58.
30. STARCKE (ibid) pp.65-75,
31. STARCKE (ibid) pp.65-75.
32. ZEUSS p.15, SHORE p.197.
33. GIBBON ch.5.
34. SHORE.
35. BENTZION HACOHEN, "Keshet Imri Emet" (Hebrew), Jerusalem 1989. See Ben-Tsion HaCohen's comments

on the letter "DALETH" and on the "HOLEM" sign. The name GAD in Hebrew could be rendered as "Goth" since the sign accounting for the "a" sound (holem) in "Gad" was then rendered as "o". In addition an unaccented "d" was pronounced "like an English "th". Thus Gad = Goth.

36. "VaYechi" Sulam edition s.553-554

Chapter Twelve: References

1. Franz. ALTHEIM, "GDH". "Geschichte Der Hunnen", Berlin 1962, vol. i, ch.2 .
2. (ibid)
3. (ibid)
4. (ibid)
5. G. RAWLINSON, G. Translation and Commentary to the 'History of Herodotus,' 1858 London, vol. 3, p.214. n.4
6. WOLFRAM, Herwig. "History of the Goths," Germany 1979, tran., USA 1988.
7. ALTHEIM, "GDH" (ibid) vol. I p.54ff
8. Encyc. Britt. 1955 "Archaeology. Iron Age", quotes J. L. Myres, Ed. MEYER " Geschichte des Altums", vol. I, p.891
9. CAESAR, "The Gallic Wars" 6;31
10. W. Montgomery MCGOVERN, "The Early Empires of Central Asia," USA, 1939, p.486ff
11. C. S. MONCRIEFF, "Translation of Widsuth,". London 1921 p.124
12. MCGOVERN (ibid)
13. MCGOVERN p.405
14. T.K. DERBY, "A Short History of Norway", London, 1954, p.26
15. DERBY (ibid) p.26 .
16. DERBY (ibid)
17. SAXO GRAMMATICUS. "The First Nine Books of Saxo Grammaticus of the Danish History," Translated, London 1894.
18. DERBY (ibid) p.26
19. B. Philip LOZINSKI, "The Original Homeland of the Parthians," 1953, The Hague, Netherlands, p.33ff.
20. F. de ROUGEMONT. "L'Âge du Bronze," Paris 1866, p.32ff
21. ALTHEIM, "GDH" (bid) vol. 2, p.91
22. Allen H. GODBEY, "The Lost Tribes a Myth. Suggestions towards Rewriting Hebrew History," Durham, USA 1930, p.382

23. M. ROSTOVTZEFF, "The Animal Style in South Russia and China," New York 1973, p.104
24. ROSTOVTZEFF (ibid), p.104
25. Victor STARCKE, "Denmark in World History," 1946, trans. 1962, 1968 USA, p.80ff.
26. (ibid) p.80ff.
27. Kemp MALONE, editor of "WIDSITH", Anglistica (vol. xiii), Copenhagen 1962, p.211 Wrosnan: Vraeson, Wrsy
28. S.G. OLSEN "The Incredible Nordic Origins," 1981, p. 114.
29. (ibid) p.113
30. (ibid) p.110
31. Paul SENSTIUS, "Die Stamme der Israeliten und Germanen," 1931, Leipzig.
32. Nechamah Sarah G. NADBORNY, The Twelve Dimensions of Israel", Jerusalem, 1995.
33. Fishel MAEL, "Sefer Shivtei Israel" (5757) based on a Midrash, p. 327.
34. MAEL (ibid) p.328.

Chapter Thirteen: References

1. Eldad HaDani (story 2) in Epstein p.42. Abraham EPSHTEIN, "Eldad Ha Dani", (Hebrew); Pressburg (Austria Hungary) 1891. Abraham EPSHTEIN, "Kadmoniot HaYehudim; Braytot Atikot. Eldad Ha Dani," Jerusalem 1957.
2. MAZAR, Encyclopedia Biblica, "Yair"
3. Eduard MEYER, "Geschichtes DES Altums", , Stuttgart 1931, 2nd volume p.374 quotes an inscription of king Palamu of Sma'al (Smal) calling himself "King of the DA(NA)NIM. The bracketed letters (NA) apparently do not appear in the original. The Danites (or Danes) were also known as Denau and as Dananu i.e. in Hebrew: "King of the Danes from the Tribe of Dan".
4. Michael C. ASTOUR, "Hellenosemitica. An Ethnic and Cultural Study in West Semitic Study on Mycenean Greece", Leiden 1967, p.8 n.7.
5. Roughly speaking, early Greek history in the formative period has it that native groups known in Greece proper as Pelasgians and as Ionians on the west coast of Anatolia together with the Aeolians (a related group) after the coming of the Danaioi created Mycenean civilization. Mycenean civilization was destroyed and its leaders fled to the north to re establish themselves as Dorians. The Myceneans were

replaced by the Pelopid dynasty from Anatolia and the Achaeans. After the 1100s the Dorians returned and re-established their suzerainty. {For reference sources see Martin BERNAL, "Black Athena", UK, vol. 1 1987, vol.2 1991} The Dorians referred to their action as "the return of the Heraclids" meaning the return of the sons of followers of Hercules. Hercules was a hero of the Danaioi. Hercules is based on the figure of Samson the judge hero of the Tribe of Dan and there exist many similarities between the two figures.

6. Edward TRIPP, "The Meridian Handbook of Classical Mythology", USA, 1970, "Apollo".
7. Yigal YADIN, "And Dan Why Did He Remain In Ships?" Australian Journal of Biblical Archaeology, vol.1, no.1, 1968, p.18.
8. N.K. SANDARS, "The Sea Peoples. Warriors of the Ancient Mediterranean", 1985, London, p.162.
9. SANDARS (ibid) p.162, YADIN (ibid) p.18.
10. SANDARS (ibid) p.162.
11. Allen H. GODBEY., "The Lost Tribes a Myth. Suggestions Towards Rewriting Hebrew History," Durham, USA 1930, p.58, SANDARS (ibid) p.162.
12. Robert. GRAVES, "Greek Myths," London 1958, p.714.
13. Not only do Samson and Sandon sound similar but they also may be understood to have the same meaning. Mopsus was allegedly fathered by Apollo who was a sun god for the Greeks and Samson in pagan eyes could easily have been identified with either Hercules or Apollo or both together. Even in Hebrew the name "Samson" may be interpreted to mean "Strength ("on") of the sun ("samas")", i.e. "Samas-on" = Samson. "Sandon" may be understood to have a similar meaning:
"PAULYS Realencyclopadie der Classischen Altertumswissenschaft," Stuttgart, 1901. "Sandon": 2268;10 Dor San=San Dor=San Don. cf. Astour (ibid) p.91 Dio nysus, p.65, Shandash=Sandon.
14. Othniel MARGALITH, "The Sea Peoples In The Bible" (Hebrew), Tel Aviv, Israel, 1988, p.97.
15. Elitsur (Daat Mikra) on Judges p.161, Radak, Ralbag.
16. Trude & Moshe DOTHAN, "People of the Sea", New York, USA, 1992, p.174.
17. DOTHAN (ibid) p.197.
18. John Linton MYRES,. "Who Were The Greeks?" Berkely, California, USA, 1930, p.119, Immanuel VELIKOVSKY, "Peoples of the Sea", 1977, UK p.56.

19. VELIKOVSKY (ibid) p.56.
20. Ed. MEYER (ibid) p.374.
21. ASTOUR (ibid) (ibid) p.48.
22. H. Jacob KATZENSTEIN, "The History of Tyre", Jerusalem, 1973.
23. John STRANGE, "Caphtor/Keftiu a new investigation", Leiden 1980, p.86.
24. BRUGSCH-BEY, "Brugsch's Egypt Under The Pharoahs", London 1881 v.2 p.403.
25. STRANGE (ibid) p.45.
26. STRANGE p.90, p.96.
27. STRANGE p.112.
28. STRANGE p.33, p.111,
29. GELLING and DAVIDSON. Peter Gelling and H.E. Davidson, "The Chariot of the Sun," London 1969, p.140.
30. J. MARKALE, "Les Celts" (English Translation 1978), 1970 Paris, p.395, J.M. FLOOD, "Ireland: Its Myths and Legends", New York, 1970, ch.2.
31. W.H. POOLE, "Fifty Reasons Why The Anglo Saxons Are Israelites of The Lost Tribes of The House of Israel", London, 18-, p.208 quotes from Villaneuva and the "Four Masters".
32. FLOOD (ibid) ch.2,. The Israelite name "DAN" is also pronounceable as "DAN-A"! Different segments from the one Israelite Tribe tended to converge over the course of time in the same areas. Amongst the peoples who from Scythia migrated to Scandinavia and re-populated it were the Danes who represented another and more substantial segment of the Tribe of DAN.
33. ANNA WILKES, "Ireland: Ur of the Chaldees," London 1873 p.16, cf. Fritz MEZGER, "Angelsachsische Volker und Landernamen," Berlin 1921.
34. Charles SQUIRE, "The Mythology of Ancient Britain And Ireland", London 1909, p.14. POOLE (ibid) p.208. J.M. FLOOD, "Ireland: Its Myths And Legends", New York, 1970, ch.2, J. MARKALE (ibid) p.395.
35. MEZGER (ibid) p.10.
35. Genesis 49:16 - a pair of scales represents "judgement". The name "Dan" means "judge".
36. EPSTEIN- (ibid).
37. Dr. Moritz LEWIN, "Waren die' Zehn Stamme Israels zusuchen?", Frankfort 1901, p.48 .

38. Franz ALTHEIM, "Geschichte der Hunnen", Berlin 1962. W. Montgomery McGOVERN, "The Early Empires of Central Asia,".New York, USA 1939, p.405 .
39. ALTHEIM, GDH. McGOVERN p.405 .
40. Wiseman in D.W. THOMAS, editor. "Documents From Old Testament Times," New York 1961, p.65.
41. CAH-3 Cambridge Ancient History, 1954, vol.3 p.38
42. GODBEY (ibid) p.310
43. J. (Colonel) GARNIER, "The Ten Tribes from The Captivity Until Now", London. p.60 quoting Sharon TURNER vol. I., p.130 who himself quotes the "Vetus Chronicon Holsatiae".

Chapter Fourteen: References

1. Yair DAVIDY, "Ephraim. The Gentile Children of Israel", 2001, chapter 8.
2. Encyclopedia Judaica, "DAN". Numbers Rabah 1;10.
3. Targum Jehonathan on Gen. 49;18, Gen. Rab. 98:14
4. 2-Kings 14:28, 2-Chronicles 3;4, CAH-3. Cambridge Ancient History volume 3, "The Assyrian Empire", Edited by Bury, Cook, and Adcock. Cambridge 1954, p.153ff, Robert William ROGERS, "Cuneiform Parallels to the Old Testament", UK, 1912, p.311
5. Yair DAVIDY, "Lost Israelite Identity", Israel, 1996, p.189 ff, cf. Rabbi Moshe EISEMAN, "Yechezkiel", Artscroll, New York, 1980.
6. CAH-3 (ibid) p.153ff, ROGERS (ibid) p.311
7. J. (Colonel) GARNIER, "The Ten Tribes From The Captivity Until Now", London, p.60 quoting Sharon Turner vo.I., p.130 who himself quotes the "Vetus Chronicon Holsatiae".
8. Kaspar ZEUSS, "Die Deutschen und Die Nachbarstamme," Germany 1835, Heidelberg, Germany 1925, p.146 .
9. ZEUSS (ibid) p.146 .
10. Ernest E. HERZFELD, edited by G. Walser, "The Persian Empire. Studies in Geography and Ethnography of the Ancient Near East," Wiesbaden 1968, p.348 .
11. M. GASTER, translator of "The Chronicles of Jerahmiel, ca. 1100 1150 c.e.," New York 1971, p.183
12. Encycl. Britt. 1967, "Franks" .
13. Encycl. Britt. 1967, "Franks" .
14. MILNER (Oxonian), "Israel's Wanderings,".London 1900, p.11ff quotes from a Professor O'Curry, "The Manner and Customs of the Ancient Irish".

15. Raymond COLE, "The Migrations of Israel", USA 1980, p.44 quotes from William Camden "Tomus Idem et Alter" (1629). Mrs. Winthrop Palmer BOSWELL, "The Roots of Irish Monasticism", USA, 1969.
16. Henri HUBERT, "The Greatness and Decline of the Celts," London 1934, p.197
17. F. de ROUGEMONT, "L'Age du Bronze," Paris 1866, p.371
18. Yair DAVIDY, "Lost Israelite Identity", Israel, 1996, p.349
19. BOSWELL (ibid)
20. W.H. BENNET, "Symbols of Our Celto-Saxon Heritage", London, 1976, p.114
21. BENNET (ibid) p.116

Chapter Fiveteen: References

1. H.M. CHADWICK, "The Origin of the English Nation" Cambridge 1924.
2. Talmud Yebamot 17.

Chapter Sixteen: References

1. Yehudah KIEL, "Sefer Divrei HaYamim", p.11, n.72
2. Jared DIAMOND, "Guns, Germs, and Steel" 1997
3. A. BASCHMAKOFF, "Cinquante Siecles D'Evolution Autour de la Mer Noir", Paris 1937.
4. For additional discussion about the Khazars and more evidence testifying to their Israelite origins see the soon-to-be-published book on the subject by Yair Davidiy.
5. Cambridge Version, Cairo Geniza, published by Schecheter, 1912 see Dr. Menachem ZEHARI, "HaCuzarim" (Hebrew), Jerusalem, 1976.
   Articles in Encyclopedia Brittanica,
   Encyclopedia Judaica,
   Universal Jewish Encyclopedia,
   The Jewish Encyclopedia,
   D.M. DUNLOP, "The History of the Jewish Khazars", USA, 1951.
   Yair DAVIDIY, "The Khazars", Tribesman, issue no.2
6. W.H. POOLE, "Fifty Reasons Why the Anglo Saxons are Israelites of the Lost Tribes of the House of Israel," London 18 ., p.200
7. D'ARBOIS de Jubainville H. [D'A], "Cycle Mythologie Irlandais et le Mythologie Celtique", Paris 1884, p.89ff

8. A.M. KHAZANOV, "The Dawn of Scythian History," Iranica Antiqua, 17, Leiden 1982, p.52.
9. CHI "The Cambridge History of Iran", volume 2. "The Median and Achaemenian Periods" edited by Ilya Gershevitch, UK, 1968, p.482.
10. Widukind quoted in E. FERAL, "La Legende Arthurienne," Paris 1929, p.180
    F.L. BORCHARDT, "German Antiquity in Renaissance Myth", 1971, UK and USA
11. PRIEBSCH & COLLINSON: R. Priebsch and W.E. Collinson, "The German Language," London ca. 1936, p.43
12. Thomas ARNOLD, "BEOWULF". London 1876 p.215, Kemp MALONE, editor of "WIDSITH", Anglistica (vol. xiii), Copenhagen 1962, p.158
13. Douglas HYDE, "A Literary History of Ireland," London 1899,1967, p.46 n.3 quotes from Nennius in the time of Charlemagne and Nennius quoted from older Scottish sources.
    Yair DAVIDY, "Lost Israelite Identity. The Hebrew Ancestry of Celtic Races", Jerusalem, Israel, 1996, part three.
14. Louis HYMAN, "The Jews of Ireland," Jerusalem 1972 p.1 quotes from Eugene O'Curry 1873.

Chapter Nineteen: References

1. M. BANYAI, "The Arab Fringe. An Enquiry Concerning Muşri, Kush, Meluhha and Magan", Germany, 2004.
   Yair DAVIDI, "Lost Israelite Identity", Jerusalem, Israel, 1996
2. E.Z. MELAMED, Tarbitz 5694, 1-Chr. 7;12 cf. 7;15 re Huppim
3. Yehudah KIEL on 1-Chronicles 7; 12 (Benjamin: Huppim and Shuppim) cf 7:15 (Machir supplied Wives for Huppim and Shuppim).
4. Ben Zion LURIA, "Shaul and Benjamin," Jerusalem 1970, in Hebrew
5. Roger GRAND, "Recherches Sur L'Origine Des Francs," Paris 1965, p.171.
6. (ibid)
7. (ibid)
8. Victor STARCKE, "Denmark in World History," 1946, trans. USA, 1962, 1968, p.222
9. Gwyn JONES, "A History of the Vikings," 1984, p.230

10. Elton on SAXO GRAMMATICUS, "The First Nine Books of Saxo Grammaticus of the Danish History," London 1894, p.xcviii, p.9
11. Michael Haslock KIRKBY, "The Vikings," USA 1977, p.103
12. Bernard S. BACHRACH, "A History of the Alans in the West". Minneapolis, USA 1973.
13. Gustav FABER, "Piraten oder Staatengrunder. Normannen bis zum Bosporus", Germany 1968, p.9
14. L.G. PINE, "They Came With the Conqueror," UK 1954, p.27
15. Yair DAVIDI, "Ephraim. The Gentile Children of Israel", 2001, ch. 8
16. Cecil ROTH, "Personalities and Events in Jewish History," USA 1953, p.46
17. Radak (Rabbi David Kimchi 1160-1235 CE) on Judges 20:15
18. Ginzberg's Jewish Legends on Judges 20:15
19. "LEMPRIERE'S Classical Dictionary," 1788, 1984 London
20. J.C. DRAGAN, "We, the Thracians", Milano, Italy 1976, p.3
21. BAIGENT, LEIGH, & LINCOLN, "The Messianic Legacy", 1986, 1987,
22. Adolf SCHULTEN, "Tartessos", Hamburg 1950 p.492.

Chapter Twenty: References

1. Hans Joachim DIESNER, "The Great Migrations", Leipzig 1978, translated 1982, London p.123.
2. H.M. CHADWICK, "The Origin of the English Nation" UK, 1924, p.206. Ptolemy
3. Nahum SLOUSCHZ, "Ba Eyay Ha Yam," (Hebrew), New York 1919 p.48.
4. Moran in William Foxwell ALBRIGHT, "The Bible and the Ancient Near East," "Essays in Honour of William Foxwell Albright," edited by G.E. Wright. New York 1961 p.54ff.
5. Kaspar ZEUSS, "Die Deutschen und Die Nachbarstamme," 1835, Heidelberg, 1925 p.48, E.O.G. TURVILLE-PETRIE, "Myth and Religion of the North. The Religion of Ancient Scandinavia," London 1964, p.190.
6. PROCOPIUS GIBBON, "The Decline and Fall of the Roman Empire", ch.5: "A STRIKING RESEMBLANCE OF MANNERS, COMPLEXION, RELIGION, AND LANGUAGE SEEMED TO INDICATE THAT THE VANDALS AND GOTHS

WERE ORIGINALLY ONE GREAT PEOPLE. The latter appear to have been divided into Ostrogoths, Visigoths, and Gepidae. The distinction among the Vandals was more strongly marked by the independent names of Heruli, Burgundians, Lombards, and a variety of petty states, many of which, in a future age, expanded themselves into powerful monarchies".

7. GIBBON (ibid).
8. Victor STARCKE, "Denmark in World History," 1946, trans. by 1962, 1968 USA, p.60.
9. The equation of the Wusun with the Asii seems to be unanimously accepted since the Asii in Roman accounts exactly parallel the Wusun in Chinese ones. Other equations of interest and generally respected are:
    As and Alans: Rene GROUSSET, "The Empire of the Steppes", 1939, trans. USA, 1970, p.552, n.75.
    Alans and As: V. MINORSKY, "Hudud al Alam," translated and explained by V. MINORSKY, edited by C.E. Bosworth. London 1970, p.445.
    Alans and Aorsi: Eduard MEYER, "Geschichtes des Altums", 2nd volume, Stuttgart 1931, p.890.
    Arsi = Aorsi: Franz ALTHEIM, "Geschichte der Hunnen", Berlin 1962, vol.1 p.69.
    As and Asi and Arsi: B. Philip LOZINSKI, "The Original Homeland of the Parthians," 1953, p.17.
    As and Alans: LOZINSKI (ibid) p.18.
    Ansi and Arsi: LOZINSKI (ibid) p.40.
10. STARKE (ibid) p.76.
11. MINORSKY (ibid) p.432.
12. D.M. DUNLOP, "The History of the Jewish Khazars", USA 1951, London 1954, p.93.
13. Encyclopedia Judaica, "Menorah".
14. Gwyn JONES, "A History of the Vikings," Oxford, New York 1984, p.22.
15. J. Otto MAENCHEN-HELFER, "The World of the Huns", edited by M. Knight, USA 1973, p.127.
16. SHORE, T.W. "Origins of the Anglo Saxon Race," London 1906, p.36.
17. CAMPBELL, J. "The Anglo Saxons". New York 1982, p.33.
18. Ritchie GIRVAN, "Beowulf of the Seventh Century," London 1935, p.53.
    R.H. HODGKIN "A History of the Anglo-Saxons," Oxford 1935, p.214- 215.

19. Jean Francoise LE PETIT. "Le Grande Chronicle Ancienne et Moderne de Holland, Zeelande, Utrecht, Frise, Oversyseel; et de Groenungham,". Dordrecht, 1601.
20. W. Montgomery McGOVERN, "The Early Empires of Central Asia," New York, USA 1939, p.476, Franz ALTHEIM, "Alexander Und Asien", Germany 1953, p.243.
21. McGOVERN (ibid) ALTHEIM (ibid)
22. Pliny N.H. 37;11, J. SVENNUNG, "Scandinavia und Scandia," Lund 1963, p.66, ZEUSS (ibid) p.157.
23. Yair DAVIDI, "Lost Isreaelite Identity", 2001, ch.19, Donald, A. MACKENZIE, "Scottish Folk Lore and Folk Life. Studies in Race, Culture, and Tradition", London & Glasgow, 1935.
24. ibid.
25. Isaac MOZESON, "The Word".

Chapter Twenty-One: References

1. W. Montgomery McGOVERN, "The Early Empires of Central Asia," New York, 1939, p.476 Franz ALTHEIM, "Alexander und Asien", Germany 1953, p.243
2. F. de ROUGEMONT, "L'Age du Bronze," Paris 1866.
3. Charles FORSTER, "The Monuments, with a New Key For the Recovery of the Lost Tribes," London 1859, p.320.
4. Ferdinand LOT, "Les Invasions Germaniques," Paris 1935, p.22.
5. Procopious, Gothic Wars 1;3.
6. F.L. BORCHARDT, "German Antiquity in Renaissance Myth", 1971 London and USA
7. Nahum SLOUSCHZ, "Les Hebreo-Pheniciens. Introduction a ire Des Origines de la Colonisation Hebraique dans les Pays Mediteranee," Paris 1909, p.61 Massimo PALLOTINO, "The Etruscans," 1942, 1978 UK p.70.
8. Yair DAVIDY, "Lost Israelite Identity", 1996
9. Kaspar ZEUSS, "Die Deutschen und Die Nachbarstamme," 1835, Heidelberg, 1925.
10. H.M. CHADWICK, "The Origin of the English Nation" Cambridge 1924.

Chapter Twenty-Two: References

1. Helene KOPPEJAN, "Strange Parallel", 1984, UK
2. David Miller brought this fact to our attention.
3. E.B. "Netherlands".
4. Zevi CHASDOI. "The Tribes of Jacob and the Preserved of Israel" (Hebrew), Haifa 1928.
5. B. Philip LOZINSKI, "The Original Homeland of the Parthians,". 1953, Netherlands.
6. Niels Clausen LUKMAN, "Skoldung Und Skilfinge". "Hunnen Und Herulerkonige in Oostorlischer Uberliersering," Copenhagen 1943.
7. Kaspar ZEUSS, "Die Deutschen und Die Nachbarstamme,". Germany 1835, Heidelberg, Germany 1925 p.57
    H.M. CHADWICK, "The Origin of the English Nation" Cambridge 1924, p.9.

Chapter Twenty-Three: References

1. N.F.K.: S. Nickels, H. Kallas, P. Friedman. "Finland. An Introduction," UK 1968, p.19
    John H. WUORINEN, "A History of Finland," New York & London 1965, p.12
2. Jewish Encyclopedia, "Khazars",
    cf. Charles FORSTER, "The Monuments, with a New Key for the Recovery of the Lost Tribes," London 1859, p.308.
3. Franz ALTHEIM, "Geschichte der Hunnen", Berlin 1962, p.277.
4. Abraham POLAK, "KAZARIA" (Hebrew), Tel Aviv 1951 p.318
5. Y. KIEL (1-Chronicles in Hebrew) "Sepher Divrei HaYamim", Daat Mikra, Jerusalem, Israel on 1-Chronicles 7:30,40.
6. V.O. KLUCHEVSKY, "A History of Russia," N.Y. 1960, p.58
7. S.G. OLSEN "The Incredible Nordic Origins" 1982, UK p.113

Chapter Twenty-Four: References

1. R. H. EISENBERG, "A Matter of Return", Jerusalem 1980, p.137

Chapter Twenty-Five: References

1. Brian BRANSTON, "The Lost Gods of England", .UK, 1957, p. 15 ff.

2. Louis David LEVINE, "Contributions to the Historical Geography of the Zagros in the Neo-Assyrian Period," Michigan, USA, 1969, p. 108

3. D.D. LUCKENBILL, "The Annals of Sennacherib," Chicago 1924.

4. H.W. BELLEW, "An Inquiry into the Ethnography of Afghanistan" London 1891, Austria 1973.
   Hugh SCHONFIELD, "The Essene Odyssey," UK, 1984, p.107

5. SCHONFIELD (ibid) p.124 ff.

6. (ibid)

7. Irma HAYNMAN, "The Syncretic Creed of Hellenized Jews from Tanais (Northern Black Sea Region)," Jerusalem, 1994.

8. Arthur J. ZUCKERMAN, "A Jewish Princedom in Feudal France, 768- 900". New York 1972, p.131 n.38 "Aimerico," p.433 "Aimericus," p.180 "Maghario." See note 38 below:

9. Leonid S. CHEKIN, "Samarcha, City of Khazaria," in Central Asiatic Journal vol. 33, nos. 1-2, 1989, Wiesbaden.

10. W.H. FASKER, "Israel's Racial Origin and Migrations," London 1934, p.56

11. MIEROW on JORDANES (ca. 551 CE) "The Gothic History", Introduction and Commentary by C.C. MIEROW, New York 1915, p.56

12. Fitz MEZGER, "Angelsachsische Volker und Landernamen," Berlin 1921, p.12

13. Kemp MALONE, editor of "WIDSITH", Anglistica (vol. xiii), Copenhagen 1962, p.184, Widsuth 42

14. Gudmund SHÜTTE, "The Problem of the Hraid Goths" in APS, vol. Viii, 1933 34 Copenhagen, p.248

15. Zaharias P. THUNDY, "Millenium. Apocalypse and Antichrist," USA, 1998, p.105

16. MEZGER (ibid) "Galatian" p.14 Lat. Galaad

17. Jean Francoise LE PETIT, "Le Grande Chronicle Ancienne et Moderne de Holland, Zeelande, Utrecht, Frise, Oversyseel; et de Groenungham", Dordrecht, 1601, p.28ff

18. Fred J. KOESLAG of Gouda, Holland, quoting Emmius and Furmerius, supplied this information to me.

19. P. PEYREFITTE, "The Jews," 1967 New York, Peyrefitte says that Messene (one of Napolean Bonaparte's best generals) was of Jewish origin and that his name is a form of Manesseh.

20. L.A. WADDEL, "The British Edda," London 1930, p.331

21. Y. KIEL "Sefer Yehoshua", series "Daat Mikra" Commentary, Jerusalem, 1970.
22. Quoted verbatim in S. Gusten OLSEN, "The Incredible Nordic Origins," UK 1981, p.61
23. Y. KIEL (ibid) p.182
24 Encyclopedia. Biblica "Yair", Benjamin Mazar
25. Henri HUBERT "The Greatness and Decline of the Celts," London 1934, p.197
26. H. D'ARBOIS DE JUBAINVILLE, "Cycle Mythologie Irlandais et le Mythologie Celtique", Paris 1884, p.89ff.
27. THUNDY (ibid) p. 108, 116.
28. MEZGER (ibid) p.19.
29. MEZGER (ibid) p.19.
30. "Lempriere's Classical Dictionary," 1788, 1984 London, "Pictae", Servius on Virgil, "Aenid" 4v.146
31. D.M. DUNLOP, "The History of the Jewish Khazars", USA, 1951, London 1954, p. 7ff.
32. J. Otto MAENCHEN-HELFER, "The World of the Huns", USA 1973, p.50 quotes a version of Virgil.
33. MEZGER (ibid) p.24
34. ZUCKERMAN (ibid)
35. Barry FELL, "American Saga," 1980, p.5
36. Arthur William WHATMORE, "Insulae Britannicae", 1913 UK, 1971 USA/UK, p.49.
37. Ian WILSON, "The Colombus Myth," UK 1991, p.166ff
38. ZUCKERMAN (ibid) p.375 Al Makhiri (Ha Makhiri came to be known as "AYMERI", as "Maghario," (p.180) or "Magharius", as "Aymeri, p.121 n.16., and as "Aimerico", and "Aimericus".
39. ZUCKERMAN (ibid) p.131 n.38, p.433. See note 8 above.
40. Herman L. HOEH, "COMPENDIUM of World History", USA, 1962, 1967, vol.1.
Sources for information quoted here derived from a Spanish work by Bartholome Gutierrez (1886) that was commissioned by the Spanish Hapsburg monarchs of Spain and reflects ancient traditions that are also found in other works. It is based on Mythologies that (at least to a degree) correspond with historical reality.

Chapter Twenty-Six: References

1. F.R. KLAEBER, "Beowulf," USA, 1922, p.xliii, Gwyn JONES, "A History of the Vikings," Oxford, New York 1984 p.38.

Fritz MEZGER, "Angelsachsische Volker und Landernamen," Berlin 1921 p.12

2. Raymond COLE, "The Migrations of Israel", USA 1980 (1988) p.56 quotes from H.B. Hannay who identified the Chorasmians with the Sacae in the region of Kiev.
3. B. Philip LOZINSKI,. "The Original Homeland of the Parthians," 1953, Netherlands.
4. Thomas ARNOLD, "BEOWULF", London 1876, p.219 .
5. Leon POLIAKOV, "The Arian Myth," London 1974
6. Herodotus bk.iv. Herodotus says that the Scythians called themselves Scoloti, and in that area "d" and "t" frequently interchanged, thus "Skiold" equals "Scolot."
7. Samuel (Bochart) BOCHARTUS, "Geographia Sacra; seu Phaleg et Canaan", Frankfort 1681, 1692. "Phaleg "
8. JORDANES (ca. 551 c.e.) "The Gothic History", Introduction and Commentary by C.C. MIEROW, New York 1915, ii, MIEROW p.51 .
9. SAXO GRAMMATICUS, "The First Nine Books of Saxo Grammaticus of the Danish History," Translated by Oliver Elton with notes, London 1894.
10. Isaac E. MOZESON, "The Word," New York 1989 p.15, "Adonis
11. R. PRIEBSCH and W.E. COLLINSON, "The German Language," London ca. 1936, p.47
12. Kaspar ZEUSS, "Die Deutschen und Die Nachbarstamme," Germany 1835, Heidelberg 1925 p.75
13. (ibid) p. 59, p.28.   Lemprieure, "Ingaevones
14. Yehudah KIEL, "Sepher Divrei Hayamim" ("The Book of Chronicles" in Hebrew), Jerusalem 1986.
15. C. M. WHITE, "The Assyrians in the Modern World", 1990, Australia, quoting Kachur 1975;2 C.M. White p.28
16. Robert GRAVES, "Greek Myths," London 1958 p.457
17. "Paulys Realencyclopadie der Classischen Altertums-wissenschaft," Stuttgart, 1901 entry, "Saxionacus.
18. T.W. SHORE, "Origins of the Anglo Saxon Race," London 1906, p.12
19. Rev. William, WARRINGTON. "The History of Wales". London 1805, p.23
20. M. ROSTOWZEW," Skythien und der Bosphorus", vol.i, p.303
21. Winston S. CHURCHILL, "A History of the English Speaking Peoples", vol.1 "The Birth of Britain", UK (1956), 1963. p.45 discusses the question and presents

the case for many of the native British having survived, yet even according to him, they were obviously only a protected minority.

22. Calvin KEPHART, "Races of Mankind, Their Origin and Migration," N.Y. 1960, p.437
23. A.S. Esmonde CLEARY, "The Ending of Roman Britain" London 1989, p.204 .
24. CLEARY (ibid)
25. KEPHART (ibid) p.438, n.314, "Based on the statistics of the U.S. Department of Labour and the assumption that 2/3 of the.immigrants from England had had such antecedents".

Chapter Twenty-Seven References

1. Leon POLIAKOV, "The Arian Myth," London 1974, p.38ff.
2. Leon POLIAKOV, (ibid)
3. Fishel MAEL, "Safer Shivtei Yisroel", by Baltimore, USA, 5757, p.490. For a more complete explanation see the article "MANASSEH BECAME GREATER LATER" in the magazine "Brit-Am Truth" no.7.

Bibliography

AHARONI, Jochanan. "Archaeology of the Land of Israel", (Hebrew), Jerusalem, Israel 1978.

ALBRIGHT, William Foxwell. "The Bible and the Ancient Near East," "Essays in Honour of William Foxwell Albright," edited by G.E. Wright. New York 1961.

ALTHEIM, Franz. "GDH". "Geschichte Der Hunnen". Berlin 1962.

ALTHEIM, Franz. "Der Urspring Der Etrusker", Baden Berlin 1950.

ALTHEIM, Franz. "Alexander Und Asien", Germany 1953.

ALTHEIM, Franz and Ruth Stiehl. "Ein Asiatischer Staat", Germany 1954

ANDERSON, A. "Alexander's Gate, Gog and Magog and the Enclosed Nations", Cambridge, Massachusetts, USA 1932.

Anderson, Inguar. "A History Of Sweden", London 1956.

APARTIAN, Dibar. "Les Pays de Langue Francaise Selon LaProphetie" USA 1961, 1982.

APS. ACTA PHILOLOGICA SCANDINAVICAE. "The Origin of the Cimbrians", by Gudmund Schutte, pp.91 96. Copenhagen 1931-1932.

ARNOLD, Thomas. "BEOWULF", London 1876.

ASKOWITZ, Dora. "The Toleration and Persecution of the Jews in the Roman Empire", New York 1915.

ASTOUR, MICHAEL C. "Hellenosemitica. An Ethnic And Cultural Study In West Semitic Study On Mycenean Greece", Leiden 1967.

ASTOUR, MICHAEL C. "Ezekiel's Prophecy of Gog and the Cuthean legend of Naram-Sin", Journal of Biblical Literature, vol.95/4 (1976), pp.567-99

D'AUVERGNE, La Tour. "Origines Gauloises", Hamburg, 1801.

AVI YONAH, M. "The Beth Shean Valley" (Hebrew), 1962 in "The 17th Archaeological Convention. I.E.S."

BACHRACH, Bernard S. "A History of the Alans in the West", Minneapolis, USA 1973.

BAKER, John R. "RACE", Oxford UK 1974 (N.Y. and London).

B-G, BARING-GOULD, S. "Germany", New York 1886.

BANYAI, M. "The Arab Fringe. An Enquiry Concerning Muşri, Kush, Meluhha and Magan", Germany, 2004.

BARRETT, Clive. "The Viking Gods", 1989 UK

BARTHOLD, "Barthold's Iran," –a translation from the Russian by G.K. Nariman, Bombay, India.

BASCHMAKOFF, A. "Cinquante Siecles D'Evolution Autour de la Mer Noir", Paris 1937.

BASSET, Steve "The Origins of Anglo-Saxon Kingdoms", UK 1989.

BELLEW, H.W. "An Inquiry into the Ethnography of Afghanistan", Original edition, London 1891. Reprinted in Austria 1973.

BENNET, W.H. "Symbols of Our Celto-Saxon Heritage", London, 1976

BEN-ZVI, I. "The Exiled and the Redeemed", London 1958.

BERNAL, Martin. "Black Athena", vol. 1 1987, vol.2, UK, 1991.

BEVERIDGE, John. Introduction and Notes to the "HEIMSKRINGLA. The OLD SAGAS", by Snorre Sturlason, translated by S. Laing.

BHARGAVA, Purochottam hal. "India in the Vedic Age", Lucknow, India, 1956.

BLL. Michael BAIGENT, Richard LEIGH, & Henry LINCOLN. "Hold Blood, Holy Grail", London 1982; N.Y. 1983.

BLL Baigent, Leigh, & Lincoln. "The Messianic Legacy", 1986, 1987 UK

BLOCHET, E. "Les Germaniques Sujets de Darius", in Revue D'Assyriologie Orientals", Tome xxi, Volume no.4, Paris 1924.

BOCHARTUS, Samuel (Bochart). "Geographia Sacra; seuPhaleg etCanaan", Frankfort 1681, 1692.

BORCHARDT, F.L. "German Antiquity in Renaissance Myth", 1971 London and USA

BOSWELL, Mrs. Winthrop Palmer. "The Roots of Irish Monasticism", USA, 1969

BOYCE, Mary. "A History of Zoroastrianism", Leiden/Koln 1975.

BRADLEY, Henry. "The Story of the Goths", London 1887.

BRAND, John. (Edited, revised and greatly enlarged by Sir Henry Ellis). "Observations on the Popular Antiquities of Great Britain", London 1841.

BRANSTON, Brian. "The Lost Gods of England", London 1957.

B & J. BRINTON, Daniel and JASTROW, Morris. " The Cradle of the Semites", Philadelphia 1890.

BRONDAL, Virgo. "Mots 'Scythes' en Nordique Primitif", in APS, COPENHAGEN 1928 29.

BRUGSCH B. "Brugsch's Egypt Under the Pharoahs", trans. by P. Smith. London 1881.

BRUNNHOFER, Dr. Hermann. "Iran unt Turan," Leipzig, 1889.

BURY, J.B. "The Invasion of Europe by the Barbarians", New York 1967.

CAESAR, Julius. "The Gallic War", Translated by H.J. Edwards, London 1917.

CAESAR, Julius. "The Gallic War", Translated by Rex Warner, London 1960.

CAH-3. Cambridge Ancient History volume 3, "The Assyrian Empire", Edited by Bury, Cook, and Adcock. Cambridge 1954.

CAH-4. Cambridge Ancient History volume 4, "The Persian Empire and the West", Edited by Bury, Cook, and Adcock. 1926.

CAMERON, George C. "A History of Early Iran", New York 1968.

CAMPBELL, J. "The Anglo Saxons", New York 1982.

CARRINGTON, C.E. "The British Overseas", Cambridge UK 1950.

CHADWICK, H.M. "The Origin of the English Nation", Cambridge 1924.

CHAMICH, Michael. "History of Armenia", translated by J. Avdall, vol.I , Calcutta 1827.

Chasdoi see Kasdoi.

CHEKIN, Leonid S. "Samarcha, City of Khazaria," in Central Asiatic Journal vol. 33, nos. 1-2, 1989, Wiesbaden.

CHI. "The Cambridge History of Iran". volume 2. "The Median and Achaemenian Periods", Edited by Ilya Gershevitch. United Kingdom 1968.

CHURCHILL, Winston S. "A History of the English Speaking Peoples", vol.1 "The Birth of Britain", UK (1956), 1963.

CLEARY, A.S. Esmonde, "The Ending of Roman Britain", London 1989.

CMW. **C.M. White.** "The Assyrians in the Modern World", 1990, Australia.

COLE, Raymond. "The Migrations of Israel", Eugene, Oregon, USA 1980.

COLLEDGE, M.A.R. "The Parthians", London 1967.

COLLINS, Steven M. ~The "Lost" Ten Tribes Of Israel...Found!~, Oregon, USA, 1995.

COLLINS, Steven M. "Parthia. The Forgotten Ancient Superpower and its Role in Biblical History", USA, 2003

CRAIGIE, W.A. "The Religion of Ancient Scandinavia", London 1906.

CULICAN, William. "The Medes and Persians", UK 1965.

Curtius, see Rooke.

DALTON, O.M. Introduction to "The History of the Franks by Gregory of Tours", volume I, London 1927.

DANDAMAYEB, M.A. "Data of the Babylonian Documents From the Sixth Centuries to the Fifth Centuries B.C. on the Sakas", in Harmatta J.

D'A. D'arbois de Jubainville H. "Cycle Mythologie Irlandais et le Mythologie Celtique", Paris 1884.

DARMESTETTER, James. "The Zend Avesta", Oxford, 1895.

DAVIDI, Yair. "Ephraim. The Gentile Children of Israel", Jerusalem 1995, 2nd edition: Jerusalem, Israel, 2001.

DAVIDI, Yair. "Joseph. The Israelite Destiny of America", Jerusalem, 2001

DAVIDI, Yair. "Origin. You Too Are From Israel. You Too Are The People", Jerusalem 2002

DAVIDI, Yair. "Biblical Truth. The Lost Ten Tribes in the West According to the Book of Genesis", Jerusalem 2002

DAVIDY, Yair. "Lost Israelite Identity. The Hebrew Ancestry of Celtic Races", Jerusalem, Israel, 1996

DAVIDY, Yair. "The Tribes. The Israelite Origins of Western Peoples", Hebron, Israel, 1993, 2nd edition: Jerusalem, Israel, 1993

DAVIDSON, H.R. Ellis. "Gods and Myths of Northern Europe", UK 1964.

DAVIDSON, H.R. Ellis. "The Viking Road to Byzantium", London 1976.

DAVIDSON, H.R. Ellis. see Gelling and Davidson.

DAVIES, Nina M. "Ancient Egyptian Paintings", Chicago, USA 1936.

DERBY, T.K. "A Short History of Norway", London, 1954

DIESNER, Hans Joachim. "The Great Migrations", Leipzig 1978. Translated by C.S.V. Salt. 1982, London.

DIODORUS of SICILY (**Diodorus Siculus**, ca. 50 b.c.e.) translated by U. Oldfather, London 1968.

DIXON, R.B. "The Racial History of Man", N.Y. & London 1923.

DOANE, T.W. "Bible Myths and Their Parallels in Other Religions", New York 1882.

DOLLINGER, Frieder. "Baldur und Bibel", Nurnberg, Germany 1921.

DOTHAN, Trude & Moshe. "People of the Sea", New York, USA, 1992.

DRAGAN, J.C. "We, the Thracians", Milano, Italy 1976.

DRUMMOND, W. "Origins or Remarks on the Origin of Several Empires, States, and Countries", volumes I, II, 1824 London.

DUNLOP, D.M. "The History of the Jewish Khazars", New Jersey, USA 1951, London 1954.

EISENBERG, R. H. "A Matter of Return", Jerusalem 1980

ELAT, Moshe. "Economic Relations in the Lands of the Bible ca. 1000 539 b.c." (Hebrew), Jerusalem , Israel 1977.

Encyclopedia Americana. New York 1977.

ENCYCLOPEDIA BIBLICA. (Hebrew), Jerusalem 1968.

Encyclopedia Brittanica. 1955, 1966 London.

Encyclopedia OF Islam, Leiden 1954.

Encyclopedia Judaica Jerusalem 1971.

EPSHTEIN, Abraham. "Eldad Ha Dani", (Hebrew); Pressburg (Austria Hungary) 1891.

EPSHTEIN, Abraham, "Kadmoniot HaYehudim; Braytot Atikot. Eldad Ha Dani," Jerusalem 1957.

EUTROPIUS. "Abridgement of Roman History", Translated by J. Swatson, London 1902.

FABER, Gustav. "Piraten oder Staatengrunder. Normannen bis zum Bosporus," Guterston, Germany 1968.

FASKER, W.H. "Israel's Racial Origin and Migrations," London 1934.

FELIKS, Dr. Jehuda. "The Animal World of the Bible," Tel Aviv 1962.

FELIKS, Yehuda. "Heredity and Environment", Techumin v.3, Israel 1982.

FERAL, E. "La Legende Arthurienne," Paris 1929.

FILMER, W.E. "Our Scythian Ancestors," an eight page pamphlet printed in Kent. United Kingdom.

FISHBERG, Maurice. "The Jews: A Study of Race and Environment," New York 1911.

FISHER, D.J.Y. "The Anglo-Saxon Age," London 1973.

FLETCHER, Arnold. "Afghanistan. Highway of Conquest," London 1965.

FLINDERS-PETRIE, W.M. "Egypt and Israel," London 1912.

FLOOD, J.M. "Ireland: Its Myths And Legends", New York, 1970.

FOGELMAN, Eva "Consience and Courage. Rescuers of Jews During the Holocaust", NY, 1994.

FORSTER, Charles. "The Monuments, with a New Key For the Recovery of the Lost Tribes," London 1859.

FRYE, Richard N. "The Heritage of Persia," USA 1963.

GARNIER, J. (Colonel). "The Ten Tribes From The Captivity Until Now", London.

GASTER, M. translator of "The Chronicles of Jerahmiel, ca. 1100-1150 c.e.," New York 1971.

GAUL, James H. "Observations of the Bronze Age in theYenissei Valley, Siberia," Studies in the Anthropology of Oceania and Asia, USA in honour of R.B. Dixon ,1943.

GAYRE R. of Gayre. "The Syro-Mesopotamian Ethnology as Revealed in Genesis X", Edinburgh 1973.

GELLING and DAVIDSON. Peter Gelling and H.E. Davidson, "The Chariot of the Sun," London 1969.

GEOFFREY of MONMOUTH. "History of the Kings of Britain," translation of Sebastian Evans, revised by Charles W. Dunn 1958.

GERSHEVITCH, Ilya, "Old Iranian Literature," Leiden 1968.

GIBBON, Edward. "The Decline and Fall of the Roman Empire," (1776-81). "The Portable Gibbon," edited by D.A. Sanders, USA 1952.

GILBERT, Adrian, Alan WILSON, and Baram BLACKETT, "The Holy Kingdom", UK, 1998

GIMBUTAS, M. "The Slavs," New York 1971.

GINZBERG, Louis. "The Legends of the Jews," USA 1911.

GIORDANO, Ralph. "Wenn Hitler den Krieg gewonten hatte", Germany, 1988.

GIRVAN, Ritchie. "Beowulf of the Seventh Century," London 1935.

GNOLI, Gherardo. "Zoroaster's Time and Homeland. A Study on theOrigins of Mazdaism," Naples, Italy 1980.

GOBINEAU, Le Comte de GOBINEAU. "Histoire Des Perses", Paris 1869.

GODBEY, Allen H. "The Lost Tribes a Myth. Suggestions Towards Rewriting Hebrew History," Durham, USA 1930.

GOLDEN, Peter B. "Khazar Studies," Budapest 1980.

GORDON, E.V. "An Introduction to Old Norse," Oxford 1937.

GOW, Andrew Colin. "The Red Jews. Anti-Semitism in an Apocalyptic Age 1200-1600" NY 1995, published by E.J. Brill.

GRAND, Roger. "Recherches Sur L'Origine Des Francs,". Paris 1965.

GRAVES, Robert. "Greek Myths," London 1958.

GROUSSET, Rene. "The Empire of the Steppes", 1939. Trans. N. Walford, USA 1970.

HACHMANN, Rolf. "The Germanic Peoples", trans. J. Hogarth, London 1971.

HACOHEN, Bentzion. "Keshet Imri Emet" (Hebrew), Jerusalem 1989.

HALPERIN, Israel. "Atlas Etz Haim" (Hebrew), vol.2, Israel 1985

HAMEL, A.G. van Hamel. "Odin Hanging on the Tree", in APS, Copenhagen 1932.

HAMMOND, N.G.L. "A History of Macedonia," Oxford 1972.

HARKAVY, Abraham Eliyahu. "HAYEHUDIM VISAFAT HASLAVIM", (Hebrew) Vilna 1867.

HARMATTA, J. editor of "Prolegomena. In the Sources on the History of Pre-Islamic Asia," Budapest 1979.

HAUGEN, Einar. "The Scandinavian Languages," London 1967.

HAYNMAN, IRMA. "The Syncretic Creed of Hellenized Jews From Tanais (Northern Black Sea Region)", Proceedings of the Eleventh World Congress of Jewish Studies; Division B: The History of the Jewish People; Volume 1, Second Temple Period To Modern Times. Jerusalem 1994, World Union of Jewish Studies.

HAWKES, Jacquetta and Christopher. "Prehistoric Britain," UK 1953.

HAYES and MILLER, J.H. Hayes and J.M. Miller, editors "Israelite and Judaean History," London 1977.

HERODOTUS (ca.430 b.c.e.) The History of Herodotus. translated and Annotated by G. Rawlinson, London 1858.

HERRMAN, Georigina. "Lapis lazuli: The Early Phases of Its Trade", Iraq, vol.30, 1968, pp.21.

HERZFELD, Ernest E. from Posthumous Papers edited by G. Walser. "The Persian Empire. Studies in Geography and Ethnography of the Ancient Near East," Wiesbaden 1968.

HILDEBRAND, Hans. "Scandinavian Art," London 1883.

HOCHAM, Amos. "Sefer Yishayahu," ("The Book of Isaiah") (Hebrew), vol.1. Jerusalem 1984.

HODDINOTT, R.F. "The Thracians," Spain 1981.

HODGKIN, Thomas. "Italy and Her Invaders. The Visigoth Invasion," 1880, 1928 UK

HODGKIN, R.H. "A History of the Anglo Saxons," Oxford 1935.

HOEH, Herman L. "Compendium of World History", A Dissertation Presented to The Faculty of the Ambassador College Graduate School of Theology In Partial Fulfillment of the Requirements for the Degree Doctor of Theology, 1962 (1963-1965, 1967 Edition), USA.

HOLDICH, Colonel Sir Thomas. "The Gates of India. Being an Historical Narrative", London, 1910

HOPE & HOPE. A. Guy Hope & Tanet Hope. "Symbols of the Nations," Washington 1973.

HOPE, Murry. "Atlantis. Myth or Reality?", UK 1991.

HOROVITZ, Josef. "Hebrew Iranian Synchronism," Bombay 1931.

HUBERT, Henri. "The Rise of the Celt", Trans. M.R. Dodrie, London 1934.

HUBERT, Henri. "The Greatness and Decline of the Celts," London 1934.

HULLEY, John C.L. "Comets, Jews, and Christians," Jerusalem, Israel, 1996.

HYDE, Douglas. "A Literary History of Ireland," London 1899,1967.

HYMAN, Louis. "The Jews of Ireland," Jerusalem 1972.

JACOBSTAHT. P. "Early Celtic Art," Oxford 1944.

JAMES, E.O. "The Old Testament in the Light of Anthropology," London 1935.

JAZDZEWSKI, Konrad. "Poland," London 1965.

JENSEN, Ole Klinst. "Denmark Before the Vikings," London 1962.

JESSELL, E.E. "The Unknown History of the Jew," London 1909.

The Jewish Encyclopedia, London 1901.

JONES, Gwyn. "A History of the Vikings," Oxford, New York 1984.

JORDANES (ca. 551 c.e.) "The Gothic History", Introduction and Commentary by C.C. Mierow, New York 1915.

JOSEPHUS, "Jewish Antiquities", trans. H.J. Thakeray.

JUSTIN. "Justin's History of the World"; extracted from Trogus Pompeius. Translated by J.S. Watson, London 1902.

KAPLAN, Rabbi Aryeh. "The Living Torah. The Five Books of Moses," Translation and Commentary, New York 1981.

KARSH, EPHRAIM. "Fabricating Israeli History. The 'New Historians'", USA, 1997.

KASDOI, Kasdoi, Zevi. "The Tribes of Jacob and the Preserved of Israel" (Hebrew), Haifa 1928.

KATZENSTEIN, H. Jacob, "The History of Tyre", Jerusalem, 1973.

KASDOI Kasdoi, Zevi. "HAMITYAHADIM", (Hebrew), Haifa 1929.

KENYON, Kathleen. "Royal Cities of the Old Testament," London 1971.

KEPHART, Calvin. "Races of Mankind, Their Origin and Migration," N.Y. 1960.

KHAZANOV, A.M. "The Dawn of Scythian History," Iranica Antiqua. 17, Leiden 1982.

KIEL, Yehudah. "Sefer Divrei HaYamim" (The Book of Chronicles), Daat Mikra, Jerusalem, Israel.

KIEL, Yehudah, "Safer Yehoshua" (Hebrew). M.H. Kook, Jerusalem 1970.

KIEL, Yehudah. "Sepher Divrei Hayamim" ("The Book of Chronicles") (Hebrew), Jerusalem 1986.

K.H. KINDER & HILGEMANN. Hermann Kinder and Werner Hilgeman, "The Penguin Atlas of World History," volume I. Trans. E.A. Menze, UK 1974.

KIRKBY, Michael Haslock. "The Vikings," USA 1977.

KLAEBER, F.R. "Beowulf," USA 1922.

K. J. KLINDT JENSEN, Ole. "Denmark Before the Vikings," London 1957.

KLUCHEVSKY, V.O. "A History of Russia," translated by C.J. Hogarth, N.Y. 1960.

KNOBEL, August. "Die Volktagel der Genesis," Giesson 1850.

KOBLER, Franz. "The Vision Was There. A History of the British Movement for the Restoration of Palestine," London 1956.

KOESTLER, Arthur. "The Thirteenth Tribe. The Khazar Empire and Its Heritage," New York 1967.

KORKANER, I. "Jordanes," Helsinki 1975.

KUHN, Hans. "Grenzen vor und Fruhgeschichtler Ortsnamen," Darmstadt 1963.

LAURING, Palle. "Land of the Tollund Man," New York 1958.

LAW, David A. "The Ten Lost Tribes of Israel", USA, 1991

LEMPRIERE. "Lempriere's Classical Dictionary," 1788 1984 London

LE PETIT, Jean Francoise. "Le Grande Chronicle Ancienne et Moderne de Holland, Zeelande, Utrecht, Frise, Oversyseel; et de Groenungham," Dordrecht, 1601.

LESTRANGE. "The Geographical Part of the Nuzhat Al Qulub composed by Hamd Mustawfi of Qazwin in 740 (1340)," Translated by G. Le Strange, London 1919.

LEVINE, Louis David. "Contributions to the Historical Geography of the Zagros in the Neo Assyrian Period," Michigan, USA 1969.

LEWIN, Dr. Moritz. "Waren die' Zehn Stamme Israels zusuchen?", Frankfort 1901.

LICHTENSTEIN (I.Z. Hirshenzohin). "Sheva Chochmot," (Hebrew), London 1912.

LOT, Ferdinand. "Les Invasions Germaniques," Paris 1935.

LOZINSKI, B. Philip. "The Original Homeland of the Parthians," Originally a paper read in Washington 1953. The Hague, Netherlands.

LUCKENBILL, D.D. "Ancient Records of Assyria and Babylon," USA 1968.

LUCKENBILL, D.D. "The Annals of Sennacherib," Chicago 1924.

LUKMAN, Niels Clausen. "Skoldung Und Skilfinge". "Hunnen Und Herulerkonige in Oostorlischer Uberliersering," Copenhagen 1943.

LURIA, Ben Zion "Shaul and Benjamin," Jerusalem 1970, in Hebrew

MACKENDRICK. P. "The Dacian Stones Speak", USA 1975

MACKENZIE, D.A. "Teutonic Myth and Legend," London 1912.

MACKENZIE, DONALD, A. "Scottish Folk Lore And Folk Life. Studies in Race, Culture, And Tradition", London & Glasgow, 1935.

MH MAENCHEN-HELFER, J. Otto. "The World of the Huns", edited by M. Knight, USA 1973.

MAJUNDAR, Ramesh C. "The Classical Accounts of India," Calcutta, 1960.

MALLET, M. "Northern Antiquities of the Ancient Scandinavians," translated by Bishop Percy. London 1882.

MALLET, M. "Introduction a l'Histoire de Danemarc," Copenhagen 1755.

MALONE, Kemp. editor of "WIDSITH", Anglistica (vol. xiii), Copenhagen 1962.

MANDEVILLE, Sir John. "Travels", 1st printed ca. 1499, London 1903.

MARGALITH, Othniel. "The Sea Peoples In The Bible" (Hebrew), Tel Aviv, Israel, 1988.

MARKALE, J. "Les Celts" (English Translation 1978), 1970 Paris.

MATHIASSEN, Therkel. English Summary from 'Norwest jaellands Oldtidsbelyggelse,': The Prehistoric Settlement of Northwest Jutland," Copenhagen 1959.

McCRINDLE, J.W. "Ancient India as Described by Megasthenes and Arrian," Calcutta, India 1960.

McCRINDLE, J.W. "Ancient India as Described by Ptolemy," London 1885.

McCRINDLE, J.W. "The Invasion of India by Alexander the Great," Westminster, UK

McGOVERN, W. Montgomery. "The Early Empires of Central Asia," New York, USA 1939.

McNAIR, RAYMOND F. "Key To Northwest European Origins", Unpublished Thesis, California, USA

McNAIR, RAYMOND F. "America And Britain In Prophecy", 1996, USA

MELIN, Bengt. "Die Heimat Der Kimbern," Uppsala 1960.

MENASSEH BEN ISRAEL. "Conciliator" (1632). Translated (from Spanish) by E.H. Linder, in 5602 1842, London.

MEYER, Eduard. "Geschichtes DES Altums", 2nd volume, Stuttgart 1931.

MEZGER, Fritz. "Angelsachsische Volker und Landernamen," Berlin 1921.

MH. see Maenchen Helfer.

MIEROW, C.C. see Jordanes.

MIESSES, Mathias. "Les Juifs et les Etablissements Puniques Afrique du Nord," Paris 1933.

MILLER, Rabbi Avigdor. "A Nation is Born", USA.

MILNER (OXONIAN). "Israel's Wanderings," London 1900.

MILTON, John. "The Works of John Milton, vol. v, book 3. (1669), "The History of England," London 1867.

MINNS, E.H. "Scythians and Greeks," New York 1965.

MINORSKY, V. "Hudud al Alam," Translated and Explained by V. Minorsky, edited by C.E. Bosworth. London 1970.

MIRKIN, M.A. Commentary and Editor of Midrash Rabah (Hebrew), Tel Aviv 1980.

MONCRIEFF, C.S. "Translation of Widsuth,". London 1921.

MONGAIT, A.L. "Archaeology in the USSR., 1961, 1972. London.

MORANT, G. M. "The Races of Central Europe," London 1939.

MORSE, Arthur D. "While 6 Million Died. A Chronicle of American Apathy", USA, 1967, 1968

MOSES OF CHORENE. "History of the Armenians," trans. by W. Thomas, U.S. 1978.

MOZESON, Isaac E. "The Word," New York 1989.

MURRAY, M.A. "The Witch Cult in Western Europe," UK 1921.

MUSSET, Lucien. "Les Invasions: Les Vagues Germaniques," Paris 1969.

MYRES, John Linton. "Who Were the Greeks?", Berkely, California, 1930.

MYRES, J. N. L. "The English Settlements," USA, 1986.

NA'AMAN, Nadav. "Population Changes in Palestine Following Assyrian Deportations" (Hebrew), in Cathedra, Jerusalem 54, December 1985.

NAGER, Dr. Yose "Mi Anachnu?" Israel, 2003

NED. "A New English Dictionary on Historical Principles," Oxford 1901.

NEUBAUER, Adolphe. "La Geographie De Talmud," Paris 1868.

NEUBAUER, Adolphe. A. (Dr.). "Where Are the Ten Tribes Now?", in Jewish Quarterly Review, no.1, London iii, 1889.

NEWMAN, Louis Israel. "Jewish Influence On Christian Reform Movements," USA 1925.

N.F.K. S. Nickels, H. Kallas, P. Friedman. "Finland. An Introduction," UK 1968.

NIBBI, Alessandra. "The Sea Peoples and Egypt," New Jersey, USA 1975.

ODED, Bustenay. "Mass Deportations and Deportees in the Neo-Assyrian Empire," Weisbaden, Germany, 1979.

OLSEN, S. Gusten. "The Incredible Nordic Origins," UK 1981.

OLMSTEAD, A.T. "History of the Persian Empire", USA, 1948

ORTELLIUS, Abraham. "Theatrum Orbis", (Atlas with annotation), Antwerp 1570.

OWEN, Gale R. "Rites and Religions of the Anglo-Saxons," New Jersey, USA 1981.

PALLOTINO, Massimo. "The Etruscans," 1942, 1978 UK

PARSONS, F.G. "The Earlier Inhabitants of London," London 1927.

PAUL, Dr. R. "The Life of Alfred the Great", translated (from German) by S. Thorpe, London 1889.

PAULYS. "Paulys Realencyclopadie der Classischen Altertums-wissenschaft," Stuttgart, 1901.

PAYNE, Robert. "The Life & Death of Adolf Hitler", USA, 1973

PEDERSON, Holgar. "L'Origine des Runes", Societe Royale der Antiquaires du Nord. No. 24. Copenhagen 1920.

PEYREFITTE, P. "The Jews," 1967 New York.

PHILIP, Mats. "Birka at the Silkroad, 1997, article on the Internet

PHILLIPS, E.D. "The Royal Hordes: Nomad Peoples of the Steppes," London 1965.

PINE, L.G. "They Came With The Conqueror," UK 1954.

PITT, R.G. "The Tragedy of the Norse Gods," London 1893.

PLINY, "Natural History", (d. ca. 79 c.e.) trans. H. Rackman, UK 1961.

PLUTARCH (ca. 90 c.e.) "The Lives of the Noble Grecians and Romans," trans. by J. Dryden, revised by A.H. Clough. New York 1864.

POISSON, Georges. "Les Aryens," Paris 1934.

POLAK, Abraham. "KAZARIA" (Hebrew), Tel Aviv 1951.

POLIAKOV, Leon. "The Arian Myth," London 1974.

POOLE, W.H. "Fifty Reasons Why the Anglo-Saxons are Israelites of the Lost Tribes of the House of Israel," London 18 .

POWELL, T.G.E. "The Celts," London 1958, 1980.

PRIEBSCH, & COLLINSON. R. Priebsch and W.E. Collinson. "The German Language," London ca. 1936.

PRUSEK, Jaroslav. "Chinese States and the Northern Barbarians in the Period 1400-300 b.c.," Dordrecht, Holland. 1971.

RAWLINSON, G. Translation and Commentary to the 'History of Herodotus,' 1858 London.

REINACH, Adolph. "Noe Sangariou. Etude Sur le Deluge en Phrygie et Le Syncretisme Judeo-Phrygien," Paris 1913.

RENAULD-KRANTZ, P. "Odin" in "Les Vikings et leurCivilisation," edited by Regis Boyer, Paris 1976.

RICHMOND, I.A. "Roman Britain," Middlesex, UK 1958.

RIPLEY, W.Z. "The Races of Europe," London 1899.

ROBERTSON, J.M. "The Germans", London 1916.

ROGERS, Robert William, "Cuneiform Parallels to the Old Testament", UK, 1912

ROOKE, "Translation of 'Arrian's History of Alexander's Expedition",' 1814. Prefix with Mr. Le Clerc's Criticism upon Quintius Curtius.

ROSTOWZEW, M. "Skythien und der Bosphorus," Berlin 1931.

ROSTOVTZEFF, M. "The Animal Style in South Russia and China," New York 1973.

ROSTOVTZEFF, M. "Iranians and Greeks in South Russia", Oxford 1922.

ROTH, Cecil. "PEJH". "Personalities and Events in Jewish History," Philadelphia, USA 1953, 5714.

ROTH, CECIL. "History of the Jews in England," Oxford 1964.

ROTH, ERICH. "Sind Wir Germanen Das Eines Irrtums," Kassel, Germany 1967.

ROUGEMONT. F. de Rougemont. "L'Age du Bronze," Paris 1866.

RUBINSTEIN, William D. "The Myth of Rescue: Why the Democracies Could Not Have Saved More Jews From The Nazis", 1997, UK, USA.

SANDARS, N.K. "The Sea Peoples". "Warriors of the Ancient Mediterranean", 1985, London.

SARKAR, Professor Benoy Kumar. "The Positive Background of Hindu Sociology," Allahabad 1914.

SAXO GRAMMATICUS. "The First Nine Books of Saxo Grammaticus of the Danish History," Translated by Oliver Elton (Elton & Powell) with notes. London 1894.

SAYCE, A.H. "Who Were the Amorites?", article in Ancient Egypt, 1924 September part iii.

SAYCE, A.H. "Assyria," London 1885.

SAYCE, A.H. "The Races of the Old Testament," London 1925.

SCHONFIELD, Hugh. "The Essene Odyssey," Dorset, UK 1984.

SCHRADER, Eberhard. "The Cuneiform Inscriptions and the Old Testament", London 1888

SCHULTEN, Adolf. "Tartessos," Hamburg 1950.

SCHULZE, Wilhelm. "Samstag" in Zeitschrift Fur Zvergleichende Sprachforschungun, vol.xxxiii (1895).

SCOTT, Franklin D. "Sweden. The Nation's History," 1988 USA

SEDGEFIELD, W.J. "Beowulf," Manchester 1913.

SENSTIUS, Parl. "Die Stamme der Israeliten und Germanen," 1931, Leipzig.

SHORE, T.W. "Origins of the Anglo-Saxon Race," London 1906.

SHUTTE, Gudmund. "The Problem of the Hraid Goths", in APS, vol. Viii, 1933 34 Copenhagen.

SIMPSON, W.D. "The Province of Mar," Aberdeen 1943.

SLOUSCHZ, Nahum, "Les Hebreo-Pheniciens. Introduction a ire Des Origines de la Colonisation Hebraique dans les Pays Mediteranee," Paris 1909.

SLOUSCHZ, Nahum. "Ba Eyay Ha Yam," (Hebrew), New York 1919.

SMITH, Reginald A. "A Guide to Antiquities of the Early Iron Age," Cambridge 1982.

Snorre Sturlassen, see Beveridge.

SPEER, Albert. "Inside The Third Reich", New York, 1971.

SQUIRE, Charles. "Celtic Myth and Legend, and Poetry," London 1905.

SQUIRE, Charles. "The Mythology of Ancient Britain And Ireland", London 1909.

STARCKE, Victor. "Denmark in World History," 1946. Trans. by F.N. Stagg and I. Nixon, 1962, 1968 USA

STRABO, "The Geography of Strabo", (d. ca. 21 c.e.), Trans. H.L. Jones, UK 1923.

STRANGE, John. "Caphtor/Keftiu a new investigation", Leiden 1980.

SULIMERSKI, Tadeusz. "Prehistoric Russia -an Outline," London 1970.

SULIMERSKI, Tadeusz. "Scythian Antiquities in Western Asia. The Appearance of the Assyrians", in "Artibus Asiae vol. xvii, Ascona, vol. 17, Switzerland 1954.

SVENNUNG, J. "Scandinavia und Scandia," Lund 1963.

SVENSSON, Orjan. "De Blekingska Runornas Hemlicheter", Sweden, 2001

SYKES, Christopher, "Orde Wingate," 1959, UK

SYKES, Sir Percy. "A History of Afghanistan," London 1940.

T. H. TACHERA-HITOVA, Margarita. "Eastern Cults in Moesia Inferior and Thrace, 5th Century B.C. 4th Century A.D.", Leiden 1983.

TACITUS. "The Agricola and the Germania," Trans. by H. Mattingly, revised by S.A. Handford. UK 1970.

TALBOT Rice, T. "The Scythians," London 1957.

TARDY, I. "The Caucasian Peoples and Their Neighbours in 1404", Acta Orientalia 32:1978

TAYLOR, A.J.P. "English History 1914-1945", Oxford 1965,

TAYLOR, Miles. "John Bull and the Iconography. Public Opinion in England c. 1712-1929", article in 'Past and Present' no.134, February 1992.

THOMAS, D.W. editor. "Documents From Old Testament Times," New York 1961.

THOMPSON, E.A. "A History of Attila and the Huns", Oxford 1948.

THUNDY, Zaharias P. "Millenium. Apocalypse and Antichrist," USA, 1998.

TODD, Malcolm. "The Northern Barbarians," London 1975.

TOWNSEND, Peter. "Duel of Eagles", 1971

T-P. Turville Petrie, E.O.G. "Myth and Religion of the North. The Religion of Ancient Scandinavia," London 1964.

T-P. Turville Petrie, G. "The Heroic Age of Scandinavia," London 1951.

TRIPP, Edward. "The Meridian Handbook of Classical Mythology", USA, 1970.

TSCAN, Joseph. Introduction and Notes to "The Chronicle of the Slavs by Helmold, Priest of Breslau," (ca. 1150 c.e.), New York 1966.

Universal Jewish Encyclopedia 1939.

UNVALA, Janshedj Manetchi. "Observations on the Religion of Parthians," Bombay 1925.

VAN L. DE L.: VAN LOHUIZEN de Leeuw, Johanna Engelberta. "The 'Scythian' Period," Leiden 1949.

VELIKOVSKY, Immanuel, "Earth in Upheaval", UK 1956, 1978.

VELIKOVSKY, IMMANUEL. "Peoples of the Sea", 1977, UK

VERCOUTTER, Jean. "L'Egypte et le Monde Egeen Prehellenique," Le Caire, France, 1956.

VERNADSKY, G. "The Origins of Russia," 1959, Oxford.

VERNADSKY, George. "Ancient Russia," 1943, USA

WADDEL, L.A. "Phoenecian Origins of Britons, Scots, and Anglo-Saxons," London 1925.

WADDEL, L.A. "The British Edda," London 1930.

WALKER, Mack. "Germany and the Emigration 1816- 1885", Harvard, USA 1964.

WANEFSKY, Rabbi David, "The Prophets Speak To Us Anew," New York 1952.

WARRINGTON. Rev. William. "The History of Wales", London 1805.

WASSERSTEIN, Bernard, "Britain and the Jews of Europe," 1939-1945", 1979.

WEISSMAN, Chaim Bell. "Giants and Giantism", Jewish Sources of the MS Cotton Vitellius Axv". Thesis for Ph.D. Purdue Univ.,1978 USA

WELLS, C.M. "The German Policy of Augustus," Oxford 1972.

WHATMORE, Arthur William. "Insulae Britannicae," 1913 UK, 1971 USA/UK

WHITELOCK, Dorothy. "The Beginnings of English Society," UK 1953, 1959.

WIGHTMAN, Edith Mary. "Rome, Trier and the Treveri," London 1970.

WILKES, Anna. "Ireland: Ur of the Chaldees," London 1873.

WILSON, D.M. "The Anglo Saxons," London 1960.

WILSON, Ian. "The Colombus Myth," UK 1991.

WINBOLT, S.E. "Britain Under the Romans," 1945, UK

WISEMAN, D.J. editor of "Peoples of Old Testament Times," Oxford 1973.

WOLFRAM, Herwig. "History of the Goths," Germany 1979, tran. T.J. Dunlop, USA 1988.

Worrel, W.H. "A Study OF Races IN The Ancient Near East," Cambridge 1927.

WUORINEN, John H. "A History of Finland," New York & London 1965.

WYMAN, David S. "The Abandonment of the Jews", USA. 1985

YADIN, Yigal. "And Dan Why Did He Remain In Ships?" Australian Journal of Biblical Archaeology, vol.1, no.1, 1968.

ZEITSCHRIFT, "Zeitschrift Fur Assyriologie", Berlin and Leipzig 1929, Strasbourg 1909.

ZEUSS, Kaspar. "Die Deutschen und Die Nachbarstamme," Germany 1835, Heidelberg, Germany 1925.

ZEHARI, Dr. Menachem "HaCuzarim" (Hebrew), Jerusalem, 1976.

ZUCKERMAN, Arthur J. "A Jewish Princedom in Feudal France, 768-900", New York 1972.

INDEX